THE HARVEST

THE HARVEST

Spiritual Nourishment for the Church Year

The Collected Works of St Ignatius (Brianchaninov)—Volume 4

Bishop Ignatius (Brianchaninov)

Translated from the Russian by Helen Tsolaki
Edited by Holy Trinity Monastery

Holy Trinity Publications
The Printshop of St Job of Pochaev
Holy Trinity Monastery
Jordanville, New York
2025

Printed with the blessing of His Grace,
Bishop Luke of Syracuse
and Abbot of Holy Trinity Monastery

Translated from the third edition of the "Ascetic sermons"
(St Petersburg: I. L. Tuzov, Gostiny Dvor, No. 45, 1905).

PRINTSHOP OF
SAINT JOB OF POCHAEV

An imprint of

Holy Trinity Publications
Holy Trinity Monastery
1407 Robinson Road, Jordanville, NY 13361
www.HolyTrinityPublications.com

ISBN: 978-0-88465-506-0 (paperback)
ISBN: 978-0-88465-515-2 (ePub)

Library of Congress Control Number: 2025939823

Cover Art: "Flax Harvesting" Emile Clause, 1904; Digital Source: ARTGEN, Alamy Stock Photo, ID 2RAMNK1.

Printed in the United States of America
by Versa Press Inc. 1465 Spring Bay Road, East Peoria, IL, 61611
versapress.com

Contents

Foreword

What you have in your hand completes the English translation of the five volume *Collected Works of St Ignatius (Brianchaninov)*, albeit it is actually the fourth volume in the Russian original. This concludes a labor of over half a century since the *Arena* was first published in 1970, which was actually the fifth and final volume in the Russian original.

In this new volume the saint instructs us on the meaning and practice of Christian asceticism, drawing upon the ever-changing kaleidoscope of the Church calendar with its seasons of feasting and fasting. We are reminded of the Apostle Paul who wrote that "whatever a man sows, that he will also reap. For he who sows to his flesh will of the flesh reap corruption, but he who sows to the Spirit will of the Spirit reap everlasting life. And let us not grow weary while doing good, for in due season we shall reap [a harvest] if we do not lose heart" (Gal 6:7–9). St Ignatius is nourishing the reader with his teaching so as to bring a harvest of blessings that will prepare us to one day enter fully the kingdom of heaven.

Holy Trinity Monastery
Pascha 2025

Preface

In 1863 several of my sermons were published. We present here an edited and expanded collection of my sermons and talks, some of which were delivered in person, others written to be read in church and or in the monastic cell. In the process of collecting them together, their character became more clearly defined, and the title "Ascetic Sermons" was found to be appropriate for this material.

Those who are familiar with the "Ascetic Experiences" I wrote while an archimandrite will clearly see that the way of thinking set forth there flows naturally from the monastic way of life and is inseparable from it. The sermons serve as a supplement to the description of the spiritual Christian struggle, and to a great extent explain it. It by no means follows that only monastics should read them: they are suitable to be read by all Orthodox Christians who wish to become familiar with the ascetic life according to the understanding of the holy Fathers and of the Church.

Bishop Ignatius
1866

Address to the Diocese

This was given in the Stavropol Cathedral after his arrival to the diocese on January 5, 1858.

Peace to this city! (see Matt 10:11–13).

I give this greeting, dear brothers, according to the exhortation of my Lord, having arrived with my pastoral staff in the blessed city of Stavropol, to preach in this city and in the surrounding towns and villages and say that "the kingdom of heaven is at hand" (Matt 10:7).

The kingdom of heaven, "the kingdom of God is within you" (Luke 17:21). The kingdom of heaven is the peace of Christ. In the soul in which, due to obedience to God, the passions have subsided, God reigns and the peace of Christ reigns.

But the peace of Christ bears no relation to the peace of this age; the Lord does not give His peace in the same way that peace is obtained by the customs of fallen humanity (see John 14:27). Unity of a vain, even ill-intentioned purpose, often introduces a temporary and soul-destroying agreement between people. But the peace of Christ is holy. The peace of Christ is all in Christ. The peace of Christ is sown in the soul through the Word of God, grows through cultivation of the field of the heart by means of the commandments of Christ, and is fed by and grows from this invisible but not effortless struggle. Through the action of the Holy Spirit, the peace of Christ envelops the mind, heart, and body of the whole Christian, unites into one whole these parts that have been cut apart and separated by sin; it unites with God the man who has come to peace within himself and with himself, making himself one and whole, as he was before the fall. I ask for such peace for myself and for you too, dear brothers, from our Lord Jesus Christ, the only Giver of true and holy peace.

"The peace of God, which surpasses all understanding," according to the living and precise understanding of the apostle, "will guard" for Christ "your hearts and minds" (Phil 4:7); may it guard for Him our earthly activities and our eternal lot which depends on them. Amen.

1. Hear Him

Sermon on Epiphany

"This is My beloved Son, in whom I am well pleased. Hear Him!" (Matt 3:17; 17:5).

This was the voice of the pre-eternal God the Father speaking to men of the pre-eternal God the Son, when the Son, by the will of the Father and through the action of the Spirit, had become man of the Virgin, and was accomplishing the salvation of fallen mankind. Brothers! Let us show obedience to the Son of God, as God desires of us, and may the goodwill of God be upon us.

Perhaps someone might say, "Even if I wanted to listen to the Son of God, how could I, when it is nearly two thousand years since our Lord Jesus Christ was on earth in the flesh, preaching His all-holy teaching?"

It is very simple for us to be with Christ constantly, to hear His most sweet voice continually, to be nourished by His life-creating teaching: the Lord Jesus Christ is still with us to this day. He is with us in His holy Gospel; He is with us by means of the holy mysteries of the Church; He *is* through His omnipresence and His omnipotence; He *is* most abundantly, as befits an absolute and perfect God. The Lord clearly demonstrates His presence with us through the liberation of souls from captivity to sin, through the distribution of the gifts of the Holy Spirit, and through many signs and miracles.

Those who wish to approach the Lord and to be united with Him in a most blessed eternal union should begin this holy work by carefully studying the words of God; they should start by studying the Gospel, in which Christ is concealed and from out of which Christ speaks and acts. The words of the Gospel "are spirit, and they are life" (John 6:63). They convert the carnal person into a spiritual person, and they revive the soul deadened by sin and worldly vanity. They are "spirit and life": beware of explaining the great word of the Spirit using your reason, which crawls along the ground; beware of explaining the word filled with the terrible power of God in a way that can easily present itself to your dead soul, your dead heart, your dead mind. The word spoken by the Holy Spirit can only be explained by the Holy Spirit.

If you wish to approach the Lord to hear His Divine teaching, to be revived and saved by Him, you should approach and stand before the Lord with the greatest reverence and the most holy fear, as His radiant angels, His cherubim and seraphim, stand before Him. With your humility, you will turn the earth on which you stand into heaven. And the Lord will speak to you from His holy Gospel, as He did to His beloved disciples. And may the holy Fathers who have interpreted the holy Gospel through the gift of the Holy Spirit be your guides toward correct and true understanding of the holy Gospel.

It is disastrous to approach the Gospel, to approach the Lord Jesus Christ Who lives in the Gospel, without proper reverence, with impudence and arrogance. The Lord accepts only the humble who are full of awareness of their own sinfulness and insignificance, full of repentance; from the proud He turns away. The averting of the face of the Lord from an impudent tempter—which is what I call an irreverent, thoughtless, or indifferent hearer—strikes the tempter with eternal death. The God-inspired Elder Symeon proclaimed God the Word incarnate. "Behold, this Child is destined for the fall and rising of many in Israel, and for a sign which will be spoken against" (Luke 2:34). The Word of God is a "stone," a stone of immense size and weight, "And whoever falls on this stone will be broken" with irreparable destruction (Matt 21:44).

Brothers, let us be reverent and active hearers of the Word of God. Let us show obedience to the Heavenly Father, Who proclaimed His all-holy Word to us today from the holy Gospel: "This is My beloved Son, in whom I am well pleased. Hear Him!" (Matt 17:5). Let us hear Him! Let us hear Him, and may the goodwill of the Heavenly Father be upon us unto the ages of ages. Amen.

2. On Repentance

First Sermon on the Sunday after Epiphany

"Repent, for the kingdom of heaven is at hand" (Matt 4:17).

With these deep and blessed words began the preaching to fallen humanity of the Word made man. Superficially, this appears to be a simple teaching. But it should be understood from the context of our own lives. It then becomes apparent that the whole Gospel is expressed by these brief, simple words. Thus the holy apostle Paul, speaking of the good news which he preached across almost the whole known world of the time, said that he testified both to Jews and to Greeks "repentance toward God and faith toward our Lord Jesus Christ" (Acts 20:21).

Brothers! In order to believe in our Lord Jesus Christ, repentance is necessary; to dwell in this saving faith, repentance is necessary; to progress in it, repentance is necessary; to inherit the heavenly kingdom, repentance is necessary.

All this is set forth with the greatest clarity in Holy Scripture. Holy Scripture teaches us that God sent "His Son into the world ... that the world through Him might be saved," that "He who believes in Him is not condemned; but he who does not believe is condemned already." "The light"— Christ—"has come into the world, and men loved darkness rather than light, because their deeds were evil. For everyone practicing evil hates the light and does not come to the light, lest his deeds should be exposed" (John 3:17–20). Scripture bears witness to the person afflicted with the passion of vanity: "How can you believe, who receive honor from one another, and do not seek the honor that comes from the only God?" (John 5:44). Those possessed with the passion of avarice not only did not believe in the Lord but even mocked Him (Luke 16:9,14) when He preached the most needful and holy teaching of the remembrance of eternity, and of arranging earthly matters in accordance with the eternal purpose of man. Those carried away by the passion of cruel envy not only did not believe in the

Lord but plotted to kill Him and then committed deicide (see Matt 27:18). All those infected with vain and sinful passions, according to the true witness of the Bible, refuse to participate in the spiritual marriage of the Son of God, and make themselves unworthy of blessed union with Him (see Matt 22:5). "You cannot serve God and mammon" (Luke 16:13). You cannot serve two masters, God and sin, at the same time. "Repent, for the kingdom of heaven is at hand!" (Matt 4:17). "Repent, and believe in the gospel" (Mark 1:15).

But even someone who has believed in Christ, and has resolved to demonstrate his faith constantly through his actions and behavior, also needs repentance. What do you think, brothers, is the first fruit of living faith? What is the first fruit of keeping the commandments of Christ? I borrow the answer from St Symeon the New Theologian, who drew the knowledge of the truth he spoke from his own holy experiences. He said, "The strict keeping of the commandments teaches us our own weakness."[1] Exactly! As soon as a believer in Christ begins to fulfill the most holy commandments of the Gospel, or, in other words, to carry out the works of the renewed nature, then, suddenly, his fallen nature, until then hidden from view, is revealed to him and begins to fight persistently against the Gospel. The life of a struggler for Christ is filled with invisible falls. He cannot help confessing together with the apostle: "I delight in the law of God according to the inward man. But I see another law in my members, warring against the law of my mind, and bringing me into captivity to the law of sin which is in my members. O wretched man that I am!" (Rom 7:22–24). From such self-perception there arises within the Christian a blessed poverty of spirit, a reasonable spiritual mourning, creating a contrite and humble heart, which "God shall not despise" (Ps 50:19). When a person lives in accordance with the Gospel, the repentance to which it calls us appears as if naturally within him. Thus repentance is necessary not only in order to believe in Christ, but also in order to keep the faith, to make progress in Christ; it is necessary for a living faith in Christ. "Repent, for the kingdom of heaven is at hand!"

It remains to explain why, in the words of the Lord that we are examining, there is such a close connection between the call to repentance and the proclamation of the closeness of the kingdom of heaven. Why is there no intervening ascetic effort placed between them, no intervening circumstance? The reason is that our Lord Jesus Christ—"The Lamb of God who takes away the sin of the world" (John 1:29)—did everything for our salvation: He reconciled us with God, and He prepared and attained for us the kingdom of heaven. Only one task is asked of us humans in the work of our salvation: the task of receiving the salvation God has given to us freely and completely, the task of repentance. The kingdom of heaven and the heavenly King are inexpressibly close to us—far closer than we suppose. "Behold, I stand at the door" of the human heart, proclaims this King, and I knock on it with My most holy and all-powerful Word: "If anyone hears My voice and opens the door, I will come in to him and dine with him, and he with Me" (Rev 3:20). It is repentance that opens the doors of the heart to the heavenly King. "Repent, for the kingdom of heaven is at hand." Amen.

3. On Repentance

Second Sermon on the Sunday after Epiphany

"Repent, for the kingdom of heaven is at hand" (Matt 4:17).

Repentance is the first commandment of the New Testament; it is the primary virtue that leads to all the other Christian virtues. Both the Forerunner of the Saviour and the Saviour Himself began their preaching to fallen humanity by calling us to repentance and promising the Heavenly Kingdom to those who repented sincerely. "Repent, for the kingdom of heaven is at hand" (Matt 3:2; Matt 4:17). Repentance gives its powerful right hand to a person who finds himself in a deep abyss, in the hell of falling into sin—it draws him out of there and raises him above the earth; it does not leave him until it leads him, saved, through the gates of eternity.

After calling on the grace of God for aid in our feeble-mindedness, we will try to investigate the meaning of repentance, so as to receive this gift offered to us by God Himself, and, after receiving it, to work out our salvation by means of it.

Two qualities, two abilities have been planted by the merciful God in human nature, with the help of which, after its fall and alienation from God, it can arise from its fallen state and restore its communion with God. These two qualities are repentance and faith, and it is to them that God turns for the salvation of men. He offers them the free choice to use these two qualities toward salvation. Man perished by his own free will and he is allowed to be saved by his own free will. "Repent and believe" (Mark 1:15).

In return for repentance, God grants forgiveness of sins and access to Himself, and He opens Himself to faith and grants the only knowledge of God of which a person is capable, and that he cannot possibly acquire by his own means. Faith brings the mind knowledge that is far beyond reason: by way of judgments and investigations, the mind acquires only the knowledge that is within its comprehension, whereas faith gives it knowledge that is beyond its comprehension. Such is all revealed knowledge of God and of the mysteries of Christianity. Repentance brings forth in the heart grace-filled feelings that are alien to fallen human nature, and teaches the mind and the heart how to serve God truly, how to make the one sacrifice to God that He receives from fallen man: contrition and humility of spirit (Ps 50:19). The human spirit that has arrived at this state enters into communion with the Spirit of God, and that is what constitutes the renewal and salvation of man.

St Symeon the New Theologian says the following of faith: "There is nothing that prevents us from having faith. For if we want it with all our heart, it will immediately become active in us, since it is God's gift to us and a pre-eminent characteristic of our nature, even though it is also subject to our individual power of free will. That is why even Scythians and other outlandish peoples have faith in each other's words."[2] A distinction should be made between this natural faith that allows us to believe in God and the active faith that appears in the soul from fulfillment of the commandments of the Gospel, as well as the living faith that is poured out into the heart by the Holy Spirit.[3] Anyone can believe in God and in the Gospel (Mark 1:14–15. Acts 20:21); active faith is acquired by those who struggle for Christ; living faith is a gift of God, acquired only by the saints of God. In exactly the same way, repentance is natural to us. It is an action of our conscience. It consists in recognition of one's sins and regret for them. Just as, by natural tendency and conviction, when we want, we trust each other, so also, by natural tendency and conviction, when we want, we repent before one another for sins against each other. Repentance, in satisfying a natural demand of the heart, brings it tranquility and joy. It restores disturbed peace and order between people, resolves doubts and confusions, heals the soul from enmity and resentment. But we only repent before one another when we want to; without our will the natural capacity for repentance remains inactive.

After creating man and giving him all the means to preserve life, the unfathomable God left the choice between life and death to his free will; in the same way, God, unfathomable both in His goodness and in His reason, after accomplishing the redemption, left it to our will whether we accepted or rejected it. He had placed within us the natural capacity for repentance: He willed to make use of the means we use to destroy enmity and restore peace between each other, as a means for destroying the enmity and restoring peace between God and mankind, between the rejected and lost creation and its almighty Creator. "Repent!" He says to all people, calling them to Himself. Your salvation has been accomplished by God; your death has been trampled on and destroyed by God, without any participation, cooperation or effort from you: reject voluntarily the death that you accepted voluntarily. Voluntarily accept the blessed eternal life that you rejected voluntarily. To do this, make use in good time of the capacity for repentance that was placed within you, the capacity that depends entirely on your will. Nothing difficult or new is being placed on you: use the ability to be reconciled amongst yourselves to reconcile yourselves with God.

Just as the original faith consists in believing the words of God, so the original repentance consists in consciousness of one's sins and one's sinfulness, in regret for them, and in bringing this awareness and sorrow before God through sincere confession and heartfelt prayer and with resolution and the promise to abandon the sinful life and to live in accordance with the commandments of the Gospel. Such repentance is followed by forgiveness of sins, reconciliation with God, and adoption by God, according to the clear testimony of Holy Scripture, which says: "I have acknowledged my transgression and my sin have I not hid; I said, Against myself will I confess my transgression unto the Lord, and so Thou forgavest the irreverence of my heart" (Ps 31:5). Such repentance was demanded of those adopting Christianity before their baptism (Acts 2:38); through such repentance the souls of Christians are healed after baptism from the wounds with which sin has defiled them (1 John 1:9).

The Gospel is accepted through faith (Mark 1:15); living in accordance with the teachings of the Gospel strengthens faith—faith from hearsay, which is theoretical, gradually turns people toward active, practical faith. A similar thing happens with repentance through living in accordance with the commandments of the Gospel. The inherent light of fallen nature, as damaged by sin, illumines the activity of man weakly; in this light, we see few of our sins; we see only the most flagrant and tangible of them. But when our behavior is illumined by the light of Christ's commandments, our view of ourselves changes: we start to see in ourselves a multitude of shortcomings that we had previously not noticed at all. The extent of our damage through sin then appears in our mind's eye in startling variety. There is then revealed to us both the sinfulness that constitutes the lamentable legacy we share with other people and the individual sinfulness possessed by each person due to the negligent, thoughtless life that precedes the change to a life of piety. As the incentives for repentance increase, repentance itself is strengthened and deepened. It cleanses the eye of the soul. The cleansed eye sees more stains on the garment of the soul than it saw when it was poisoned and ulcerated with sin: it is natural that repentance is strengthened and deepened from these sights. It acts incomparably more in experienced ascetics than in those beginning their struggle. Spiritual progress in a Christian is progress in repentance, because progress in repentance appears due to particularly painstaking fulfillment of the Gospel commandments. All the saints abounded in a feeling of repentance; they concentrated their activity on repentance, and they kept the commandments, as payment of that terrible debt (see Luke 17:10) that is unpaid even with constant payment, that due to the perfection of the Creditor and the weakness of the debtors remains unpayable even if it were to be paid incessantly. Repentance in mature Christians acquires a special, broad meaning. When St Isaac the Syrian was asked, "What is repentance?" he answered, "A contrite and humble heart."[4] This great teacher of perfect Christians said, "If we are all sinners, and not a single one of us is beyond temptation, there is no virtue greater than repentance. It can never be completed. It always becomes anyone who wants to acquire salvation, both sinners and righteous. There are no limits at which it could be deemed to be complete; and for this reason, repentance cannot be limited either in time, nor in works (of an ascetic), until death itself."[5]

When the grace of God has descended upon the faith of a Christian, he is elevated to a way of living that is beyond nature. In exactly the same way, when repentance is covered with divine grace, one who practices it is elevated to a way of living that is beyond nature. Enveloped with the feeling of and thirst for repentance, the holy Fathers would confine themselves for its sake in a locked cell, and give themselves over to weeping and sobbing from contemplation of their sinfulness and that of all humanity; they would forget food because of their lamentations, and they would roar, from their great sorrow, like lions wounded by hunters. Having learned the virtue of repentance offered in silence, they said, "Without silence there is no perfect repentance."[6] Others from among the Fathers, having contemplated their sinfulness, submissively endured slanders, humiliations, persecution, and even death, weeping and condemning themselves as if guilty of what they were accused of. The holy martyrs, accepting terrible tortures and execution, saw in them the longed-for purification from their sinfulness. While grace revealed their election and their holiness with manifest signs, they concerned themselves with repentance. Thus the martyr Timothy, after saying openly to his torturer: "The Spirit of Jesus Christ abides in me," and also that angels of God were present during his torture and strengthened him, invited his young wife, Maura, to join him in martyrdom with the following words: "Leave transitory things, Maura, and come with me to this wonderful struggle for which we will have the honour of receiving crowns from God our Saviour, and He will forgive us all our sins when we willingly give ourselves up to death for Him." Maura, filled with the Holy Spirit, stood boldly in front of the torturer and confessed Christ. At the command of the governor, the martyr's hair was torn out. She said to the governor, "Now I have learned, Governor, that my Christ has adopted me for His own, not remembering my sin committed in ignorance and consisting in the fact that I, hearing your evil advice, adorned my hair in order to seduce my blessed husband. You did right to tear out my hair: through its uprooting a great sin has been taken from me." When at the torturer's command Maura's fingers were cut off, she said to him, "With this you have also done me a good deed: by removing my fingers, with which I put on vain adornments, you caused my release from a second sin." When the martyr was thrown into a cauldron of boiling water, she said to the governor, "Again I thank you for giving the order for me to be washed from the sins I committed in the world, so that I may approach my God with a pure heart and receive the crown of life." The blessed Maura endured an arduous martyrdom, confessing her sinfulness and accepting martyrdom as purification from it. She thought and spoke in this way even though the boiling cauldron did not cause her any harm and she endured the amputation of her fingers without any pain. Saints Timothy and Maura ended their lives crucified on crosses opposite one another. Before her repose the martyr said to the people gathered there: "Brothers and sisters! Remember that we acted as humans when living among humans; also, that we having carried out the work of God, being servants of God, now receive crowns from our Lord Jesus Christ. And you, living in accordance with human nature, must also try to do what is pleasing to God, so that you may receive forgiveness of sins and crowns from that same Master."[7] The above words of St Isaac are accurate and true: "Repentance is humility of the heart." Because of their deep humility, it was as if the greatest servants of God did not see the grace-filled gifts in which they abounded—they saw only their own sinfulness, which had already been cleansed by divine grace as shown by its obvious presence of grace in those chosen vessels. Among the qualities in which holy people excel, it is noticeable that they always have before their eyes their own sin, even if it has been forgiven by God—they weep for it as if it had only just been committed and did not yet deserve forgiveness. Thus St David, weeping, says, "For I know my fault, and my sin is ever before me" (Ps 50:5 LXX). It is said of the holy apostle Peter that he remembered his denial of the Lord his whole life long, and every night, when the rooster crowed, Peter gave himself up to bitter weeping just as he wept and cried on the night of the betrayal itself (see Matt 26:75). St Sisoes the Great, the Egyptian hermit, was filled with the gifts of the Holy Spirit; but as he approached his repose, he expressed the desire to remain a little longer in earthly life in order to perfect himself in repentance.[8] This is how the greatest saints of God viewed repentance: this view developed within them from continual and painstaking cleansing through repentance through which the ineffable greatness of God, the insignificance of mankind, and the gravity of his fall are gradually revealed to a person.

With our feeble powers, or rather, through the great mercy of God, the arena of repentance is expressed here as a painting in words. Let each person examine himself in accordance with this outline, and determine his place in the arena of repentance. Blessed are they who, having heeded the call of God, have acknowledged their sinfulness, repent of the sins they have committed and of their sinful life, and have resolved to confess these things, to expel from themselves the wrongful love of sin by sincerely denouncing it, and to begin a way of life opposite to the sinful one, a way of life according to the will of God and the teaching of the Gospel. Blessed are they who, laboring in repentance, have seen within themselves, with the eye of the soul and through divine grace, the fall of man in general and their own fallenness in particular, have seen that we are all poisoned by sin, that our very nature is poisoned by it, and have seen the action upon themselves and upon humanity of the fallen angels and the burdensome captivity in which we find ourselves with these enemies of God and of ourselves. People who see this spiritual sight can be completely immersed in a boundless sea of repentance.[9] A hundred times blessed are they who, having been cleansed through repentance, have been able in their purity to acquire for themselves the unfathomable humility of Christ, to be crucified with Christ, and from their involuntary, or apparently voluntary cross given by Christ, they cry out to Him: "we receive the due reward" for our sins: "Lord, remember" us "when You come into Your kingdom" (Luke 23:42), at the hour of our separation from the body, at the boundary with eternity.

The saving gift of God, repentance, demands that we accept it with the greatest reverence and care. Negligent, arrogant behavior in relation to the gifts of God leads to terrible calamities. This is natural. How can the most terrible spiritual, fundamental, and eternal calamity not arise when we accept a gift from God and then reject the necessary investigation both into the gift itself and into the use we should make of it? Unfortunately, many people act most negligently and ignorantly with the great gift of repentance. They do not want to acknowledge that repentance is not compatible with a voluntarily sinful life. Remaining in a sinful life due to sympathy with it and attachment to it, they resort to repentance at certain times, only to immerse themselves again in sinful filth after washing themselves for a moment. What terrible self-deception! What terrible mockery of the gift of God! What terrible blasphemy of God! "The latter end is worse for them than the beginning" (2 Pet 2:20). Through such hypocritical repentance, such playing with and mockery of the great sacrament, a sinful life is imprinted and consolidated and becomes an inalienable possession of a person. The following words of St John the Theologian are addressed to voluntary lovers of sin: "Whoever sins has neither seen Him nor known Him. Little children, let no one deceive you. He who practices righteousness is righteous, just as He is righteous. He who sins is of the devil, for the devil has sinned from the beginning. For this purpose the Son of God was manifested, that He might destroy the works of the devil. Whoever has been born of God does not sin, for His seed remains in him; and he cannot sin because he has been born of God. In this the children of God and the children of the devil are manifest" (1 John 3:6–10). It is manifest who are the children of God and the children of the devil; the sign of the difference between them is obvious; deception is impossible. Those voluntarily living a sinful life, those who are drowning in bodily pleasures, are children of the devil, even if they call themselves Christians; the sign of the children of God, on the other hand, consists in the fact that they live in accordance with the testament of the Gospel and the holy Church, and they quickly heal through repentance the sins into which they fall through weakness. Not even a righteous man can be wholly free from sin: healing through repentance is also essential for him, as witnessed by the same holy apostle John. "If we say that we have no sin, we deceive ourselves, and the truth is not in us" (1 John 1:8). The Christians of the early Church, who abandoned the faith of the pagans, also abandoned their way of life (1 Pet 4:3–4). The holy apostle Peter calls this way of life a "flood of dissipation" (1 Pet 4:4). Even without mentioning folk entertainments, all the institutions of the pagans were in various ways serving sensuality which, like a flood, submerged the whole of society. A sinful, depraved way of life was the life of the pagans; it was the soul of their society. This way of life has no place within Christianity.

Let us love repentance, and we will be granted salvation. Let us receive from the hand of the Lord the lifelong gift of repentance, and we will receive at the appropriate time the eternal gift of salvation. The most good "God has also granted ... repentance to life" (Acts 11:18). He gives blessedness in eternity to those who have truly repented, been reconciled with Him, and been adopted by Him through repentance: "Salvation is of the Lord" (Ps 3:9). To Him be glory unto the ages of ages. Amen.

4. The Character of the Pharisee and of the Tax Collector

First Sermon on the Sunday of the Pharisee and the Tax Collector

Dear brothers! In the Gospel that has just been read, we heard the parable of our Lord Jesus Christ on the pharisee and the tax collector (see Luke 18:9–14).

Why did the Lord preach this parable? He preached it to people who are seduced and deluded by conceit, who rely upon and hope in their own righteousness and their own good works, who look upon their neighbors from a position of conceit and self-delusion, disparage them, that is, have a low opinion of them, and despise, condemn, and speak evil of them, both within their souls and openly before other people.

Why has the holy Church set this Gospel to be read before the beginning of the period of Great Lent? With the aim of guarding us from conceit and from disparaging our neighbors, both of which make it completely impossible for a feeling of repentance to be adopted in the heart. If fasting does not bear the fruit of repentance, then the effort of fasting is in vain. Not only that: it will cause us harm by strengthening conceit and self-assurance within us. Such is the nature of all bodily ascetic efforts and visible good works. If we think that in accomplishing these things we are making a sacrifice for God and not weeping over our unpayable debt, then the good works and ascetic efforts become within us the begetters of soul-destroying pride.

"Two men went up to the temple to pray," thus the Lord began His parable, "one a Pharisee and the other a tax collector" (Luke 18:9–14). Then the Lord Who sees inside hearts recounted the thoughts that expressed the secret pledge of the heart of each of the men praying, the thoughts with which each of them portrayed his relationship with God.

The pharisee was satisfied with himself, deeming himself worthy of God, pleasing to God. "God, I thank You," he said "within himself," that is, he said in thought in the course of invisible self-examination. What is the pharisee praising God for? Is it for the boundless greatness of God, provoking amazement and bewilderment among all reason-endowed creation? Is it for the incomprehensible and ineffable mercy of God in allowing insignificant creation, man, to converse with God? Is it for the innumerable blessings of God poured out on mankind? No. "I thank You," says the pharisee, "that I am not like other men." The pharisee in his blindness gives praise to God for his state of self-satisfaction and self-deception. What an audacious and evil form of boasting! This is praise to God that is unworthy of God, praise to God that is filled with slander of God. It was not God who gave the pharisee the state for which he praises himself: that emerged from the acceptance and adoption of false notions. The father of false notions, who destroys the soul with eternal death, is the fallen angel (John 8:44). That is the one under whose influence the disposition of the pharisee formed. Self-deception is always linked with what the holy fathers call "diabolical deception": it consists in accepting lies instead of truth and in being carried away by lies. In his self-deception, the pharisee has a dark view of humanity: "I am not like other men—extortioners, unjust, adulterers, or even as this tax collector." Where did he obtain such knowledge which he expresses with such certainty and confidence? How could he know so precisely and in such detail the behavior and conscience of all people so as to make such a serious and all-encompassing accusation about them? How could he know about the behavior and conscience of the tax collector who entered the church together with him, who held no conversation with him and told him nothing about himself? It is obvious that the verdict was made hastily, and it was made not because other people and the tax collector were as the pharisee describes them but because the disease of self-deception and self-satisfaction presented them as such to the pharisee. Then the pharisee lists his own virtues: "I fast twice a week; I give tithes of all that I possess." The pharisee looked upon his own deeds as sacrifices, as services to God; such a view is common to all pharisees. For them, it is in vain that God proclaims in both the Old and the New Testaments, "I desire mercy and not sacrifice" (Matt 9:13; Hos 6:6). The Lord pointed out to them this expression of God's will in holy Scripture more than once. He said to them that they would never have fallen into condemnation of innocent people if they had understood this expression of the will of God (see Matt 12:7), because mercy not only does not condemn the innocent but views the guilty with sympathy; it condescends to them as far as possible, as weak and sick members, and it is concerned not with punishment but with healing. The embittered, blind pharisees, stubbornly rejecting mercy, want somehow to coerce God and offer sacrifices to Him that He does not accept. They also demand the same behavior from other people; when they do not see this behavior in them, they are tempted and they judge. It is characteristic of the pharisees to be scandalized by those in whom they do not see pharisaism; it is characteristic of them to be scandalized by those who, disdaining self-love and people-pleasing, try to please God in simplicity and in the secrecy of their hearts; it is characteristic of them to see sin and evil intent where it is not; it is characteristic of them to condemn, to hate, and to persecute true servants of God. By whom were they scandalized, whom did they condemn, in whom did they see sin, whom did they persecute with frenzied malice? From the narrative of the Gospel, we find that their persecution and hatred was always suffered by repentant sinners who had been reconciled with God and had become righteous through repentance, or disciples and followers of God incarnate, but above all by the incarnate, all-perfect God Himself. The pharisees had a false understanding of the Law of God. They studied the Law by letter alone and not through experience, not through obeying the Law; they did not achieve humility, to which a person is led through true knowledge of God, but remarkable pomposity and arrogance. They attached far more significance than was appropriate to rules about rituals and symbolism but paid no heed to the commandments of God, which constituted the essence of the Law. Misinterpreting the meaning of the Law in accordance with their false reason and corrupted hearts, they at the same time as serving and pleasing self-love alone wrongly appeared to themselves and to others to be serving and pleasing God. They strove to serve and please God by fulfilling their own will and their own understanding, probably believing them to be good and true which is unnatural to fallen human nature, and not by painstaking pursuit and fulfillment of the will of God. With this kind of behavior, a person almost always does evil believing it to be good, and even when he does good, he does it from within himself which is why he ascribes it to himself just as the pharisee in this parable did. In this way, even goodness becomes the cause of evil, bringing conceit to the person and sowing, feeding, and growing within it the most pernicious of the sins: pride.

There are completely different consequences from living in accordance with the commandments of the Gospel. Someone who sets himself the aim in life of fulfilling the will of God tries in detail and with precision to ascertain this all-holy will by studying holy Scripture, especially the New Testament, very carefully, by reading the writings of the holy Fathers, by conversing with and visiting Christians who are advanced in the spiritual life, and by keeping the commandments of the Gospel both in his external behavior and in his mind and heart. "The law of freedom," said St Mark the Ascetic, "is studied by means of true knowledge, it is understood through practice of the commandments, and is fulfilled through the mercy of Christ."[10] When a Christian starts living according to the will of God that is good, acceptable, and perfect (see Rom 12:2), or according to the commandments of the New Testament, then the fallenness and weakness of human nature are suddenly revealed to him.[11] Weakness prevents him from keeping the commandments of God in a pure and holy way, as God asks of him, and his fallenness resists fulfillment of these commandments, often with great cruelty. It wills and demands that the fallen human will and the fallen human reason are fulfilled. The strivings of this will and the notions of this reason assume the appearance of the most lofty truth and the greatest virtue. Knowledge of the internal battle, exposure, and revelation of the sin living within, and knowledge of its strong power over good intentions and strivings give the Christian a true understanding of himself and of humanity. He sees the fallenness of humanity in himself; he sees in his own experience the impossibility of rising from this fallenness in his own strength alone; he gains true humility, he begins to offer to God the most heartfelt prayer for help from a contrite heart, which God always hears. "Teach me to do Thy will" (Ps 142:10); "teach me Thy statutes" (Ps 118:12); "O hide not Thy commandments from me" (Ps 118:19); "sustain Thou me in Thy words" (Ps 118:28); "Take from me the way of injustice, and by Thy Law have mercy upon me" (Ps 118:29). Having learned through experience that the commandments of God are kept only with the abundant help of the grace of God, and constantly praying for this help for himself, a Christian cannot but ascribe all his good works to the grace of God. Together with this, he cannot avoid acknowledging that he is a sinner. On the one hand he has discovered through experience that he is fallen and is unable to keep the commandments of God by his own strength alone; on the other hand, in the very fulfillment of God's commandments, with the help of grace, he sees his incessant sins caused by human weakness and fallenness. This can be seen very clearly from the testimony of the holy apostle Paul about himself. In one of his epistles he says: "I labored more abundantly than they all, yet not I, but the grace of God which was with me" (1 Cor 15:10), and in another: "Christ Jesus came into the world to save sinners, of whom I am chief" (1 Tim 1:15). Such is God-pleasing righteousness. It is produced in a person through the divine grace that has come upon him, and it pleases God with works of God-given righteousness. A righteous man who is pleasing to God does not cease to acknowledge that he is a sinner, not only due to his obvious sins, but also due to his natural righteousness in its lamentable fallen state mixed with evil and defiled by sin. Blessed is he who is righteous in God's justice, whose hope is concentrated on Christ, the source of his righteousness. Unhappy is he who is satisfied with his own human righteousness: he has no need of Christ, Who proclaimed of Himself, "For I did not come to call the righteous, but sinners, to repentance" (Matt 9:13). St Pimen the Great said, "A person who has sinned and repented is more pleasant to me than one who has not sinned and not repented: The former, in deeming himself a sinner, has a good thought, whereas the latter, deeming himself righteous, has a false thought."[12] An adopted false thought makes all the life that is based on it worthless. This has been shown through experience: obvious sinners, tax collectors, and harlots believed in Christ, but the pharisees rejected Him. Conceit and pride essentially consist in the rejection of God and worship of the self. They are a subtle kind of idol-worship that is hard to discern and hard to reject. The pharisees were superficially the closest and keenest servants and adherents of true worship of God, but in essence they had completely alienated themselves from God, making themselves His enemies and children of Satan (John 8:44). When the promised Messiah, Whom suffering humanity had awaited for several thousand years, appeared among them with incontestable testimonies of His God, they did not accept Him. Recognizing Him, they consciously delivered Him to a shameful death and made themselves murderers of God (Matt 27:42).

The Gospel does not mention either the sinfulness or the righteousness of the tax collector, but merely sets before us the example of the form of his prayer, which consists exclusively in recognizing his sinfulness and asking God most humbly for mercy. The reason for showing this is obvious. All people, without exception, are sinful before God; all need forgiveness and mercy for their salvation, and God, in His boundless perfection, forgives all sins, small and great. Before the perfection of God, all people are equal in terms of righteousness in which they can differ only between themselves (see Rom 4:1–6). Declaring oneself to be righteous is no different from not seeing one's sins, or from self-deception. And because of this, all people without exception when they come to the church of God to stand before the face of God, or when they resolve to do this in the seclusion of a cell, must prepare themselves to acknowledge their own sinfulness, and solely from this acknowledgment to offer prayer to God. Otherwise our prayers will not be accepted.[13] "And the tax collector, standing afar off," the Gospel recounts, "would not so much as raise his eyes to heaven, but beat his breast, saying, 'God, be merciful to me a sinner!'" (Luke 18:13). With these words the Gospel teaches us that during prayer the humble disposition of the soul must be matched by the attitude of the body. We should not allow our eyes to roam freely: let them be constantly directed at the ground, so that the mind and heart can be directed constantly to God. The tax collector had a stooped appearance, so vividly did he feel the burden of his sins. And anyone who feels vividly this most oppressive burden on the soul will involuntarily adopt a bent and mourning appearance, as the holy David said: "I am brought into great torment and misery; I go mourning all the day long. For my loins are filled with sores, and there is no healing in my flesh" (Ps 37:7–8). It is impossible not to observe that the place where the tax collector chooses to stand—afar off—is pointed out by the Gospel in contrast to the place chosen by the pharisee who, of course, stood at the front in order to serve for the edification of the people gathered there and attract their attention to himself for their benefit (see Luke 18:9–14). This is the way in which vainglory usually justifies and conceals its actions. The bodily attitude adopted by the tax collector in line with the thoughts within his heart is in contrast to that adopted by the pharisee, which also corresponded to the impulse of his soul produced by thoughts of pride. The tax collector, acknowledging himself to be a sinner, did not dare to raise his eyes to heaven; the pharisee, deeming himself a righteous man, freely raised his arrogant eye upwards. The tax collector, because of the weight of sin felt by him, appeared to be burdened with a heavy load; the body of the pharisee assumed a contrasting appearance to this; encouraged, straightened, inspired by self-confidence and self-assurance. The face of the tax collector was covered with sorrow; the face of the pharisee shone with complacency. Occasionally, pharisees stand within the church but at a distance , especially when they are people of rank, then they suddenly appear in front of the people, in order to impress them more deeply both with the appearance of their rank and with the preceding appearance of humility. Their faces do not always express complacency; they adopt various appearances, depending on need; but they are always false.

The Lord Who sees people's hearts concluded the parable with the following words: "I tell you that this man" (the tax collector) "rather than the other" (the pharisee) "went home justified before God. For all those who exalt themselves will be humbled, and those who humble themselves will be exalted." This means that the tax collector was justified because he resorted to the justification granted by God, but the pharisee was condemned because he rejected the justification granted by God and wanted to remain in his own fallen human justice. "To be humbled" means to acknowledge one's fallenness, one's sinfulness, for which reason humans made themselves into outcasts devoid of all virtue; "to be exalted" means to ascribe to oneself righteousness, and other virtues even if only to a certain extent. Our virtue, our righteousness, the price by which every person is valued and which is given for each person is our Lord Jesus Christ.

The poison, the completely poisonous behavior of the pharisees, consists in the fact that "all their works they do to be seen by men" (Matt 23:5). The basis of their behavior is the quest for glory among men; the means for attaining the goal is hypocrisy. Hypocrisy constitutes the character of the pharisees. The Lord called hypocrisy their "leaven" (Luke 12:1). All the behavior of the pharisees is fed by hypocrisy; their every act has a spirit of hypocrisy. Hypocrisy, born of vainglory, that is of seeking praise and human glory feeds vainglory with its successes. When vainglory reaches maturity, it turns from bursts of action into a constant striving and then develops into the mad and blind passion of pride. Pride is the spiritual death of the soul: when a soul is enveloped by pride, it is incapable either of humility or of repentance or of mercy or any spiritual thought or feeling that delivers a living knowledge of the Redeemer and adoption by Him. In order to avoid the terrible poison passed on by the leaven of the pharisees, let us, as exhorted by the Gospel (see Matt 6:1–6), strive to fulfill the divine commandments for God alone, concealing our good works with the utmost care from the pernicious gaze of men. Let us act on earth for God and for heaven and not for other people. We will also act for people, but not in order to draw from them praise of ourselves, but to bring them true service and benefit for which they often tear their benefactors to pieces just as dumb and ferocious animals often tear to pieces those who care for and feed them. This is what happened to the holy apostles and to many other saints of God. Let us pay heed to ourselves vigilantly, noticing our shortcomings and our sins. Let us pray to God to reveal our fallenness and our sinfulness to us. Constant striving to fulfill the will of God will gradually destroy our self-satisfaction and will clothe us in blessed poverty of spirit. Clothed in this holy and grace-filled garment, we will learn how to stand before God in a way that pleases Him, like the humble tax collector who is praised in the Gospel. By praying to God from the depths and sincerity of the heartfelt recognition of our sinfulness, we will surely receive forgiveness of sins and an abundance of true blessings—temporal and eternal: "for everyone who exalts himself will be humbled" by the almighty and all-blessed right hand of the Lord God, our Creator and Saviour. Amen.

5. On Prayer and Repentance

Second Sermon on the Sunday of the Pharisee and the Tax Collector

Today's Gospel (Luke 18:9–14) describes the prayer of the tax collector which attracted the mercy of God toward him. This prayer consisted of the following few words: "God, be merciful to me a sinner" (Luke 18:13). It is worth noting both that such a short prayer was heard by God and that it was said in the temple, during the public divine service, while psalms and other prayers were being read and sung. This prayer is commended by the Gospel and brought out as an example of prayer. It therefore becomes our sacred duty to examine it devoutly.

Why did the tax collector not choose some grand and moving psalm in order to pour out his heart before God, but turn to such a short prayer, repeating only this throughout the whole divine service? We borrow our answer from the holy Fathers.[14] "When true repentance germinates within the soul, when humility and contrition of spirit appear within it from the sinfulness revealed before its eyes: then verbosity becomes unnatural to it, impossible for it." Concentrating within itself, directing all its attention to its wretched situation, the soul begins to cry out to God with the shortest of prayers.

The sight of a person's sinfulness is vast when God grants him to see it: it cannot be portrayed through eloquence or verbosity but is more accurately expressed as the sighing and wailing of the soul clothed in the briefest and simplest words. A person who wishes to reveal within himself a feeling of deep repentance uses a short prayer as a tool for reaching such a state, pronouncing it with all possible care and reverence. Abandoning many words, even holy ones, the mind can free itself completely from distraction, and strive with all its strength toward self-contemplation. "In your prayer, do not allow yourself to speak much," says St John of the Ladder, "so that your mind does not turn aside to examine the words. One word from the tax collector moved God to have mercy on him, and one faithful utterance saved the thief. Verbosity in prayer often brings the mind to distraction and dreaminess, but with reticence, it can usually be collected again."[15]

Because of the great benefit of brief, attentive, focused prayer, the holy Church teaches her children to learn any short prayer at an early stage. A person who has become accustomed to such prayer has a prayerbook ready anytime and anywhere. Whether traveling or sitting at table or doing handiwork or in human company, he can cry out to God. If it is not possible for him to pray with the lips, he can pray in his mind. In this context the convenience of a short prayer is obvious: when we are occupied, it is very easy to lose the meaning and sequence of prolonged prayer, but a short prayer is always kept intact. After leaving it for a short while, it is possible to return to it again without any difficulty. Even during divine services, it is helpful to repeat a short prayer within our hearts: this not only does not distract attention from the prayer to God being read and sung in the church, but even facilitates particularly close attention to it, keeping the mind from distraction. If the mind does not keep itself in a state of self-observation with a brief prayer, filling the soul with a feeling of repentance, it will easily succumb to distraction; during divine services, if it leaves unattended the readings and singing, it will turn aside to empty thoughts and dreaming. This is what happened to the pharisee in the parable: he paid only superficial attention to the divine service and was distracted by sinful thoughts. The sinful thoughts not only removed all merit from his prayer, which was already weak, but turned it into a means to condemn the one who was praying. The prayer of the pharisee was rejected by God: the pharisee left the temple stamped with the seal of the wrath of God not understanding and not sensing his spiritual poverty because his heart, which was dead to repentance, was filled with self-satisfaction and self-deception. When praying a short prayer becomes a habit from frequent, repeated use, it becomes as if natural to a person. When we listen attentively to something that particularly concerns us, we make various exclamations, which not only do not hinder us from paying attention, but even increase our focus: in exactly the same way, when we acquire the habit of brief prayer, we express with it our sympathy with and attention to the communal prayers and singing we hear.

Throughout Great Lent, the prayer "God, cleanse me a sinner" is frequently repeated at all services so that everyone present in the church can hear it. What is the purpose of such frequent repetition of the same prayer? It is so that we may learn to repeat it frequently. It is with the same aim that another short prayer is often repeated: "Lord have mercy."

Having commended the prayer of the tax collector, the Saviour of the world subsequently permitted and granted us to pray using His all-holy name. The prayer in the name of the Lord Jesus, using His name and as established by Him, is called the Jesus prayer. During the era of the Old Testament, man turned toward God, Whom he did not yet know specifically; since the new era began, in the New Testament, in a most bountiful enrichment, we have been granted to turn to the God-Man as to a mediator between God and mankind, as to a mediator who unites divinity with humanity, as to a mediator who has explained God to humans in as much detail and as fully as they can comprehend, who "has declared" God (John 1:18). The Old Testament prayer "God, have mercy on me, a sinner" is equivalent to the New Testament prayer "Lord Jesus Christ, Son of God, have mercy on me, a sinner." The Old Testament servants of God used the former prayer; those of the New Testament, while also using the former prayer, used the latter more because the God-Man was well pleased to give His human name a special wonderworking spiritual power. For continuous entreaty, the prayer "Lord have mercy" is also used. This is a shortened version of the prayer of Jesus and replaces it in situations when it would be difficult to say the whole Jesus prayer such as in an instance of fright, of unexpected joy, of severe illness, or of a spiritual vision. In the latter case, the exclamation "Lord have mercy" serves for the mind as an echo of those grace-filled understandings that appear to it after it has been cleansed, that exceed its comprehension and cannot be expressed in words.[16]

In all these prayers, what is the meaning of the verb "have mercy" or "be merciful"? It signifies a person's recognition of his perdition; it is the feeling of that mercy, that pity for oneself, which the Lord commanded us to feel toward ourselves, and which is felt only by a very few; it means asking for the mercy of God without which there is no hope of salvation for one who is lost. The mercy of God is nothing other than the grace of the all-holy Spirit; we sinners must ask it of God constantly and persistently. "Have mercy, my Lord, on the disastrous state into which I have fallen, losing Your grace, and establish Your grace once more within me. With Your 'governing Spirit' (Ps 50:14 LXX), the Spirit of Your strength, strengthen me that I may resist temptations brought by the devil, and temptations arising from my fallen nature. Send me a Spirit of chastity that I may arise from the state of madness in which I find myself, and redirect me on my spiritual path. Grant me the Spirit of fear of You that I may fear You as befits the most feeble creature to fear his great God and Creator, that through my reverence toward You I may devoutly keep Your commandments. Place in my heart love toward You that I may no longer absent myself from You and no longer be carried away by irresistible attraction to vile sin. Grant me Your peace that it may keep my soul in undisturbed tranquility, and not allow my thoughts to wander needlessly around the world, causing me harm and agitation, but focus them on self-contemplation and raise them up to Your throne. Grant me a Spirit of meekness that I may keep myself from anger and hatred and always be filled with kindness toward my brothers. Grant me a spirit of humble-mindedness that I may not be filled with pride, or dream about myself, or seek praise and glory among men, but remember that I am dust and ashes, a fallen being, who has been thrown down to earth because of my unworthiness, and will be taken from this body and this world by death, and presented before Your dread and impartial judgment.[17] 'God, be merciful to me, a sinner! Lord, Jesus Christ, Son of God, have mercy on me! Lord have mercy!'"

Many people say these short prayers with the greatest haste, troubling only to complete the required number of them. By praying in this way, they do not allow the prayer to penetrate the heart and to have its characteristic effect of tender emotion. The holy Fathers justly note that people who pray in this way are praying to the air and not to God.[18] Why are we bored in the church of God? Because we have not felt the effect of prayer. Why do we rush to the table laden with food? Because we know from experience the importance of material food. Why do we not rush to the church of God but try to arrive later when a significant proportion of the divine service has already been completed? Because we do not know from experience the importance of prayer, which acts as nourishment for the soul, and gives it spiritual strength. We do not know from experience the importance of prayer because we pray hurriedly, superficially, without paying attention. The effect on the soul of prolonged but inattentive prayer is similar to the effect of plentiful rain on an iron rooftop, from which all the water runs down, however much pours onto it, without having any effect on the roof. Attentive prayer, on the other hand, can be compared to the beneficial rain that irrigates a sown field, gives nourishment to the plants and ensures a rich harvest. To correct a grievous sin that takes all the fruit of his struggle from the ascetic of prayer, the students and friends of holy prayer, the holy Fathers, enjoin us to pronounce the words both of short prayers and of all prayers in general with particular unhurriedness, while paying close attention to the words of the prayer.[19] Such attention is possible if prayers are read unhurriedly; if they are read in a hurry, there is no room for attention. Prayer that is devoid of attention is devoid of its essence of life. It is then like a body that has been abandoned by its soul: it does not have the sweet fragrance of humility; it does not ascend toward God; struck and mortified by distraction, it crawls around in the earthly decay and stench imparted by those praying negligently and coldly. The attention of the mind during prayer is reflected in the heart by blessed sorrow for one's sins, which is the repentance to which God calls us. When the heart is filled with a feeling of repentance, it in turn draws the mind toward particular attentiveness. Following after attentiveness and tender reverence, all the gifts of the Holy Spirit enter the soul, making it a temple of God.

Let us acquire two qualities for our prayer: attentiveness and repentance. With them, as with two wings, may it fly up to heaven, may it stand before the face of God, may it obtain forgiveness for us. The prayer of the tax collector had these two qualities. Imbued with the consciousness of his sinfulness, he did not find in his deeds any hope of receiving salvation; he saw this hope only in the mercy of God, Who calls all sinners to repentance and grants salvation in return for repentance alone. As a sinner without any good deeds of his own, the tax collector took the last place in the temple; as a sinner unworthy of heaven, he did not dare to raise his eyes to heaven. He directed his gaze to the ground and beating his heart in repentance from the depths of his heart, with all his soul he pronounced the prayer that is combined with a confession: "God, have mercy on me, a sinner."

The prayer was so effective and powerful that the sinner left the temple of God justified. Our Lord, the Saviour of mankind and Seer of hearts, bore witness to this, and the prophecy of the prophet came true for the repentant sinner: "For the Lord shall build up Zion," the human soul destroyed by its fall, "and reveal Himself in His glory. He hath regarded the prayer of the humble, and hath not despised their petition. Let this be written for another generation," let this be written for the instruction of all humanity, let it be written for the edification of all Christians and their descendants! And may the "people built up" in repentance and attentive prayer, feeling their renewal through the grace of God, "praise the Lord" (Ps 101:17–19), Who was pleased to take human form and to save mankind through His wondrous providence and His wondrous teaching. Amen.

6. On Repentance

Sermon on the Sunday of the Prodigal Son

Dear brothers! The holy Church, that loving mother of believers, who gave birth to them for salvation and takes upon herself every care so that her children may not be deprived of their legacy, Heaven, preparing them for the approaching ascetic effort of Great Lent, has ordained that we read today at the divine Liturgy the parable of our Lord Jesus Christ on the prodigal son (Luke 15:11–32).

In what does the ascetic effort of holy Great Lent consist? It consists in repentance. We are approaching a period of time chiefly devoted to repentance, as if standing before its gates, and we sing a hymn filled with emotion: "Open to us the doors of repentance, O Giver of life!" What more does the parable of our Lord we have just heard in the Gospel reveal to us? It reveals the unfathomable, eternal mercy of the Heavenly Father toward sinners who offer repentance. "There is joy in the presence of the angels of God over one sinner who repents" (Luke 15:10), the Lord proclaimed to men, calling them to repentance, and, so that these words of His were imprinted more powerfully in the hearts of those who heard Him, He was pleased to supplement them with a parable.

"A certain rich man"—as the parable in the Gospel relates—"had two sons. The younger of them asked his father to give him the part of his inheritance that was due to him. The father fulfilled this wish. A few days later, the younger son took the property he had acquired and went away to a distant land where he squandered it, living a dissolute life. When he had spent it all, a famine arose in that land. The son of the rich man not only began to be in want but found himself in a disastrous state. In this extremity he attached himself to one of the local inhabitants, who sent him to the field to care for his pigs. Unhappy, tormented with hunger, he would have been glad to fill his belly with the coarse fodder with which the pigs were fed, but this proved to be impossible. In this state he finally came to himself and, remembering the plenty with which his father's home was filled, decided to return there. In his thoughts he prepared to mollify his father by acknowledging his sin and his unworthiness and humbly asking to be counted not as a member of his father's family but as one of his father's servants and hirelings. With this pledge in his heart, the younger son started on his way. He was still far from his parents' house when his father saw him: he saw him, took pity on him, and ran toward him, threw himself on his neck, and began kissing him. When the son made the confession and the request he had prepared, the father ordered his servants, 'Bring the best clothing and put it on him, put a ring on his finger and shoes on his feet. Fetch and slaughter the fatted calf: we will eat and be merry. This son of mine was dead but has come back to life; he was lost but has been found.' The older son, who had always been obedient to his father's will and had been out in the fields, returned home during the feast. He found his father's behavior toward the younger son strange. But the father, inspired by the justice of love beside which all other justice is meager and paltry, said to him, 'My son! You are always with me, and all that is mine is yours. But you ought to have rejoiced and made merry because your brother was dead, and has come back to life; was lost, but has been found!'" (Luke 15:11–32).

The younger son, as the holy Fathers explain,[20] can serve as an image of the whole of the fallen race of man and of every human and sinner. The portion of the inheritance due to the younger son represents the gifts of God with which every person, and primarily every Christian, is filled. The most exquisite of these gifts are the mind and the heart, in particular the grace of the Holy Spirit granted to every Christian. The son's request of the father to give him his due portion of the inheritance, in order to use it willfully, signifies man's intent to cease to obey God and to follow his own designs and desires. The father's agreement to give away the inheritance signifies the free agency with which God has honored man in using the gifts of God. The distant land is the life of sin that takes us far away and alienates us from God. Squandering the inheritance means depleting the powers of the mind, heart, and body, in particular offending and driving away from oneself the Holy Spirit through sinful acts. The destitution of the younger son signifies the emptiness of the soul that results from a sinful life. The permanent inhabitants of the distant land are the "rulers of the darkness of this age" (Eph 6:12), fallen souls who remain constantly in their fallen state, in alienation from God; a sinner submits to their influence. The herd of unclean animals signifies the sinful thoughts and feelings that wander in the soul of a sinner and graze in its pastures; they are the inevitable consequence of sinful behavior. In vain do some people think that they can suppress these thoughts and feelings by fulfilling them: they cannot be realized; and fulfilling the passion-filled intentions and dreams a person can have does not destroy them but invigorates them with twice the strength. Man is created for Heaven: only what is truly good can serve for him as satisfying, life-giving food. Evil, which deceptively attracts toward itself the taste of a heart that is damaged by the fall, is capable only of deranging natural human attributes.

How terrible is the emptiness of a soul that is living a sinful life! Unbearable is the torment from passionate sinful thoughts and feelings, when they seethe like maggots in the soul, when they tear to pieces the soul that has submitted to them, the soul that is constrained by them. Sometimes a sinner who is tormented by cruel thoughts, impossible dreams and desires, despairs; sometimes he makes an attempt on his own life, both temporary and eternal. Blessed is the sinner who, at this difficult time, comes to himself, and remembers the boundless love of the Heavenly Father, remembers the immense spiritual richness in which the house of the Heavenly Father abounds—that is, the holy Church. Blessed is the sinner who, horrified with his sinfulness, conceives a desire to save himself by means of repentance from the heaviness that weighs him down.

From the Gospel parable we learn that in order for a person to repent successfully and fruitfully, it is essential for him to see his sin, acknowledge it, repent of it, and confess it. God sees a person who turns to Him with such a pledge from the heart, "when he (is) still a great way off" (Luke 15:20): He sees, and already hurries toward him, embraces him, and kisses him with His grace. The repentant person has barely finished making the confession of his sin when the merciful Lord commands His servants—those who serve at the altar and the holy Angels—to clothe him in the shining garment of purity, to put a ring on his hand—testimony of renewed union with the earthly and heavenly Church, to put shoes on his feet, so that his activity be protected from spiritual thorns (this is the significance of the shoes) by means of firm decisions through the commandments of Christ. To complete the act of love, a table of love is set for the son who has returned, for which the fatted calf is slaughtered. This table represents the ecclesiastical table, at which there is offered to the sinner reconciled with God imperishable spiritual food and drink: Christ, long promised to mankind, prepared by the ineffable mercy of God for fallen humanity from the very moment of the fall.

The Gospel parable is the teaching of God. It is deep and exalted, despite the remarkable simplicity of the human word with which the Word of God was pleased to be clothed. The holy Church was wise to appoint this parable to be read across the land as Great Lent approaches. What news could be more comforting for a sinner standing in confusion before the gates of repentance than that of the eternal and ineffable mercy of the Heavenly Father toward repentant sinners? This mercy is so great that it amazed the holy Angels themselves—the firstborn sons of the Heavenly Father who have never transgressed against a single one of His commandments. With their bright and elevated minds, they could not comprehend the incomprehensible mercy of God toward fallen humanity. With regard to this subject they needed revelation from on high, through which they learned that they should "celebrate and be glad, because" their younger "brother" (the human race) "was dead and is alive again: he was lost and is found," through the Redeemer. "There will be ... joy" before the angels of God even "over one sinner who repents" (Luke 15:7).

Dear brothers! Let us use the time appointed by the holy Church to prepare accordingly for the ascetic efforts of Great Lent. Let us use it to contemplate the great mercy of God toward mankind and toward every person who wishes to be reconciled and united with God through true repentance. The time of our earthly life is priceless: during this time we decide our eternal lot. May it be given to us to decide it unto our salvation and joy, so that our joy may be eternal and united with the joy of God's holy Angels! May the joy of the Angels and of mankind be fulfilled and completed through fulfillment of the will of the Heavenly Father! For "it is not the will of your Father who is in heaven that one of these little ones"—people lessened and disparaged by sin—"should perish" (Matt 18:14). Amen.

7. On the Second Coming of Christ

Sermon on Meatfare Sunday

"When the Son of Man comes in His glory" (Matt 25:31).

Dear brothers! Not long ago we contemplated our Lord Jesus Christ born in a cave, wrapped in swaddling-cloths, laid in a manger (Luke 2:7), taking upon Himself, together with His humanity, all human weaknesses apart from sin; not long ago we contemplated Him persecuted by Herod, fleeing from the murderers' sword to Egypt, returning to Judea, not daring to remain there, settling in Nazareth, a poor town of little importance in little-known Galilee, receiving baptism on an equal footing with people in need of baptism, preaching repentance and the approach of the kingdom of heaven (Matt 2:1–23; 3:13–17; 4:17). We contemplated this not long ago, and we now prepare ourselves for a new, amazing sight. In order to become worthy of this sight, as far as humanly possible, we intend to purify our spiritual eyes—our minds and our hearts—through the ascetic effort of fasting. We intend to refine our very flesh through fasting, so that the veil that covers our spiritual nature is not excessively thick and impenetrable, and no longer prevents us from seeing with the necessary purity, faith, and tenderness our Saviour crucified for us, breaking down on the cross the "middle wall" separating us from God (Eph 2:14). And we will also see another sight, a terrifying and terrible event: the second coming on earth of our Lord Jesus Christ. We can contemplate the first coming with reverent commemoration; the second is presented vividly and powerfully to our imagination by the Word of God. This image has the capacity to strike our souls with the fear of God for the sake of our salvation, to waken us from deep negligence about our eternal lot as if from a deep sleep into which our fleshly life has lulled us. "When the Son of Man comes in His glory ... " (Matt 25:31).

The first coming of our Lord to earth and His existence there were filled with a deep, constant humility. The Lord left unheeded everything that the world respects and values. He did not will to appear in the brilliance and the thunder of earthly glory; He did not will to appear surrounded by splendor and magnificence; He did not will to appear amongst the noise of festivities and jubilation. He came to the earth as to a land to which the transgressors of God's commandments had been exiled; He stayed and acted there as in a land of sorrows to which the transgressors against the commandment in God's paradise were banished from paradise on high; He lived and acted there as the Redeemer of the fallen becoming a partaker in all the tribulations suffered by transgressing humanity. He was as one of the destitute who are trampled on by other people. He was a wanderer with nowhere to lay His head (see Matt 8:20). He was persecuted and dishonored; and He constantly returned good for evil: "For the Son of Man did not come to destroy men's lives but to save them" (Luke 9:56). And He ended His earthly wanderings with an agonizing and shameful death, the death of criminal transgressors, the death of slaves who even in the very means of death did not have the same rights as citizens. Such was the first coming on earth of the Son of God. At the appropriate time, His second coming to us will come to pass: "the Son of Man," who is at the same time also the Son of God, "[will come] in His glory." His first coming was the coming of the Redeemer, who submitted to all human weaknesses, raising them onto Himself to destroy them through Himself; the second coming will be the coming of the Judge to Whom men will give an account of their behavior in terms of the divine redemption granted to them by God. "When the Son of Man comes in His glory, and all the holy angels with Him .... All the nations will be gathered before Him" (Matt 25:31–32), so as to present to Him their deeds at the judgment and receive from Him accordingly reward or punishment.

When we hear that the arrival of any earthly ruler or judge is imminent, we take all measures to put our affairs in order and earn approval: we should be even more concerned with the judgment of Christ at which the eternal lot of each of us will be decided. The Judge is frightening, inexpressibly frightening. He is frightening in His greatness, He is frightening in His omnipotence, He is frightening because He sees into the depths of the human soul, and not a single secret human thought, not even the most subtle sensation is hidden from Him. Justifications have no place at His judgment: not only no-one who has been mortified by sin but "no man living" a life of righteousness will "be justified" (Ps 142:2). You will "prevail," cries the God-inspired prophet to the Judge Who is coming, "when Thou art judged" (Ps 50:6). All people will be seized with trembling when they stand before the face of the Judge, not only sinners but also the righteous. The sinners will tremble from despair, from anticipation of the torments that await them, from that extraordinary fear that causes within them a revolution capable of changing the universe. They will cry out to the mountains and the rocks: "Fall on us and hide us from the face of Him who sits on the throne and from the wrath of the Lamb! For the great day of His wrath has come, and who is able to stand?" (Rev 6:16–17). They will tremble, and they will give praise although it will be too late. When the Creator concealed His inaccessible and unbearable glory beneath a cloak of humility, only the created being was able freely to have thoughts and feelings, to speak words and to have actions at his disposal. But when the Creator appears in His glory, the freedom of His creation will fade before the greatness of His glory, just as this freedom under any other particular circumstances, while remaining ours, can be destroyed by the force of circumstance. The most hardened enemies of the Lord, members of the Sanhedrin itself who crucified Him and swore hatred toward Him, will cry out with hymns of praise when they meet the Judge, as the Lord Himself prophesied to them: "You will see the Son of Man sitting at the right hand of the Power, and coming on the clouds of heaven" (Matt 26:64). "For I say to you, you shall see Me no more till you say, 'Blessed is He who comes in the name of the Lord!'" (Matt 23:39). The righteous will tremble from the boundless glory of the Judge Who appears: they will see their virtues, but, in the light of the Highest Virtue, these virtues will appear to them as the tattered rags of beggars: in their virtues they will not see a pledge of their forgiveness—they will expect forgiveness only due to the eternal mercy of God. The very angels of God will be confused and afraid (Luke 21:26–27) when God, Who "has committed all judgment to the Son, that all should honor the Son just as they honor the Father" (John 5:22–23), reveals Himself in His glory. Insentient material nature will not be able to endure the gaze of the Son of God: "the sky receded as a scroll when it is rolled up, and every mountain and island was moved out of its place" (Rev 6:14).

At the judgment of Christ, by way of justification mercy will be demanded, and only mercy, as an active expression of love and as empirical proof of love, will earn forgiveness. "I desire mercy and not sacrifice" (Matt 9:13), proclaimed the future dread and impartial Judge. Mercy will obtain justification for those who love it, and it will commit to condemnation those who reject it. It will stand with audacity before the Lord, and it will bring before Him all its workers. It will bring those who achieved it by material means, those who fed their starving brothers, received wanderers into their homes, clothed the naked, visited the sick and the imprisoned. Mercy will bring before Christ those who have cultivated it secretly within their souls and pardoned their neighbor, guarding themselves from judging him for his stumbling-blocks, forgiving him for insults and offence, bestowing upon him a blessing in return for an oath, a good work in return for an evil deed. Mercy will bring before Christ pastors of the church who have preached to their brothers the imperishable food, the Word of God, who have clothed those made naked by sin with the garments of virtue, who have given spiritual healing to the sick of soul, who have patiently taught those imprisoned in the dungeons of unbelief or of dark delusion. Mercy will bring before Christ humble monks who have gained secret and essential knowledge of Christ living within them, who have longed with a blessed hunger for the truth of the Gospel, who have sought to clothe themselves in reverence and holiness, who have cleansed themselves even from the most subtle human ailments, the predilections of everyday life, and by this means attained the freedom of the Gospel. Mercy will also bring before Christ those who have been able to have mercy simply on themselves, practicing self-examination and releasing themselves through repentance from the poverty, the illness, the darkness of sin. Repentance is impossible for a hardened heart: it is necessary for a heart to soften, to be filled with sympathy and mercy toward its own disastrous state of sinfulness. When a heart is enveloped and filled with mercy, only then does it become capable of repentance; only then, after ceasing to condemn its neighbors, can it turn to self-examination, and, condemning itself in a way that leads to salvation, apply to its sores the healing of repentance. Christ redeemed all people and each person by means of Himself. A person who proves to be capable only of mercy toward himself, and shows this mercy, feeding his hungry soul with the Word of God, giving it to drink of sensations emanating from the Holy Spirit, distracting it from disastrous wandering from one type of sin to another, bringing it into a home of reverence and virtue, clothing it with good deeds, healing former sins by confessing them and by carrying out activity opposite to them, escaping from the dungeon of a carnal mind and a carnal state into a spiritual mind and state—this person will be recognized as having done all this for Jesus Christ the Lord Himself. Mercy will bring before Christ all those who have shown mercy, and will obtain from Christ forgiveness and eternal bliss for them. "Come," He says to them, "you blessed of My Father, inherit the kingdom prepared for you from the foundation of the world: for I was hungry and you gave Me food; I was thirsty and you gave Me drink; I was a stranger and you took Me in; I was naked and you clothed Me; I was sick and you visited Me; I was in prison and you came to Me." "Assuredly, I say to you, inasmuch as you did it to one of the least of these My brethren, you did it to Me" (Matt 25:34–36, 40).

It is not known on what day and at what hour the Son of God will end life on earth through His coming to give judgment; it is not known on what day and at what hour the earthly life of each one of us will be cut short at the command of the Son of God, and we will be called to be parted from our bodies and to give account for our earthly life, at that personal judgment, before the general judgment that awaits man after his death. Dear brothers! Let us remain vigilant and prepare ourselves for the dread judgment that awaits us at the border with eternity for the irreversible decision about our lot unto the ages. Let us prepare ourselves, arming ourselves with all the virtues, especially mercy, which includes in itself and crowns all virtues just as love—the stimulating reason for mercy—is the "bond of" Christian "perfection" (Col 3:14). Mercy makes people who are filled with it God-like (see Matt 5:44,48; Luke 6:32,36). "Blessed are the merciful, for they shall obtain mercy; for judgment is without mercy to the one who has shown no mercy" (Matt 5:7; Jas 2:13). Amen.

8. The Precondition for Entering Great Lent

Sermon on Cheesefare Sunday

Dear brothers! We have already reached the gates of the holy fast; they are ready to open before us. Already, as appointed by the holy Church, we have heard in today's reading of the holy Gospel the instructions of our Lord Jesus Christ on the right way to approach the ascetic effort of fasting.

"If you forgive men their trespasses," proclaims the Gospel teaching we have just heard, "your heavenly Father will also forgive you. But if you do not forgive men their trespasses, neither will your Father forgive your trespasses" (Matt 6:14–15). This is the information with which the holy Church meets us at the gates of the fast. This is the precondition it offers us on the very threshold of the spiritual hall of repentance. We intend to show our repentance for various sinful passions by means of various bodily deprivations: the Gospel demands mercy of us before the sacrifice so that the sacrifice may be pleasing to God.

If you wish to approach the ascetic struggle of fasting and prayer, if you wish to reap abundant fruits from your repentance, listen to the word of God, listen to the testament of God, and let go, forgive your neighbors their sins toward you. "If you forgive men their trespasses, your heavenly Father will also forgive you. But if you do not forgive men their trespasses, neither will your Father forgive your trespasses." Amen.

9. Preparation for the Mystery of Confession

Talk on the Monday of the First Week of Great Lent

Introduction

Dear brothers! We have found refuge in the holy fast. Let us now dedicate a period of time to especial, attentive, thorough self-examination: the gates of repentance are opening wide for us.

We are inhabitants of a holy monastery, the closest disciples of Christ, eternal children of the Church, constantly to be found at her spiritual breast: we ought not to need a special time for paying attention to ourselves, for cleansing our sinful blemishes with confession and repentance; all our life ought to consist of constant attentiveness, constant repentance, if our life were in keeping with our name. The model of purity that we must attain is perfect. It is our Lord Jesus Christ. "As He who called you is holy," says the Apostle, "you also be holy in all your conduct, because it is written, 'Be holy, for I am holy'" (1 Pet 1:15–16). According to the eternal perfection of the model of purity, the arena of repentance and purification is eternal. If a person passed through this arena with all possible diligence and zeal—even that person would not be able to attain perfect purification. Even if his life continued in constant repentance for thousands of years, he would not attain full purification. The greatest of the holy monks recognized at their deaths that they not only had not perfected but had not even begun repentance.[21] And we, with our weaknesses that are constantly growing and multiplying, will be very far on the day of our departure from earthly life from that holiness with which our venerable Fathers—chosen vessels of God, dwellers in the wilderness—left their bodies. They are now dwellers in heaven as a reward for painstakingly remaining in a state of repentance throughout their wandering across the wilderness of earthly life.

So, people who spend their life in constant attentiveness, constantly observing their souls, noticing within themselves the varied activity of sin, constantly healing themselves from this poison with repentance, do not attain full spiritual perfection. What then can be said of people who live negligently, occupying themselves with continual amusements, never thinking, or thinking very rarely, in passing, about the matter that they should think about most of all: their salvation? I will say of them what has already been said; I will pronounce the verdict already pronounced on them. I will say this with sorrow in my heart, but I will say truly because I am merely repeating the words of the Apostle, the words of God. "A widow ... who lives in pleasure is dead while she lives" (1 Tim 5:5–6). Do not think that these words refer only to widows in the flesh. They refer much more to me and to you who have renounced the world to serve Christ: a monk is a true widow to whom the world should be dead. Monk, secret widow, listen to my poor words. Did you call yourself dead to the world and to this vain age in order to live for God and for blessed eternity? Look deeply into Scripture, look deeply into yourself, check the state of your soul against the state foreordained for it in the Scriptures, and say, are you really dead to the world? Has your mortification at least begun? Have you felt yourself being revived by God? Have your thoughts and wishes moved on to the age to come? It is a very rare person who can answer these questions in the affirmative; each one of us would sooner admit the justice of a terrible verdict pronounced upon him. This verdict is burdensome to the ears and heart of carnal and worldly people; but it is better to hear it here, while our wandering on earth continues, and the arena of repentance and correction has not ended. If my words produce fear and grief within you, this fear is blessed, this sorrow is desired! "For godly sorrow," says the Apostle, "produces repentance leading to salvation, not to be regretted" (2 Cor 7:10). If it exerts influence for a time, this sorrow will lead to flight from sorrow and torment, terrible both in their eternity and in the awful torture they bring that is inexpressible in words and incomprehensible to our minds and sensations.

Let each one of us look deeply into himself; let each one of us verify within himself the words that I will say for the salvation of your souls and of my soul.

We are destined for paradise, heaven, and eternal blessedness if we live here virtuously, fulfilling the vows we made at our baptism and repeated at our tonsure into monasticism with the addition of vows of poverty and chastity. But we pay no attention to the blessedness that is prepared for us like one sleeping who is unaware of his surroundings and of the pleasures and delights of this life that await him when he wakes; we never think of the ineffable good things of the future: our thoughts are always on earth, always with earthly pleasures, earthly cares. Are we not dead in our souls, although we appear to be alive to ourselves and to those who have carnal wisdom, and seeing only with carnal eyes.[22]

If we live an earthly life full of sins and sinful pleasures, we are destined for hell, eternal fire, the unsleeping worm that gnaws and torments incessantly. Yet we seek these very pleasures, we pursue them; our desires and thoughts are with them. We live as if there were no hell, as if we were immortal, eternally on earth, as if we had attained eternal blessedness. In vain does the Word of God ring out with threats, in vain does it proclaim fearful eternal torments. We see the death of our brothers, we participate in their burial: this makes no impression on us as if death were the lot of other people, not ours at all. We, like the dead, possess neither remembrance nor premonition of death, neither remembrance nor premonition of the future. It is as if we were dead. "You have a name that you are alive, but you are dead" (Rev 3:1), the true Word of God testifies of every carnal person.

The Son of God came down to earth for us, trampled on our death by means of His own death, became life for us and at the same time the way to this life. He asks us to crucify our "flesh with its passions and desires" (Gal 5:24), and He asks this not because He Himself needs it, but because we need it: only in a body that is dead to sin can the existence of a grace-filled life be revealed.[23] But we hear only the sounds of the words; the soul does not understand or accept the words themselves: for us it is as if they were being spoken in an unknown foreign language. And this is not surprising: it is the direct consequence of our spiritual state. A person who is dead in the body is not capable of physical feelings: whether he is glorified or is given great riches, whether he is stripped naked or humiliations are heaped upon him, he is insensible to everything. In the same way, a person who is dead in the soul cannot understand spiritual words, he cannot sense spiritual good things, he cannot have the necessary remembrance of death and of eternal torments, the necessary knowledge of the vanity of this world and this age, although this knowledge is so clear and tangible: he is injured and deadened by sin, he is already a stranger to God and to blessedness, he is already stamped as a victim of hades. The life of the body depends on the presence within it of the soul; the life of the soul depends on the presence within it of the Holy Spirit.

Will I be able to glorify worthily the unfathomable goodness of God, His ineffable patience, His ineffable love for mankind? Shall I, like the Prophet (Ps 148), call upon ranks of angels, all the tribes of people to glorify Him, all beasts and cattle, the birds of the heavens, reptiles and creeping things, fish wandering in the wide expanses of water, and with them all inanimate creation? And then every created thing, united into one mouth, one voice of praise, will not be able to hymn worthily the goodness of God that is beyond words, beyond comprehension. Come, brothers, let us venerate and fall down at the feet of this goodness: until now it has patiently borne our transgressions, until now it has awaited our conversion, until now it has extended its embrace to us, calling the wanderers in the wilderness and in the impassable thickets of sin, accepting repentant sinners, making them sons and daughters of God. Now, after hearing its voice, the voice calling you to repentance, "do not harden your hearts" (Heb 3:15); "he who has ears to hear" (Matt 13:9) do not remain deaf. "Awake, you who sleep" the deep sleep of negligence and carelessness for your salvation! "Arise from the dead" (Eph 5:14), you who are dead from insensibility and bitterness, from a life that is wholly sacrificed to the flesh, to sin, and to corruption. May I see in you the movement of a life awakened by the word that proclaims repentance. May I hear your voice as the voice of lamentation, the voice of your weeping, the voice of your repentance so that I may satisfy myself that there is still a sign, a remnant of life within you. May the Lord, seeing that you have spent all the days of your life without fruit, grant you another day that you may be saved without effort; a day on which, through sincere confession before your spiritual father, you can throw down the whole burden of your sins.

Part One

As an institution of the omnipotent God, repentance is omnipotent. There is no sin that can stand before the face of repentance. It is a gift given to fallen human nature; it is a remnant of our original innocence like a consciousness of this purity and a mourning for its loss; it is a reclamation of baptism; it is a link between earth and heaven, a ladder to heaven. It cleanses and effaces every sin. Even if you were burdened with the gravest sins, you should never stop yourself from turning toward repentance. The immeasurable ocean absorbs both the waters of a broad river that flows majestically through many lands and the modest flow of a little stream that is hardly noticeable: in the same way, in the depths of God's goodness, grave falls into sin disappear just as completely as the smallest, most insignificant transgressions. Be assured of this by the parable of the five hundred denarii and the fifty denarii, both amounts equally forgiven: the creditor is infinitely rich, while the debtors are all bankrupt (Luke 7:41–42). Even a small sin remains uneffaced if the sinner neglects to repent for it, believing it to be insignificant; and a great sin is completely wiped away by means of repentance through the boundless goodness and omnipotence of God. Remember St David, who fell into both adultery and murder. Negligence stole imperceptibly into the soul of the righteous man; from this negligence was born unguardedness of bodily sensations and his unguarded gaze unexpectedly fell on a means of temptation: the object of temptation roused in the holy soul a sinful desire; the desire was followed by a sinful act; the act of adultery was followed by vainglorious shame. The shame by which human pride was ashamed of the sin led to a new sinful desire, the desire to hide his fall into sin, the desire to preserve the appearance of righteousness before men. This was the reason that murder was committed. For a long time David remained in bitterness, unfeeling, as if innocent of any sin. It was necessary for God Himself to expose him. The prophet Nathan exposed the sinner at the command of God—and David had hardly said, "I have sinned against the Lord," when the answer came from the Lord: "The Lord ... has put away your sin" (2 Kgdms 12:13). Omnipotent repentance has saved whole cities and kingdoms, it has revoked judgments already given by God. Thus the populous city of Nineveh, condemned to destruction by God's prophet, averted this by sincere repentance—and in vain did the prophet, sitting not far away from Nineveh, await its destruction, the fulfillment of his prophecy (Jonah 3:1–4:5). Thus the impious king of Israel, Ahab, a worshiper of idols and persecutor and murderer of the worshipers of the true God, had already been condemned to execution as announced by the great Elijah; but Ahab was moved and shed tears, remaining however in impiety. This short-lived tender emotion, these few tears did not remain without effect: "Ahab humbled himself before Me," the Lord said to the prophet Elijah, "I will not bring the evil in his days. But in the days of his son, I will bring evil upon his house" (3 Kgdms 20:29). All of Holy Scripture and the whole history of the Church are filled with countless examples demonstrating the great power of repentance. A certain bandit, recounts Palladius in the *Lausiac History*, was caught in the act of committing a crime and was brought to Arsenoitis, a town in the Thebaid. After many torments, he was condemned to death by beheading. When he went with soldiers to the place where he had committed the crime, which was six miles away from the town, a monk unknown to him followed him, wanting to watch his execution. The bandit, seeing the monk following him, said to him, "Abba! Don't you have a cell and handiwork to do?" The monk answered, "I do." To this the thief replied, "Why don't you sit in your cell and weep for your sins?" The monk replied, "Brother, I am very lazy; my soul does not have repentance. That is why I came to see how you die. Perhaps with the help of this sight I will come to repentance." Then the bandit said to him, "Abba, for the sake of God, stay in your cell, bless and praise Christ the Saviour: since the time when He became man and died for us sinners, man has no longer suffered death."

And here is another story, just as moving and instructive: "Near a certain town there lived a hermit who possessed the divine gift of discernment. In that town there lived a harlot who was known to all the inhabitants. One day the hermit saw extending from the women's monastery in the town up to heaven a bright path along which a soul walked in great joy, led by angels, and approached the gates of heaven. He sent his disciple to the women's monastery to find out who had passed away there. The disciple returned with the news that in the monastery no-one had died, but the well-known harlot had died suddenly before the monastery gates after coming there from the town. Perplexed, the hermit began praying to God to explain the vision to him. 'Yes,' was God's reply to the holy elder, 'you saw ascending to heaven the soul of the woman who had been a harlot. She had conceived a firm intention to repent and to reform, and she had gone to the monastery with the resolve to enter it. The fact that she died before the gates of the monastery without managing to fulfil her intention was the decision of God. But God took her intention as the actual deed.'"

In these two stories we see the promise of the Gospel being realized in practice. And how many of these experiences the Gospel itself presents! The tax collector, burdened with sins, came to the temple of God, and because of his humility and his repentance he came out of the temple justified. Another tax collector, Zacchaeus, had barely expressed his intention to reform, when he was called a son of Abraham in a verdict over him from God: "Today salvation has come to this house" (Luke 19:9). The harlot who fell at the feet of the Saviour, transforming love for sin into love for God, heard: "Her sins, which are many, are forgiven, for she loved much" (Luke 7:47). The thief who was crucified at the right hand of the God-Man received salvation in the last moments of his turbulent life. No sooner had he humbled himself, no sooner had he acknowledged himself to be worthy of condemnation than his spiritual eyes opened, and he recognized the God-Man in the crucified man next to him; after recognizing Him, he confessed; no sooner had he confessed than he received a promise of eternal blessedness. This was an event that was in complete conformity with the teaching of the Gospel. "He who believes in Me," said the Lord, "though he may die, he shall live" (John 11:26). He openly and clearly proclaimed of Himself, "For I did not come to call the righteous, but sinners, to repentance" (Matt 9:13).

Do not think that those sinners who lived in the time of our Saviour's presence on earth were especially fortunate. Fortunate were those who hastened to confess their sins and to repent; on the other hand, those who rejected the healing of repentance and remained in sin perished from their unrepentance, from their bitterness. Nothing and no-one prevent us even now from enjoying the happiness of repentant sinners before Jesus Christ the Lord Himself. He said of Himself to those who believe in Him, "lo, I am with you always, even to the end of the age" (Matt 28:20). When you stand before your spiritual father, he will confirm to you the truth that has been proclaimed to us: "Lo, child," he will say, "Christ stands invisible, accepting your confession."[24] Standing before Christ Himself, request of Him and receive from Him great and rich mercy—the forgiveness of sins.

Why should we delay? Why stop, enter into doubt and uncertainty in which the devil delights and which gives him more power over us? You will say that numerous grave sins over a long period of time are leading you to doubt and uncertainty; from continually falling into sin the strength of your soul has become exhausted and you feel a weakening of your very will. Yes, your sins are grave. For any physician your condition is incurable, but not for this Physician, the Lord, Who is almighty and eternally merciful. Your unbelieving timidity would still be to some extent forgivable if you might expect the Physician to turn His eyes away from you and reject you with disdain and wrath. But He does not reject you; on the contrary, He calls you to Him, implores you to approach Him. He will not rebuke you: no cruel word will leave His lips: He calls you to Him only in order to grant you forgiveness and healing. "Come now, and let us reason together," says the Lord, "although your sins are like crimson, I shall make them white like snow, and although they are as scarlet, I shall make them white like wool" (Isa 1:18). The purpose of the coming of Christ on earth was to free human souls from the sin that possesses them and to restore in us the fallen divine image. "Behold!," John the Forerunner testifies of Jesus, "The Lamb of God who takes away the sin of the world" (John 1:29). The healing of bodily illnesses was merely evidence of the healing of the soul from sin. When the paralytic was brought before the Lord, He said to the sick man, "Son, be of good cheer; your sins are forgiven you" (Matt 9:2). Some of the scribes who were present thought that he was blaspheming. Jesus, seeing their thoughts, said, "Why do you think evil in your hearts? For which is easier, to say, 'Your sins are forgiven you,' or to say, 'Arise and walk'? But that you may know that the Son of Man has power on earth to forgive sins"—then He said to the paralytic, "Arise, take up your bed, and go to your house." And he arose and departed to his house" (Matt 9:4–7). If you are so weakened through sin that you have lost the will for good; if you are leprous, deaf, and blind of soul; if you have obeyed the devil to such an extent that you have completely come under his control and, acting by the force of the enemy, you resemble one possessed: even then, do not hesitate to approach for repentance, and you will hear, "your sins are forgiven you." Your Creator is also the Creator of your heart, your mind and your will. Have you spoiled or defiled them with sin? The Creator can re-create a pure heart from a defiled heart, or renew a darkened or deranged mind through His almighty Truth. He can confirm in goodness your suffering and exhausted will that is in the power of sin, and in this way will return to your soul the joy of the hope of salvation, that is contained in victories of the will over sin.

Let the following evil thought enter no-one's mind: "It is easy to receive forgiveness through repentance: ease in receiving forgiveness allows one not to be strict with oneself, it allows one to give oneself up to sinful delights. Even more: it looks with leniency on the resumption of grave falls into sin." No! It is not on this condition that sins are forgiven following repentance. This gift is granted in order that a person who has fallen into grave sins should abandon them. This is clear from the very words of the Saviour: after forgiving the harlot brought to judgment before Him by the pharisees, He said to her, "go, and sin no more" (John 8:11). The Lord gave the same command to the man He healed at Bethesda: He gave a command together with a threat of greater punishment if the command were disobeyed: "See, you have been made well," He said, "Sin no more, lest a worse thing come upon you" (John 5:14). This is how the holy desert Fathers understood and fulfilled the words of the God-Man, and how they taught the brothers. Abba Pimen gave the following reply to the question "What does repentance from sin mean?": "It consists in repenting from sin and not repeating it. Those who act thus are called pure and righteous because they have given up their sins and become righteous people."[25] The great instructor of monastics St Isaac the Syrian says of people who repeat their falls into sin, "Anyone who falls again into the same sin in the hope of repentance walks before God with guile; to such a person is sent sudden death, and he does not receive the time he was counting on in order to restore his virtue."[26] This is understood to mean mortal sins, rather than those half-formed intentions due to weakness that are covered by daily repentance and were not entirely foreign even to the saints. If due to an unfortunate habit or weakness you are carried away somehow forcibly by the flesh or by blood, and you cannot stand firm against the mortal sins primarily referred to as "falls," even then do not give yourself up to despair, into which an uninterrupted series of falls so forcefully draw a man. For such cases, we have the wise exhortation of St Sisoes the Great. A brother said to him one day with sorrow in his heart, "Father! What shall I do? I have fallen." The elder answered him, "Get up again." The brother said, "I did get up again, and again I fell." The elder replied, "Get up again." The brother objected, "How long should I go on getting up and falling again?" The elder said, "Until your end."[27] A true servant of God preserves himself not only from sinful acts and words, he guards himself even from sinful thoughts and feelings. In return for faithfulness to the Lord, he is honored with special spiritual gifts. The holy Silouan, an ascetic of Scetis and then of Sinai, abounded in them; when he was asked by what means he gained grace, Silouan would answer, "I never allowed into my heart thoughts that would anger God."[28]

A person who has kept himself from mortal sins must not think that he has little need of repentance. Your sins may be insignificant in your eyes, but you do not know what their weight is on the scales of God's justice. "Human judgement is one thing and the judgement of God is another," said a certain holy hermit discussing his monastic and ascetic work as he approached his demise.[29] The lawgiver of the people of Israel, the God-seer, holy Moses, radiant with the rays of prophecy, of wonderworking, and of visible glory, spoke a thoughtless word before the people when grieved by their obstinacy (Num 20:10–12). He only "spake unadvisedly with his lips" (Ps 105:33), to use the expression of the holy Psalmist; he said a word of disbelief, while remaining full of faith in his heart; he spoke this word with his lips, acknowledging the impiety and unbelief of a people unworthy of miracles and blessings—as if supposing that the grace of God, weakened by the impiety of the people, were not powerful enough in itself to perform the miracle. A sin that was apparently unimportant and forgivable, the sin of a holy man, rich in good deeds and grace-filled gifts, was judged otherwise by God: not only does it merit exposure, not only is it recorded in the books of Holy Scripture for the information of the whole people of Israel and of everyone in the whole world who was to believe in the true God—it also earned a temporary punishment. Moses, who knew the power of prayer and the unending mercy of God, in vain resorted to prayer and entreaty to

God (Deut 3:23–25); Moses, who more than once had averted the wrath of God from the whole people of Israel, prayed for the decision pronounced regarding him to be revoked; he prayed and was not heard, "But the Lord disregarded me on your account," said Moses, telling the people about the consequences of his prayer, "and would not listen to me" (Deut 3:26). In Scripture nothing is said without a holy purpose. In guessing the purpose of Scripture in the present circumstance, we will not by any means sin if we acknowledge that it serves as an exhortation and a warning to us not to consider even our minor sins to be minor and to take the greatest care to avoid them and to cleanse ourselves from them through repentance. How often we sin through ignorance! How often we sin through weakness! How often we sin by being carried away by pleasure, by the example of others, by indulgence toward others! How often we permit the stumbling-blocks of judging our neighbor, of hard-heartedness toward him! We remain unconcerned, but the manuscripts where our sins are written are multiplying. The righteous Job knew about this, and every day he offered prayers and sacrifices to God for his children, saying, "Lest my sons consider evil things in their mind against God. Therefore Job did this continually" (Job 1:5). The sign of a righteous man is that he has a firm distrust of his own righteousness and remains in a state of constant repentance.

When we avoid an amusement that dazzles us, when we become absorbed in ourselves and begin to contemplate ourselves, checking the state of our souls against how they should be according to the teachings of Holy Scripture: then we ourselves recognize that our minor sins are not minor but grave and terrible, worthy of constant tears and repentance. We open the Holy Scripture, we see how we should be. The holy apostle Paul says, "The first man was of the earth, made of dust; the second Man is the Lord from heaven ... And as we have borne the image of the man of dust, we shall also bear the image of the heavenly Man" (1 Cor 15:47,49). On being granted existence, beginning to exist, we at that very moment clothe ourselves in the image of our forefather Adam, in his fallen image; we are conceived and born with a body that is subject to illnesses and destruction, with a soul that is subject to sin; we are conceived and born possessing the seed of sin sown in all our nature, with the poison of sin spread throughout all the members of our soul and our body. "I was conceived in wickedness, and in sins did my mother bear me" (Ps 50:7). In this way the whole human race became and becomes defiled, is deadened by the sin with which we were infected in our very roots, in our forefather. In our re-creation through redemption, it was necessary to remove the root that was constantly passing on the mortal infection to all the branches, and to replace it with a root that would give us life, incorruption, holiness; the human race needed a new forebear, and the "Lord from heaven" made himself that Forebear. He deigned to be a descendant of Adam in the flesh, conceived from the Virgin without seed and without passion. In being born on earth, Adam and many other people anticipated Jesus; but through His birth from death and from the grave, which is resurrection, Jesus anticipated Adam and all people (Matt 27:53). He made Himself the Firstborn of the human race (Col 1:18); He is the first person to have ascended into heaven. There He sat at the right hand of God (Acts 7:55–56). Adam and the other holy forebears of Jesus in the flesh were made His descendants through birth in the Spirit in the regeneration (Matt 19:28). He is the Father of the age to come, the Progenitor of the holy generation of the chosen people. In order that we who began our existence in the image of the old Adam may pass over from his outcast descendants to the blessed descendants of the New Adam, we must be born again from on High. "Unless one is born of water and the Spirit," the New Adam, our Lord Jesus Christ, tells us, "he cannot enter the kingdom of God" (John 3:5). We are born to a new life full of grace "through holy baptism," through which we pass over to be descendants of the Lord Jesus Christ, and receive adoption by the Father of the new age, as the Apostle said: "For as many of you as were baptized into Christ have put on Christ." "You received the Spirit of adoption by whom we cry out, 'Abba, Father'" (Gal 3:27; Rom 8:15). But in order to remain in this adoption, we must live not according to the flesh, but according to the Spirit: "For as many as are led by the Spirit of God, these are sons of God" (Rom 8:14). On the other hand, "now if anyone does not have the Spirit of Christ, he is not His" (Rom 8:9). Is this sign of adoption preserved in us? Does the Spirit bear witness "with our spirit that we are children of God?" (Rom 8:16). By this sign the holy desert Fathers would put themselves to the test and examine themselves; this self-examination would plunge them into an abyss of repentance and weeping. Let us hear how St Macarius of Egypt, justifiably called the Great, discourses upon this subject:

> "Just as the body," he says, "does not possess its life of itself, but from without, that is, from the earth, and cannot live without external means: in the same way the soul, if it is not regenerated from here in that world of the living, if it is not fed spiritually there and, making progress in the Lord, does not grow spiritually, if it does not clothe itself in a garment of heavenly beauty taken from Divinity itself; then it is impossible for

> it to live in joy and peace. The nature of God contains within itself the bread of life in accordance with these words: 'I am the bread of life' (John 6:35) and 'wine [that] maketh a man's heart glad' (Ps 103:15) and 'the oil of gladness' (Ps 44:8), as well as the diverse food of the Spirit and the heavenly garment of light that proceeds from God Himself. It is in these things that the eternal life of the soul consists. Woe betide the body when it is left solely to its own nature, for it is destroyed and it dies. Woe betide the soul, too, when it is left solely to its own nature, hoping only in its own works, and having no communion with the Spirit of God, for it dies without being vouchsafed eternal, divine life ... If you have become the throne of God, and the heavenly Charioteer has seated Himself upon you; if your whole soul has become a spiritual eye and has become all light; if you have been nourished with the heavenly food of the Spirit, and given the water of life to drink, and have clothed yourself in a garment of mystical light; if your inner man has gained all of this, and is sure of this: then truly you are already living the eternal life, your soul rests from now with the Lord. Truly you have gained and accepted from the Lord what you need to live a true life. But if you see none of this within yourself, then weep, grieve and cry out bitterly because you have not yet become a partaker in eternal and spiritual riches, you have not yet acquired true life. Have a care for your spiritual poverty and beseech the Lord day and night, as someone who is in the terrible destitution of sin. O, when did we concern ourselves and have care for our poverty! O, when did we not live in carelessness like those who abound in wealth and spiritual gifts!"[30]

The desire to gain true repentance was a motive for holy monks who had felt poverty of spirit to withdraw into deep seclusion, to shut themselves in their cells, to hide away in caves and in canyons. But such a view of one's poverty, such a view of the deadening of the soul through sin, is given to someone who has already made considerable progress in the monastic struggle. This inspires a person to resolve to renounce the world conclusively, to die to the world, in order to give himself up completely to the search for eternal life within himself.

Let us turn to a different sign by which self-examination is more accessible for those of us who are beginners. The Lord said in the holy Gospel, "If anyone loves Me, he will keep My word. He who does not love

Me does not keep My words" (John 14:23–24). "If you keep My commandments, you will abide in My love" (John 15:10). A person who keeps Christ's commandments is of Christ; someone who does not keep them does not belong to Christ. To examine our conscience, our spiritual state, in accordance with the commandments of the Gospel is very easy, extremely salutary, and wholly reliable. For example, let us examine whether we have fulfilled the commandments of Christ set forth in Chapter Five of the Gospel according to Matthew. Have we been angry with a neighbor for no reason? Have we quarreled or are we still quarreling with anyone? Is resentment acting within us? Have we uttered reproachful or abusive words? Did we refrain from sensual looks, feelings, or thoughts? Did we return evil for evil? Were we so meek that we did not resist evil? Did we love our enemies? Did we bless those who cursed us? Did we do good to those who hated us? Did we pray for those causing us distress? Of course, even these few questions will trouble and expose our conscience. So what might happen after further and more thorough examination? Our eyes will be opened to our sins, a feeling of constant sorrow for our unworthiness will be implanted in our hearts; we will learn to grieve for those sins that in our darkened state appeared minor, but in actual fact deprive us of adoption by God and blessed eternity. The Lord Himself bore witness to this and other things. After commanding us to love our enemies, He also explained why this love is essential for us: "that you may be sons of your Father in heaven" (Matt 5:45). Breaking even the smallest Gospel commandment entails a sad consequence: "Whoever therefore breaks one of the least of these commandments," said the Lord, "and teaches men so, shall be called least in the kingdom of heaven" (Matt 5:19), that is, will not become a partaker in it.[31] And complete disregard for the commandments of the Gospel, as if to moral admonitions that it is permissible not to follow, draws after it certain ruin. Fulfillment of the commandments cannot be replaced with any ascetic struggles. Even miracles are no substitute for it. "Many," says the Saviour, "will say to Me in that day, 'Lord, Lord, have we not prophesied in Your name, cast out demons in Your name, and done many wonders in Your name?' And then I will declare to them, 'I never knew you; depart from Me, you who practice lawlessness!'" (Matt 7:22–23). The structure of a soul based not on keeping the commandments but only on ascetic struggles is precarious and vain; it can endure neither tribulations that come from other people, nor temptations by demons; it is a stranger to light, and full of darkness and self-deception. 'But everyone who hears these sayings of Mine,' proclaims the

Word of God incarnate, 'and does not do them, will be like a foolish man who built his house on the sand: and the rain descended, the floods came, and the winds blew and beat on that house; and it fell. And great was its fall'" (Matt 7:26–27).

Part Two

Repentance is essential for everyone. Let us all make use of the precious time we have been granted through the mercy of the Lord. Let us all be immersed in blessed repentance. Let us occupy ourselves particularly with it during this week that we have set aside and appointed to prepare for the sacrament of confession and for the mystery of communion that follows it. Let us carry out this preparation with the greatest possible attentiveness. Let us not sacrifice this week to mindless diversions: we have already sacrificed enough to that. We have occupied ourselves enough with our own perdition. Let us now devote ourselves to our salvation. Let us open the book of our conscience often; let us scrutinize the stains of our sins and prepare them for cleansing through confession. Do not spare your sins! Do not consider any fault to be unimportant, forgivable; do not deem any habit or practice to be innocent if it has been condemned by Scripture. Blame yourself, so as to receive abundant justification from God. Resolve to lay bare your wounds with openness before your spiritual father. Do not leave within your heart any secret friendship, secret connection with sin, concealing it, postponing its revelation until the future. Otherwise your repentance will not be true, it will be hypocritical—there will remain in your soul a pledge, a reason to continue a sinful life. Unconfessed sins are easily repeated, as if committed in impenetrable darkness.[32] Hate sin resolutely. Betray it by revealing it, and it will run far from you; expose it as an enemy, and you will receive from on high the strength to resist and conquer it.

Place within yourself the firm intention to lead a life that is pleasing to God and quickly to repent of those half-formed intentions that arise within you either through weakness or through the cunning of the enemy or by chance. "Not to fall is characteristic only of angels; it is characteristic of humans to fall and rise again; after falling, to remain in a state of fallenness is characteristic only of devils."[33] Resolve to be a faithful servant of Christ every day of your life. A faithful servant fulfills the will of his master exactly; when he sins in something, he immediately repents, is sorrowful, asks forgiveness, makes amends for the fault by correcting it. Abhor the acts, life, and attributes of a traitor. Do not pursue a friendship with enemies of your God, your Creator, your Redeemer. Do not betray Him for pieces of silver or for ambition, or for gluttony, or for sensual pleasure.

Use this week to examine your past behavior. Plan for yourself forms of correction: consider what vices you must give up, what virtues you must plant in your body and soul. Do not do this only once in the course of the week: reflect on it several times every day; what you have forgotten today, you will remember tomorrow. The Lord Himself, seeing your zeal, will send you good thoughts, and will open your eyes to your shortcomings. The more you immerse yourself in self-examination, the more comprehensive your confession and repentance will be, and the more perceptibly and abundantly the renewal granted through confession of sins will pour into your soul.

"In a full stomach there is no sense of the mysteries of God."[34] Wishing to dedicate this week to spiritual occupations and reflections, we abstain from surfeit, from all excess, and if possible, from pleasure in food and drink. Let us show in our bodies that we are followers of the Lord, Who was crucified for us. Let us fatigue the flesh by standing in church services. When the flesh feels weary and exhausted and demands rest, admonish it in this way: "I remember the Lord Who suffered for me and I want you, my flesh, to participate, at least in the smallest way, in those sufferings felt by the most sacred flesh of Christ when He was crucified on the wood of the cross. Your pleasures are ruinous both to you and to the soul: they awaken the carnal mind, love of the vain world and of temporal earthly life; they crush spiritual impulses, remembrance of death and of eternity; they strengthen the passions; they weaken the very faith in Christ. Strictness toward you brings countless benefits: it cleanses the mind; it revives the soul; it even makes you, mortal flesh, light and capable of spiritual effort and of spiritual feeling. The martyrs brought their blood to the foot of the cross of Christ; the holy hermits brought their arduous struggles that, if not exactly the same, were similar to martyrdom. Let me also offer at least a slight weariness of my body. By wearying the flesh, I will at least a little resemble the Lord Who was crucified for my sake. By wearying the flesh, I will punish myself at least a little for satisfying the sinful desires of the flesh. By wearying the flesh, I will show in practice that I am angry with myself for the faults I have committed, I condemn myself and I sincerely want and look for correction. Even you yourself, my flesh oppressed by fasting, vigils, and standing in church, plead for abundant forgiveness for yourself and for my soul."

If in the course of this week we eat to surfeit, if we are carried away with pleasing the capricious desires of the flesh, then can we really expect to examine ourselves as we should in order to offer unhypocritical repentance? Is it possible to believe that we are abandoning our vices and being confirmed in virtue if we are doing the work of turning away from sin and toward God with hypocrisy, coldness, and negligence? No! Coldness and negligence expose an unreliable, bad will. Let us fear the words of the Lord: "So then, because you are lukewarm, and neither cold nor hot, I will vomit you out of My mouth" (Rev 3:16). Let us be zealous!

In all good beginnings we need the help of God; we need it even more to overthrow the yoke of sin, to start off on the right and holy path. The help of God is requested with heartfelt, attentive prayer. The holy Fathers exhort us to pray that we may be granted to see our sins that we may be sent from on high the good and saving thought of confessing our sins.[35] Both the one and the other are gifts from God, or, to be precise, all actions that result in blessed repentance necessarily require the help of God. Pray to the Lord God to grant you to pass this week in reverence and attentiveness, to examine yourself, to see your sins. Pray to the Lord that He may place enmity between you and the seed of the serpent (Gen 3:15), which is sin; pray to Him that He may inspire you with courage in the struggle with yourself, with your injured nature, with the death living within you. Pray to God that He Himself may fight for you, and thus always achieve victory for you; it is impossible for the Lord not to be victorious. If we are conquered, this means that we fight alone and that the Lord is not fighting together with us against our enemies either due to our irresolute disposition or because we deserve to be abandoned for our negligence, for our coldness toward Him, for our attachment to the world and its delights. Pray to the Lord that He may help you to confess all your sins to your spiritual father in all sincerity, rejecting pernicious shame, and to hear absolution from his lips with living faith, as from the lips of God. Finally, pray to the Lord that, having been cleansed through repentance, you may not return to the abyss, the stench of sin, to darkness and hell, but begin a God-pleasing, watchful way of life—the way by which every stranger and wanderer on earth may achieve eternal, blessed rest. Ask for all of the above in prayer: "without Me you can do nothing" (John 15:5).

Most of all, pray that you may be granted "a contrite spirit; a contrite and humble heart" (Ps 50:19 LXX), streams of tears to wash away the filth of sin. When the heart is pierced with saving sorrow for sins, then the life-creating waters of tears flow from the eyes. These tears revive the action of the waters of baptism in the soul and body and are themselves called "baptism." The waters of baptism wash away the sin of the first parents, and, in the case of those baptized as adults, their own sins committed before baptism; the waters of tears wash away the sins committed after baptism.[36] Pray to receive these waters, show your desire to acquire them by forcing yourself to shed them. Prepare for confession and holy communion with tears. Wash, soften, revive with tears the field of your heart; use them to make clear the image of God, to restore the likeness that has been darkened and disfigured by irregular lines and dingy colors. He who accepted the tears of the harlot and released her sinful bonds (Luke 7:36–50) will also release your fetters. He who shed His sacred tears for Jerusalem which stubbornly rejected the salvation that had come down from God, and rushed headlong to its ruin (see Luke 13:31–35) will rejoice at the tears you shed with the desire of gaining salvation. He Who shed His holy tears on hearing of the death of His friend Lazarus (John 11:35), Who raised Lazarus who had been dead for four days and already stank (John 11:38–44), will look mercifully on your tears, He will raise your sinful soul from the dead even if all its members are bound with winding-sheets, even if it also stinks from deep-rooted, long-lasting sinful habits, even if at the entrance to the heart there is a heavy stone of bitterness and insensibility. He will order the stone to be rolled away, He will destroy your thoughts and feelings bound by death—may you walk in spiritual progress and freedom from passion.[37]

You are preparing for an important sacrament, one of the seven main sacraments of the Church—holy confession, which in mystical Christian teaching on the sacraments is called a second baptism. You are coming for spiritual healing; do not go away unhealed. A wondrous and extraordinary judgment awaits you, at which your sins will be weighed up and evaluated, and instead of the punishments you deserve, you will be given justification, purity, holiness. "'Come now, and let us reason together,' says the Lord," calling us to this judgment, "although your sins are like crimson, I shall make them white like snow, and although they are as scarlet, I shall make them white like wool" (Isa 1:18). God incarnate has taken your punishments on Himself (John 1:29), and gives you, in His eternal goodness, His holiness, asking of you only that you acknowledge your sins. It is impossible to forgive someone who has not acknowledged his sins, as by not acknowledging them, he expresses that he does not admit his guilt, does not need forgiveness and rejects it.

Immerse yourself in reverent and pious contemplation of the sacrament, a sacrament that is eminently great and marvelous. Immerse yourself in contemplation of God's eternal love for the fallen human race. "But God demonstrates His own love toward us, in that while we were still sinners, Christ died for us. Much more then, having now been justified by His blood, we shall be saved from wrath through Him" (Rom 5:8–9). And we save ourselves from wrath through repentance, which corrects our faults, supports us throughout our wanderings on earth, and extricates us from any fall into sin however deep it may be. The power and effect of repentance remain inexhaustible until the end of our life. Even if someone falls every day, even if he commits every transgression—repentance will take him into its embrace so as to purify and heal him, and make him righteous and holy. It only remains ineffective if its almighty power is rejected with ill-judged stubbornness and blind despair.

And marvel that in this sacrament it is not an immortal angel, fearful in its very holiness, that is appointed its servant, but a human being who is subject to the passions in a similar way to us, afflicted with the shared sicknesses of our race, needing repentance no less than you. This person serves by means of the visible instrument of grace when cleansing your sins but needs the service of another in the cleansing of his own sins. When you fall down before the sacred image of Christ, to confess your sins before your spiritual father, he will humbly say to you in accordance with the tradition of the holy Church: "I am only a witness to testify before the Lord about all you say to me."[38] The goodness of God catches you from all sides for your salvation, surrounds and encircles you with all the means to approach and come close to God.

Conclusion

Such reflections are essential to preparing oneself properly for the mystery of confession. Make straight the crooked paths of your mind and your heart, cleanse them from all slyness and hypocrisy. If you do not do this, you will only increase your sins; you will add to earlier sins one that is far graver. I am afraid to say exactly what this sin is, but for the sake of your salvation I will tell you; I will tell you so that each of you, after hearing how grave and terrible this sin is, may take fright and flee its infernal jaws. Have you fallen into condemnation, gluttony, or anger? Have you fallen into adultery? Then you have sinned as a human being. But if you approach the mystery of repentance with negligence, with slyness and secretiveness, then you commit a satanic undertaking, you mock the Almighty and All-seeing God Who created you and created and granted you the grace of repentance to help you to dwell within the shelter and the state of creation, Who at the end will judge you and will consider how you have used His ineffable gifts. In the service of confession, the holy Church places in the mouth of the spiritual father the following very important words of caution to the repenting person: "Behold, child, Christ stands invisibly, accepting your confession. Be not ashamed nor afraid, and hide nothing from me. Do not hesitate, but fear not to tell all that you have done, that you may receive forgiveness from our Lord Jesus Christ. If you hide anything from me, you will have a double sin."[39]

Do not accept the evil thought that will say to you: "How will you tell your spiritual father a foul and base sin? Hide it now and tell it at your next confession, when enough time has passed, and you will be less ashamed to speak of your sin, as it will be long past and you will barely remember it." Recognize the voice of the serpent of old (Rev 12:9) that came in the form of a thief to "steal" good thoughts from you, to "kill" you with evil cunning advice, and to "destroy" you (John 10:10) by taking away the salvation that the Lord offers to you "freely" (Rom 3:24) in repentance. This voice sounds like the one that once penetrated paradise and took our forebearers away from there. Son of Adam! Now it is trying to penetrate your soul, so that you cannot enter paradise. Turn away from it, do not listen to it, do not taste the poison that is fatal for your soul.

Filled with meek faith, courageous selflessness, humble simplicity and sincerity, approach the holy sacrament of confession. Believe that for the almighty Lord and Physician, all wounds, both small and great, are equally insignificant, equally curable. His almighty Word heals, resurrects, leads into paradise with one word. For the Creator, labor is unnecessary. He speaks His will and all of creation, visible and invisible, hastens to fulfill the command of the Creator. This will is spoken and our sins, written by us and by our enemies on eternal manuscripts, are wiped away.

With faith, selflessness is not difficult. Reject false, ruinous shame, reject this repository of sins; reject its mother, which is pride; blame yourself and condemn yourself. Bow your head with a contrite spirit, with tears and weeping, tell your sins to God in detail through your spiritual father, and with the help of the servants of God's sacrament, the grace of the Holy Spirit will come over you, bringing remission of sins into the house of your soul and, in their place, justice from God and eternal salvation, that you may be blessed and may glorify the Father and the Son and the Holy Spirit, now and ever and to the ages of ages. Amen.

—Sergiev Hermitage, 1845

10. On the Harm Caused by Hypocrisy

Sermon on the Wednesday of the First Week of Great Lent

"When you fast, do not be like the hypocrites" (Matt 6:16).

Dear brothers! Our Lord Jesus Christ, after exhorting us to forgive our neighbors before beginning the ascetic struggle of fasting, told us to take care to guard the fasting itself from hypocrisy. Just as a maggot that has grown inside a fruit destroys the whole of the inside of the fruit, leaving only its husk, so too hypocrisy destroys the whole essence of virtue. Hypocrisy is born from vainglory (Matt 6:1,2,4,16). Vainglory is the vain desire and quest for the temporal praise of men. Vainglory results from deep ignorance of God or from completely forgetting about God, eternity, and heavenly glory, and that is why in its darkness, it strives insatiably to gain earthly, temporal glory. This glory, like earthly life, appears to it to be its eternal, inalienable property. Vainglory, which seeks not virtue itself but only praise for virtue, takes care and labors only to give an impression of virtue in human eyes. And the hypocrite stands before humanity, clothed in a doubly deceptive garment. His outward appearance shows virtue that in essence he does not possess at all; in his soul complacency and arrogance can be seen, because it is above all within himself that he is deluded and deceived. He morbidly enjoys the vainglory that is destroying him, he morbidly enjoys deceiving his neighbors, he morbidly and ill-fatedly enjoys successful hypocrisy. At the same time, he becomes a stranger to God. Before God "every high-hearted man is unclean" (Prov 16:2 LXX [Prov 16:2]).

Vainglory and the hypocrisy it gives birth to are destructive in their very origin: they deprive a person of any heavenly reward, giving him only the longed-for vain human praise that he has chosen. This is the verdict of our Lord on vainglorious hypocrites. Exhorting His disciples to carry out good works in secret, the Lord says: "Take heed that you do not do your charitable deeds before men, to be seen by them. Otherwise you have no reward from your Father in heaven. Therefore, when you do a charitable deed, do not sound a trumpet before you as the hypocrites do in the synagogues and in the streets, that they may have glory from men. ... And when you pray, you shall not be like the hypocrites. For they love to pray standing in the synagogues and on the corners of the streets, that they may be seen by men. ... Moreover, when you fast, do not be like the hypocrites, with a sad countenance. For they disfigure their faces that they may appear to men to be fasting. Assuredly, I say to you, they have their reward. But you, when you fast, anoint your head and wash your face, so that you do not appear to men to be fasting, but to your Father who is in the secret place; and your Father who sees in secret will reward you openly" (Matt 6:1–2,5,16–18).

Vainglory and hypocrisy are disastrous when they develop and mature, when they prevail over a person, when they turn into a rule of behavior and are integrated into the person's character. They produce the pharisee who seeks with frenzied and blind determination to commit all manner of transgressions and evil deeds; they produce the pharisee who needs to give an impression of virtue solely in order to be immersed more freely and more fully in evil deeds. The darkened and embittered pharisees committed the most terrible of all human crimes; they committed deicide. And if it were possible for a worse crime to exist, they would not have hesitated; they would have attempted that too.

Such is the sorry picture of spiritual devastation, spiritual calamities caused by vainglory and hypocrisy in fallen human nature. Our Redeemer, our Lord Jesus Christ, Who has given us the most effective treatment for all our ailments, whether of body or soul, tells us to cure the passion of hypocrisy at its root where it begins: with vainglory. Vainglory hungers and thirsts for human glory: the Lord commanded us to destroy it by means of the hunger that characterizes it. He commanded us to take away from vainglory its food and drink—human praise; He told us painstakingly to hide all good deeds from human eyes, to bring all good deeds, even love for our neighbors, wholly as an offering to God alone. And the Old Testament teaching the holy truth to the mystical Israel by depicting prototypes prescribes the following: "Now every gift of your grain offering you shall season with salt; you shall not allow the salt of the Lord's covenant to be lacking from your grain offerings. With every gift you shall offer salt to the Lord your God" (Lev 2:13). Salt in every gift, in every offering to the God of Israel, corresponds to a Christian's thought and aim of pleasing God in every good deed.

The holy Fathers, the teachers of the Church, in the light of Christ, in the light of the Holy Spirit, who have looked into the depths of the human heart and have seen in those depths how the various passions function, call vainglory a multifaceted passion that is most subtle and difficult to perceive.[40] All other passions disturb a person's peace and are immediately exposed by the conscience; the passion of vainglory, on the other hand, deludes the fallen son of Adam and brings him a sort of enjoyment, presenting itself as a spiritual consolation, a reward for a good deed he has done. All other passions directly disrupt their opposite virtues: thus, abstinence is disrupted by gluttony, meekness by anger, generosity by avarice. Vainglory, obviously, does not disturb a single virtue; by robbing a person of the remembrance of God, of the ineffable greatness of God and of His ineffable holiness, before which the very "heaven is not pure" (Job 15:15), it entices the fallen person to look at himself with approval and satisfaction and to be in love with himself. "I am not like other men," he says (Luke 18:11). In the blindness of his self-satisfaction, a vainglorious person thanks God, forgetting that fallen mankind can only offer thanks to God from seeing the multitude of his own sins and weaknesses, together with the ineffable good works of the Creator toward His creation, His lost creation. Vainglory rejoices when it sees that a person is enriched with virtues: it hopes to turn every virtue into a sin; it hopes to make every virtue a cause and reason for the person to be condemned at the judgment-seat of Christ. It attempts to prophesy. It dares to strive to work miracles, and resolves to tempt the Lord. Devoid of any spiritual gift, it seeks to present itself as possessing gifts, or at least to inspire in people the suspicion that it is in some way above nature; with this deception it seeks to console itself, with disastrous results. It accompanies an ascetic in his fasting, in his prayers, in his almsgiving, in his vigils, in his prostrations, attempting to take away the offering he has made to God, and to render it worthless, defiling it by seeking to please men. It follows the servant of Christ in the solitude of his cell, in his seclusion; unable to bring to the ascetic the soul-destroying praise of onlookers, it brings praise to him in his thoughts, it paints a seductive picture of human glory in his imagination. It often acts without thoughts or dreams, known solely by the absence in the heart of blessed tender emotion, of blessed remembrance of and grief for sins. "If you do not have weeping in your heart," said a certain great Father, "you have vainglory."[41]

Let us resist with determination, with self-denial, the soul-destroying and flattering passion of vainglory. Let us resist it by securing on the rock of Christ's commandments our feeble hearts that easily waver due to the influences and actions of various passions, as if from the winds. If we have rejected and continue to reject vainglory, we will already be safe from another terrible passion, that of hypocrisy. We will carry out our good works and our ascetic efforts in secret, as taught by the Saviour. When we take part in the services of the church, let us beware of manifesting any particular rushes of piety in ourselves that distinguish us sharply from our brothers. "Take care," says Saint John of the Ladder, "when you are among your brothers, not to appear more righteous than them in any way. Otherwise you will commit two evils: You will hurt your brothers with your feigned zeal, and you will inevitably give yourself an excuse for arrogance. Be zealous in your soul, not revealing your zeal either by a movement of your body, or by your appearance, your words or any allusion."[42] If in solitary seclusion, in solitary prayer, in reading and reflection that is edifying to the soul, a vainglorious thought, penetrating through the locked door, penetrating our very minds, our very hearts, presents human glory to us, like a painted harlot, to attract us—then let us immediately raise our thoughts to heaven, before God. When the human mind lights up with spiritual contemplation of the glory and greatness of God, and descends from there to contemplation of itself: then it no longer sees human greatness. It sees human poverty, sinfulness, sickness, fallenness; it sees a death sentence that has been pronounced upon everyone; it sees the decay and stench of everything in the course of the gradual completion of the sentence that no-one escapes. It acquires a sound understanding of humanity that is free of vainglorious delusion, and it exclaims together with Job: Master, Lord, "now my eye sees You. Therefore I depreciate myself, and I waste away. I regard myself as dust and ashes" (Job 42:5–6). True humility comes from the knowledge of God. Amen.

11. Your Body Is the Temple of the Holy Spirit

Sermon on the Friday of the First Week of Great Lent

"Your body is the temple of the Holy Spirit who is in you" (1 Cor 6:19).

Dear brothers! At this time when we are preparing to become communicants in the most holy Body and the most holy Blood of the God-Man, it is a good time for us to consider what significance our own bodies have. Their significance is remarkably great. It is expressed by the holy Apostle Paul in this way: "Your body is the temple of the Holy Spirit who is in you."

Brothers! Have we paid due attention to the significance of our bodies? Have we perhaps looked at this subject lightly and superficially as if it did not require any scrutiny? Yet God tells us through the lips of the Apostle: "Your body is the temple of the Holy Spirit who is in you."

The human body was taken from the earth (Gen 2:7), but it was not created for the earth. It fell into decay, but it was not created for decay. Created and adorned by the Creator for eternity and as eternal, it was animated immediately after creation with an eternal and holy soul, together with which it was taken away from earth to radiant paradise in order to dwell there for spiritual work, for spiritual enjoyment; it was incapable of carnal pleasures. It could not have come from the hands of the All-holy Creator otherwise than entirely pure and holy; it was sin that subsequently distorted and disfigured it. The eye of this body was so pure that it did not see the nakedness of its other members which, in their turn, did not have anything that would necessitate being covered. The soul was not prey to or disturbed by passions; nor did they disturb the body. The blood did not boil with rage or become cold from sorrow or despondency. Death was unnatural to this body, as were diseases; it had no need of protecting itself against the elements; it did not fetter or imprison the soul: it was a wondrous, eternally new garment for it.

Man fell. Sin struck both his soul and his body with death. The power of death over mankind is so universal and so mighty that not a single member of the great human family has avoided it; every human being is born with the beginning of death already within him. He may be exposed to it at any hour throughout his earthly life, and will certainly be subject to it at his appointed hour. It would not be wholly inaccurate to call all wanderers on earth walking corpses. What is our life on earth other than a constant battle with death? In such a state we cannot possibly infer what the state of natural man was before his fall; from our bodies, we cannot possibly form an opinion about the bodies of the first humans. We can only contemplate the primitive blessed and immortal state from divine revelation. We can see the empirical, full demonstration of it in our Lord Jesus Christ and, in part, in those chosen by God who have manifested not only in their souls but also in their bodies the power of the redemption granted by the God-Man to mankind.

The body of Adam would not drown in water or burn up in fire; it was inaccessible to death.[43] Such was the body of the new Adam, our Lord Jesus Christ; it tasted death, but only because He willed it. While tasting death, it did not cease to be alive because when it was separated from the soul, it was not separated from the Divinity. It was taken up into heaven, echoing in abundance the way the body of Adam was taken up into paradise. There to heaven is where it will bring the bodies of true Christians: "Wherever the" (most holy) "body is, there the" (spiritual) "eagles will be gathered together" (Luke 17:37). Although we see now that the bodies of the departed fathers and brothers are lowered down into a dark grave, and are covered with earth, we believe and know that these bodies will not remain forever on earth. They will rise from the dead. Moreover, the risen righteous and the living righteous—by righteous I mean true Christians—will not remain on the earth: on the last day of this transient world, at the beginning of the unending day of eternity, they will be carried away with their bodies into the air, to meet the Lord, "and thus [they] shall always be" there, in heaven, "with the Lord" (1 Cor 15:51–52; 1 Thess 4:15–17). The body "sown" like a seed in the grave "in corruption" will be raised "in incorruption," it will be raised "in glory," it will be raised "in power" (1 Cor 15:42–43); the "terrestrial body" will become a "celestial body," the "natural body" a "spiritual body" (1 Cor 15:40,44).

This is the destination of the human body. It is born infected with sin and death; it is born unto death in the image of that body that became the body of the first man who was created from dust and returned to dust, and who was lost; but it is reborn in the baptismal font unto salvation in the image of the body taken on by the heavenly Man, conceived and born of the Holy Spirit and the most pure Virgin: "as many of you as were baptized into Christ have put on Christ" (Gal 3:27). By means of the wondrous mystery of the Eucharist, our body is united with the body of Christ Himself; our body is united with the body of God, our blood with the blood of God. "He who eats My flesh and drinks My blood," says the Lord, "abides in Me, and I in him" (John 6:56). He who eats the most holy body of Christ and drinks the most holy blood of Christ comes, by such fullness of partaking, to perfect unity with the God-Man. His body becomes the body of the God-Man, his blood becomes the blood of the God-Man. The true Christian sleeps in the Lord, and the Lord sleeps in him; the Christian is clothed in Christ, and again Christ is within the Christian. Contemplating this greatness of Christians, the Apostle cries out to us: "Your bodies are members of Christ" (1 Cor 6:15). "The body is ... for the Lord, and the Lord for the body" (1 Cor 6:13). "Put on the Lord Jesus Christ, and make no provision for the flesh, to fulfill its lusts" (Rom 13:14). "The gifts of the Holy Spirit," says a certain great saint of God,[44] "are already natural to renewed nature." It is already natural to the body that is one with the body of Christ to be the temple of the Holy Spirit: where there is Christ, there is also the Holy Spirit, unconfused with and inseparable from Christ.

Many true servants of God have manifested the presence of the Holy Spirit in their bodies in the course of their earthly lives, and in this way have shown in practice that the bodies of Christians should and can be temples of the Holy Spirit. The shadow of the Apostle Peter healed the sick (Acts 5:15); items made of linen that the Apostle Paul had for his own use were brought to the sick, and the sick were healed by touching them while unclean spirits left the people they had been tormenting (Acts 19:12). A viper, that most poisonous of snakes, bit the Apostle but he remained unharmed, somehow not affected at all by the bite of the snake (Acts 28:3–6). Some saints have walked on water, have traveled substantial distances within the shortest time, as if on wings; when at prayer they have been raised up in body from the earth, as if somehow, as a certain holy writer puts it,[45] anticipating their future experience of being caught up into the air (1 Thess 4:17) and confirming the capacity for this to happen. The Holy Spirit acted not only in their souls but in their very bodies. Just as various passions seethe in the bodies of humans who have been reduced to the likeness of unreasoning beasts; so, on the other hand, in sanctified bodies the grace of God wells up and runs over, permeating the body with a heavenly and spiritual sweetness and at the same time deadening it to sin. After the soul is separated from such a body, decay dare not touch it because, despite the absence of the soul, the Holy Spirit is also present, revealed by various signs worthy and characteristic of it.

Why are our bodies foreign to spiritual sanctification? Why are our bodies capable only of animal feelings, while the Holy Spirit has borne witness that "there is one kind of flesh of men, another flesh of animals" (1 Cor 15:39)? Because we do not heed the warning of our Lord, Who said, "But take heed to yourselves, lest your hearts be weighed down with carousing, drunkenness, and cares of this life" (Luke 21:34). We have weighed down our hearts, our souls have cleaved to the earth: such a state of spirit brings the body down into corpulence, and we fail to learn in practice that our "flesh" can "rejoice in the living God" (Ps 83:3): Let us lift up our hearts, and our bodies will follow them. Let us love the Lord in the way He commanded us to love Him, "with all your heart, with all your soul, with all your mind, and with all your strength" (Mark 12:30) which is impossible to achieve without the participation of the body. Let us make our bodies spiritual, heavenly. Let us save them from passing unhappily from prison to prison: from the prison of the grave to the prison of hades. We have the essential duty to achieve this: we were originally created for heaven, and then after the fall, we were redeemed for heaven. We belong entirely to God, not to ourselves. "You are not your own," the Apostle tells us, "For you were bought at a price," the price of the priceless blood of the Son of God. "Therefore glorify God in your body and in your spirit, which are God's." For "your body," not only your soul, "is the temple of the Holy Spirit who is in you" (1 Cor 6:19–20). Amen.

12. On Receiving the Body and Blood of Christ

Talk in the First Week of Great Lent

This talk was given at Sergiev Hermitage, in the church of St Sergius, on the Saturday of the first week of Great Lent, 1840.

Dear brothers in Christ! Now your hearts hear the comforting voice of God the Word incarnate: "He who eats My flesh and drinks My blood abides in Me, and I in him" (John 6:56). Now you feel the fulfillment of these words in practice. Understand your glory; examine your present worthiness. Each of you is a vessel of the divine mystery; each of you is mystically and at the same time materially a temple in which the Son of God dwells with His pre-eternal Father and His venerated Spirit. You are now no longer your own: you are God's. You have been bought by Him at the price of the blood of His Son (1 Cor 6:19–20). You cannot belong to an alien yoke. If any of you was darkened by sin, he has now become a righteous man through the righteousness of the Son of God.

This glory of yours, these riches, this righteousness, will they only remain with you while you are in the church, or until a short time after you have left the church? Will you really give yourselves up again to the work of corruption? Will Christ, after entering your hearts with the holy Mysteries, have to turn away from them because of the many sinful thoughts, intentions, words, and actions that you permit yourselves? No! May this sad betrayal of the Saviour, this treachery against the Saviour, not happen! Remain temples of God, serve the Lord Who has entered into you by keeping His holy commandments assiduously—and He will abide in you (see 1 John 3:24). He will keep you from all stumbling-blocks on the path of earthly life, and He will lead you through a peaceful and non-frightening death to the refuge of blessed eternity. Amen.

13 On Orthodoxy

Homily on the First Sunday of Great Lent

Dear brothers! It is quite natural to begin our homily on the Sunday of Orthodoxy with this question: what is Orthodoxy?

Orthodoxy is the true knowledge and worship of God; Orthodoxy is the glorification of God with true knowledge and worship of Him; Orthodoxy is the glorification by God of man, the true servant of God, and the giving by Him of the grace of the All-holy Spirit. The Spirit is the glory of Christians (John 7:39). Where there is no Spirit, there is no Orthodoxy.

There is no Orthodoxy in studying and human philosophizing in which reigns what is falsely called knowledge (1 Tim 6:20), a fruit of the fall. Orthodoxy is the teaching of the Holy Spirit given by God to mankind for salvation. Where there is no Orthodoxy, there is no salvation. "Whosoever will be saved, before all things it is necessary that he hold the Catholic Faith. Which Faith except every one do keep whole and undefiled: without doubt he shall perish everlastingly."[46]

The teaching of the Holy Spirit is a precious treasure, contained in Holy Scripture and in the holy Tradition of the Orthodox Church. The teaching of the Holy Spirit is a precious treasure because it constitutes the pledge of our salvation. Our blessed portion in eternity is precious, irreplaceable, incomparable with anything else for each of us; equally precious and beyond all price is the pledge of our blessedness—the teaching of the Holy Spirit.

In order to keep this pledge for us, the holy Church today enumerates for all to hear those teachings begotten of and promulgated by Satan that are an expression of enmity toward God, that plot against our salvation and steal it from us. The Church denounces these teachings as it would ravenous wolves (see Matt 7:15), deadly snakes, thieves, and murderers; protecting us from them and calling out of perdition those deluded by them, it anathematizes these teachings and those who persistently adhere to them.

The word "anathema" means excommunication, casting out. When the Church declares a teaching to be anathema, this means that the teaching contains within it blasphemy against the Holy Spirit, and for the sake of salvation it must be rejected and eliminated, as poison is eliminated from food. When a person is anathematized, this means that the person has irrevocably adopted a blasphemous teaching and through it deprives of salvation not only himself but also those neighbors to whom he communicates his way of thinking. When a person intends to abandon a blasphemous teaching and to accept the teaching of the Orthodox Church, then he is obliged, by the canons of the Orthodox Church, to pronounce anathema against the false teaching that he previously upheld that was leading him to perdition, alienating him from God, and keeping him in enmity toward God, in blasphemy against the Holy Spirit, in communion with Satan.

The significance of anathema is that of a spiritual, ecclesiastical treatment of a disease of the human spirit that causes eternal death. Eternal death is caused by all human teachings that introduce into the teaching about God, revealed by God, their theorizing drawn from falsely named knowledge, from carnal-mindedness, that general inheritance of fallen spirits and fallen people. Human theorizing that has been introduced into the teaching of the Christian faith is called heresy, and to adopt this teaching is to adopt false doctrine.[47]

The apostle includes heresies among the works of the flesh (Gal 5:20). This is due to their source, being "carnally minded," which is "death," "enmity against God; for it is not subject to the law of God, nor indeed can be" (Rom 8:6–7). Heresies are also among the works of the flesh due to their consequences. Alienating the spirit of a person from God, uniting it with the spirit of Satan through their main sin, blasphemy, they expose it to enslavement to the passions, as one left behind by God, betrayed by its own fallen nature. "Their foolish hearts were darkened," says the Apostle of the wise men who turned away from true knowledge of God. "Professing to be wise, they became fools," they "exchanged the truth of God for the lie." "For this reason God gave them up to vile passions" (Rom 1: 21–22; 25–26). Various licentious passions are meant by "vile passions." The behavior of the heretics was depraved: Apollinarius had an adulterous relationship,[48] Eutychius was particularly enslaved by the passion of avarice,[49] Arius was depraved to an unbelievable extent. When his poem, *Thalia*, was read aloud at the first Council of Nicaea, the Fathers of the council covered their ears, refusing to listen to the shameful words that could never have come to the mind of a devout person. The *Thalia* was burned. Fortunately for Christianity, every copy of it has been destroyed; we have been left with the historical record that this work breathed frenzied depravity.[50] The works of many more recent heretics are similar to the *Thalia*, combining terrible blasphemy with expressions of terrible, inhuman depravity and blasphemy. Blessed are those who have never heard or read these excretions from hell. When one reads them, the connection between the spirit of the heretics and the spirit of Satan is obvious.

Heresies, being works of the flesh, the fruit of a carnal mind, are devised by fallen spirits. "Flee from these ungodly heresies" says St Ignatius the God-Bearer, "they are the inventions of that serpent, the devil"[51] [*First epistle to the Trallians*]. One should not be surprised at this: the fallen spirits descended from the heights of spiritual virtue; they fell more deeply into a carnal mind than humans did. Humans have the possibility of moving from the carnal mind to the spiritual; fallen spirits are deprived of this possibility. Humans are not subject to such a powerful influence from the carnal mind because the natural goodness in them is not destroyed, as in the spirits, by the fall. In humans, good is mixed with evil, and that is why it is diluted; in fallen spirits evil alone prevails and acts. The carnal mind has reached its full development in the realm of the spirits. Their main sin is a frenzied hatred of God, expressed by terrible, unceasing blasphemy. They became proud even before God Himself; they turned the obedience to God that is natural to creation into uninterrupted opposition, irreconcilable hostility. For this reason their fall was deep, and the plague of eternal death with which they have been struck is incurable. Their essential passion is pride; they are dominated by monstrous and foolish vainglory; they find pleasure in all types of sin, they move constantly among these sins passing from one to another. They crawl along in love for money, in gluttony, and in adultery.[52] Since they do not have the possibility of committing carnal sins bodily, they commit them in dreams and in feelings; they have adopted in their bodiless nature vices that are characteristic of the flesh; they have developed within themselves these vices that are unnatural to them far more than they can be developed among humans.[53] "You are fallen from heaven," says the Prophet of the fallen cherubim, "who rose up in the morning! He ... is crushed to the earth. For you said in your mind, 'I will ascend into heaven; I will place my throne above the stars of heaven. ... I will be like the Most High.' But now you shall descend to Hades, to the foundations of the earth. But you shall be cast forth on the mountains like a ... dead person" (Isa14:12–15, 19).

Having within them the source of all sins, fallen spirits strive to draw us into all sins, aiming and thirsting for our destruction. They draw us into various ways of pleasing the flesh, into greed, into ambition, painting the most captivating pictures to us of the objects of these passions. In particular, they strive to draw us into pride as a result of which enmity toward God and blasphemy grow like plants from seeds. The sin of blasphemy, which forms the essence of every heresy, is the gravest sin being inherent to the rejected spirits and constituting their most distinctive characteristic. The fallen spirits strive to conceal all sins with a plausible guise known in ascetic writings of the Fathers as "justifications."[54] They do this with the aim of captivating people, so that they agree more easily to accept sin. They behave in just the same way with blasphemy: they strive to conceal it with grand designations, lavish eloquence, and lofty philosophy. What a terrible weapon heresy is in the hands of spirits! By means of heresy, they have destroyed whole peoples stealing Christianity from them unnoticed, replacing it with heretical teaching, hiding the deadly teaching by designating it as the purified, true, resurrected Christianity. Heresy is a sin that is committed predominantly in the mind. This sin, after being accepted by the mind, is communicated to the spirit, spreads to the body, defiles our very bodies that have the capacity both to receive sanctification through communion with the grace of God and to be defiled and infected by communion with fallen spirits. This sin is little noticed and little known by those who do not know Christianity in all particulars, and that is why it easily catches in its nets simplicity, ignorance, and indifferent or superficial profession of Christianity. Those caught by heresy in the past include St Joannicius the Great, St Gerasimos of the Jordan, and several other saints of God. If holy men who led lives that were exclusively concerned with their salvation could not immediately discern blasphemy concealed by a guise, then what can be said about those who live their lives in earthly cares, and have very inadequate understanding of the faith? How can they discern a deadly heresy when it stands before them in the guise of wisdom, justice, and holiness? That is the reason why whole human societies and whole peoples have easily bent their necks under the yoke of heresy. For this very reason the return from heresy to Orthodoxy is very difficult, much more difficult than from unbelief or idolatry. Heresies that are closer to atheism are easier to recognize and to abandon than heresies that are less remote from the Orthodox faith and are therefore more hidden. The Roman emperor and equal to the apostles Constantine wrote a letter to St Alexander, the patriarch of Alexandria and denouncer of the heresy of Arius, exhorting him to stop the discussions that were disturbing the peace because of "empty" words. With these words, referred to as "empty," the divinity of the Lord Jesus Christ was being rejected and Christianity was being destroyed.[55] Thus ignorance, even in a holy man, an adherent of piety, was deceived by the snare of a heresy that was beyond his comprehension.

Heresy, a grave sin, a deadly sin, is healed quickly and decisively, as a sin of the mind, by sincerely and whole-heartedly declaring it be anathema. St John of the Ladder says, "The holy Orthodox Church receives heretics when they sincerely anathematize their heresy and quickly permits them to receive the holy Mysteries, whereas it orders those who have fallen into fornication, even after they have repented and abandoned their sin, to abstain from the holy Mysteries for many years, in accordance with the apostolic canons."[56] The impression produced by carnal sin remains in the person even after he has confessed the sin, and has given it up; the impression produced by heresy is quickly destroyed after the heresy has been rejected. Sincerely and decisively anathematizing the heresy is the treatment that definitively and decisively liberates the soul from heresy. Without this treatment, the poison of blasphemy remains in the human spirit, and it incessantly shakes it with perplexities and doubts produced by persistent sympathy with the heresy; there remain thoughts that "exalt [themselves] against the knowledge of ... Christ" (2 Cor 10:5), making salvation difficult for a person who is possessed by them and by recalcitrance and opposition to Christ, and who is living in communion with Satan. Treatment for the terrible disease of heresy by means of anathema was always recognized as necessary by the holy Church. When the blessed Theodoret, bishop of Cyrrhus, stood before the fathers of the Fourth Ecumenical Council wishing to defend himself against the accusations made against him, the fathers asked him first of all to anathematize the heretic Nestorius. Theodoret, who had rejected Nestorius, but not very decisively, wanted to explain himself. The fathers again demanded of him that he decisively, without reservation, anathematize Nestorius and his teaching. Theodoret again expressed the wish to explain himself, but the fathers again demanded that he anathematize Nestorius, threatening that they would otherwise declare Theodoret himself a heretic. Theodoret anathematized Nestorius and all heretical teachings of the time. Then the fathers praised God and proclaimed Theodoret an Orthodox pastor and Theodoret no longer asked to give explanations, having expelled from his soul the reasons that had provoked the need for them.[57] Such is the relationship of the human spirit to the terrible disease of heresy.

Having heard today the formidable proclamation of spiritual healing, let us take it in its true interpretation and applying it to our souls reject sincerely and decisively those fatal teachings that the Church will strike with anathema for our salvation. If we have always rejected them, then let us be confirmed in the voice of the Church in our rejection of them. The spiritual freedom, lightness, and strength we will inevitably feel within ourselves will show us the correctness of the action of the church and the truth of the teaching it proclaims.

The Church proclaims:

"We bless and praise those who have submitted their understanding in obedience to Divine revelation and have struggled for it. Following Holy Scripture and the Tradition of the early Church, we excommunicate and anathematize those who oppose the truth, if they have not repented before the Lord who awaited their conversion and repentance.

To those who deny the existence of God and assert that this world is self-existing, that all things happen in it by chance without God's providence: anathema.

To those who say that God is not a spirit, but flesh, and also who do not recognize Him as righteous, merciful, all-wise, omniscient, and who utter similar blasphemies: anathema.

To those who dare to say that the Son of God is not consubstantial and equal in honor with the Father and the Holy Spirit, who do not confess that the Father, Son, and Holy Spirit are one God: anathema.

To those who say that the coming into the world of the Son of God in the flesh, His voluntary passion, death, and resurrection are not necessary for our salvation and expiation of sin: anathema.

To those who do not accept the grace of redemption preached in the Gospel as the only means of our justification before God: anathema.

To those who dare to say that the most-pure Virgin Mary was not a virgin before childbirth, during childbirth, and after childbirth: anathema.

To those who do not believe that the Holy Spirit inspired the prophets and apostles, and through them instructed us in the true path to salvation, having testified to it by miracles, that He now dwells in the hearts of faithful and sincere Christians, guiding them into all truth: anathema.

To those who reject the immortality of the soul, and deny that the world will end, there will be a future judgment and eternal rewards for the virtuous in heaven, and condemnation for sins: anathema.

To those who reject the sacraments of the holy Church of Christ: anathema.

To those who reject the Councils of the Holy Fathers and their traditions that are in accordance with Divine revelation and are piously preserved by the Orthodox Catholic Church: anathema."[58]

The Truth of God was made man in order to save us from perishing by accepting and adopting the fatal lie. "If you abide in My word," it says, if you accept My teaching, and remain faithful to it, "you are My disciples indeed. And you shall know the truth, and the truth shall make you free" (John 8:31–32). Remaining faithful to the teaching of Christ is possible only for one who decisively rejects, and continues to reject, any teachings devised and in the process of being devised by rejected spirits and people who are hostile to the teaching of Christ and the teaching of God, and slander its unity and its inviolability. The revealed teaching of God is preserved in its integral unity solely and exclusively in the bosom of the Eastern Orthodox Church. Amen.

14. The Meaning of Fasting

Sermon on the Second Sunday of Great Lent

"Take heed to yourselves, lest your hearts be weighed down with carousing [and] drunkenness" (Luke 21:34).

Dear brothers! It is beneficial to us during the holy days of Great Lent not only to suppress our bodies with fasting but also to talk about fasting; it is beneficial to us during the holy days of Lent to turn all necessary attention to the warning against surfeit and satiety given to us by the Lord Himself: "Take heed to yourselves," He says, "lest your hearts be weighed down with carousing [and] drunkenness."

The institution of fasting is an institution of God. The first commandment God gave to mankind was to fast. It was essential to us in paradise, before our fall: how much more necessary it is after the fall. The commandment to fast given in paradise is repeated in the Gospel. Let us turn our thoughts to the divine institution of fasting and, through this contemplation, revive in our souls the ascetic struggle of fasting.

The ascetic effort of fasting does not belong exclusively to the body; fasting is beneficial and necessary not only for the body but primarily for the mind and the heart. "Take heed to yourselves, lest your hearts be weighed down with carousing [and] drunkenness." With these words the Saviour of the world has revealed to us the consequence, worthy of particular attention, of excessive eating and drinking, a terrible, soul-destroying consequence. When the stomach is pleased, the heart is burdened, grows coarse, becomes embittered; the mind loses its lightness and spirituality; the person becomes carnal. What is meant by a carnal person? Holy Scripture uses the word "carnal" of that unhappy person who is pinned down to the earth, who is not capable of spiritual thoughts and feelings. "My Spirit shall not remain with these people forever, for they are flesh" (Gen 6:3), God testified. A carnal person is not capable of revering God. Even a spiritual person exposed to satiety loses his holiness, loses somehow his very capacity to know God and to serve Him. "So Jacob," says Holy Scripture, calling Jacob a true servant of God, "ate and was filled, and the beloved kicked; he grew fat, he grew thick, he is obese. Then he forsook God who made him and stood back from God his Saviour" (Deut 32:15). This is the state in which a struggler finds himself when he excludes fasting from his ascetic efforts. The corpulence and sluggishness imparted to the body by abundance and lack of moderation in food are transferred little by little from the body to the heart and from the heart to the mind. Then these eyes of the soul, the heart and the mind, become blind; eternity is hidden from them; earthly life appears to the ailing eyesight to be endless. The earthly wandering is guided by notions and feelings, and the unhappy blind wanderer together with the outcast serpent goes "on [his] belly" and he eats "dust all the days of" his earthly "life" (Gen 3:14). Breaking the fast threatens the disciple of Christ with falling away from Christ.

Such a bad effect on a person arising from excessive or even imprudent and incautious eating explains why mankind needed the commandment to fast even when in a state of innocence amongst the delights of paradise. This commandment enabled the newly created people made up of two natures, the bodily and the spiritual, to be kept in a spiritual state; it enabled them to keep the two natures in balance, giving a preponderance to the spiritual nature. With the help of this commandment, man was able to stand unceasingly before God in thought and heart and could be inaccessible to vain intentions and dreams.

The commandment about fasting is all the more necessary for fallen mankind. An attraction to the earth, to the brief earthly life, to its sweetness, its greatness and glory, even an inclination toward sin have become characteristic of fallen nature just as disordered influences and feelings are characteristic of a disease that produces them. We are pinned down to the earth, we cleave to it with all our souls, and not only in body; we have become completely carnal, deprived of spiritual feelings, incapable of heavenly thoughts. The commandment to fast again appears as the first, the most necessary commandment for us. Only with the help of fasting can we tear ourselves away from the earth. Only with the help of fasting can we resist the alluring power of earthly pleasures. Only with the help of fasting can we break off our alliance with sin. Only with the help of fasting can our spirits be liberated from the heavy fetters of the flesh. Only with the help of fasting can our thoughts rise up from the ground and look toward God. The greater the extent to which we lay the blessed yoke of fasting upon ourselves, the greater the freedom our spirit acquires; it strives to enter the realm of spirits that is natural to it, it begins to turn often to contemplation of God, to be absorbed in unfathomable and marvelous contemplation of Him, and to linger in it. If the objects of the material world, illuminated by the rays of the material sun, inevitably absorb radiance from it and emit it, then how can our spirit fail to be enlightened when, after casting aside the coarse, thick curtain of carnality by means of fasting, it stands directly before God, the Sun of Righteousness? It is enlightened! It is enlightened and it is changed. New, divine thoughts arise within it, mysteries until now unknown to it are revealed. "The heavens declare" to it "the glory of God" (Ps 18:2) "and the firmament showeth" the omnipotence of the hands that created it; all created things, visible and invisible, preach aloud the ineffable mercy of the Creator; our spirit tastes and sees spiritually "that the Lord is good" (Ps 33:9). The grace-filled lightness and refinement of the spirit are imparted to the body: the body, following the spirit, is drawn to spiritual feelings, and prefers the incorruptible food for which it was created to the perishable food to which it has fallen. At first the body has difficulty in submitting to the healing and the power of fasting; at first it revolts against the institution of fasting, it sets our spirit against it, arming itself with various ideas derived from our false knowledge: but when it has been subdued and healed by fasting, it already feels and thinks differently. Its relations to surfeit are like the feelings of a recovered invalid toward the harmful foods that he longed for desperately during his illness; its relations to surfeit resemble the attitude one might have toward a poison discovered and already apparent that takes away the spirit's prevalence over the flesh, and lowers a person from a likeness to and affinity with an angel to a likeness to and affinity with dumb animals. Spiritual warriors who achieve victory over the flesh by means of fasting and who stand before the face of the Lord to learn greater mysteries and more exalted virtues can hear from His lips what He taught about the great virtue of fasting and the secret He revealed of that state that gradually develops from satiety and surfeit: "Take heed to yourselves, lest your hearts be weighed down with carousing [and] drunkenness." The victors are reminded to keep carefully by their sides the weapon with which they achieved the victory. And the victory is achieved, and the spoils acquired through the victory are preserved by means of one and the same weapon: fasting.

When an ascetic of Christ who is illuminated from on High and taught by his own devout experiences turns to consider the ascetic effort of fasting, he finds it necessary not only to refrain from surfeit and constant satiety, but also to be strict about the types of food eaten. This fastidiousness seems excessive in a superficial, cursory glance at oneself; but in fact the type of food is particularly important. In paradise, it was only a particular type that was forbidden (Gen 2:17). In our vale of tears (Ps 83:7), on earth, we find that indiscriminate eating in terms of food type creates far more distress to the soul than excess in terms of quantity. We must not think that it is only the fruit of the vine that acts on our minds and our souls; every type of food has its own characteristic effect on the blood, the brain, the whole body, and through the body also on the spirit. A person who takes good care of himself, practicing the ascetic struggle of fasting, will definitely find it beneficial for both body and soul to abstain from continual consumption of meats and even fish; he will lovingly kiss and submit to the fasting rules of the holy Church.

The holy Fathers called fasting the foundation of all virtues because it keeps the proper clarity and soberness in our minds, and the proper refinement and spirituality in our hearts. A person who shakes the foundation of virtues shakes the whole building of virtues.

Brothers! Let us pass the time of the holy fast with zeal and assiduity. The deprivations that are apparently undergone by our bodies from the rules of fasting are insignificant in comparison with the spiritual benefit that they can bring. Through fasting we release our bodies from luxurious and rich meals and our hearts from the earth and from corruption, from that deep and pernicious forgetfulness through which we separate ourselves from the eternity that awaits us and is ready to come over us. Let us strive toward God both in spirit and in body. Let us fear the carnal state produced by breaking the fast, let us fear the complete incapacity to revere and know God that results from contempt for the fast. This disastrous incapacity is the beginning of eternal death. It appears in us when, by neglecting God's commandment to fast, we act in such a way that our hearts are "weighed down with carousing [and] drunkenness." Amen.

15. On Taking up One's Cross

Sermon on the Third Sunday of Great Lent

"Whoever desires to come after Me, let him deny himself, and take up his cross, and follow Me," said the Lord to His disciples when calling them to follow Him, as we heard in today's Gospel (Mark 8:34).

Dear brothers! We too are disciples of our Lord Jesus Christ, because we are Christians. We too are called before the face of the Lord into this holy church to hear His teaching. We stand before the face of the Lord; His eyes are fastened on us. Our souls are bared before Him; our secret thoughts and hidden feelings are manifest to Him. He sees all our intentions; He sees the good things done and the sins committed by us from our youth; He sees our whole lives past and future; "deeds not yet done" by us are already written in His "book."[59] He foresees the hour of our transition into immeasurable eternity, and proclaims to us for our salvation His all-holy commandment: "Whoever desires to come after Me, let him deny himself, and take up his cross, and follow Me."

With the power of living faith let us raise the eyes of our minds toward the Lord, and we will see Him. We will see Him Who is present everywhere, present with us. Let us open our hearts, rolling away from the entrance the heavy stone of bitterness; let us hear, consider, accept, and assimilate within ourselves the teaching of our Lord.

What is meant by "denying oneself"? To deny oneself means to abandon a sinful life. Sin, by means of which our fall took place, has so enveloped our whole nature that it has become almost natural to us; renouncing sin has begun to mean renouncing nature; to renounce nature means to renounce oneself. The eternal death that has struck our souls has turned into life for us. It demands its food, which is sin, and its pleasure, which is sin; it is by means of such food and such pleasure that eternal death maintains and preserves its dominion over mankind. But fallen man believes that the dominion of death maintained and developed within him is the development and progress of life. Thus someone who is infected with a deadly disease is overcome by the strong demands of the disease, and seeks food that aggravates the disease as if it were not only necessary but a very agreeable pleasure. Against this eternal death that constitutes life for mankind made sick by the terrible fall, the Lord pronounces His judgment: "For whoever desires to save his life," developing in it the life of the fall or eternal death, "will lose it, but whoever loses his life for My sake and the gospel's," mortifying sinful desires within himself and abstaining from sinful pleasure, "will save it" (Mark 8:35). Indicating the whole world that is before our eyes, with all its beauties and charms, the Lord says, "For what will it profit a man if he gains the whole world, and loses his own soul?" (Mark 8:36). What is the use for a person, what has he gained, if he possesses not just something insignificant but even the whole visible world? This visible world is nothing but a temporary hostel for mankind. There is not a single object on earth and there is not a single benefit that we can see as our own property. Everything is taken away from us by inexorable and inevitable death and often even before death by unforeseen obstacles and upheavals. We even take off our bodies on the threshold to eternity. Our property, our belongings, and our treasure are our soul, and our soul alone. "What will a man give in exchange for his soul?" (Mark 8:37), says the Word of God. Nothing can compensate for the loss of a soul when it is destroyed by eternal death seductively presenting itself as life.

What is meant by taking up one's cross? The cross was an instrument of abusive punishment for common people and for prisoners who were deprived of citizens' rights. The proud world, the world hostile to Christ, deprives Christ's disciples of the rights enjoyed by sons of the world. "If you were of the world," says the Lord to His followers, "the world would love its own. Yet because you are not of the world, but I chose you out of the world, therefore the world hates you" (John 15:19). "They will put you out of the synagogues; ... whoever kills you will think that he offers God service" (John 16:2–3). To take up one's cross means graciously to endure the taunts and abuse that the world heaps upon the followers of Christ, the sorrows and persecutions with which the sin-loving and blind world persecutes the followers of Christ. "For this is commendable," says the holy apostle Peter, "if because of conscience toward God one endures grief, suffering wrongfully" (1 Peter 2:19). "For to this you were called" (1 Peter 2:21) by the Lord, Who proclaimed to His beloved disciples, "In the world you will have tribulation; but be of good cheer, I have overcome the world" (John 16:33).

To take up one's cross means valiantly to endure hard unseen labor, unseen torment, and martyrdom, for the sake of the Gospel, while fighting our own passions and the sin living within us, fighting evil spirits that rise up against us in fury and bitterly oppose us, when we resolve to throw off the yoke of sin and submit to the yoke of Christ. "For we do not wrestle against flesh and blood, but against principalities, against powers, against the rulers of the darkness of this age, against spiritual hosts of wickedness in the heavenly places" (Eph 6:12). "For the weapons of our warfare are not carnal but mighty in God for pulling down strongholds, casting down arguments and every high thing that exalts itself against the knowledge of God, bringing every thought into captivity to the obedience of Christ" (2 Cor 10:4–5). After gaining victory in this invisible but arduous battle, the apostle exclaimed: "But God forbid that I should boast except in the cross of our Lord Jesus Christ, by whom the world has been crucified to me, and I to the world" (Gal 6:14).

To take up one's cross means to submit with obedience and patience to those temporary sorrows and adversities that divine Providence permits for the cleansing of our sins. The cross then serves as a person's ladder from earth to heaven. The thief mentioned in the Gospel climbed this ladder from among the most terrible crimes up into the most radiant abode of paradise: from his cross he spoke words that were full of humility; through humility he entered into knowledge of God, and through knowledge of God he acquired heaven. "We receive the due reward of our deeds," he said; "Lord, remember me when You come into Your kingdom" (Luke 23:41–42). Let us, too, dear brothers, when we are surrounded by tribulations, repeat the words of the thief, words that amount to the price of paradise. Or, like Job, let us bless as a just person the one who chastises us, together with the merciful Lord. "If we accepted good things from the Lord's hand," says this suffering man, "shall we not endure evil things?" (Job 2:15 LXX [2:10]). "As it seemed good to the Lord, so also it came to pass. Blessed be the name of the Lord" (Job 1:21LXX). May it happen to us as in the true promise of God: "Blessed is the man who endures temptation; for when he has been approved, he will receive the crown of life which the Lord has promised to those who love Him" (Jas 1:12).

To take up one's cross means to submit voluntarily and with zeal to the deprivations and ascetic struggles with which the unreasoning urges of our flesh are curbed. It was this crucifixion of the flesh to which the holy apostle Paul resorted: "I discipline my body," he says, "and bring it into subjection, lest, when I have preached to others, I myself should become disqualified" (1 Cor 9:27). "Those who are in the flesh," that is those who do not curb their flesh but allow it to predominate over the spirit, "cannot please God"

(Rom 8:8). And for this reason, living in the flesh, we must not live for the flesh. "If you live according to the flesh you will die" an eternal death; "but if by the Spirit you put to death the deeds of the body, you will live" an eternal, blessed life (Rom 8:13). The flesh is substantially curbed by the spirit; but the spirit can only exercise dominion over the flesh when the latter is prepared for submission by crucifixion. The flesh is crucified through fasting, vigils, prostrations, and other bodily labor placed on it with prudence and moderation. Prudent and measured bodily ascetic effort liberates the body from heaviness and corpulence, enhances its strength, and keeps it constantly light and capable of activity. "Those who are Christ's," says the Apostle, "have crucified the flesh with its passions and desires" (Gal 5:24).

What is meant by taking up the cross, and in particular taking up *one's own* cross? This means that every Christian must patiently endure precisely those very insults and persecutions by the world that befall him and not any others. It means that every Christian must fight with courage and constancy precisely those passions and those sinful thoughts that arise within him. It means that every Christian must, with obedience, with dedication to the will of God, with confession of the justice and mercy of God, with thanksgiving to God, endure precisely those sorrows and deprivations permitted to him by divine Providence, and not some others depicted and suggested to him in pride-filled daydreams. It means to be content with precisely those bodily ascetic efforts that correspond to our bodily strength, of which our flesh has need in order to keep it in order, and by no means to strive, carried away by the zeal of vainglory, in the words of St John of the Ladder,[60] toward stricter fasting, longer vigils, and other lack of moderation in ascetic efforts that destroys bodily health and leads the spirit toward conceit and self-deception. All mankind labors and suffers on earth; but how diverse these sufferings are! How varied are the passions that fight against us! How varied are the sorrows and temptations that God sends us for our healing to cleanse us from our sins! What differences there are between people in their own bodily strength, in their health! Yes, every person has his or her *own* cross. And every Christian is commanded to accept this, his *own* cross, with self-denial and to follow Christ. Anyone who has accepted his own cross and denied himself has been reconciled with himself, with his circumstances, with his situation, external and internal; he alone can follow Christ wisely and properly.

What is meant by following Christ? It means to study the Gospel, to have the Gospel as one's sole guide in the activity of the mind, the heart, and the body. It means to take one's way of thinking from the Gospel, to attune the feelings of one's heart to the Gospel and to follow the expression of the Gospel in all one's actions and in every movement, hidden and visible. To follow Christ in this way is only possible, we repeat, for a person who, after avoiding being cheated by "false humility" (Col 2:18), wants to acquire true humility from the place where it abides—in obedience and submission to God. A person who has entered obedience to God, obedience combined with complete self-denial, has taken up *his own* cross, has recognized and confessed this cross to be *his own*.

Dear brothers! When we make a prostration today in body before the honorable cross of the Lord, in accordance with the canons of the holy Church, let us also make a prostration to it in spirit. Let us honor the honorable cross of Christ—the weapon of victory and the sign of the glory of Christ—each of us confessing from his own cross: "[I] receive the due reward of [my] deeds! Lord, remember me when You come into Your kingdom" (Luke 23:41-42). With recognition of our sinfulness, thanksgiving to God, obedience to the will of God, we make our cross—an instrument of torture and a mark of dishonor—into a weapon of victory and a mark of glory like the cross of the Lord. Let us open up paradise for ourselves by means of the cross. Let us not allow ourselves pernicious grumbling, in particular let us not allow ourselves the soul-destroying blasphemy that is often heard from the lips of a blind, embittered sinner suffering and struggling on his cross, trying in vain to save himself from the cross. With grumbling and blasphemy, the cross becomes an unbearable weight, enticing into hell the person crucified on it. "What have I done?" cries the unrepentant sinner, and he reproaches unjustly and mercilessly the just and merciful God, condemning and rejecting divine Providence; seeing the Son of God crucified, he mockingly and cunningly demands of Him: "If You are the Christ, save Yourself and us" (Luke 23:39), "come down from the cross" (Matt 27:40). But our Lord Jesus Christ "was pleased to ascend the Cross in the flesh and to endure death"[61] in order to reconcile mankind with God, and through death to save mankind from eternal death. Preparing the holy apostles for the great event that was to occur, for the redemption of the human race through the passion and shameful death of God made man, the Lord told them beforehand that it was necessary for him to be betrayed into the hands of sinners, to suffer greatly, to be killed and to rise. This prophecy appeared strange and impossible to some of the holy apostles. The Lord then called His disciples before Him and said to them: "Whoever desires to come after Me, let him deny himself, and take up his cross, and follow Me." Amen.

16. The Effect of Fasting on Fallen Spirits

Sermon for the Fourth Sunday of Great Lent

"This kind," says the Lord to His apostles of evil spirits, "can come out" from those possessed by them "by nothing but prayer and fasting" (Mark 9:29).

Here is a new characteristic of fasting. Fasting is accepted by God when it is preceded by a great virtue: mercy; a reward is prepared in heaven for fasting when it is free of hypocrisy and vainglory; fasting works when it is attended by another great virtue: prayer. And how does it work? It not only curbs the passions in the human body, it also enters into battle with evil spirits and vanquishes them.

How can fasting which is a bodily ascesis have any effect in the battle against spirits, either on its own or together with prayer? And how, on the other hand, can bodiless spirits submit to the effect of fasting on them?

The reason for the effect of fasting on evil spirits lies in its powerful effect on our own spirits. A body that is subdued through fasting gives the human spirit freedom, strength, soberness, purity, and discretion. Only with such a disposition can our spirit resist its invisible enemies. "But when they," demons, "troubled me," says the God-inspired David, "I put on sackcloth, and humbled my soul with fasting, and my prayer shall turn into mine own bosom" (Ps 34:13). Fasting gives soberness to the mind and prayer is a weapon of the mind by which it chases away invisible adversaries. Fasting humbles the soul, liberating it from the bitterness and arrogance that arise from a surfeit of food, and the prayer of a person who is fasting becomes especially powerful and is not said superficially but from within the soul itself, from the depths of the heart, guiding and lifting it up toward God.

The dark spirits of evil committed two grave offences:[62] The first was the reason for their expulsion from the assembly of the holy angels; the second was the reason for their irrevocable rejection. In heaven they rebelled against God; their leader, blinded by conceit, wanted to become equal to God. Thrown down from heaven to earth for this offence, they envied the blessedness of newly created man and committed another offence: they deceived man and enticed him to his fall. The second evil deed of the fallen angels definitively decided their fate: it fixed them in evil; it caused the grace of God to be withdrawn completely from them; they gave themselves up to themselves, to their own evil, to the sin conceived and borne within themselves that they allowed to penetrate their nature. Not a single good thought, not a single good feeling ever comes to an outcast angel. He is wholly, completely immersed in evil, desires evil, and contrives evil. Burning with an insatiable thirst for evil, he seeks to be sated with evil, and he cannot. Every evil thing that is and has been done by him seems to him to be insufficient compared to the evil that he imagines, that his insatiable thirst for evil seeks. Created together with the radiant angels, for his offences he was cast down lower than all beasts of the earth. "Because you have done this"—that is, killed man—said the wrathful God to Satan, on finding him in the place of transgression, in paradise, next to the people he had just led to their downfall, "you are cursed more than all cattle, and more than every beast of the field; on your belly you shall go, and you shall eat dust all the days of your life" (Gen 3:14). The bodiless spirit is condemned to have only earthly, passion-filled thoughts and feelings. All his life, all his treasure, lies in these. The spirit lacks the capacity for spiritual occupation; he is completely enveloped in carnal preoccupations. In his thoughts, the spirit is brought down from the assembly of spirits to a carnal state, and he ranks below all cattle and every beast of the field. The cattle and the beasts act in accordance with the laws of their nature, but when the fallen spirit acts within the nature of cattle and beasts, he is acting within a nature that is not his own and is degrading to him. He neither wants nor is able to act appropriately in this nature: he constantly abuses it. This sinful materiality of the fallen angel subjects him to the effect of fasting which liberates our spirit from the dominion of the flesh. The fallen angel approaching a person who is fasting no longer sees the material predominance he desires and needs; he can no longer stir up the blood that has been cooled beneficially by fasting; he can no longer arouse the flesh that is loath to play games being curbed by fasting; the mind and the heart no longer obey him, having acquired a particular spiritual vigor due to fasting. Seeing resistance, the proud fallen spirit retreats because he cannot endure opposition and contradiction. He likes quick agreement, rapid submission. Although he "goes on his belly," although he eats only dust, the thought that he resembles God has not left him: he seeks veneration and worshipers. He once dared to show the Son of God "all the kingdoms of the world in a moment of time" and promised to give Him all "authority" over them "and their glory" asking for worship of himself in return (Luke 4:5–8); and now he does not cease to tempt the followers of the Son of God with the charms of the world, depicting them in daydreams in the most vivid colors, with the aim of deceiving us in any way possible and forcing us to worship him. "Resist the devil and he will flee from you," said the holy apostle James (Jas 4:7); another apostle says, "take the shield of faith with which you will be able to quench all the fiery darts of the wicked one" (Eph 6:16). Through the power of faith, let us raise our mind's eye to eternity, to the unspeakable blessedness that awaits the righteous in eternity, and to the equally unspeakable tortures that await the unrepentant and stubborn followers of the serpent. Such contemplation is only possible for us when our body has been brought into order and kept in order through fasting, when, in the pure prayer that is only possible with fasting, we cleave to the Lord and become "one spirit with Him" (1 Cor 6:17). "The serpent always crawls on the earth in accordance with the sentence pronounced on him from on High," says St John Chrysostom. "If you want to be safe from his poisonous bite, be always higher than the earth."[63] Then you will be able to resist him, and he in his pride, unable to endure opposition, will run away from you.

But where are the people possessed with an unclean spirit? Where are the people being tormented and tortured by one, like the boy tormented and tortured in today's Gospel? There seem not to be any, or they are very rare: this is how a person reasons who views everything superficially and sacrifices his earthly life to distraction and sinful pleasures. The holy Fathers argue otherwise. "After the devil and his demons had brought about man's exile from paradise and from God by making him transgress," they say, "they found they could inwardly derange—to a greater or lesser extent—anyone's reason whenever they wanted to."[64] Just as the body of the boy in the Gospel account underwent tortures and torments from the evil spirit, the soul also suffers from it, especially by submitting voluntarily to his influence and accepting as truth the murderous lie that it constantly presents to us for our perdition, concealing it with the guise of truth to deceive us more easily and to have greater success in evil. "Be sober, be vigilant," the holy apostle Peter warns us, "because your adversary the devil walks about like a roaring lion, seeking whom he may devour. Resist him, steadfast in the faith" (1 Pet 5:8–9). With what weapons does the fallen angel act against us? Predominantly with sinful thoughts and sinful daydreams. He flees from those who oppose him and he shakes, torments, and destroys those who do not recognize him, who converse with him and trust him. Just as he himself goes on his belly and is incapable of spiritual thoughts, so in our imaginations he paints pictures of this transient world with its charms and delights and at the same time converses with the soul about realizing impossible dreams. He offers us earthly glory, he offers us riches, he offers us surfeit, he offers us the enjoyment of carnal pleasures for which, as St Basil the Great puts it, he not only acquired sympathy but of which he, while created a bodiless spirit, became the begetter.[65] He offers all this in our imaginations and at the same time points out unlawful means of realizing unlawful daydreams. He causes us to fall into sadness, despondency, and despair—in short, he vigilantly concerns himself with our ruin by plausible and implausible means: both through obvious sin and through sin concealed by a mask of goodness, anointed with an incentive of pleasure. "This is the victory that has overcome the world—our faith" (1 John 5:4), says St John the Theologian. Faith, the weapon of victory over the world, is at the same time the weapon of victory over the fallen angels. Who, when looking with the eye of faith at eternity as proclaimed by the word of God, does not become indifferent to the transient benefits of the world? Who, while being a true disciple of our Lord Jesus Christ, will want to trample on His all-holy commandments for the sake of a sin that seems to be alluring before being tasted but turns out to be foul and deadly? What power could a fascinating image of earthly advantages and pleasures, or even a terrible image of earthly calamities, painted by evil spirits to bring the viewer into despondency and despair, have over a disciple of Christ, when the power of the Word of God has imprinted in his soul the majestic image of eternity, before which any earthly painting is colorless and worthless? St John the Theologian, who proclaimed that "the victory that has overcome the world" is "our faith," greets in the following way the true children of Christ who have overcome the world with victory over the fallen angel and the assembly of spirits that serve him: "I have written to you, young men," he says, "because ... you have overcome the wicked one" (1 John 2:14). Young men here means Christians who have been renewed by divine grace. When a servant of Christ shows the necessary courage and constancy in the fight against evil spirits, then divine grace descends into his soul, and grants victory: then his "youth is renewed like the eagle's" (Ps 102:5), that ageless youth with which he was adorned by the Creator when he was created, and which he replaced with incurable decrepitude at his voluntary fall. "Do not love the world or the things in the world. If anyone loves the world, the love of the Father is not in him. For all that is in the world—the lust of the flesh, the lust of the eyes, and the pride of life—is not of the Father but is of the world. And the world is passing away, and the lust of it; but he who does the will of God abides forever" (1 John 2:15–17).

Dear brothers! Why can we not also be victors over the world and over the ruler of the world? They have been conquered by people like us, clothed in flesh and in the weaknesses of humanity; he has been conquered not only by valiant men but also by frail old men and weak women and small children; they have conquered him and left us no excuse for becoming subject to him. They were faced with the same world with its temptations; the same invisible serpents crept around them, applying all their efforts to drag their souls down into the dust and keep them there. But the hearts and thoughts of the victors were up in heaven. Guarding their bodies by fasting, they curbed and stopped within themselves the attraction to earthly pleasure. By means of fasting, they made it possible for their spirits to be in a state of constant soberness and vigilance, to follow and observe the diverse machinations of the devil. By lightening their bodies and their very spirits through fasting, they made it possible for their spirits to cleave to the Lord in pure and constant prayer (Ps 134:3), to receive divine aid, to revive their faith by hearing, and to turn their faith by hearing into spiritual strength—and in this strength to achieve complete victory over the world and the spirits of evil. Such faith, as St John the Theologian teaches us, even calling it boldness toward God and basing his teaching about it on his own sacred experiences, is acquired through prayer that is heard (1 John 5:14–15). By faith such as this, the righteous somehow see the invisible God, says the holy apostle Paul (Heb 11:27). When they see God, it is natural that the transient world should hide from their view, as if nonexistent. And the ruler of the world has nothing to lean on for his battle. "Be sober, be vigilant; because your adversary the devil walks about like a roaring lion, seeking whom he may devour. Resist him, steadfast in the faith" (1 Pet 5:8–9), taking up "the shield of faith" (Eph 6:16), of active faith, of living faith, of grace-filled faith, of which only that soldier for Christ is capable who has prepared for the battle with evil spirits by forgiving his neighbors their sins, that is, through mercy and humility, and has entered this battle wielding the weapons of fasting and prayer. Amen.

17. The Spiritual Tools of Almsgiving, Fasting, and Prayer

Sermon on the Fifth Sunday of Great Lent

"Prayer," says the Archangel Raphael to Tobit, "is good with fasting, almsgiving, and righteousness" (Tob 12:8). Such fasting is indeed a great good. It is good for sinners as the only door by which to exit the carnal state or to enter and remain in the saving pasture of repentance. It is a great good, not only for sinners, but also for the righteous: it is a great weapon in their hands. Throughout their earthly wanderings, they do not abandon it, and through it they keep themselves in purity and holiness. They base their fasting on mercy; they lay their fasting on a foundation of prayer; with the prayer of faith (Jas 5:15) they receive whatever they ask (Mark 11:24).

Our flesh—as St Mark the Ascetic notes[66] —is taken from the earth and like the earth it requires cultivation. Just as seeds sown in a field that has not been tilled with agricultural tools disappear without bearing any fruit, so prayer remains fruitless if the flesh is not prepared for it, if the heart is not prepared by fasting. The distraction and burden of thoughts, the coldness and hardening of the heart, vain and sinful dreams that constantly appear in the imagination, destroy the prayer of a person who is satiated. And conversely, just as weeds flourish in a field that has carefully been tilled with agricultural tools, but not sown with good seed, so the weeds of conceit and pride spring up in the heart of someone who is fasting, if he, satisfied with bodily ascesis alone, does not guard his mind with the spiritual ascesis of prayer. Pride and conceit in an unreasonably strict faster are always combined with disparagement and condemnation of his neighbor, with a particular tendency to be tempted, in the end, with self-deception, arrogance, and perdition. Fasting is a powerful tool when it is left to itself. When it is turned from a tool into an aim in itself, a means of vainglory, then it becomes an ascetic's instrument of suicide. This is the kind of fasting practiced by the pharisees, and they fasted a great deal but to their own detriment (see Matt 9:14). "I did not choose this fast, and such a day for a man to humble his soul; nor if you should bow your neck like a ring and spread sackcloth and ashes under yourself, could you thus call such a fast acceptable. I did not choose such a fast," says the Lord; "rather, loose every bond of wrongdoing; untie the knots of violent dealings; cancel the debts of the oppressed; and tear apart every unjust contract. Break your bread for the hungry, and bring the homeless poor into your house. If you see a naked man, clothe him, nor shall you disregard your offspring in your own household. Then your light shall break forth as the morning, and your healing shall spring forth quickly. Your righteousness shall go before you, and the glory of God shall cover you. Then you shall cry out, and God will hear you. While you are still speaking" your prayer, "He will say, 'Behold, I am here'" (Isa 58:5–9). The prophet demands that fasting be both preceded and accompanied by mercy; he promises that the prayer of an ascetic who accompanies fasting with mercy will be heard quickly, and that such a person will be worthy of visitation by God's grace.

Generally, the Holy Spirit rules that fasting be combined with prayer. "Turn to Me with all your heart," the Lord appeals to sinners through the lips of another prophet, exhorting and encouraging them to repentance, "with fasting and wailing and with mourning; rend your heart and not your garments. Return to the Lord your God ... Sound the trumpet in Zion, sanctify a fast, call a solemn assembly" (Joel 2:12–13,15). The experience of the power of fasting and prayer is shown by the repentant Ninevites. God had already pronounced His decision about them and the prophet Jonah had already proclaimed it to them; the prophet, after leaving the city, kept looking back intently, expecting at any hour the events of the terrible prophecy. But the Ninevites took refuge in repentance, demonstrating that it was genuine by abandoning their wicked deeds, by strict fasting and earnest prayer—"And God had a change of heart about the evil which He said He would do to them, and He did not do it" (Jonah 3:10). In the New Testament, the Lord proclaimed that fasting would become an ascesis common to all His disciples "when the bridegroom" of heaven, the Lord was "taken away from them" through His ascension into heaven (Luke 5:35). And how can the disciples of the Lord Jesus not fast on earth, how can they not weep, how can they not clothe themselves in garments of sorrow, when their Treasure, the only Treasure, is far from them, and the path to Him is filled with difficulties, filled with terrible and evil robbers?

All the saints of God spent their earthly lives in fasting and prayer. Thus, according to the testimony of the Gospel, St Anna the prophetess, the daughter of Phanuel, never left the temple, serving God with fasting and prayers day and night (Luke 2:37). Holy Scripture says of the great Judith that she "fasted every day of her widowhood" (Jdt 8:6), she had an empirical understanding of prayer; she saw its power, through prayer she achieved a living faith in God, and through faith she accomplished a wondrous feat. "I chastened my soul with fasting" (Ps 68:11), says the God-inspired David—how powerful this struggle is! "I humbled my soul with fasting" (Ps 34:13)—this is how this struggle counters the complacency and arrogance that result from surfeit. By means of fasting "my prayer shall turn into mine own bosom" (Ps 34:13); without it, prayer is a regrettable sacrifice to the intellectual diversion that is inseparable from a surfeit of food. Listing the signs of true servants of God, the holy apostle Paul includes being in a state of fasting and prayer (Rom 12:12; Col 4:2). Of himself he testifies that he has spent his life on earth in constant ascetic struggles, deprivations, and tribulations; he mentions both the hunger and thirst to which he has been subjected by circumstances (2 Cor 11:27), and the constant voluntary fasting with which he has curbed his body (1 Cor 9:27). And when the evangelist Luke describes in Acts the communal life in Jerusalem, after the ascension into heaven of our Lord Jesus Christ, of the holy Apostles and of the Most-holy Virgin Mother of God and the other women who followed the Lord during His wanderings on earth, he says, "These all continued with one accord in prayer and supplication" (Acts 1:14). From these words it is clear that their prayers were very long and constant, which is impossible to achieve without fasting. Such was the life of the apostles! Such was the life of the martyrs! Such was the life of the monastic saints! It was and is a union of prayer with constant fasting. Their mercy and love toward their brothers, toward those who loved them and those who hated them, was divine as if going beyond human nature, as if taken from the bosom of the Lord Himself. They not only felt sympathy for all those in need, whether in body or in soul; they not only forgave all insults and the most serious offences: they lay down their souls to save their neighbors and their enemies.

In critical and difficult situations in life before starting a major undertaking, when great tribulations approached, the saints of God intensified their fasting and their prayers. Our Saviour, our Lord Jesus Christ set us the example on both these points. Before beginning to preach for the salvation of mankind, the Lord withdrew to the wilderness, and there he stayed in fasting for forty days and forty nights. "He fasted," says St Theophylact, "to show us that fasting is a great tool both in time of temptations and against demons. Just as an increase in food serves as the beginning of all sin, so abstinence serves as the beginning of all virtue."[67] The guide in the ascesis of fasting and in the ascesis against the devil is the Holy Spirit.[68] Before choosing the twelve apostles who were to catch the whole world for faith and salvation, the Lord went up a remote mountain, and remained in prayer all night (Luke 6:12); before the raising of Lazarus, the Lord turned to thank the Father for hearing His prayer. "I know," he said, "that You always hear Me" because the will of the Father and of the Son is a single united divine will, "but because of the people who are standing by I said this, that they may believe that You sent Me" (John 11:42). In exactly the same way, before choosing the apostles, the Lord also had no need of prayer, but turned to and remained in prayer all night, showing by His actions, according to the holy Fathers,[69] an example for our actions, showing us that God accepts even our brief prayers, but that especially long and intensive prayer is helpful, needful, and essential for us before important events and undertakings. Before the sufferings and the death on the cross to which the Lord was pleased to submit Himself for the redemption of mankind, He came to the garden of Gethsemane, to the place where His betrayal was to take place (Matt 26:36), as a voluntary sacrifice made according to the single indivisible will of the Father and of the Son. In this way He showed us that we must accept any misfortune sent to us from on high as our inalienable property, accept it with selflessness, with obedience to the will of God, with faith in the omnipotent God Who watches over us vigilantly, Who numbers all our hairs (Matt 10:30), from Whom "my bones are not hid," as the Prophet says, "which thou didst make in secret, and my substance in the nether regions of the earth" (Ps 138:15). The Lord shows us a means by which we can and must strengthen the weakness of human nature at times when misfortune descends. He turns to intensified prayer. He tells the disciples overcome by sleep to "watch and pray, lest you enter into temptation" (Matt 26:41). Prayer is essential in order that a misfortune that is on the way does not envelop a person, take possession of him, and swallow him up. Prayer is essential during misfortune, to overcome it. Spiritual strength and that divine unwavering peace is brought by prayer. Satan strives to shake and destroy with thoughts of sorrow, hopelessness, and despair a person who is undergoing misfortune appointed by God. Prayer is needed so that our faith may not weaken during the misfortune. We need prayer so that amidst the sorrow we may feel, as proclaimed by the apostle, "all joy" which he told us to have when we "fall into various trials" (Jas 1:2). Grace-filled consolation from prayer can be received only by someone who has been cleansed by fasting, and it can be retained only by someone who has maintained his purity through fasting.

True servants of the Lord have followed the example of the Lord. Already in the Old Testament, St David, led by the Spirit of Christ, intensified his fasting and his prayers in especially difficult circumstances in his life (2 Kgdms/2 Sam 12:16; Ps 34:13). Like him, the holy prophet Daniel, perceiving from the book of the prophet Jeremiah that the years appointed by God for the captive Jews to remain in Babylon had passed, and that the time had arrived for them to return to Jerusalem, turned with intense prayer to God for the salvation of the Jews strengthening his prayer with fasting: "I set my face toward the Lord God to seek Him in prayer and supplication, with fasting, sackcloth, and ashes. So I prayed to the Lord my God and made confession" (Dan 9:3–4). The state into which fasting and prayer bring a person is especially open to receiving God's blessings and divine revelations. Thus the almsgiving, prayer, and fasting of Cornelius the centurion were revealed before God (Acts 10:4), and obtained for him the greatest blessing: knowledge of Christ. "I was fasting ... and at the ninth hour I prayed in my house," the Centurion said of himself to the Apostle Peter, "and behold, a man stood before me in bright clothing" (Acts 10:30). This was an angel. Thus when the Apostle Peter was praying and had become hungry a great sheet appeared, let down from the heavens, to represent the whole gentile world, accepted by God unto faith in Christ and unto salvation in Christ (Acts 10:11). Thus the Holy Spirit revealed to The Apostles "as they ministered to the Lord and fasted" (Acts 13:2) that he had chosen Paul and Barnabas to preach Christianity to the gentiles, and ordered that they be sent out to this ministry. The apostles, after hearing the command of the Holy Spirit while praying and fasting, again resorted to prayer and fasting, so that the command received with the help of fasting and prayer might also be fulfilled with the same help. "Then, having fasted and prayed, and laid hands on them, they sent them away" (Acts 13:3), says the author of the Acts of the Apostles. Everyone knows how successful the ministry of Paul and Barnabas was. It succeeded in spreading Christianity throughout the whole known world of the time. There are countless examples to show us that all those who have pleased God have been made worthy of divine revelations when they liberate themselves from material things by fasting, and with pure prayer, with clear minds that are not contaminated by a single daydream, not distracted by any irrelevant thought, stand before God in deep reverence and in the peace of the invisible and unknowable God.

Dear brothers! Having learned the meaning and the power of the spiritual tools of almsgiving, fasting, and prayer, let us make haste to gird ourselves with these tools. Let us acquire mercy; let us put on kindness, following the teaching and the conviction of the apostle (Col 3:12). May mercy be a distinctive trait of our character, a constant distinguishing feature of our behavior.[70] We will not look for righteousness outside mercy.[71] Mercy that comes from damaged human nature is contrary to truth: on the other hand, the mercy that streams out in great abundance from the commandments of the Gospel is united inseparably with the truth of God and constitutes its expression (Ps 84:11–14; Ps 88:15). Let us subdue our bodies by moderating the amount and the type of food we consume; not only during the holy fasting periods appointed by the holy Church, but also at other times let us consume food with prudence, in proportion to essential need, to support our bodily strength and our physical health. Having enslaved the body to the spirit by means of fasting, having made our spirit like an angel in terms of goodness, let us inspire it with prayer: may our spirit acquire the blessed habit of flying up quickly and frequently to God and asking for God's blessing on our undertakings and God's help in all we do.[72] We will not be slow to see God as the helper and the guide of our activity. And not only this: by raising our thoughts often to God, we will gradually clear our spiritual path from all iniquities, great and small, committed in thoughts and in feelings. Who among those calling upon God would dare to call upon Him to help with a depraved act? Who, when presenting his request to be considered by the King of kings, will not first take care to ensure that the request is worthy of the eye of the King and God that penetrates the secret depths of our hearts and sees with unique clarity everything visible and invisible? "If we ask anything according to His will," in this only "He hears us," says the apostle (1 John 5:14). Who turns constantly to God and does not acquire the conviction and the feeling that he lives before the eyes of God, that the all-seeing, omnipresent God sees his every deed, every movement of his soul? The inevitable consequence of such a conviction and feeling is the spiritual progress of the Christian. May the merciful Lord grant us this progress to the glory of His Name and unto our salvation. Amen.

18. The Lord's Entrance into Jerusalem

First Homily on Palm Sunday

"Rejoice greatly, O daughter of Zion! Proclaim it aloud, O daughter of Jerusalem! Behold, your King comes to you; He is righteous and saving; He is gentle and mounted upon a donkey, even a young foal" (Zech 9:9).

More than four hundred years before it took place, God's prophet made this prophecy about the event we remember and celebrate today. Our Lord Jesus Christ, after completing His teaching on earth, made a solemn entrance into the royal city of Jerusalem, the city of the worship of the true God, the city of God. The Lord made this entrance as a King and a conqueror, so as to crown His ministry with a definitive act of ascesis: destroying death by means of death, removing the curse from the human race, and taking this curse upon Himself. He made the entrance into the royal city on "a donkey's colt" (John 12:15) "on which no one [had] ever sat" (Luke 19:30) in order to return to mankind the royal dignity lost by our forefather, to return this dignity by ascending the cross (Luke 19:30). The untamed colt was tamed beneath the wondrous Rider. The apostles laid their garments upon the colt; the many people who came out to meet and accompany the Lord cried in joy: "Hosanna to the Son of David!" (Matt 21:9) "Blessed is the King who comes in the name of the Lord!" (Luke 19:38). It was at a sign from the Lord, and not by chance, not through human knowledge and will that He was proclaimed King in the name of the Lord. Four days later, the same people cried of the One proclaimed King today: "Crucify Him, crucify Him!" (Luke 23:21). "We have no king but Caesar!" (John 19:15).

What could be the meaning of the Lord's entrance into Jerusalem on an untamed colt? According to the holy Fathers, this has a deep, prophetic meaning. The all-seeing Lord already saw the approaching final apostasy of the Jews. He had already prophesied about this deviation at the time when the law had been given to the Israelites on Mount Sinai, speaking through the lips of their inspired Lawgiver. "They sinned," says Moses of the future sin of the Jews against the God-Man, as if it had already been committed, "They sinned; the blameworthy children are not His ... Is this how you repay the Lord, O foolish and unwise people? For they are a nation void of counsel, nor is there understanding in them. For their vineyard is of the vineyard of Sodom, and their vine is of Gomorrah" (Deut 32:5–6,28,32). On the other hand, "Rejoice, O Heavens, together with Him"—the Son of God—and worship Him, all the sons of God; Rejoice, O Gentiles, with His people; and let all the angels of God be strong with Him" (Deut 32:43). The entrance into Jerusalem on an unbroken colt is a reiteration of the prophecy of Moses, a reiteration not in words, but in symbols. Moses prophesied that the gentiles would rejoice in the Lord, and the Jews would be rejected. Here the untamed colt "on which no one has ever sat" represents the gentiles. The clothing of the apostles is the teaching of Christ, preached by them to the gentiles, and the Lord is seated spiritually above the gentiles becoming their God. He led them into Jerusalem: into the bosom of His Church, into the eternal city of God not made by hands, into the city of salvation and blessedness. The rejected Jews were there in person. They proclaimed Him "King of Israel" (John 12:13) with their lips, but in their souls, in their Sanhedrin, they had already decided to murder the Saviour (Matt 26:3–4).

And the "donkey's colt" has yet another meaning. It represents every person who is led by dumb, animal desires, deprived of his spiritual freedom, tied down by a predilection for and habit of carnal living. The teaching of Christ releases the donkey from its tether, that is, from fulfillment of its sinful and carnal will. Then the apostles lead the donkey to Christ, they lay garments upon it, the Lord sits on it and enters Jerusalem. This means that after abandoning a sinful way of life, a person is brought to the Gospel, and is clothed, as if in the garments of the apostles, in the most detailed and precise knowledge of Christ and of His commandments. Then the Lord is seated on him in the sense that He appears to him and dwells within him spiritually, just as He promised: "He who has My commandments and keeps them, it is he who loves Me. And he who loves Me will be loved by My Father, and I will love him and manifest Myself to him. and My Father will love him, and We will come to him and make Our home with him" (John 14:21,23). The entrance of the Lord comes with a peace that transcends description and comprehension, a grace-filled peace, worthy of its bearer, the Lord. This peace bears no relation to the natural tranquility of fallen man who can feel tranquility and satisfaction from carnal pleasure, who can consider his very insensibility, his eternal death, to be tranquility. The Lord sits on the natural characteristics of a person who has submitted himself to Him and assimilated His most holy teaching and leads him, sitting on him, to the spiritual city of God, to the city of peace, to Jerusalem, the founder of which is not man but God.

The Holy Spirit welcomes the soul that has borne the Lord. He offers it spiritual, incorruptible, eternal joy. "Rejoice greatly, O daughter of Zion," daughter of the holy Church because you belong to no-one except God. "Proclaim it aloud, O daughter of Jerusalem! Behold, your King comes to you; He is righteous and saving; He is gentle and mounted upon a donkey, even a young foal." You, feeling within you the grace-filled peace of Christ and becoming a daughter of this peace, have been renewed with spiritual youth and have experienced the Kingdom of Christ. The passions have already been curbed within you through the grace-filled might of the Rider directing you. Your natural characteristics cannot break their own natural laws, they cannot turn into unrestrained passions. Taking from the Lord all your thoughts, all your feelings, all your actions, you can and must declare the "name" of the Lord "unto [your] brethren," and sing of the Lord "in the midst of the church" (Ps 21:23). You, born of the Holy Spirit and daughter of the Spirit, are able to contemplate the spiritual coming of your King and the righteousness of your King. He is "gentle and lowly in heart" (Matt 11:29), and "He will guide the meek unto judgment, He shall teach the meek His ways" (Ps 24:9). Our God is a Spirit incomparable with any created spirit and in every way eternally different from all creation; the holy created spirits are His thrones and chariots. He sits and rides on the cherubim; He sits and rides on those blessed human souls that have submitted themselves to Him and have brought Him their natural characteristics as a burnt offering. Upon such souls the King rides, entering the holy city of God and bringing into it holy souls. "Hosanna in the highest! Blessed is He who comes, the King of Israel." Amen.

19. Lift Up the Gates

Second Homily on Palm Sunday

"Lift up your gates, O ye princes, and be ye lift up, ye everlasting doors, and the King of glory shall come in" (Ps 23:7). The Holy Spirit commands and proclaims this through the lips of the inspired prophet.

Dear brothers! God expresses His most holy will to dwell within us. It especially befits the will of our great God to be proclaimed on this feast-day, on which we remember the entrance of the Lord into the city of Jerusalem, into the city of peace, the city of true ministry to God. Jerusalem represents a devout soul. "Lift up your gates, O ye princes, and be ye lift up, ye everlasting doors, and the King of glory shall come in."

The word of the Spirit must be understood and explained spiritually, as the holy apostle says (1 Cor 2:14). Let us call for divine grace from on high, and let us examine in the Lord His appeal to us: "Lift up your gates, O ye princes, and be ye lift up, ye everlasting doors, and the King of glory shall come in."

Who are the "princes" to whom the word of God refers here? The soul and body of a person, all his strengths and capabilities, his life, are possessed and ruled by his mind. The mind is the master, the emperor, the priest, the prince of a small world—of a person. Our Lord Jesus Christ is the Truth of God. Just as the Truth is accepted solely by the mind, so the word of God, which invites men to accept the Saviour, addresses their head, their spirit, their mind, and says, "Lift up your gates, O ye princes." The essence of our salvation consists in directing the mind toward the Truth, and in the mind dwelling in the holy Truth that is Christ.

Which gates are we asked to lift up, so as to allow the King of Glory to enter the God-given city, the person? These gates are sin: "Your sins," says the prophet, "stand between you and your God, and He turned His face from you because of your sins" (Isa 59:2).

The gates are referred to as "everlasting" because the sin with which we were infected at our roots, in our forefathers, is infinite. The Saviour brought an end to it, but even now, sin is infinite and everlasting in those who do not recognize the Saviour, or who recognize Him with their lips but deny Him with their way of life. "Lift up your gates, O ye princes, and be ye lift up, ye everlasting doors."

Again, what does the expression "lift up" mean in God's invitation and command? Gates are usually opened, but here they are commanded to be lifted up. Yes! For these gates—for sin—the word "open" was found to be insufficient, and it was necessary to use the word "lift up": the gates had to be taken, removed, and completely destroyed. "Repentance from sin," says a certain great Father, "consists in recognizing one's sin, repenting of it, and not repeating it."[73] Only to the soul that rejects sin with determination and cleanses itself completely through repentance will the "King of glory ... come in."

The Holy Spirit not only commands us to lift up the gates but also commands the gates to be lifted up: "be ye lift up, ye everlasting doors." This signifies that in order to abandon sin and a sinful way of life, initially a person's own will and strength is essential; but forgiveness of a person's sins, his liberation from the force of sinful habits, and his cleansing from sinful traits adopted by fallen nature are all accomplished through the action of the all-holy and almighty Spirit of God. "Be ye lift up, ye everlasting doors!" When the "eternal doors" are lifted up, the "King of glory" comes into the soul.

Longed-for and joyful for Jerusalem was the entrance into that city of our Redeemer, Saviour, Lord, and God that we commemorate and celebrate. Dear brothers! We can all have the honor of this great happiness if we desire and strive with all our hearts to acquire it. Let us turn away from sin because of which the Lord turns away from us; let us turn away from sin through sincere and true repentance. May our thoughts, the feelings in our hearts, our words, and deeds express the commandments of Christ which teach the definitive avoidance of evil and the right, God-pleasing way to do good. In this way we will make ourselves into a home, church, city worthy of Christ. "If anyone loves Me," He says, "he will keep My word; and My Father will love him, and We will come to him and make Our home with him" (John 14:23). "Lift up your gates, O ye princes, and be ye lift up, ye everlasting doors, and the King of glory shall come in." Amen.

20. On the Holy Mysteries of Christ

Homily at the Liturgy on Great Thursday

"Bread strengtheneth man's heart" (Ps 103:15), the prophet said prophetically of a certain wondrous bread that, unlike the usual material bread that strengthens the body, was to strengthen the heart of man. Our heart needs strengthening. It was shaken terribly at our fall, and it cannot stop shaking on its own. It is continually shaken by various passions. In vain does fallen man proclaim, in his blindness, the steadfastness of human will. This steadfastness does not exist. The will is carried away by the force of the sin that prevails over it. How needful is the prophesied wondrous bread, to strengthen the wavering, weakened human heart.[74]

The human heart is strengthened by "the bread which [comes] down from heaven" (John 6:58), "the bread of life" (John 6:48). This bread is our Lord Jesus Christ. He says, "I am the living bread which came down from heaven. If anyone eats of this bread, he will live forever; and the bread that I shall give is My flesh, which I shall give for the life of the world" (John 6:51). "He who eats My flesh and drinks My blood abides in Me, and I in him" (John 6:56).

What a strange institution! It is natural to the human mind to be perplexed at an institution that transcends nature and is incomprehensible. It was heard by people who were darkened by their carnal minds and by unbelief, did not wait to receive an explanation from God of the divine institution, and pronounced their own judgment on it to their condemnation and ruin. "This is a hard saying," they said, "who can understand it?" "From that time many of His disciples," who bore the name of disciples in vain, "went back and walked with Him no more" (John 6:60,66). And now those who merely bear the name of Christians, keep the external Christian customs, but in their lives and in their hearts are not Christians, offend the great mystery with their doubts. The "saying" would have been "hard" if it had been spoken by a man; it would have been impossible to obey if it had been spoken by a man. The word was spoken by God Who in His unlimited goodness put on humanity for the salvation of mankind; and this is why the word is filled with goodness. The word was spoken by God, Who, in His unlimited goodness, put on humanity for the salvation of mankind; and this is why attention to the word and judgment of it must not be superficial. We must accept the word in faith, with our whole heart, just as we must accept God incarnate. The putting on of humanity by God is incomprehensible to men; equally incomprehensible are the institutions and actions of the God-Man: they assimilate to God the man conceived in wickedness and born in sins (Ps 50:7), the man doomed to eternal perdition and eternal torment in the prisons and abysses of hell, they make him into a god in grace, they raise him up to heaven to live there eternally in perpetual blessedness. Those who condemned the word and the institution of the God-Man, who rejected the word and the institution, who condemned and rejected the Word, the Spirit and the life (John 6:63), also condemned and rejected the institution with which the Spirit and the life are taught to the disciples of Christ. "Most assuredly, I say to you," says the Lord, "unless you eat the flesh of the Son of Man and drink His blood, you have no life in you" (John 6:53). "One should learn," says St John Chrysostom, "the wondrous quality and action of the holy Mysteries: what are they? For what reason have they been given to us? What is their benefit? We are one body with the body of our Lord Jesus Christ, we are 'bones of (His) bones, and flesh of (His) flesh' (Gen 2:23). Those who are initiated into the mystery pay attention to what is being said: we are united with the all-holy flesh of the Lord not only through love but also through the mystery itself. The most holy flesh of the Lord becomes our food! He gave us this food, wanting to show us the love He has for us. He has mixed himself together with us, and kneaded into us His body, that we may be joined with Him, as the body is joined to the head: such is the nature of ineffable love. Prefiguring the Lord, Job said of his servants, who particularly loved him, that they, to explain their great love for him, said, 'Who may give us his meat to be satisfied?' (Job 31:31). Christ did this for us, leading us into the greatest love, and revealing His love to us by granting those who wished not only to see Him, but to touch Him and to consume Him and be united with Him, and to fulfill every desire."[75] The Lord, after taking the place for us of our forefather Adam, from whom we are descended unto death and becoming our Progenitor, replaces the flesh and blood we have taken from Adam with His own flesh and blood. When we devoutly contemplate the redemption of mankind through the incarnation of God, such action of the Lord, while incomprehensible and beyond nature, at the same time becomes both clear and natural. The worthless flesh and blood of fallen and rejected nature must be replaced with the nature that the God-Man renewed through His most holy flesh and blood.[76]

"The good, all-good and supremely good God," theologizes St John Damascene, "being all goodness, in the boundless richness of His goodness, did not suffer that goodness, that is His nature, to be alone, and that no-one should partake in this nature."[77] This is how the human mind illumined by the light of the Holy Spirit sees the actions of God; this is how this mind explains the actions of God; this is how this mind explains the actions of God for itself: the actions of God and the origins of the actions of God are comprehensible in detail and in full certainty only to God. The human mind that is enlightened from on high produces the following blessed prophecy:[78] The goodwill of God was fulfilled so that the most perfect goodness, that is, the essence of God, might be reflected in other beings just as the sun is reflected in objects touched by its rays. It was for this purpose that God originally created spirits and the world they inhabit, then the sensory world, and finally man, belonging in soul to the created spirits, and belonging in body, in which the soul is clothed, to the sensory world. God Who is life, life itself, poured life from himself into everything living and everything that existed. The life of the world is the reflection in it of life itself: God. Both the spirits and man and all other creation came out of the hands of the Creator in a perfect state, perfect within the limits of their nature, filled with unadulterated goodness, without the slightest trace of evil. The goodness in creation, corresponding to their natures, was a reflection of the boundless goodness of the limitless Creator. The limited perfection of creation was a reflection of the most perfect perfection that is the quality of the one Trinity. The spirits and mankind became the closest and clearest reflection of God in all creation. The Creator traced His image in their very essence; He adorned this image with qualities similar to those that constitute the essence of God in their boundlessness and totality. God is goodness. He also made His reason-endowed creatures good. God is wisdom. He made His reason-endowed creatures wise. In a definitive last touch to the likeness, He gave His reason-endowed creatures His Holy Spirit, in this uniting their spirit, their whole essence with Himself.

Evil appeared from the free will of reason-endowed creatures. The spirits conceived evil within themselves and gave birth to it in its negative being. They spread the poison of evil to the whole human race, infecting with evil the root of the race, the forefather, captivating him with the promise of a position equal to that of God. Here the goodness of God appears in a most striking manifestation. In order to extricate humanity from the fall and from perdition, the tri-hypostatic God is made man in one of His Persons. In and with Himself He renews man, and through this unites him far more closely with Himself than at creation. The Son of God by nature, after being made man and becoming the Progenitor of men, made them sons of God in grace. The animal-like conception and birth to which men were subjected after the fall is rejected: it is covered, as it were, by the birth from the Holy Spirit in baptism. The people who are reborn turn from flesh into spirit, not in nature but in quality: "That which is born of the flesh is flesh, and that which is born of the Spirit is spirit" (John 3:6). Christians who were born from Adam unto death are born through baptism unto life; they are born of God and they are born already children of God. Their existence is called and is "regeneration" (Matt 19:28; Titus 3:5). It is existence unto eternal life completely different from existence unto death; it is a second existence granted after the loss of the first existence through the fall that led to eternal death. For the state of regeneration, an appropriate food has been granted. Just as birth unto regeneration is birth from the Holy Spirit, so the food given to the renewed person is prepared by the Holy Spirit. This food is the body and blood of the God-Man. "The flesh of the Lord is the life-creating Spirit," said St John Damascene, "since it is conceived from the life-creating Spirit: I say this not to destroy (not to reject) the nature of the body, but wishing to show all its divine and life-creating quality."[79]

The God-Man, being the all-perfect God, was superficially, in terms of the physical human sensations caused by the fall, only a man. Holy people who have been made children of God through baptism, who have become a spirit that preserves and develops the adoption and the spiritual state of a God-pleasing way of life, remained, to people with the external human sensations that followed the fall, ordinary people, no different from any other. The holy Mysteries of Christ that are the body and blood of the God-Man, that are Spirit, preserve in terms of physical sensations the external appearance of bread and wine. They look, smell, feel and taste like bread and wine. It is by their action that they are revealed as and are holy Mysteries. In the same way, God was revealed while concealed by human nature. He was revealed and bore witness to Himself through His actions. In this way the saints of God, the vessels of the Spirit, revealed themselves. They were revealed and exposed through their actions. An appearance that is deeply humble, hidden by simplicity, free from sophistication, unaffected by impact, has an action that is beyond nature, divine. It is through divine action that the merit of a marvelously humble appearance is manifest. Yes,

God humbled Himself inconceivably through His incarnation and His life on earth. All His actions were unspeakably humble, unspeakably beautiful, and great in their humility. The same also applies to the holy Mysteries. What could be superficially more humble, more ordinary than food offered to renewed people, than that extraordinary, wondrous, awe-inspiring food in which the Holy Spirit, the God-Man are given for people to eat? "He who eats My flesh and drinks My blood," He says, "he who feeds on Me will live forever" (John 6:56–58). "Those who receive the most holy body and blood," said a great Father, "stand with angels and archangels, and with the powers of heaven, clothed in the regal purple robe of Christ, girded with spiritual arms. In this I have not yet said anything great: they are clothed in the King Himself."[80] In the institution of the Old Testament sacrifices, it was permitted to use for food the meats that had been prepared on the fire, but it was forbidden to use blood. The reason for the prohibition was given: "For the life of all flesh is in its blood" (Lev 17:11). When the Sacrifice of the New Testament, prefigured by the weak shadows that were the sacrifices of the Old Testament, was made by the Priest of priests, the Lord, Who was both the Sacrifice and the Priest: then God gave a new commandment about the sacrificial blood. "Drink from it, all of you," the Lord commands everyone, calling upon everyone, "For this is My blood of the new covenant" (Matt 26:27–28). Everyone is invited to consume the blood of Christ. The invitation is made for the same reason that the former prohibition was made. In the blood of Christ is His life. During communion with the holy Mysteries, a communicant clearly senses that the soul of Christ touches his soul and is united with it. Without words, without instruction in words, the soul begins to sense within itself a peace, meekness, humility, love for all, indifference toward things that are subject to decay and transient, sympathy with the age to come, that are alien to its fallen nature. All these sensations are transferred into the soul from the soul of Christ, as He said: "learn from Me, for I am gentle and lowly in heart, and you will find rest for your souls" (Matt 11:29). "Learn not from angels, nor from men, nor from books. Learn from Me," says St John of the Ladder, explaining the words of the Saviour, "from My adoption of you, from My radiance and action within you, that I am meek and humble in heart, and in thought, and in form of thoughts, and you will find rest from the internal battle, relief to your soul from the burden and confusion caused by its designs brought from the region of fallen spirits."[81] Such is the action of the holy Mysteries: acting upon us, they at the same time act upon our invisible and indefatigable enemies, the demons, protecting from them their vessel, that is, the person who worthily contains the holy Mysteries within himself. A food that appears to be material, taken by the mouth, acts against spirits and binds them as if with fetters. The table on which bread and wine appear to be presented fights with spirits and tramples upon them. "Thou hast prepared a table before me," exclaims the Prophet to God in delight, indicating from afar the Christian altar, "against them that trouble me" (Ps 22:5).[82] This action of the holy Mysteries is especially well known to monks who live a silent life and are subjected to more intensive invasion of demonic thoughts. "They burn," as St Pimen the Great expresses it, based on his personal experience, "with the poison of evil demons, and they await Saturdays and days of rest with impatience, so as to come to the sources of living water—to the body and blood of the Lord—and to be cleansed by them from the bitterness the enemy has given them to drink."[83] Even the fallen spirits know the power of the holy Mysteries. They tremble before it, hate it, and envy the communicants with that envy of which only demons are capable. They often make a frenzied attack on a person preparing for communion, plunder his thoughts, place indifference and bitterness in his heart, bring up gravely sinful memories and dreams, try to defile his conscience, and bring him into doubt and to impede communion; after he has received communion, the spirits often carry out a similar attack on the Christian, again with the aim of causing him to fall into doubt and confusion, of shaking his faith, of sowing the thought that communion in the holy Mysteries does not bring any benefit. This invisible battle to which evil spirits subject people receiving communion serves as evidence of the great importance and benefit of the holy Mysteries. Precious is the treasure that a person's enemies make so much effort to prevent him from receiving. Precious is the treasure that a person's enemies try so frantically to carry away from him. Let us stand firm in our faith and resist our adversaries courageously. Let us endeavor, when preparing to receive the holy Mysteries, to keep all possible vigilance over ourselves; let us try, after receiving the holy Mysteries, to preserve this vigilance. Let us not be afraid of the storm produced in our souls by the attack of the spirits. Let us not allow despondency and confusion to possess us. The action of the holy Mysteries will not fail to appear in the soul of a patient struggler, as the sun appears in the sky when the clouds have cleared. "Mine eye hath looked upon mine enemies" (Ps 53:9), said St David, after the disturbances produced by them in his soul had passed. May the communicant in the holy Mysteries also utter this confession, after liberating himself from the invasion of the spirits, which the action of the holy Mysteries reveals to him even more clearly. Everyone who receives communion with attentiveness and reverence, with proper preparation, with faith, feels a change within himself, if not immediately after communion, then after some time. A marvelous peace descends on the mind and the heart; the members of the body are clothed in calmness; the sign of grace lies on the face; the thoughts and feelings are bound by holy, spiritual fetters that prevent thoughtless lack of inhibition and carelessness, restraining them. In a constantly devout and mindful life, the action of the holy Mysteries becomes clearer, more perceptible, and more abundant. This action is likened in Scripture to the anointing of the head, that is, the mind, with spiritual oil; it is likened to a sovereign, royal cup, giving the soul sensations to drink that come from the Holy Spirit, from Christ. In a constantly devout and mindful life, the incomprehensible mercy of God is made partly comprehensible, appearing to mankind by giving it heavenly food. This "mercy" of God "will follow" unto salvation, through its power beyond nature, for the person who receives communion as often and as worthily as possible, "all the days" of his earthly "life," he will "dwell" in the heavenly "house of the Lord unto" the eternal "length of days" (Ps 22:5–6).

The material bread represents heavenly bread, and the wine represents a true spiritual drink. The action of material bread and wine represents the action of the body and blood of Christ.[84] Bread, taken as food, releases juices into the body, by means of digestion, in a way that is unknown and incomprehensible to man. The way the action happens is unknown and incomprehensible: the consequences of the action, and therefore the action itself, are obvious. Similar to the action of the bread is that of the wine, which acts primarily on the blood. It releases substances that change the state of the blood, and through the blood act on the soul, the mind, and the heart. The action of material bread and wine is material. Bread sustains and strengthens the body; wine, acting on the blood, stimulates activity within it, and assists the bread in feeding and strengthening the body. If the body is deprived of material food, it must necessarily become a victim of death. The spiritual bread—the body of Christ—strengthens the heart of man, his whole being, his will, and his mind, and gives the right direction to the desires and urges of the soul and the body; it liberates people's natural attributes from the diseases with which they were infected after the fall, that are called passions, that is, sufferings and illnesses. The spiritual drink assists the spiritual food. It delivers to the soul the quality of the attributes of Christ. Christ took upon Himself all human attributes apart from sin: the attributes of the human soul of Christ are free from the harm brought by sin, and pure. Because of the union with the Divinity, they are also divine. The soul of one who drinks the blood of Christ drinks its fill of these deified attributes. "Just as material wine," says St Mark, "spreads throughout all the members of the drinker's body, and wine is in him and he is in the wine, so a person who drinks the blood of Christ drinks his fill of the Spirit of Divinity, and he becomes part of the perfect soul (of Christ), and this soul becomes part of him. Becoming holy in this way, he becomes worthy of the Lord."[85] A person who withdraws from communion in the holy Mysteries alienates himself from Christ, is left to himself, to his nature that has been struck with eternal death. Christ alone destroys eternal death within a person in his mind and heart. As omnipotent God, He enters into the inaccessible treasure-houses of a person, and there He defeats death by death. If this is not done, eternal death will remain within the person, as the beginning and the pledge of eternal perdition. It is not possible for someone who keeps within himself its beginning and its pledge, eternal death, to escape that eternal perdition.

Oh, how understandable, how natural is the invitation of the most merciful Lord to taste His most holy Body and Blood, to be nourished by them. This invitation is most compelling; it is connected with great promises but also with great threats. The Lord, in His ineffable love for us, saved us with Himself, substituting our condemnation to death with His condemnation to death, our defiled dignity with His most holy dignity. Through this same ineffable love, in the marvelous order and system determined by this love, He calls upon us to be united closely with Himself through communion in the holy Mysteries, as a true, necessary condition of our salvation. "Do not labor for the food which perishes," He says, "but for the food which endures to everlasting life, which the Son of Man will give you" (John 6:27). "My Father gives you the true bread from heaven. For the bread of God is He who comes down from heaven and gives life to the world" (John 6:32–33). "I am the bread of life" (John 6:48). "I am the living bread which came down from heaven. If anyone eats of this bread, he will live forever; and the bread that I shall give is My flesh, which I shall give for the life of the world" (John 6:51). "For My flesh is food indeed, and My blood is drink indeed" (John 6:55). "Most assuredly, I say to you, unless you eat the flesh of the Son of Man and drink His blood, you have no life in you" (John 6:53). Communion of the holy Mysteries is appointed daily.[86] Daily communion in the life of Christ should enliven the Christian daily with new spiritual life. "What else does frequent communion with life mean," says St Basil the Great, "but frequent enlivening?"[87] What else does frequent communion mean but renewal within oneself of the attributes of the God-Man, and renewal of oneself through these attributes? Renewal that is constantly sustained and nourished is assimilated. From it and through it the decrepitude acquired through the fall is eradicated; eternal death is conquered and mortified by eternal life, living in Christ, imparted by Christ; life, Christ, comes to dwell within a person.

That special action of the word of God described by the holy apostle Paul is also shared by the holy Mysteries. This is natural. Just as in the word of God Christ acts, the Holy Spirit acts, and Christ and the Holy Spirit act together, from Their single, equally holy origin in one nature, the Father; so They act in the holy Mysteries. "For the word of God is living and powerful, and sharper than any two-edged sword, piercing even to the division of soul and spirit, and of joints and marrow, and is a discerner of the thoughts and intents of the heart" (Heb 4:12). The same should be said of the holy Mysteries. "They enter our being," says St John Damascene, "to preserve and cleanse us from all defilement, to ward off all harm from us. If they find false gold within us, they purify it with the fire of judgement, that we may not be judged with the world in the age to come: they purify us with illnesses and with all kinds of misfortune."[88] A communicant of the holy Mysteries needs to know that by taking them he "eats and drinks judgment to himself" (1 Cor 11:29), as the Apostle says. This judgment justifies those who live a God-pleasing life, lavishing spiritual rewards upon them: but it judges the sinfulness of those who do not please God sufficiently, and heals the sinfulness with transient punishments to impede eternal ones; it strikes with terrible punishments those who dare to approach the holy Mysteries while willfully leading a sinful life that is against the commandments of Christ.

On this basis, those who wish to approach the holy Mysteries are commanded to prepare themselves very thoroughly. "But let a man examine himself," says the Apostle, "and so let him eat of the bread and drink of the cup" (1 Cor 11:28). He should immerse himself in self-examination, and carefully consider and examine himself; he should purify himself from sins, and eradicate them from himself through repentance and confession; he should correct even the slightest deviations from the path of the commandments of Christ by returning to this path, and placing in his soul the intention to keep to the path, and strengthen the intention by reading and studying the Word of God, by the most heartfelt prayers and by communion in the holy Mysteries. He should consider human insignificance, poverty, sinfulness, and the fall on the one hand, and on the other hand the greatness of God, the ineffable goodness of the Saviour Who for our sake gave up His body to be killed, His blood to be spilled—the ineffable goodness of the Saviour, Who nourishes us with His flesh and blood thus leading us into close union with Himself. By examining and judging himself in this way, the Christian experiences contrition of the heart and prepares himself for worthy communion of the holy Mysteries through sincere consciousness of his unworthiness. Such self-examination is set forth by the holy Fathers in the prayers before holy communion, helping our dull eyesight and the bitterness with which we clothe our souls as if in wedding garments and in the humility so beloved of our Saviour. "He who humbles himself will be exalted" (Luke 18:14), says the Saviour, and "if anyone eats of this bread, he will live forever" (John 6:51).

Worthy communion in the holy Mysteries is possible only when a person lives a consistently devout life, or after he has decisively repented of and abandoned a sinful way life, giving evidence of repentance as stipulated by the holy Church. A dissipated, careless way of life that is not illumined and governed by the word of God, that is directed by the imaginings of a person's own reason, by the urges of the sin-loving heart and body, making the person a Christian in name alone, deprives him of the basic knowledge of God and of himself, and deprives him of the necessary understanding of the holy Mysteries, of proper preparation before receiving them, of the proper disposition and state when receiving, and of the necessary preservation of this state afterwards. "For he who eats and drinks in an unworthy manner eats and drinks judgment to himself, not discerning the Lord's body" (1 Cor 11:29), not ascribing the necessary value to it, not preparing his vessel to receive the greatest, most holy treasure. The salvific treasure is at the same time a most awe-inspiring treasure in its ineffable holiness. The judgment of God would not smite us if we lived an attentive life in accordance with the commandments of Christ, carefully keeping them and healing transgressions of them by means of repentance. "For if we would judge ourselves, we would not be judged" (1 Cor 11:31). Thoughtlessness and an insufficiently virtuous life are smitten by the judgment of God, prompted by unworthy communion in the holy Mysteries; they are smitten with mercy, with temporary punishments that have the goal of salvation in eternity. "But when we are judged, we are chastened by the Lord, that we may not be condemned with the world" (1 Cor 11:32). Listing the punishments to which the Corinthians were subjected for unworthy communion in the holy Mysteries while leading an insufficiently devout life, the Apostle says, "For this reason," that is, because they were not sufficiently worthy of communion in the holy Mysteries, "many are weak and sick among you, and many sleep" (1 Cor 11:30)—that is, a significant number are dying.

Unworthy communion in the holy Mysteries has a different significance when a person willfully and intentionally leads a sinful life, when he falls into mortal sin, loss of faith or heresy. Those who receive communion in such a state as this commit an offence attracting punishments that are no longer corrective but drastic, attracting eternal torment.[89] This offence is similar to that committed by the murderers of the God-Man[90] who showered Him with abuse, struck Him on the cheeks, covered His face with spit, and mutilated His body with cruel beatings, nails, and crucifixion. "Therefore whoever eats this bread or drinks this cup of the Lord in an unworthy manner will be guilty of the body and blood of the Lord" (1 Cor 11:27). "A certain fearful expectation of judgment, and fiery indignation ... will devour the adversaries. Anyone who has rejected Moses' law dies without mercy on the testimony of two or three witnesses. Of how much worse punishment, do you suppose, will he be thought worthy who has trampled the Son of God underfoot, counted the blood of the covenant by which he was sanctified a common thing, and insulted the Spirit of grace?" (Heb 10:27–29). "But let a man examine himself" (1 Cor 11:28), let him consider himself before approaching the holy Mysteries—and, if he is bogged down in the filth of sin, let him avoid a terrible communion so as not to compound and crown his sins with the gravest sin of all: blasphemy against the holy Mysteries of Christ, blasphemy against Christ. Before daring to enter into marriage with the Son of God, let him concern himself with the garment of his soul. When we repent, it is washed, it is cleaned, by the ineffable mercy of the Lord, from the stains of sin, as if they had never been. St Mark the Ascetic made the following observation: "Because an interval of times elapses between sowing and reaping, we begin to think there will be no requital."[91] Almost everyone who receives communion unworthily is subject to unbelief of this kind. Approaching the Mysteries of Christ from the stench of sin, and falling down into the stench of sin after receiving them, because they do not see the immediate punishment hanging over them, they think that no punishment will ever follow. This is a mistaken conclusion. It was foretold that the Jews would suffer drastic punishment for deicide; but the punishment followed several decades after this most terrible crime was committed (Matt 23:34–24:2). The ineffable mercy and long-suffering of God still waited for their repentance, just as it also waits for our repentance. The punishment is postponed again and again, but it will certainly strike unrepentant, intentional, persistent sinners. We see its beginning most often in sudden death, or in death following the kind of illness that precludes repentance. The punishment itself takes place in the land beyond the grave. "Do not be deceived, God is not mocked; for whatever a man sows, that he will also reap. For he who sows to his flesh will of the flesh reap corruption, but he who sows to the Spirit will of the Spirit reap everlasting life" (Gal 6:7–8).

The sacrament of the Eucharist[92] was instituted by the God-Man today, after He had eaten the symbolic Passover lamb and the supper that followed it, and before He went out to the sufferings that brought our salvation. The twelve apostles participated in the supper. To commemorate and celebrate the great event, the holy Church, on Great Thursday, gathers her children in her bosom for the Divine Liturgy, at around mid-day or, sometimes, in the evening, so that the sacrament and communion in the holy Mysteries may be completed at the same time at which the Lord for the first time celebrated the sacrament, and proclaimed the invitation to eat His body and blood. In this way the great event, through the very setting in which it is remembered, is imprinted vividly in our souls, and the command of the Lord to "do this in remembrance of Me" (1 Cor 11:24) is fulfilled with particular fidelity. "The Lord," says St Basil the Great, borrowing both from Holy Scripture and from holy Tradition, "when He was about to go forth to His voluntary and ever-memorable and life-creating death, in the night in which He gave Himself for the life of the world, taking bread in His holy and most pure hands, showing it to Thee, the God and Father, giving thanks, blessing it, sanctifying it, breaking it, He gave it to His holy disciples and apostles, saying: Take, eat: this is My Body, which is broken for you for the remission of sins. Likewise also taking the cup of the fruit of the vine, mingling it, giving thanks, blessing it, and sanctifying it: He gave it to His holy disciples and apostles, saying: Drink of it, all of you: This is My Blood of the New Testament, which is shed for you and for many, for the remission of sins."[93] This body and blood are the true body and blood of the God-Man, taken by Him from the All-holy Virgin; this body and blood are divine, as they are truly united with the Divinity.[94] "It is not that the body that ascended into heaven," says St John Damascene, "comes down from there, but that the very bread and wine are turned into the Body and Blood of God. If you ask how this happens, then it is enough for you to hear that this happens through the Holy Spirit, in the same way that the Lord made flesh for Himself and within Himself from the Holy Mother of God through the Holy Spirit. Moreover, we do not know anything: we know only that the word of God is true, it acts, and it is all-powerful. The manner of His action is incomprehensible to us."[95]

"Do this in remembrance of Me" (Luke 22:19), says the Saviour of the world to His chosen disciples, gathering with them in the upper room for the mystical supper. And the command of the Lord is fulfilled to this day throughout the universe in all churches that belong to the Orthodox Church. What a mighty command! It was given to twelve simple fishermen and tax collectors: it was given at a humble supper, the last before death, at which many bitter prophecies were uttered, soon to be fulfilled, it was given in the stillness and dusk of the evening, in the privacy of the upper room that was a separate part of the house—and it takes effect to this day throughout the whole earth, across the centuries and the millennia. The Divine Liturgy, throughout its length, by means of all its rites, presents a series and a chain of remembrances about the Lord. The very preparation of the bread and wine for sanctification begins with these remembrances. Before the Divine Liturgy begins, the priest, robed in all his vestments, completes the *proskomide*; this is the name for bringing the bread and wine and preparing them into the form needed in order to celebrate the Liturgy. The priest takes the prosphora and, marking on it three times the sign of the cross, he says three times the words: "In remembrance of our Lord and God and Saviour, Jesus Christ." During further actions he says that the Lord "was led as a sheep to the slaughter, and as a lamb is silent before his shearers, so He opens not His mouth" (Isa 53:7). Various events from the Passion of the Lord are also remembered. The prepared bread and wine, sanctified by the most holy remembrances, receive the meaning and the name of images of the body and blood of Christ.[96] The Divine Liturgy then begins. After the invocation of the Holy Spirit by the bishop or priest and their sanctification, these images of the body and blood of Christ are transformed into the body and blood of Christ. During this great mystery, the following hymn is sung: "We praise Thee, we bless Thee, we give thanks unto Thee, and we pray to Thee, O our God."[97] This hymn is a repetition of the blessing, thanks and praise uttered by the Lord when He sanctified the bread and wine and turned it into His body and blood at the mystical supper. There is no place for any other words at the time of the great sacrament. The sacrament is incomprehensible, inexplicable. Before it both the human mind and that of the angels should be reverent, and out of their abundant reverence they should keep silence. If words and speech are allowed, then only to express thanks and praise, which are as powerful as and equivalent to reverent silence. Only thanksgiving and praise to God can, inexplicably, express how precious, holy, sublime, divine the gift is.

The greatness of the sacrament places corresponding obligations upon us. We must present not only our souls but also our bodies as "a living sacrifice, holy, acceptable to God" (Rom 12:1). "The body is ... for the Lord, and the Lord for the body" (1 Cor 6:13). "Your bodies are members of Christ" (1 Cor 6:15), says the apostle. The purpose of man in soul and in body is to be the dwelling-place of God (2 Cor 6:16), a vessel of divinity (1 Thess 4:4). Both the soul and the body must be disposed toward conformity with this purpose. It is completely impossible to receive God into one's soul after taking one's disposition from Satan. It is impossible to receive God into a body that is ruled by impure desires. God forbids us, with terrible threats, to receive Him in this state. Those who trample on the prohibition of God, on the greatness of God, on God Himself, commit a sin of immense gravity.

Let us set our bodies free from corpulence and from sinful lusts, desires, and passions. Let us purify our souls both from those passions that pertain exclusively to them: from anger, avarice, vainglory, and other similar passions and from those with which the body infects the soul such as gluttony and sensuality. Let us purify our spirits from the pollution peculiar to them, from false and blasphemous thoughts and from the erroneous sensations that lead to self-deception, blindness, and mortification by eternal death. We are set free through the holy Truth (John 8:32). We are set free and purified by abstinence from overindulgence in food and drink, by vigils, standing in prayer and making prostrations, and by curbing careless and curious looks, touch, hearing, and other physical senses through which sin enters the soul and defiles both soul and body. We are set free and purified by the Word of God (1 Cor 11:29). Let us satiate ourselves with reading the word of God, let us revive and activate within ourselves the Word of God by acting in accordance with the will and testament of the Lord proclaimed to us in the Word of God. With devout thoughts and contemplation, let us rekindle in our memory the sufferings of our Saviour, His death on the cross, through which we were redeemed from eternal death, His earthly life—that constant expression of humility and love—that he spent amid deprivations and sorrows. Let us make a firm resolution to spend our brief wandering on earth in a wise and God-pleasing way. Let us spend it in preparing ourselves for eternity, for the judgment of God. To achieve this, it is essential to keep careful vigilance over ourselves, and painstakingly to dispose ourselves toward the teaching of the Gospel, and, through repentance, to correct negligence and deviations from this teaching. Terrible is the jubilation of the sons of the world, their continual distraction and their great concern for things that perish, their rapture with the delusion of the vain world. This is a state that leads to perdition. Eternal death has already opened the dark jaws of hell to its willing victims, ready to chew and swallow them up, as soon as God allows it, when the long-suffering of God, Who awaits the repentance of sinners, is exhausted, when God finally withdraws from the unrepentant sinners. Let us be afraid of falling into such a terrible state. Let us immediately direct all our efforts toward our God, in good time, in order to be adopted by Him forever, and in our adoption by Him to acquire our salvation and blessedness in time and for eternity. With a way of life such as this, when it is constant, demonstrating that we are true to God, the grace of God comes over us, strengthens our wavering effort, changes and regenerates it, and grants us a new effort that is powerful, spiritual, heavenly, and leads quickly to abundant progress. And with his own struggle—and, without revealing itself, grace contributes to a person's own struggle—the servant of God, while still fighting the passions, can already receive communion in the body and blood of Christ, when he receives them with a broken spirit and in full recognition of his unworthiness. The body and blood of Christ help his ascetic effort which is a martyric effort. They purify and teach him through their merciful, divine judgment, burning and eradicating the filth within him that he can neither see nor eradicate for himself. When grace has come over the struggler, the body and blood of Christ revive him and awake within him new, higher thoughts and sensations previously unknown to him; they reveal divine mysteries, fill him with the actions of the Holy Spirit, and bring humility incomparable, in its depth and in the marvelous peace of mind it confers, with the humility brought by sufferings resulting from the oppression of the passions and of fallen spirits. "He who is joined to the Lord is one spirit with Him" (1 Cor 6:17). The Lord is the Spirit, and the Lord unites with Himself a person who has become attached to Him, makes him a spirit, although the person remains in the body. That person becomes spiritual, taking spiritual qualities from the Spirit of the Lord, while the animal-like characteristics with which he was infected at the fall are detached and fall away from him, like a scab from a healing wound. A life lived according to the commandments of the Gospel, and prayer with a contrite spirit, leads to union with the Lord: this union takes place through the grace of God and through communion in the most holy and divine body and blood of Christ.

God fed His chosen people, the Israelites, with manna that fell from the heavens, when they were traveling in the desert from Egypt to the Promised Land: "He rained down manna ... upon them for to eat," says the

Scripture, "and gave them bread of heaven. Angel's bread did man eat" (Ps 77:24–25). This bread prefigured Christ, Who feeds with His word (Matt 4:4), His body and blood, Christians wandering in the vale of persecution, walking and proceeding up to their mountainous homeland in the face of numerous different obstacles, sufferings, and adversities. Egypt signifies humanity's state of fallenness, of enslavement to sin and to fallen spirits. The exodus from Egypt represents the rejection of a sinful life, the acceptance of belief in Christ, and the beginning of a way of life according to the commandments of Christ. The Promised Land means heaven; traveling across the wilderness means earthly life; the bread of heaven is Christ. "For the bread of God is He who comes down from heaven and gives life to the world" (John 6:33). "Your fathers," says Christ of the old Israel to the new Israel, "ate the manna in the wilderness, and are dead. This is the bread which comes down from heaven, that one may eat of it and not die" (John 6:49–50) an eternal death either in the course of life on earth or after the soul is separated from the body at its death. Amen.

21. The Lord Crucified

Homily at Vespers on Great Friday

"The whole crowd who came together to that sight, seeing what had been done, beat their breasts and returned" (Luke 23:48).

What was the sight that brought onlookers to complete bewilderment? What was the sight that sealed the lips of onlookers with silence and at the same time shocked their souls? They came to see it so as to satisfy their curiosity; they went away beating their breasts and in terrible confusion ... What was this sight?

It was not only people who looked on this sight: all the angels of God looked on it with horror and deepest reverence; the things of heaven no longer held their attention; their gaze was turned, riveted toward the sight that was being revealed on earth. The sun saw things never seen by it, and, not able to endure what it saw, hid its rays, as a person covers his eyes from a sight he cannot endure. It clothed itself in a deep darkness, expressing a sorrow as bitter as death. The earth quaked and shook from the event that had occurred on it. The temple of the Old Testament tore its great veil in the same way that precious garments are torn and are not spared in the event of an irreversible, definitive calamity. "The whole crowd who came together to that sight, seeing what had been done, beat their breasts and returned" ... What was this sight?

It was the sight that we now contemplate in remembrance, in the church service we have celebrated, in the holy Image that lies before our eyes. The sight was the Son of God, Who descended from the heavens and was made man for the salvation of men, abused and killed by men.

What feeling, if not one of horror, must envelop one's heart at this sight? What state, if not one of complete bewilderment, must take over one's mind? What word can be spoken at this sight? Will every human word not die on a person's lips before it passes them? "The whole crowd who came together to that sight, seeing what had been done, beat their breasts and returned."

They returned beating their breasts; they returned in bewilderment and horror, those who had come to see the Saviour hanging on the wood of the cross, like a ripe and reddening fruit, to see Him out of curiosity, out of an arrogant and false conceit. Faith was silent within them. The darkened sun proclaimed it to them. The shaking earth proclaimed it to them, and so did the stones crashing open and rising above the graves of the dead who had suddenly come to life through the death of the Saviour. They returned in horror, those who were vainly curious: in horror not because of the deicide that had been committed—in horror from the terrible sight and from the voice of quaking, inanimate nature, expressing its knowledge of God before men who did not know Him. They "beat their breasts and returned" in horror for themselves, for their own flesh and blood, for the sake of which the blood of the God-Man had been spilt and His body tortured.

At the time when the Jews, who had remained assured of the Law, boasting of broad and precise knowledge of it, were perplexed at seeing the event that had been foretold by the Law and the Prophets, seeing the voluntary Sacrifice for which they had unconsciously been the priests; at the time when the Jews were bewildered and returned home, troubled by fear and by a dark foreboding of their own disaster—there stood before the cross and the Sacrifice a gentile, a centurion. It was impossible for him to leave, because he commanded the guard keeping watch over the Sacrifice: this happy opportunity was given to him because there was hidden in his heart a faith that was visible to the Knower of hearts. When the natural world proclaimed its confession of God, the centurion gave an answer to the mysterious voice of nature and to the mysterious confession by making a clear and public confession. "Truly this was the Son of God," he said of the executed wanderer who hung before his eyes, recognizing God in Him (Matt 27:54).

The Jews, who had been proud of their knowledge of the letter of the Law and of their external ritual righteousness, were bewildered at the sight of the Son of Man and the Son of God crucified. On the one hand they were shocked by the signs—the earthquake, the tearing of the veil of the temple, the profound darkness that had descended in the middle of the day; on the other hand, they were blinded and embittered by carnal reason and by proud self-deception, imagining the Messiah in the brilliance of earthly glory, a magnificent king, a conqueror of the universe, at the head of a great army, among a host of luxurious courtiers. Meanwhile a centurion, a gentile, was confessing the executed wanderer to be God: meanwhile a criminal prisoner was confessing Him as God. "Come down from the cross!" said the blinded high priests and scribes of the Jewish people to the God-Man, not understanding what an all-holy Sacrifice, what an all-holy and all-powerful Burnt Offering they had brought to God, "come down from the cross, that we may see and believe" (Mark 15:30,32): at the same time the coarse, ignorant thief recognized Him as God, as one who had ascended the cross because of His divine righteousness and not because of His sin. With his bodily eyes he saw a man stripped naked, crucified alongside him, subject to the same fate as himself, a helpless pauper, condemned by both the spiritual and the civil authorities, tormented and punished, and still being tormented and punished by all the expressions of hatred: with the eyes of his humble heart, he saw God. The powerful, the glorious, the wise, the righteous people of the world were showering God with abuse and with mockery; the thief turned to Him with a timely and brief prayer: "Lord, remember me when You come into Your kingdom" (Luke 23:42).

Before the cross and the Lord crucified on it stood the Ever-Virgin Mother of God. Her heart was pierced through with sorrow as if by a sword: the prophecy of the holy elder Symeon was fulfilled.[98] But she knew that the redemption of the human race was being accomplished on the cross, she knew that her Son, the Son of God, deigned to ascend the cross and to offer Himself as a sacrifice for rejected mankind; she knew that the Lord, after accomplishing the redemption of mankind through death, would raise up humanity and make it rise again with Himself; she knew this—and kept silence. She kept silence before the greatness of the event; she kept silence from an abundance of sorrow: she kept silence before the will of God that was being accomplished, against which there is no voice.

The beloved disciple of the Lord also stood before the cross. He looked up to the height of the cross, and in the unfathomable love of the voluntary Sacrifice he beheld divine Love. Divine Love is the source of Theology. It is a gift of the Holy Spirit and Theology is a gift of the Holy Spirit (Rom 5:5). Divine Love revealed to the apostles the mysterious significance of the redemption. "For the love of God compels us," explains the disciple and messenger of Christ, "because we judge thus: that if One died for all, then all died" (2 Cor 5:14). In the endless love that the Lord has for mankind and of which only the Lord is capable, all of mankind suffered on the cross and died in the person of the Lord. If mankind suffered in Him, then it was justified in Him; if mankind died in Him, then it was also brought to life in Him. The death of the Lord became a source of life.

Suddenly the voice of the crucified Lord was heard saying to the Ever-Virgin: "Woman, behold your son"; then to the beloved disciple: "Behold your mother" (John 19:26–27). Destroying on the wood of the cross the sin committed by the forebears at the tree in paradise, and giving new life to humanity through the life-giving death, the Lord earns the right to be the new Progenitor of the human race, and proclaims His mother to be the mother of His disciple and of all His disciples, all Christians. The old Adam is replaced by the new Adam, the fallen Eve by the all-pure Mary. "For if by the one man's offense," says the Apostle, "many died, much more the grace of God and the gift by the grace of the one Man, Jesus Christ, abounded to many" (Rom 5:15). By our Lord Jesus Christ countless and unspeakable good works have been granted to the human race: not only the redemption of man but his adoption by God.

After being illumined by contemplation of the great event, let us return, dear brothers, to our homes, and let us take away with us profound, saving thoughts, letting them penetrate our hearts. We have remembered, we have vividly contemplated the action of Divine Love, an action beyond words, beyond comprehension. It was to this Love that the martyrs responded when they shed streams of their blood like water; it was to this Love that the holy monastics responded with mortification of their flesh "with its passions and desires" (Gal 5:24); it was to this Love that many sinners responded with streams of tears, heartfelt lamentations, confession of their sins, taking from it healing of their souls; it was to this Love that many responded who were oppressed with sorrows and illnesses, and this Love dissolved their sorrows with divine consolation. Let us too respond to our Lord's love for us through sympathy with His love: by living in accordance with His most holy commandments. This is the sign of love He asks of us, and it is the only sign of Love He will accept from us. "If anyone loves Me, he will keep My word ... He who does not love Me does not keep My words" (John 14:23–24). If we do not respond to the Lord's love for us with love toward Him, then was the blood of the God-Man not shed for us in vain? Was His most holy Body not tortured in vain? Was the Great Sacrifice not placed on the altar of the cross and sacrificed in vain? Most powerful is its pleading on our behalf unto salvation: most powerful also is its complaint to those who disregard it. The voice of the blood of the righteous Abel has gone up from earth to heaven and stood before God with an accusation toward the one who shed it (Gen 4:10): the voice of the great Sacrifice resounds in heaven itself, at the very throne of God, on which the great Sacrifice sits. The voice of His complaint is at the same time also the decision of God that pronounces eternal punishment on the enemies of the Son of God and those who scorn Him. "What profit is there in my blood, when I go down to corruption?" (Ps 29:10), prophesies the all-holy Sacrifice, accusing the Christians redeemed by Him, who have accepted His price within themselves and have brought Him down together with themselves into the stench of sin. A terrible offence is committed by all who "take the members of Christ", their soul and body, redeemed by Christ and belonging to Christ, and "make them members of a harlot" (1 Cor 6:15) by means of various kinds of sin. "Do you not know that you are the temple of God and that the Spirit of God dwells in you? If anyone defiles the temple of God, God will destroy him" (1 Cor 3:16–17). Amen.

22. On Christianity

Sermon on the Sunday after Pascha

"Blessed are those who have not seen and yet have believed" (John 20:29).

The Lord spoke these words to His faithful disciple, who had refused to believe in the resurrection of the Lord when his brothers, the apostles, had told him of it; the Lord spoke these words to his disciple who had declared that he would not believe in the resurrection of the Lord until he personally had assured himself of this event so wondrous and so important for the whole of humanity. The other holy apostles, to whom the Lord had appeared on the very day of His resurrection, entering the chamber without opening the doors, said joyfully to the holy Apostle Thomas, "We have seen the Lord" (John 20:25). The chamber had been firmly closed and locked for fear of the Jews, who had just committed deicide and taken all measures against the resurrection that had been foretold. "Unless I see in His hands the print of the nails," answered Thomas, confused by the joyful news, "and put my finger into the print of the nails, and put my hand into His side, I will not believe" (John 20:25). This expressed not unbelief, hostile to God: this expressed unutterable joy; it expressed a soul facing the greatness of the event that changed the state of humanity. With Christ and in Christ, mankind was resurrected.

The good Lord was not slow to give his beloved disciple the proof he desired. One week after His first appearance to the apostles, the Lord appeared to them again, when they were again together, and Thomas was with them. The doors were locked, as before, for fear of the Jews. The apostles suddenly saw the Lord standing among them. "Peace to you," He said to them. Then, turning to Thomas, He said to him, "Reach your finger here, and look at My hands; and reach your hand here, and put it into My side. Do not be unbelieving, but believing" (John 20:26–27). With these words the Lord showed that He had also been present among His disciples, omnipresent in His divinity, when Thomas, supposing that He was absent, had expressed his doubts about what they had told him of the resurrection. Thomas had wanted to be sure about the resurrection, but now he received incomparably greater evidence, whereupon he no longer needed any proof of the resurrection. "My Lord and my God!" exclaimed Thomas. "After assuring myself of Your divinity, I no longer seek proof of the resurrection. For You, as omnipotent God, all actions are possible that are beyond human comprehension."

In answer to the confession of the apostle, the Lord blessed "those who have not seen and yet have believed." The Lord also mentioned us, He remembered all those who have not seen Him with their bodily eyes. He also remembered us, who are far away from Him in place and time. He remembered us at a time when He stood among His holy apostles, after taking on human nature, sacrificing himself for humanity and already glorified with the glory of the resurrection. The Lord did not forget even us, who are present here in His church, remembering the event from which we are separated by eighteen centuries.[99] We too are blessed, who have not seen Him but believe in Him. Those of us who believe in Him are blessed. The essence of the matter is in faith. This is what brings a person closer to God, and to adoption by God; this is what presents the person before the face of God and, on the last day of the life of this world, at the beginning of the eternal day, places him at the right hand of the throne of God, to see God in eternity, for eternal delight in God, to reign with Him eternally.

"Blessed are those who have not seen and yet have believed." With these words the Lord included together with the apostles all the faithful of the whole earth and of all times. When He offered the prayer for the apostles to His Father, before going to the sufferings that saved us, He united all true Christians with the apostles. "I do not pray for these alone," He said—I pray not only for the apostles—"but also for those who will believe in Me through their word" (John 17:20). In the same way, He makes all children of the Church partakers in the blessedness of the apostles. "But blessed are your eyes for they see, and your ears for they hear; for assuredly, I say to you that many prophets and righteous men" of the Old Testament "desired to see what you see, and did not see it, and to hear what you hear, and did not hear it" (Matt 13:16–17). The blessed eyewitnesses and servants of the Word passed down to us what they had seen and heard (Luke 1:3), when "the Word became flesh and dwelt among us," as one of the eyewitnesses of the Word says, "and we beheld His glory, the glory as of the only begotten of the Father, full of grace and truth" (John 1:14). The very clear narrative of the apostles makes us witnesses, as it were, of the events to which the apostles were witnesses. Through the sacraments of the Church we have entered into essential communion with the Lord, and we remain in this interaction through these sacraments. God, Who is invisible to our sensory eyes, is made visible by living faith to the eye of the soul: the mind (Heb 11:27). Living in accordance with the Lord's commandments reveals the Lord to us mystically. He appears spiritually within the heart, when the disciples of the Lord—that is, the understanding formed and adopted by the mind from the Gospel—gather in the heart, lock the door, so that the Jews (thoughts that are hostile to God and reject His holy teaching) may not enter there.

As participants in the situation of the holy apostles, we dare to claim that our situation is more blessed than that of the righteous men of the Old Testament. They believed in the future Redeemer: we believe in a redemption that has come and has been completed. They were promised grace-filled gifts: we have received an abundance of gifts, we hold them in our hands, we use them as we wish. The Giver of the gifts is both infinitely rich and infinitely generous. If we feel any deficiency, then that is our fault and ours alone. If we do not feel these grace-filled gifts, this comes from weakness in our faith; let me put it more clearly: it comes from rejection of it.

Why do we not have faith? Because we have not taken or wanted to take any trouble to study Christianity, to gain faith by hearing (Rom 10:17), through which a clear theoretical knowledge of Christianity is acquired, or to gain faith by works (Jas 2:18), which supplies an active knowledge of Christianity. A person who acquires these two types of knowledge is guided by them, by God Himself, as someone who has demonstrated as far as he can the sincerity of his desire to know God: he is guided to mystical, essential spiritual knowledge, always combined with living faith. "He who has My commandments and keeps them, it is he who loves Me. And he who loves Me will be loved by My Father, and I will love him and manifest Myself to him" (John 14:21).

Christianity can be likened to a wonderful, broad harbor where vessels of all sizes and all types can put in with the same convenience. This harbor will give refuge both to the humble boat of a fisherman and to the great ship of a merchant, loaded with diverse goods, to a giant battleship, equipped with countless means of destruction and death, and to the ornate yacht of a king and dignitary, appointed for grand and entertaining trips. Christianity embraces a person of any age, in any state or situation, of any abilities, at any level of education: it accepts and saves them all. "If you confess with your mouth the Lord Jesus and believe in your heart that God has raised Him from the dead, you will be saved. For with the heart one believes unto righteousness, and with the mouth confession is made unto salvation" (Rom 10:9–10). Whoever accepts Christianity, with all sincerity of heart, in the bosom of the Orthodox Church, where alone true Christianity is preserved, is saved. All people have been redeemed by a single price: by Christ: and in the act of redemption, it is only the price of redemption that has meaning. This price is paid without distinction and without partiality in return for everyone who wants to be redeemed and believes in the meaning of the price and confesses it. To confess the meaning of the price of redemption is at the same time to reject all one's own significance and merit. This price is paid on the condition of self-sacrifice. The simplest person who possesses no maturity in worldly terms has the same access to salvation through Christianity as the most learned and wise man. Christianity, as a gift of the most perfect God, fulfills everyone richly: faith from sincerity of heart takes the place of understanding in an infant or a simpleton, whereas a wise man who approaches Christianity in a legitimate way (1 Cor 3:18) will find in it an inexhaustible depth, an unattainable height of wisdom. Within Christianity is contained both true theology and genuine psychology and metaphysics. Only a Christian can gain true knowledge, accessible to mankind, about man, about both holy and rejected spirits, about the world that is invisible to our bodily eyes. Out of the instruction given by Christianity, a person develops the view of human scholarship that God has of it. "The wisdom of this world is foolishness with God. ... The Lord knows the thoughts of the wise," the thoughts of which their scholarship consists, "that they are futile" (1 Cor 3:19–20). These thoughts and this knowledge relate only to the transient and the vain; they bring a person who has them to indulge in vainglory, pride and self-deception, to ruin his life by caring about only mortal and transient matters, to lead a sinful life, and to reject and forget God and eternity. And when a person who is not illumined by the light of Christ dares to discuss spiritual subjects, then his mind wanders as if in a dark, boundless wilderness, and instead of true knowledge, which he has no possibility of acquiring, he invents opinions and dreams, and clothes them in dark and incomprehensible words with which he deceives himself and his neighbors, recognizing wisdom where in all justice there is delirium and mental derangement.

Strange and astonishing are the blindness and bitterness of those contemporaries of Christ who saw Him, heard His most holy teaching, were witnesses of His marvelous signs and did not believe in Him. Seven centuries earlier, as if from the top of a distant mountain, the prophet cried out, amazed by human insensibility, to this great multitude of living corpses: "Hearing you will hear and shall not understand, and seeing you will see and not perceive" (Matt 13:14). Just as strange is the present-day unbelief of many people in Christianity, which is radiant with the clearest truth. Scripture explains the cause of this unbelief with these words: "For the hearts of this people have grown dull" (Matt 13:15). Their hearts have become carnal, corpulent from a carnal way of life; they have become blind and deaf, they have become dead to all that is spiritual, eternal, and divine.

Studying Christianity shows its truth very clearly and decisively. The conviction acquired by proper study of Christianity, of the existence of everything invisible that is taught by Christianity, is far stronger than a conviction of the existence of something visible acquired through the senses. This conviction is so true that thousands upon thousands of people have abandoned the visible so as to gain the invisible. They did not cease to seal the conviction with blood, and they were not intimidated by the fierce punishments with which folly and frenzy attempted to force them to deny their conviction.

The most superficial glance at the institution and the spread of Christianity is astonishing. It proclaims to the whole world that the institution of Christianity is not human but divine. The Lord, after putting on humanity, was pleased to appear not in the brilliance of earthly glory but in a state of earthly humility. He was descended in the flesh from a royal tribe; but the members of that tribe had long since come down from the heights of the royal throne, had moved from the royal mansions to huts, and entered the ranks and position of the common people, earning their living by manual work. Not having taken anything from human power and glory, neither did the God-Man take anything from human wisdom. He was uneducated (John 7:15). After coming out to preach at the age of thirty, He chose twelve disciples from the same class of the common people to which He Himself also belonged. These disciples were very simple people, uneducated, illiterate young men, as the Gospel calls them in terms of their education according to the principles of fallen nature (Acts 4:13)—such were the people who were to be the founders of Christianity.

What instruction does this Teacher give and what does He prophesy to these disciples? He instructs them to recognize God incarnate in Him, to assure the whole world of this, to convert the whole world to serving and worshiping Him, destroying all the religions of the world. He instructs them and all who believe in Him to renounce the pleasures of the world and to deny themselves for the sake of belief in Him and adoption by Him. Of Himself He says that He will be punished with the dishonorable punishment given to criminals, and He will then draw everyone toward Himself. Of the disciples He says that they will be hated by all, persecuted, killed, but that they will catch all people with their teaching, overcoming and correcting both the powerful and the wise of the earth, that they are being sent out like sheep among wolves (Matt 10:16), and that in this struggle the sheep will emerge as the decisive victors.

According to the reason of the world, the institution of Christianity makes no sense: the purposes of its Founder are the impossible dream of someone carried away by imagination and ambition; the means and the tools to fulfill this dream are negligible, strange, ridiculous; in every aspect of the undertaking, it is obvious that it is impossible, that disaster is inevitable from the beginning. The Teacher had only three years to educate His disciples; no care was taken at least to acquaint them with the literacy necessary to read Holy Scripture, no provision was made for their upkeep: on the contrary, they were commanded not to be greedy (Matt 10:9–10), and instead of being given money toward their upkeep they were promised that through the providence of God everything necessary for earthly life would be provided to them.

This is the sight, incomprehensible to human reason, that is contemplated at the very foundation of Christianity: a new sight, equally wondrous, came with the events that followed immediately afterwards. These events began in Jerusalem but spread very quickly throughout the world. The God-Man was crucified on the wood of the cross. The death penalty on the cross at that time was the equivalent of today's gallows. Those criminals whom the authorities want to disgrace by the very means of their death are executed by hanging. Hanging on the cross, naked, showered with abuse, the God-Man began the conquest of men, as he had foretold: "I, if I am lifted up from the earth, will draw all peoples to Myself" (John 12:32). When He was hanging on the cross, the thief who was crucified like Him confessed Him to be the Lord, and the centurion who was guarding Him confessed Him to be the Son of God. Ten days after the ascension of the Lord into heaven, the Holy Spirit descended on the apostles: they were filled with wisdom of various kinds; these people who did not know their own language properly, who were illiterate, began speaking in all the languages of the world, working the most amazing miracles, and explaining the Scripture that they had never read. Thousands of Jews adopted Christianity. Troubled by the successes of the apostles, the Sanhedrin, which consisted of the chief priests and other highly respected and learned members of the Jewish people, called before it the uneducated apostles, interrogated them and listened to their answers and their teaching, to which they had no objections. As they could find no words to counter the words with which the truth was being told, the Sanhedrin resorted to threats, beatings, imprisonment, and stone-throwing, thus revealing their weakness and the might of their opponents. After the Sanhedrin, Herod also began to harass the apostles, and to the great approval of the Sanhedrin (Acts 12:3), cut off the head of one of them. The persecution in Jerusalem forced many of Christ's disciples to retreat from there (Acts 11:19). They spread throughout the world and sowed Christianity everywhere, watering the seeds with their blood. Within twenty years Christianity had embraced the whole known world. Within fifty years of the resurrection of Christ, Christians were so numerous that in one eastern army of the Roman emperor Trajan there were eleven thousand of them. He subjected them all without exception to the death penalty,[100] to the surprise of reasonable people, who deemed the destruction of their own army to be great folly. Romulus, who was commander of the Christian unit, was first beaten cruelly, then beheaded. Ten thousand people were crucified in the wilderness near Ararat; the rest were killed in various other ways. The act of Trajan was also subsequently imitated elsewhere.

The Roman emperors, masters of the world, set themselves against Christianity with intransigent hatred and tyranny. Neither the Celts, nor the Marcomanni, nor Attila, nor Gaiseric destroyed so many populations in the Roman Empire as the emperors who persecuted Christians.[101] The bloody conflict between wolves and lambs lasted for three centuries. The one side operated with the sword, with fire, with wild beasts, with stifling dungeons, hunger, and thirst, with all means of torture and murder; the other side fought with the power of the spirit, of faith, of God, enduring the most terrible tortures, dying nobly for their faith. The three-century struggle was crowned with victory, and at the beginning of the fourth century the Christian faith became dominant in the world. The powerful and the wise of the earth bowed down before the teaching of the uneducated fishermen; all peoples bowed down before it. The cross, previously the sign of a humiliating means of execution, became a sign of the highest honor: emperors and bishops wear it on their heads and on their breasts; it crowns the churches of the true God; it serves as a sign for every Orthodox Christian, a sign of his faith, his hope, his love. Who does not recognize in the establishment of Christianity the will of God, the power of God, the work of God, exceeding human reason and power? An impossible thing, a thing beyond nature, was accomplished; a work of God was accomplished.

This is how the history of Christianity looks when considered as a whole. More detailed study forms within us a clearer conviction of its divinity. The strongest conviction appears from living in accordance with the commandments of the Gospel, as the prophet also said: "Through Thy commandments I understood" (Ps 118:104). A conviction based on keeping the commandments is one that acts within a person's very soul: it is stronger than any external conviction. The commandments of the Gospel comfort, revive, and strengthen the soul. A person who senses their action within him gains a living faith in the Lord Jesus Christ, and this faith expresses before the Lord a pledge from the heart with a clear and decisive confession: "You have the words of eternal life. Also we have come to believe and know that You are the Christ, the Son of the living God" (John 6:68–69).

"Reach your finger here," says the Saviour to His disciple whose faith is wavering, who is stricken with confusion, "... reach your hand here, and ... do not be unbelieving, but believing" (John 20:27). "Handle Me and see" (Luke 24:39): start acting according to the guidance of My commandments, handle Me by living according to My will, and you will see Me, Who am invisible, with the spiritual sensation of your soul: everyone who handles Me in this way will assure himself of Me, and in the joy of finding Me will cry out with My beloved apostle, "My Lord and my God!" (John 20:28). Amen.

23. On the Mortification of the Human Spirit

Sermon on the Sunday of the Myrrh-bearing Women, the Third Sunday after Pascha

Today's Gospel (Mark 16:1–8; Luke 23:54–24:11; Matt 28:1–10) proclaimed the ascetic effort of the holy women who followed the God-Man during His wandering on earth and were witnesses of His sufferings and present at His burial. The burial took place on the evening of the Friday. When the rage of the Jews poured out like red-hot lava from fire-breathing Mount Etna, directed not only at the Lord but at all those close to Him; when the holy apostles were forced to go into hiding, or could only watch the astonishing events from afar; when one disciple of love—for which nothing terrible exists—remained faithfully near the Lord: then a disciple, Joseph, who had always been secret, concealing the pledge of his heart for fear of persecution by the other members of the Sanhedrin, or the council of the Jews, of which he was an honored member, suddenly trampled on all obstacles, hesitations, and doubts that had until then bound and troubled him, approached the cold and cruel Pilate, asked for the body of the One put to death by a shameful execution, received it and buried it with reverence and honor. The Gospel presents the act of Joseph as generous and courageous. This indeed it was. A member of the council, in the presence of that same council that had committed deicide, in the presence of Jerusalem, which had taken part in the deicide, took down from the cross the body of the God-Man, killed by men, and took it away to a garden near the gates and walls of the city. There, in seclusion and in silence, in the shade of trees, in a new tomb hewn out of solid rock, he lay the body with which the bodies and souls of all people had been redeemed, having liberally anointed it with perfumes and oils, and wrapped it in the cleanest shrouds, as a precious treasure is wrapped and covered up. Another member of the Sanhedrin, Nicodemus who had once come to the Lord by night and had recognized Him as sent by God, took part in the burial of the Lord. After rolling a great stone to the doors of the tomb—in the Gospel the low-lying opening to the cave is called a door—Joseph left, having completed his ministrations. The council followed Joseph's actions and, after he had left, set a watch on the tomb and sealed the stone that closed its entrance. The burial of the Lord was witnessed by both His followers and His enemies. Some members of the council, in their frenzy and fury, while committing a great atrocity, in their ignorance made the greatest sacrifice (Acts 3:17–18): by sacrificing the most holy Sacrifice, they redeemed humanity, putting to an end to the constant fruitless sacrifices, and making them and their very institution superfluous. Other council members, representing all the righteous men of the Old Testament with their God-pleasing disposition of spirit, accomplished the burial of the Redeemer of men. With this action they completed and fulfilled the devout activities of the sons of the Old Testament. From here on begins the exclusive ministry of the figures of the New Testament.

The holy women did not fail to match the courageous selflessness of Joseph. After being present at the burial on the Friday, they did not believe it was permissible on the Sabbath—the day of rest—to disturb that rest in which the body of the Lord reposed in the blessed darkness and seclusion of the tomb. The women intended to pour out their zeal toward the Lord by pouring myrrh on His body. After returning from the burial on the Friday, they immediately bought a substantial quantity of fragrant compounds and waited for daybreak on the day after the Sabbath, known as Sunday, the day of resurrection. On this day, as soon as the sun rose, the devout women set off for the tomb. On the way they remembered that a large stone had been placed across the entrance to the tomb. This worried them, and they began to say to each other, "Who will roll away the stone from the door of the tomb for us?" The stone was "very large" (Mark 16:3–4). When they came to the tomb, they saw to their astonishment that the stone had been rolled away. It had been rolled away by a radiant, powerful angel: he, after the resurrection of the Lord, had descended from heaven to the tomb that contained the One Whom the heavens cannot contain, struck the guard with terror and at the same time broke the seal and rolled away the heavy stone. He sat on the stone, awaiting the arrival of the women. When they came, he proclaimed to them the resurrection of the Lord and commanded them to tell the good news to the apostles. For their zeal toward the God-Man, for their determination to give honor to the most holy body that was being watched by an armed guard, and was also being watched closely by the hatred of the Sanhedrin, the holy women were the first people of all to receive precise and true information about the resurrection of Christ, and they became the first, powerful preachers of the resurrection, as they had heard the news from the lips of the angel. The most perfect God is impartial: all people are equal before Him, and someone who strives toward God with great selflessness is honored with special gifts from God, in particular abundance and spiritual grace.

"Who will roll away the stone from the door of the tomb for us?" These words of the holy women have their own mystical significance. This is so edifying that love for our neighbor and the desire for his spiritual benefit do not permit us to pass over it in silence.

The tomb signifies our heart. The heart was a temple; it became a tomb. Christ enters it through the sacrament of baptism, so as to dwell within us and to act through us. The heart is then consecrated as a temple of God. We take away from Christ the possibility of acting through us when we revive our "old man" (Eph 4:22), constantly following the urges of our fallen will, of our reason poisoned by lies. Christ, Who has entered through baptism, continues to be present within us, but as if wounded and mortified by our behavior. The temple of God not made with hands is turned into a confined, dark tomb. Against its entrance leans a stone that is "very large." The enemies of God place a watch on the tomb, strengthen with a seal the entrance that is closed with a stone, sealing the stone against the rock-face so that, apart from its weight, the substantial seal prevents the stone from being touched. The enemies of God themselves are watching for the mortification to be preserved. They have considered and put in place all possible barriers to preempt the resurrection, to obstruct it, and to make it impossible.

The stone signifies the ailment of the soul that preserves all other ailments intact, and that the holy fathers call "insensibility."[102] What kind of sin is this? We have not even heard of it, many will say. According to the definition of the fathers, "insensibility" is the mortification of spiritual sensations, the invisible death of the human spirit with regard to spiritual objects, at the same time as full development of life with regard to material objects. It can happen that from long physical illness all a person's strength is exhausted, all the capabilities of the body wither away: then the sickness, not finding food for itself, stops torturing the constitution; it abandons the patient, leaving him exhausted, as if dying, incapable of activity due to being exhausted by suffering, because of his terrible, mute sickliness that is not expressed by any particular affliction. The same thing also happens with the human spirit. A negligent life over a long period of time with constant distraction, with constant willful transgressions, forgetfulness of God and of eternity, paying no attention or, if any, then only the most superficial, to the commandments and teaching of the Gospel, removes from our spirit sympathy for spiritual objects, and mortifies our spirit in respect to them. Although they exist, they stop existing for it, because its life for them has stopped: all its strength is directed only toward the material, the temporal, the vain, the sinful.

Everyone who wishes to examine the state of his soul dispassionately and thoroughly will see within it the ailment of insensibility, the vastness of its significance, its weight and importance, and will confess that it is the manifestation and evidence of mortification of the spirit. When we want to read the Word of God, what tedium attacks us! How everything we read appears to us difficult to understand, unworthy of attention, strange! How we want to break free from this reading as quickly as possible! Why is this? Because we do not sympathize with the Word of God.

When we stand in prayer, what dryness, what coldness we feel! How we rush to finish our superficial prayer, filled with distractedness! Why is this? Because we are alien to God: we believe in the existence of God with a dead faith; we do not feel that He exists. Why do we forget about eternity? Are we really excluded from the number of those who must enter its immense realm? Will we not stand face to face with death, like other people? Why do we forget this? Because we have cleaved with our whole soul to material things, we never think or want to think about eternity, we have lost the precious anticipation of it, we have gained a false feeling toward our wandering on earth. This false feeling presents earthly life to us as infinite. We are so deceived and distracted by the false feeling that we arrange all our activities in conformity with it, sacrificing the capabilities of the soul and the body to decay, not concerning ourselves at all with the other world that awaits us, although we must become eternal inhabitants of that world. Why do idle talk, idle jokes, condemnation of our neighbors, and witty jokes at their expense pour out from us, as if from a fountain? Why do we spend so many hours, without becoming tired of them, on empty amusements, never getting our fill of them, and try to replace one vain occupation with another, not wanting to devote the smallest amount of time to contemplating our sins and weeping for them? Because we have acquired sympathy for sin, for everything that is vain, everything through which sin is introduced into man and kept within him; because we have lost sympathy with all occupations that introduce God-pleasing virtues into a person and increase and preserve them. Insensibility is planted within a soul by a world hostile to God and by the fallen angels that are enemies God, with the cooperation of our will. It grows and is strengthened when we live according to the principles of the world; it grows and is strengthened when we follow the reason and will of our fallen nature, when we abandon the service of God and serve Him negligently. When insensibility lingers in the soul and becomes an attribute of it, then the world and the rulers of the world are applying their seal to the stone. This seal consists in the interaction of a human spirit with fallen spirits, in the acceptance by a human spirit of impressions made on it by fallen spirits, and in submission to forced influence and domination of the rejected spirits.

"Who will roll away the stone from the door of the tomb for us?" The question is filled with concern, sorrow, and bewilderment. This concern, this sorrow, this bewilderment are felt by those souls who have turned toward the Lord, abandoning the service of the world and of sin. Before their eyes the ailment of insensibility is revealed, in all its terrible extent and significance. They wish to pray with tenderness, to read the Word of God to the exclusion of all other reading, to remain in constant contemplation of their sinfulness, in constant pain on its account, in short, they want to be adopted, to belong to God—but they encounter things that are unexpected, unknown to servants of the world, and resistance within themselves: insensibility of the heart. The heart, struck by the past negligent way of life, as if by a deadly sickness, finds no sign of life. In vain the mind gathers thoughts of death, of the judgment of God, of its many sins, of the torments of hell, the joy of paradise; in vain the mind seeks to strike these thoughts into the heart: it remains without sympathy toward them, as if hell, and paradise, and divine judgment, and sins, and the state of fallenness and perdition had no connection with the heart. It sleeps a deep sleep, a deadly sleep: it sleeps after being intoxicated with the poison of sin. "Who will roll away the stone from the door of the tomb for us?" This stone is "very large."

According to the teaching of the holy Fathers, to destroy insensibility a person needs to act against it constantly, patiently and without pause, and constantly to lead a virtuous and watchful life. Such a life fights a life of insensibility; but this death of the human spirit cannot be mortified only with a person's own strength: insensibility is destroyed through the action of divine grace. At God's command, an angel of God comes down to help the toiling and troubled soul. He rolls away the stone of bitterness from the heart, fills the heart with tenderness, and proclaims to the soul the resurrection that is the usual consequence of constant tenderness.[103] Tender emotion is the first sign that the heart has revived in relation to God and to eternity. What is tender emotion? It is the feeling within a person of mercy and compassion for himself, for his wretched state, a state of fallenness, of eternal death. It is the state of the people of Jerusalem who heard the sermon of the holy Apostle Peter: Scripture says that they "were cut to the heart" (Acts 2:37), and they immediately adopted Christianity.

The body of the Lord had no need of the fragrant myrrh brought by the myrrh-bearing women. Through the resurrection, it forestalled being anointed with myrrh. But the holy women, by buying the myrrh in good time, by arriving early, in the first rays of sunlight, to the life-bearing tomb, by disregarding their fear of the anger of the Sanhedrin and of the military watch guarding the tomb and the One who was buried there, appeared and demonstrated in practice the pledge of their hearts to the Lord. Their gift proved to be superfluous; it was rewarded a hundredfold by the appearance of the angel—a new experience for the women—and by the news, that could not have been more credible, of the resurrection of the God-Man and of humanity together with Him.

For His own sake, God does not need us to dedicate our lives, all our strength and capabilities to serving Him: it is for us that this is necessary. We bring them, like myrrh, to the tomb of the Lord. We buy the myrrh—that is, our good intention—in good time. From our youth we renounce all sacrifices to sin: this is the price we pay for the myrrh—the good intention. It is impossible to combine serving sin with serving God: the latter is destroyed by the former. Let us not allow sin to deaden sympathy within our spirit toward God and toward everything divine. Let us not allow sin to mark us with its impressions, and to gain forced domination over us. A person who enters the service of God from the days of his unspoiled youth, and remains in this service with constancy, submitting to the constant influence of the Holy Spirit, is marked with the grace-filled, holy impressions emanating from it, and, in his time, acquires an active knowledge of the resurrection of Christ, revives in spirit in Christ, and, if chosen and commanded to do so by God, becomes a preacher of the resurrection to his brothers. But a person who, through ignorance or weakness, is enslaved by sin, has interacted with fallen spirits and attached himself to them, has lost the connection in his spirit with God and with celestial beings: let this person heal himself by means of repentance. Let us not postpone our healing day after day, so that death may not steal up to us unexpectedly and carry us instantly away, so that we may not prove to be unable to enter the dwelling-places of unending rest and joy, so that we may not be caused, like worthless tares (Matt 13:30), to fall into the flame of hell that burns eternally and is never quenched. The healing of long-standing ailments is not achieved as quickly or as easily as ignorant people imagine. It is not for no reason that the mercy of God gives us time to repent; it is not for no reason that all the saints pleaded with God to grant them time to repent. Time is needed to wipe away the impressions of sin; time is needed for the impressions of the Holy Spirit to be marked; time is needed to purify oneself from pollution; time is needed to clothe oneself in the garments of virtue, to acquire the God-pleasing qualities with which all who dwell in heaven are adorned.

Christ is resurrected within a person who is prepared for this, and the tomb, or heart, is transformed anew into the temple of God. "Arise, O Lord; save me, O my God" (Ps 4:8); in this, Your mystical and at the same time real resurrection is my salvation. Amen.

24. On the Punishments of God

Sermon on the Sunday of the Paralytic, the Fourth Sunday after Pascha

"See, you have been made well. Sin no more, lest a worse thing come upon you" (John 5:14). This is the advice that the Lord gave to the paralytic healed by Him, as we heard in today's Gospel.

Dear brothers! This advice of the Lord also has a very important meaning for us. It tells us that we are subjected to illnesses and other adversities of earthly life for our sins. When God delivers us from an illness or an adversity, and we again begin to lead a sinful life, then we again subject ourselves to adversities, more serious than the first punishments and lessons sent to us by God.

Sin is the cause of all men's tribulations, both in time and in eternity. Tribulations are like a natural consequence, a natural accessory to sin, similar to the way that sufferings produced by physical ailments are an inevitable accessory to these ailments, an effect that is characteristic of them. Sin in its broadest sense, that is, the fall of mankind and his eternal death, envelops all people without exception; some sins are the regrettable inheritance of whole human societies; finally, each person has his own individual passions, his particular sins that belong exclusively to him. Sin, in all these different forms, serves as the beginning of all tribulations and adversities undergone by mankind in general, human societies, and each person in particular.

The state of fallenness, of eternal death, with which the whole of humanity is infected, struck, and killed, is the source of all other human sins, both societal and individual. Our nature, disordered by the poison of sin, has acquired the capacity to sin, and to be attracted to sin; it has submitted itself to the force of sin, it is unable to avoid producing sin from within itself, it cannot manage without it in any area of its activity. No person who has not been renewed can avoid sinning, even if he does not want to sin (Rom 7:14–25).

Three punishments have been appointed by divine justice for the sins of all of humanity. Two of them have already been meted out, one still remains. The first punishment was eternal death, which all of humanity underwent at its origin, in the forefathers, for disobedience to God in paradise. The second punishment was the worldwide flood, in response to the people allowing the flesh to prevail over the spirit, and relegating themselves to the life and dignity of dumb animals. The final punishment must be the destruction and demise of this visible world in response to people turning away from the Redeemer, and interacting consistently with the rejected angels.

Not infrequently, a particular type of sin grips whole human societies, incurring the punishment of God. Thus the sodomites were burned by fire that fell down from heaven, for their transgressive gratification of the flesh; thus the Israelites were betrayed to members of other tribes more than once for turning to idolatry; thus no stone remained on another in the magnificent Jerusalem, built of wondrous stones, and its inhabitants perished from the swords of the Romans, for rejecting the Saviour and committing deicide. Sin is contagious, and it is difficult for an individual person to stand firm against a sin by which a whole society has been captivated.

In the prolonged illness of the paralytic healed by the Lord, we see an example of personal punishment through divine justice for a sin committed personally.

Having said as much as it is necessary to know and as much as can be said here about the sinfulness of the human race as a whole and of human societies, let us now pay particular attention to the individual sinfulness of each person. This examination is completely necessary and extremely useful for us. It can have a saving influence on our activities, averting them from a path of iniquity and directing them toward the will of God. Illuminated by the law of God, we will learn that God, in His infinite mercy, is also completely just, and that He will certainly impose an appropriate punishment for a sinful life. This conviction will inspire us to apply every effort to liberate ourselves from being led astray both by our own passions and by the wicked habits of society, in order to save ourselves from the temporal and eternal punishments of God.

The holy Fathers[104] state that until their redemption all people were possessed by sin, and fulfilled the will of sin even against their own will. Following the redemption of the human race by the God-Man, those who have believed in Christ and been renewed through holy baptism are no longer constrained by sin, but are free: free either to resist sin or to follow its inspirations. Those who willingly submit again to sin lose their freedom and fall into the enforced domination of sin (Matt 12:44–45). Those who battle with sin, under the guidance of the Word of God, resist it, in time gaining full victory over sinfulness. A victory over one's own sinfulness is at the same time a victory over eternal death. After achieving this, a person can easily avoid the sinful passions of society. We see this in the holy martyrs: after overcoming sin within themselves, they resisted the error of the people, they denounced it, they did not cease to seal their holy witness with their blood. A person who is led astray and blinded by his own sin cannot avoid being led astray by a sinful disposition within society: he will not see it clearly and will not understand it as he should, he will not renounce it with selflessness because, in his heart, he belongs to it. The essence of the ascetic struggle against sin, the struggle which every Christian is obliged to pursue, consists in fighting against sin with which the body cannot avoid sympathizing, terminating our friendship with it, vanquishing it within our very soul, in our mind and in the heart. "Eternal death," says St Macarius the Great, "is found hidden within the heart: with it a person is dead, while being superficially alive. Whoever in the secrecy of his heart has passed from death to life, he will be alive unto the ages, and will never die. Even though the bodies of such people are separated from their souls for a time, they are blessed, and will rise in glory. It is for this reason that we call the death of the saints sleep."[105]

All saints without exception, although they conquered eternal death and during this temporal life had already discovered eternal life within themselves, underwent many grave tribulations and temptations (Heb 12:8). Why is this? It is inherent in sinners to invite divine punishment on themselves; but why does the rod of God not pass by the chosen people of God, but strikes them with blows? The answer to this question is given by Holy Scripture and the holy Fathers: Although in righteous men, sinfulness has been vanquished, and although eternal death has been destroyed by the presence within them of the Holy Spirit, they have not been granted immutability in goodness for the whole time of their earthly wandering: the freedom to choose between good and evil has not been taken away even from them.[106] Immutability in goodness is something that belongs to the age to come. Life on earth, until its last moment, is the arena of willing and unwilling ascetic struggle. "I discipline my body and bring it into subjection," says the great Paul, "lest, when I have preached to others, I myself should become disqualified" (1 Cor 9:27). The apostle says this of the body seasoned and blessed by divine grace, to which the bitter poison of the viper did no harm, whose clothes brought about healing. Even a body like this needed to be brought into subjection and disciplined, so that the passions mortifying it did not revive, and eternal death was not resurrected. For as long as the Christian wanders on the earth, even if he be a vessel of the Holy Spirit, that is how long eternal death may be resurrected in him, and sinfulness may again overcome both body and soul. But also, their own struggle is not enough for servants of God to curb the fallenness that lurks within their nature, constantly striving to restore its dominion: they need help from God. God assists them through His grace and with the rod of His paternal punishment, in proportion to the grace of each. The great Paul was given, as he testifies, "a thorn in the flesh ... , a messenger of Satan to buffet me, lest I be exalted above measure" (2 Cor 12:7), due to his elevated spiritual progress, the many divine revelations he experienced, the many spiritual gifts he possessed, and the many miracles he performed. Our nature is so damaged by the poison of sin that the very abundance of divine grace in a person can serve as a cause of pride and perdition for him. Paul encountered neither honour, nor glory, nor unquestioning obedience when he was preaching Christ to the world, and showing the truth of what he preached through signs: a messenger of Satan prepared for him everywhere machinations, resistance, humiliation, persecution, attacks, and death. Knowing that this happened because God permitted it, Paul exclaimed, "I take pleasure in infirmities, in reproaches, in needs, in persecutions, in distresses, for Christ's sake" (2 Cor 12:10). St Paul found it necessary to mortify his body that carnal passions would not arise through bodily weakness: the eye of divine providence saw the need for tribulations to protect the soul of Paul from pride. Even the purest human nature possesses within it something proud, notes St Macarius the Great.[107] This is the reason why servants of God subject themselves willingly to deprivations and afflictions—at the same time they are subjected to various tribulations and temptations permitted by the providence of God, assisting them in their ascetic struggle and protecting it from being defiled by sin. The way of earthly life for all the saints was arduous, thorny, full of deprivations and countless misfortunes. "Others were tortured ... Still others had trial of mockings and scourgings, yes, and of chains and imprisonment. They were stoned, they were sawn in two, were tempted, were slain with the sword. They wandered about in sheepskins and goatskins, being destitute, afflicted, tormented—of whom the world was not worthy. They wandered in deserts and mountains, in dens and caves of the earth" (Heb 11:35–38). The blessed Symeon Metaphrastis notes in his life of the great martyr Eustathios: "It is not pleasing to God that His servants, for whom He has prepared eternal, unchanging honour and glory in heaven, be honoured and glorified with vain and temporal honour in this inconstant and fickle world."[108] Why is this? It is because there is no man who could remain in the heights of earthly greatness and prosperity without harm to his soul. Even if a person were equal to the angels in virtue, he too would waver.[109] The capacity to change is implanted within us, within our souls, through our fall.[110] We cannot avoid aligning and conforming the disposition of our spirit to our external circumstances and material situation. "My soul cleaveth to the dust" (Ps 118:25; cf Ps 137:7), the prophet confesses to God in the name of every fallen person: "Your 'right hand'—Your most holy Word and Your most holy Providence—raises me from the earth, tears me away from it, and leads to salvation, dissolving my temporal well-being with tribulations and at the same time bestowing on me a grace-filled spiritual consolation, instilling an attraction toward heaven in my heart. Without this help from God, in my unhappy inclination, which I cannot resist in my own strength, my mind and heart would be attached only to material things, and I would deceive myself terribly, disastrously, forgetting eternity and the good things prepared for me there, I would lose them irrevocably."

The true servants of God accepted with obedience to God the tribulations permitted to them by divine providence, giving thanks and glorifying God. They "were well pleased," as the Apostle Paul expresses it, about their sorrows; they found them helpful, necessary, essential for themselves; they deemed it correct and beneficial that they had been permitted. They united the pursuit of their own will with the action of the will of God: they were well disposed in the precise sense of the word toward the punishments and lessons sent from God.

Such was the pledge of the heart and the way of thinking with which the saints regarded the misfortunes that befell them. Spiritual consolation and joy and renewal of the soul with sensations of the age to come were the fruits of this disposition inspired by humility. What shall we sinners say about the tribulations we encounter? First of all, what is their initial cause? The initial cause of human sufferings is, as we have seen, sin, and every sinner will do well, in the sorrows that befell him, to turn his thoughts immediately to his sins, admit and condemn them, condemn himself for his sins and recognize the sorrow as a just punishment from God. There is also another cause of tribulations: this is the mercy of God toward weak humanity. In allowing sinners to suffer sorrows, God reminds them to come to their senses, to come to a halt in the midst of their irresistible enthusiasm, to remember eternity and their relationship with it, to remember God and their obligations to Him. Tribulations that sinners are permitted to suffer serve as a sign that these sinners are not yet forgotten, not rejected by God, that the capacity to repent, to correct themselves, and to be saved can be seen in them.

Take courage, sinners punished by God. "For whom the Lord loves He chastens, and scourges every son whom He receives" (Heb 12:6). This is proclaimed to us by the Holy Scripture that teaches, consoles, and strengthens us. "Choose chastening, lest the Lord be angry, and so ye perish from the right way" (Ps 2:12): accept punishment, knowing that you are worthy of punishment; accept punishment by giving glory to the just God, Who is merciful in His justice; accept punishment by examining your past life objectively, confessing your sins and washing them away with tears of repentance, and correcting your behavior. This often needs little external correction but much secret correction: in one's way of thinking, in tendency, in motives, in intentions. You have strayed from the right way through your sins: do not lose it permanently with grumbling, with self-justification—in opposition to your conscience—to yourself and to others, with hopelessness, despair, or blasphemy. Do not turn a means of assistance given to you to raise you up to the way of godliness, and used by the Lord Himself, into a means of definitive distress, into a means of destroying yourself. Otherwise, the Lord will be angry with you. He will turn His face away from you, as from those who are alien to Him: He will not send you tribulations, like one who is forgotten and rejected (Heb 12:8); He will allow you to spend your earthly life in accordance with the lusts of your sin-loving heart, and will command death to burn you up instantly, like the tares that became the food of the fire of Gehenna through their own free will and choice (Matt 13:40–42).

Those who endure, as they should, the temptations permitted by God, draw nearer to Him, acquire boldness toward Him, and are adopted by Him, as witnessed by the apostle: "If you endure chastening, God deals with you as with sons" (Heb 12:7). God fills with spiritual blessings a person who has endured a tribulation with humility of spirit, He hears his heartfelt prayer, and often averts the rod of punishment if it is not necessary for great spiritual progress. This is what happened to the paralytic who was healed after lying for thirty-eight years in the porch of Solomon among a great number of other sick people waiting, as he did, for the healing action of an angel stirring up the water. What suffering was in this situation induced by sickness and poverty! It is clear that these people struck by disease had no other means for treatment, and therefore had decided in favor of a prolonged wait for a miracle that took place only once a year, giving true and full healing from any illness, but only to one of the sick. The illness of the paralytic was a punishment for sins, as is apparent from the instruction given by the Lord to the healed man: "See, you have been made well. Sin no more, lest a worse thing come upon you" (John 5:14).

The Lord, Who gave the healed paralytic the advice not to fall again into the same sins for which he had been punished by his illness, gave the same advice to the woman who had been a sinner and whose sins He had forgiven. "Go," said the Saviour of the world to the woman who had been condemned to death by stoning, "and sin no more" (John 8:11). The merciful Lord grants healing of the soul and of the body subject to one condition, and one only. The sin of the woman was a mortal sin; it is clear that the sin of the paralytic was also one of the mortal sins. These are the very sins that summon the punishment of God. A person who is bogged down in the abyss of mortal sins is in particular need of help from God—and this help appears openly in the form of punishment and secretly in a call to repentance. A person is called to repentance either through illness that is sent to him, as happened with the paralytic, or through persecution by people that is permitted by God, as befell David, or in some other way. In whatever form the punishment of God appears, we must accept it with humility and quickly strive to fulfill the aim for which the punishment has been sent: to turn to the healing of repentance, placing into our soul the commandment to abstain from that sin for which the hand of the Lord chastises us. Our conscience will reliably reveal this sin to us. God grants us forgiveness of the sin and salvation from the tribulation through which we are punished for it, solely subject to the condition that we abandon the sin that is destructive to us and an abomination before God.

Returning to a sin that brings the anger of God upon us and has been healed and forgiven by God causes yet greater tribulations, and predominantly eternal ones, lasting beyond the grave. For thirty-eight years the paralytic languished in sickness for his sin. This is a considerable punishment—but the Lord proclaims an even greater punishment for returning to sin. What punishment is this that is more severe than an illness that keeps the sufferer bedridden for a whole life, amid every deprivation? It is none other than the eternal torment in hell that awaits all unrepentant and uncorrected sinners. Amen.

25. On Worshiping God in Spirit and in Truth

Sermon on the Sunday of the Samaritan Woman

"The true worshipers will worship the Father in spirit and truth; for the Father is seeking such to worship Him" (John 4:23).

Dear brothers! We heard now in the Gospel that the true servants of the true God worship Him in spirit and in truth, that God "is seeking," that is wishes to have such worshipers. If God wishes to have such worshipers, then it is obvious that He will accept only worshipers and servants like these, and only they are pleasing to Him. This is a teaching given to us by the Son of God Himself. Let us believe Him. Let us embrace with all our love the most holy teaching of Christ. So as to follow it exactly, let us examine what it means to worship God the Father in spirit and in truth.

The truth is our Lord Jesus Christ, as He bears witness of Himself: "I am the way, the truth, and the life" (John 14:6). The truth is the Word of God: "Your word is truth" (John 17:17). This Word was before eternity in God, was spoken by God and to God; this Word is God: this Word is the Creator of all that exists, visible and invisible (John 1:1,3; Col 1:16). This "Word became flesh and dwelt among us, and we beheld His glory, the glory as of the only begotten of the Father, full of grace and truth" (John 1:14). "No one has seen God at any time" but the Word of God, "the only begotten Son, who is in the bosom of the Father, He has declared Him" (John 1:18). The Son of God, the Word of God, confessed God before men, and fully revealed Him to men: the Son of God revealed to men a truth that was inaccessible to them, bearing witness to and imprinting the truth clearly through the most abundant teaching of divine grace. "And of His fullness we have all received, and grace for grace. For the law was given through Moses, but grace and truth came through Jesus Christ" (John 1:16–17). This means that Jesus Christ did not simply present some more or less thorough understanding of grace and truth, but taught men grace itself, truth itself in essence, and implanted it within them. We became partakers in the nature of God (2 Pet 1:4).

The truth has a Spirit that is intrinsic to it. This spirit is called the Spirit of truth (John 15:26; John 16:13). It is the Spirit that proceeds from the Father (John 15:26). It is the Holy Spirit of God (John 14:26). It is the Spirit of the Son (Gal 4:6), that is constantly present with the Son, constituting together with the Father and the Son a single, undivided and unconfused divine essence. Acceptance of the truth is at the same time acceptance of the Holy Spirit: that is why the all-holy truth proclaims of itself that it will send the Holy Spirit from the Father to His disciples. It is natural for the Holy Spirit of truth to be present where holy truth acts, and to leave its mark on its activities. In the same way, wherever the Holy Spirit acts, the truth is revealed most abundantly, as the Lord indeed said to His disciples: "when He, the Spirit of truth, has come, He will guide you into all truth" (John 16:13). And in describing the wonderful relationship of the divine Word with the divine Spirit, The Lord said of the Spirit: "He will glorify Me, for He will take of what is Mine and declare it to you. All things that the Father has are Mine" (John 16:14–15). The Spirit proclaims and reveals to mankind the Son Who is one in nature with Him. The Spirit is attracted to people when they have faith in the Son Who is one in nature with Him. The Holy Spirit builds a true Christian spiritually and transforms him into a dwelling-place of God (Eph 2:22); He presents and establishes Christ in the inner man (Eph 3:16–17). He adopts men for God, making them resemble Christ, installing characteristics of Christ within them (John 14:6). Men who have been adopted by God address Him in their prayers as the Father, because the Holy Spirit completely clearly and perceptibly bears witness with the spirit of the person renewed by Him (Rom 8:16) of the union of this person with God and his adoption by God. "Because you are sons, God has sent forth the Spirit of His Son into your hearts, crying out, 'Abba, Father!'" (Gal 4:6). It is worshipers like these who are recognized as true worshipers of God. It is worshipers like these, who worship God in spirit and in truth, whom God seeks and accepts. Outside true Christianity, there is neither knowledge of God, nor service of God.

"No one comes to the Father except through Me," said the Lord (John 14:6). For someone who does not believe in the Lord Jesus Christ, there is no God: "Whoever denies the Son does not have the Father either" (1 John 2:23); "he who does not believe the Son shall not see life, but the wrath of God abides on him" (John 3:36). It is impossible to approach God, to enter into any interaction with God, in any way other than through our Lord Jesus Christ, the one mediator and intercessor, the means of intercourse between God and men. There is no true knowledge of the Lord Jesus Christ except through the Holy Spirit. "No one can say that Jesus is Lord except by the Holy Spirit" (1 Cor 12:3). "Now if anyone does not have the Spirit of Christ, he is not His" (Rom 8:9). Outside Christianity there is no virtue worthy of Heaven. "It is impossible," says St Mark the Ascetic, "for us to have faith in anything good or to carry it into effect except in Christ Jesus and the Holy Spirit."[111] Natural human good works are unworthy of God, as they originate in our fallen nature, in which good is mixed with evil, and is for the most part hardly noticeable in the abundance of evil. The fallen nature is capable only of evil, as God Himself bears witness: "The mind of man is diligently involved with evil things from his youth" (Gen 8:21). "You ... being evil, know how to give good gifts to your children" (Luke 11:13). This is the value in the eyes of the Gospel and of God of natural human goodness and of the actions emanating from it. In vain does our fallen nature glorify its acclaimed and great good works! Such boasting is evidence of terrible blindness. Such boasting amounts to an involuntary revelation of the quality of acclaimed human works that are prompted and fed by vainglory. Stinking of the arrogance that these whitewashed tombs give off, they are an abomination to God: it is the incense of humility that is favorable to Him.

This is why the Lord commanded fallen and blind humanity to renounce its nature, although mankind does not acknowledge its sad fall, on the contrary, it sees in it some kind of great triumph and seeks to develop this triumph. To be saved, it is essential to renounce sin. But we have adopted sin to such an extent that it has become our nature, our very soul. To renounce sin it has become essential to renounce our fallen nature, to renounce the soul (Matt 10:39), to renounce not only obviously evil deeds but also the good deeds of the "old man" (Eph 4:22) that are highly respected and glorified by the world. We must substitute our own way of thinking with the mind of Christ (1 Cor 2:16), and instead of acting under the influence of feelings and being guided by the carnal mind, we must carefully keep the commandments of Christ. "If you abide in My word, you are My disciples indeed. And you shall know the truth, and the truth shall make you free" (John 8:31–32). What great and deep words these are! The direct conclusion that follows from them is that sin keeps man enslaved solely by means of incorrect and false notions. And it is obvious that the harmful falseness of these notions consists both in the very recognition of good where there is in fact nothing good and in the failure to recognize evil where there is in fact deadly evil.

"He who is of God hears God's word" (John 8:47), says the Lord. Brothers! Let us humble ourselves before our Lord God. Unlike the embittered Jews, who rejected both the Lord and His teaching, let us show submission to the Lord by obeying His all-holy and saving teaching. Let us lay aside the way of thinking we acquired from our fallen nature and the world that is hostile to God. Let us adopt the way of thinking that the Lord offers us in His Holy Gospel. Let us follow the truth, and we will inherit the truth. The truth frees the human mind from the invisible bonds of delusion with which sin has fettered it. Not only that: after obtaining spiritual freedom for the mind and renewing and reviving it with life from on high, through the Word of God—the all-powerful truth, leads it onto the way of the commandments of Christ, and "takes from [it] the way of injustice" (Ps 118:29). The soul that has been revived by the Truth cries out together with the inspired prophet: "I ran the way of Thy commandments, when Thou didst enlarge my heart. Make the way of Thy statutes a law unto me, and I shall always seek it. Give me understanding, and I shall delve into Thy law; yea, I shall keep it with my whole heart" (Ps 118:32–34). Such a soul immediately becomes a partaker in the Holy Spirit, which cannot avoid being present where the Divine Truth is present and reigns, and which in Its mystical concord with the all-holy Truth says of Itself: "I am a part of all them that fear Thee, and of them that keep Thy commandments" (Ps 118:63).[112]

While a person remains in his fallen nature, he is submerged in the darkness of the deepest ignorance: he does not know how he must pray and what he should pray for (Rom 8:26); he is incapable of serving God. Only faith in Christ gives knowledge of the truth. Faith, expressed by keeping the commandments of Christ, draws the grace of the Holy Spirit into the heart of the believer, as the God-inspired prophet said: "I opened my mouth and sighed, because I was longing for Thy commandments" (Ps 118:131). Only a true Christian, a Christian in faith and in works, can be a true worshiper of God, worshiping and serving God as the Father, the Spirit and the Truth. Amen.

26. On Conceit and Humble-mindedness

Sermon on the Sunday of the Man Born Blind

Dear brothers! Our Lord Jesus Christ, after healing the man who had been born blind, as we heard today in the Holy Gospel, said, "For judgment I have come into this world, that those who do not see may see, and that those who see may be made blind" (John 9:39). The pharisees, who were proud wise men and righteous men of the world, could not listen to these words of the Lord indifferently. Their conceit and their high opinion of themselves made them offended. They responded to the words of the Lord with a question with which they expressed at the same time outrage, conceit, ridicule, and hatred toward the Lord, combined with contempt for Him. "Are we blind also?" they said. With His reply to the pharisees' question, the Lord showed them their spiritual state, which was the initial cause of the question. "If you were blind," He said to them, "you would have no sin; but now you say, 'We see.' Therefore your sin remains" (John 9:40–41).

What a terrible ailment of the soul conceit is. In human affairs it deprives a proud person of the help and advice of his neighbors, and in the works of God, in the work of salvation, it deprived the arrogant pharisees of old—and continues to deprive the pharisees of every era—of the most precious treasure, the gift of God brought down from heaven by the Son of God, that is divine Revelation and, together with acceptance of this Revelation, the most blessed interaction with God.

The pharisees considered themselves to have seen, that is, to be familiar to a high level with true knowledge of God, and not to need any further progress or study, and on that basis they rejected the teaching about God that came straight from God Himself.

The virtue that is opposite to pride and to its particular expression within a person's very soul—conceit—is humility. Just as pride is mainly an ailment of our spirit, a sin of the mind, so humility is a good and blessed state of the spirit, and is mainly a virtue of the mind. For this reason it is also called humble-mindedness in Holy Scripture and in the writings of the holy Fathers. What is humble-mindedness? Humble-mindedness is the correct understanding of a person about humanity. Consequently it is a person's correct understanding about himself. The direct effect of humility, or of humble-mindedness, consists in the fact that a person's correct understanding about mankind and about himself reconciles him with himself, with human society, with his passions, shortcomings, abuses, with his personal and social circumstances—it reconciles him with the earth and with heaven. Humility received its name from the inner peace that it bears in our hearts.[113] When we mean a restful, joyful, blessed state produced within us by virtue, we call it humility. When we intend to indicate the source of this state together with the state itself, then we call it humble-mindedness.

Do not think, dear brothers, that the definition we have given, whereby humble-mindedness is said to be the correct way for a person to think about mankind in general and about himself in particular, is arbitrary. The Lord Himself pointed to this definition of humility and humble-mindedness. He said: "If you ... know the truth, ... the truth shall make you free" (John 8:31–32). But what is the spiritual freedom preached by the Truth if it is not holy, grace-filled peace of the soul, holy humility, the humble-mindedness of the Gospel? The Truth of God is our Lord Jesus Christ. He proclaimed: "Learn from Me," from the Truth of God, "for I am gentle and lowly in heart, and you will find rest for your souls" (Matt 11:29). Humble-mindedness is a way for a person to think about himself and about mankind that has been inspired by Divine Truth.[114] Conceit is unfortunate and destructive self-deception; it is a lethal means by which blinded humanity deceives itself and is deceived by demons.

The views and foundations of human arrogance and human conceit are false. A proud man regards himself as an original being, and not as a creature of God; life on earth seems to him infinite, death and eternity nonexistent. Divine providence does not exist for him: he believes that human reason is the ruler of the world. All his thoughts creep along the earth; all his life is sacrificed to the earth, on which he would like to establish constant enjoyment of sin. And it is on this insane, impossible goal that the blind pharisees and Sadducees focus all their efforts.

On the other hand, a humble-minded person is accompanied on the path of earthly life by the remembrance of death, which exhorts him to act on earth with eternity in mind and, in a wondrous way, inspires his very acts with particular merit. The humble-minded person acts for the virtue and not in response to the passions and to satisfy them, and in consequence his works cannot avoid being beneficial to human society. The humble-minded person regards himself as an insignificant speck of dust in the vast universe, in the ages, generations, and events of humanity, past and future. The mind and the heart of a humble-minded person are capable of accepting the divine Christian teaching and constantly progressing in Christian virtues; his mind and heart see and feel the fallenness of human nature, and that is why they are capable of recognizing and accepting the Redeemer.

Humble-mindedness does not see merits in fallen human nature: it views humanity as a superior creation of God, but at the same time it also sees sin penetrating the whole essence of man, and poisoning this essence; humble-mindedness, recognizing the greatness of divine creation, at the same time recognizes the ugliness of creation distorted by sin; it constantly deplores this calamity. It regards the earth as the land of its exile, and strives through repentance to return to the heaven lost through conceit. But pride and conceit, having obtained the fall and perdition for mankind, do not see or recognize the fallenness in human nature: they see only merits in it, only perfections and refinement; they honor the very ailments of the soul, the very passions, as merits. Such a view of humanity makes it completely superfluous and alien to think about the Redeemer. The eyesight of the proud is a terrible blindness; and the absence of vision in the humble is a capacity to see the Truth. These words of the Lord relate to this: "For judgment I have come into this world, that those who do not see may see, and that those who see may be made blind" (John 9:39). The humble have accepted the Lord and have been enlightened with the divine Light; the proud have rejected Him, satisfied with themselves, and have been darkened further with their rejection of God and their blasphemy.

On a clear night, countless stars shine in the heavens, competing with one another in an abundance of light; but when the sun rises, the stars disappear, as if becoming completely nonexistent, although in fact they all remain in place. In the same way, human virtues, when compared to each other, have their own light, but when divine goodness appears, they disappear before the light of the Divinity. The apostle, talking of the virtues of the patriarch Abraham, says that Abraham "has something to boast about, but not before God"; in relation to God, "Abraham believed God, and it was accounted to him for righteousness" (Rom 4:2–3). This is how the pharisees ought to have acted. Instead they boasted of their descent in the flesh from Abraham, but estranged themselves from him in spirit. In contrast to the image of the actions of Abraham, they wanted to keep behind them the supposed strengths of the old man, and through this became incapable of self-knowledge and of knowledge of God; they heard the terrible judgment of the Lord: "If you were blind," that is, if you recognized your blindness, "you would have no sin; but now," being blind, "you say, 'We see.' Therefore your sin remains" (John 9:41). You have adopted it for yourselves and have imprinted it within yourselves through your conceit.

In his youth the holy Apostle Paul was a student of the pharisees; but he did not follow the bitterness and the conceit of the pharisees. He was, as he tells us for our edification, "a Hebrew of the Hebrews; concerning the law, a Pharisee; ... concerning the righteousness which is in the law, blameless. But what things were gain to me, these," he says, "I have counted loss for Christ. Yet indeed I also count all things loss for the excellence of the knowledge of Christ Jesus my Lord" (Phil 3:5–8).

Dear brothers! Let us imitate the holy Apostle Paul and the other holy saints of God: let us approach God, entirely rejecting harmful conceit, by means of humility. By means of humility let us cleave to God and attract toward ourselves the attention and mercy of our God, Who said: "upon whom will I show respect, but to the humble and the peaceful and to him who trembles at My words" (Isa 66:2). By seeing and acknowledging our sins, we number ourselves among the sinners who have loved God; by rejecting conceit, we exclude ourselves from the number of the false righteous, otherwise God will renounce us, saying: "For I did not come to call the righteous, but sinners, to repentance" (Matt 9:13). May our hearts be given to God through humility on the spiritual altar,[115] and may the priest of God on high—our mind—offer up spiritual sacrifices to Him. May it offer up the sacrifice of tender emotion, the sacrifice of contrition, the sacrifice of confession, the sacrifice of prayer, and the sacrifice of mercy, filling every sacrifice with humble-mindedness: for "a contrite and humble heart God shall not despise" (Ps 50:19). Amen.

27. The Sign of Those Chosen by God

Sermon on the Sunday of All Saints, First Sunday after Pentecost

"Therefore whoever confesses Me before men, him I will also confess before My Father who is in heaven. But whoever denies Me before men, him I will also deny before My Father who is in heaven" (Matt 10:32–33). The Lord said this to His disciples who were standing before Him at that time; the all-seeing Lord said this looking into the distant future as if to the present, and He said it to all His disciples without exception, in all times and in every land; the Lord was also saying it to us, who stand here in His church, having joined the number of His disciples through holy baptism. Just as lightning passes quickly from one part of the heavens to another without losing any of its brilliance, so the Lord's definition has reached us across eighteen centuries; it is proclaimed to us with all its power and clarity in today's Gospel. The disciples of the Lord are not simply those who are named Christians after Him, they are not just those who have taken upon themselves the vows to serve Him: disciples are those who truly confess Him to be their Lord, confess Him as sovereign Master over them and eternal King, following His teaching as the teaching of the Lord, keeping His commandments as commandments of the Lord. The confession must be made in the mind, in the heart, in word, in deed, in one's whole life. Shame, shyness, and wavering are not tolerated in this confession. The confession demands decisive self-sacrifice. It must be solemn. It must be made as if in full view, before all of humanity, before the holy angels and before the fallen angels, before the eyes of earth and of heaven. "For we have been made a spectacle to the world, both to angels and to men" (1 Cor 4:9), says the holy Apostle Paul of himself and of the other holy apostles. The apostles were not ashamed or afraid to confess the God-Man Who had been condemned to a shameful death by both the spiritual and the civil courts. They were not ashamed or afraid to confess Him before these courts, before the powerful and wise men of the earth, before tyrants and torturers, in the face of tortures and punishments, in the face of violent death. Such was the confession of the Lord that the holy martyrs brought to Him, watering the whole earth with their blood, and proclaiming the good news to the whole earth through their holy witness of true knowledge and worship of God. The holy monks confessed the Lord through their unseen martyrdom and constant self-sacrifice throughout their whole lives: they served in a union between earth and heaven, between angels and men, belonging to heaven during their presence on earth, and entering while on earth into intercourse with angels and their assemblies. Those saints of God who undertook the ascetic struggle in the world, to whom one can so justly apply the words of the Gospel: "These are in the world ... they are not of the world" (John 17:11,16), confessed the Lord with their contempt for and defiance of the principles of the world. Confession of the Lord, accompanied by decisive and complete renunciation of the world and of oneself, was a sign of all the saints.

Whoever during his wandering on earth confesses the Lord as He commanded, whoever shows through his way of life that he confesses the Lord as his Lord and God: him the Lord confesses to be His disciple and His friend, and He confesses this not only before the world but before God the Father. When God the Son confesses a person before God the Father, this means that this person is led into closer union with God (John 14:20). When a person makes a God-pleasing confession to God as stipulated by Him, this is a sign that He has chosen that person. Being numbered among the chosen is the fruit of a person's good will.

A weak, equivocal confession is not accepted; it is rejected as worthless and unworthy of God. Confession within the secrecy of the soul is not enough: it is essential to confess with the lips and in word. It is not enough to confess in word: it is essential to confess in deeds and with one's whole life. "For whoever is ashamed of Me," said the Lord, "and My words in this adulterous and sinful generation, of him the Son of Man also will be ashamed when He comes in the glory of His Father with the holy angels" (Mark 8:38). Not only must we confess the Lord, not only must we recognize His divinity and His rule—we must also confess His teaching and His commandments. The commandments are confessed by keeping them. Keeping them, despite the conventional habits in human society, is confession of "the Lord and His words" before men. Human society is called sinful and adulterous because the majority of it has turned aside to a sinful life, and has betrayed and exchanged love of God for love of sin. The customs that rule in the world and have the significance of a law above all laws are offensive and hostile to a God-pleasing way of life. A godly way of life is the object of hatred and ridicule to the proud world. In order to avoid the hatred of the world, its persecutions and its darts, a weak heart that is not established through faith tends to please other people and is unfaithful to the teaching of the Lord, excluding itself from the number of the chosen.

The Lord establishes His disciples in faithfulness to Him and to His teaching with terrible words, a terrible definition, that is proclaimed in good time. "Therefore whoever confesses Me before men, him I will also confess before My Father who is in heaven. But whoever denies Me before men, him I will also deny before My Father who is in heaven."

Dependence on human society is weaker than dependence on one's family. It is easier to turn aside from submission to the demands of society than to turn aside from submission to family demands. Family demands are supported by natural law, and, when these demands are in agreement with the law of God, this same law of God is supported by them. A servant of Christ is often perplexed by conflicting demands and does not know which should be deemed God-pleasing. The Lord satisfactorily resolves this confusion, foreseen by Him, supplementing the words quoted above with the following: "He who loves father or mother more than Me is not worthy of Me. And he who loves son or daughter more than Me is not worthy of Me" (Matt 10:37). "Whoever prefers the will of parents or of any relatives in the flesh to My will, whoever prefers their way of thinking and their philosophizing to My teaching, whoever prefers to please them rather than to please Me: he is unworthy of Me."

Difficulties and obstacles in confessing Christ that act externally on the Christian mean little in comparison with the difficulties and obstacles that he finds within himself. Sin that lives within the mind, heart, and body is directly opposed to confessing Christ by keeping His commandments, and persistently counteracts this effort. The most natural good thing, when damaged by sin, makes it more difficult to confess and tries to introduce into this confession, to mix into it, a confession of the merits of a fallen nature. Through this mixing the confession of Christ is destroyed, an incomplete fall is ascribed to fallen nature, and importance is taken away from Christ, importance which, as all-perfect, endures no contaminants, and demands recognition of the decisive harm caused to nature by the fall[116] (Gal 5:4; Gal 2:16, 21).

It is possible to turn aside from human society, from relatives, but where can one go to escape from oneself? Where can one hide from one's own nature? How can one be saved from it? To be freed from enslavement to fallen nature, the Lord commands that we crucify this nature, that is, reject its reason and its will, and nail the works of the mind and the urges of the heart to the commandments of the Gospel. In this way "those who are Christ's have crucified the flesh with its passions and desires" (Gal 5:24): they have crucified the carnal mind and the will of the fallen nature, on which the sinful desires of the soul and body, sinful life, are based and founded. In this way the world was crucified to the apostle, and the apostle to the world (Gal 6:14). St David prayed to God to be granted the strength and capacity for such crucifixion: "Nail my flesh to the fear of Thee" (Ps 118:120), that is, my carnal mind and my will, so that they remain inactive. "O stablish Thy word in Thy servant unto fear of Thee" (Ps 118:38), so that I may be guided steadily only by Your word in my seen and unseen actions. Whoever mortifies his fallen nature with the sword of Christ's teaching, "whoever loses his life for My sake and the gospel's," said the Lord, "will find it" (Matt 10:39), "will save it" (Mark 8:35). On the other hand, whoever acts according to the views and urges of fallen nature, mistakenly deeming them to be good, "who finds his life, will lose it." "He who does not take his cross," who does not take upon himself the yoke of My commandments, "and follow after Me" in selflessness, but follows himself, "is not worthy of Me" (Matt 10:38–39).

After the frightening, impartial, decisive proclamation we have heard from the lips of God, the holy Church has appointed the Lord's answer to the Apostle Peter's question to be read today, in order to explain in the most satisfactory way the fate of those chosen by God in time and in eternity. "Then Peter answered and said to Him, 'See, we have left all and followed You. Therefore what shall we have?'" (Matt 19:27). The Lord promised special honour to the twelve apostles. Just as the God-Man is the one eternal King of Israel, that is, the King of all Christians, of this spiritual Israel that is to consist of all the people on earth and to inhabit the promised land, heaven: in the same way the apostles of the God-Man, through whom all peoples are subjugated to the God-Man, naturally became the leaders and judges of this new Israel, of this eternal, heavenly people. After announcing to the apostles their importance in the condition of the regeneration (Matt 19:28) of mankind, the Lord added: "And everyone who has left houses or brothers or sisters or father or mother or wife or children or lands, for My sake and the gospel's, [shall] receive a hundredfold now in this time ... with persecutions—and in the age to come, eternal life" (Mark 10:29–30; Matt 19:29). Earthly life is called a "persecution." It is a persecution because men are thrown down to the earth and compelled to wander on it full of suffering for their offenses against God's commandment. It is a place and time of persecution for the followers of Christ because the ruler of the world rules there and the rule of sin prevails there, hostile to the followers of Christ and pursuing them with constant fierce persecution. They are subject to many different forms of torment by sin, both within themselves and from without. The fallen spirits that thirst for their perdition act against them with frenzied anger and enormous cunning; the majority of people act against them with passion, after voluntarily being enslaved by the fallen spirits, and serving as blind, wretched tools for them; their own passions and preferences act against them.

And in this temporal persecution the followers of Christ receive a hundredfold in comparison with those whom they left for the sake of Christ and His teaching. They palpably receive the grace of the most Holy Spirit. In comparison with the consolation acquired through divine grace, all joys, all pleasures of the world are as nothing; compared to spiritual richness, spiritual glory, all the riches of the world, all its glories, are as nothing; from the point of view of the saints of God, sinful and carnal pleasures are repulsive filth, filled with deadly bitterness; the situation of the glorious and rich people of the world is similar to whitewashed tombs that shine on the outside but inside are filled with decay and stench, the attributes inseparable from every corpse. A soul that is struck with eternal death, that is, alienation from Christ, can justifiably be called a corpse.

All earthly good things and advantages leave a person, remain on the earth, when he, by the inevitable and inexorable law of death, leaves the earth and moves irrevocably into eternity. Divine grace follows different rules: it accompanies a person who has acquired it here into the land beyond the grave. As soon as the person throws off the body from himself, as if it were fetters, the grace that until now was somehow constrained by the flesh develops extensively and wonderfully. Its serves as a pledge and testimony for the person chosen by God. When he stands at the judgment that awaits every person after his death, and presents his testimony and his pledge, then, in accordance with them, as a logical consequence of them, he is granted in heaven spiritual, eternal, ineffable and boundless riches, glory, delight. "In the age to come" (Mark 10:30) he will "inherit eternal life" (Matt 19:29), said the Lord, life so abundant, so exquisite, that a carnal person, who bases himself on ideas about the known when making assumptions about the unknown, cannot form any concept of it using his own judgment. May it also be granted to us, in return for faithful confession of the Lord, to inherit this life that has been prepared for all of us through the unfathomable, boundless mercy of the Lord Who has redeemed us. Amen.

28. The Precondition for Adoption of Christ

Sermon on the Saturday of the Fourth Week after Pentecost

Our Lord Jesus Christ said to the pharisees: "Those who are well have no need of a physician, but those who are sick. But go and learn what this means: 'I desire mercy and not sacrifice.' For I did not come to call the righteous, but sinners, to repentance" (Matt 9:12–13; Hos 6:6).

Dear brothers! Whoever wishes to be a true Christian, that is, to believe in Christ, to adopt Christ for himself and to be adopted by him, that person must "deny himself" (Matt 16:24). He must admit that his sins are sins, and see his righteousness as the "filthy rag" of a harlot—of a soul that has entered into a culpable relationship with sin. This is how the great prophet spoke of the righteousness of fallen man (Isa 64:6). Our righteousness that was so flawless in the state of purity, before the fall, was defiled by the fall and became worthless, just as a beautiful, precious cloth loses all virtue when it is soaked in a repulsive, stinking substance. Christ accepts him who denies himself and approaches Him from a state of self-denial; He redeems him, replacing him with Himself; He saves him, uniting him with Himself.

It is impossible to adopt Christ while keeping one's sinfulness. He is adopted only by the pure, that is, by those who after being impure have become pure by means of repentance.

The adoption of Christ is impossible not only when a person does not abandon his sinfulness; it is also impossible when a person does not abandon his righteousness. Christ denies and rejects those who are righteous in their righteousness.[117] "Go," He says, "and learn what this means: 'I desire mercy and not sacrifice.' For I did not come to call the righteous, but sinners, to repentance."

"Go"—this word encompasses the following thoughts: "Leave: you are not able to approach Me. Your way of thinking, the disposition of your spirit, do not allow you to accept Me. You need to prepare. You need to understand, to feel, to recognize, to learn, to confess your fall." This is frightening. It is explained by God's words "desire mercy and not sacrifice," which mean: "You cannot make sacrifices: all your thoughts, feelings and actions are stamped with and steeped in sin, they are united, mixed with it; all your thoughts, feelings and actions are unworthy of the all-holy God; they cannot be favorable to Him. And that is why God tells you that He not only does not demand sacrifices of you, but does not want you to make them. Come out of your disastrous deception; God wants to have mercy on you; God wants to save you; God wants to redeem you with Himself. There are no means either among men or among angels to reform humanity damaged by sin. God alone, in His omnipotence, can cure the incurable plague of eternal death. Understand how far you have fallen; understand how gravely you have been damaged, completely reject hope in yourself; feel the sympathy toward yourself that you lack only because of your conceit, self-deception, bitterness, and blindness. Acquire mercy: unite your action with regard to yourself with the action of God; assist the work of God with your works. Relent, you who have hardened hearts! Have mercy on yourselves and on all humanity: you, like all people without exception, are creatures that have been rejected by the Creator because of your willful rejection of the Creator, unfortunate creatures, crawling, troubled, suffering on earth, on this threshold of hell—creatures that are constantly multiplying on earth, constantly reaped by death, devoured by the earth—creatures that were thrown down to earth from paradise for rebelling against God. Hate your sins, abandon your sinful life. Not only this: recognize that your very nature has been distorted by sin, that the righteousness born within it and emanating from it corresponds to a disfigured and distorted nature (Ps 50:7). Regard your righteousness as a sin; regard it not as a gain but as a very great loss to you (Phil 3:7–9). This righteousness, in those who want to keep it for themselves, serves as an insurmountable obstacle to receiving the righteousness of God (Rom 10:3). Bow down your proud, falsely-named reason before the righteousness of God. It is brought down from heaven to men, brought by the incarnate God: it raises up to heaven those who, after renouncing themselves and renouncing their sins and their righteousness, immerse themselves wholly in the cleansing font of repentance, and are guided exclusively by divine righteousness.[118] May your good deeds be the fulfillment of the all-holy will of God alone, and not of your corrupt will. May they constitute a payment of your debt to God, your debt that cannot be repaid, both because of the perfection of Him to Whom you owe it, and because of your limitations, poverty, and sin."

Humility and the repentance that is borne of it are the only precondition for receiving Christ. Humility and repentance are the only price at which knowledge of Christ is purchased. Humility and repentance are the only spiritual states in which it is possible to approach Christ and adopt Him. Humility and repentance are the only sacrifices that God rewards and that He accepts from fallen humanity (Ps 50:18–19). The Lord rejects those who are infected with a proud, false opinion of themselves, who consider repentance to be unnecessary for themselves, who exclude themselves from the number of the sinners. They cannot be Christians. "Those who are well," those who falsely consider and declare themselves to be well, "have no need of a physician," says the Lord, "but those who are sick"—those who consider themselves to be sick. The Saviour of the world proclaims of Himself for all to hear: "I did not come to call the righteous, but sinners, to repentance." Amen.

29. God Is the Helper of Man in His Tribulations

Sermon on the Ninth Sunday after Pentecost

As we heard today in the Gospel (Matt 14:22–34), when the holy Apostle Peter saw the Lord walking on the choppy waters of the sea, he asked Him to command him to join Him there: "Command me to come to You on the water." After receiving the command from the almighty Lord, Peter got out of the boat and walked on the waters which were somehow firm beneath his feet. As long as Peter believed in the command of the Lord, as long as he kept in mind this command, he walked on the wet element as if on dry land. But the wind was very strong and the waves rose up high. Peter noticed this, allowed fear to enter him, which, viewed superficially, it would be possible to call natural and well-founded, and began to drown. Then he cried out to the Lord: "Lord, save me!" The Lord stretched out His hand to him, saved him from drowning, and said, "O you of little faith, why did you doubt?"

We are all walking on the unsteady waves of the sea of life that is shaken and disturbed by life's various vicissitudes. We are all walking on the waves of the sea of life, toward the gates of death, and the judgment of God. What an uncertain element is under our feet! We cannot know what may befall us at any moment. The greatest changes in our life happen unexpectedly, suddenly. Not only does death steals up on us like a thief: almost all misfortunes steal up on us in this way. The sea is beaten and shaken by strong winds arising from various directions for unknown reasons: and our life is also subject to many different attacks from evil spirits and from people led by them; we are subject to many different misfortunes due to unexpected events, or to some mysterious coincidence. It is impossible to foresee and to foreknow what evil will devise, what will serve as the cause and means of a misfortune, where temptation will come from. For the most part, it is impossible to preempt or avert these things.

And another sea, an invisible sea, is beneath the feet of our thoughts. This sea is beaten and disturbed by other winds. The sea is our heart, in which many different sensations are mingled. In fallen man, sensations are infected with sin, and that is why they usually do not function properly. It is rare that the "old man" (Eph 4:22), not renewed by God's grace, can act in accordance with the commandments of the Gospel, and then it is by forcing himself and with significant omissions. The improper action of sensations that have been infected with sin is mostly biased, but often passionate. When a sickness of the soul is moderate, then the sensations are stamped with moderate abnormality, that is, with weaknesses; but when the sickness has progressed fully, then the sensations turn into passions. Our sensations are under the influence of thoughts that either arise within us or are brought to us by the evil spirits that are the enemies of the human race. Sometimes we are overcome by sorrow, sometimes we are moved by anger, sometimes captivated by sensuality, sometimes carried away by vainglory and pride. This wind—this rush of thoughts—is often so strong that we do not find the means to resist it, we are lost, we fall into despondency and despair, and we come close to perdition.

What can we say to comfort someone who has realized that he is walking on the waves of the sea, both in his external life and in the life of the spirit? We can say that he is walking at the behest of his God. St Peter walked at this behest, for our edification, and did not drown as long as he firmly believed that he was acting at God's command. Let us also believe that God has called us from nothingness into being, that He has given and allotted to us the arena of earthly life, commanding us to do His will here and promising that His providence will watch unceasingly over His faithful servants. Let us believe that we are His creatures, that we are fully subject to His will, and that nothing happens to us without a sign from this almighty and all-holy will. Guided by this thought, we will freely and boldly complete our walk across the sea. "Are not two sparrows," says the Lord to His disciples, "sold for a copper coin? And not one of them falls to the ground apart from your Father's will. But the very hairs of your head are all numbered. Do not fear therefore; you are of more value than many sparrows" (Matt 10:29–31).

People are weak. It was to console and instruct the weak that St Peter was permitted to waver in his faith and to be exposed to danger. When faith in God is replaced by human considerations, then a person suffers in the waves of the sea of life. He is in trouble. He sees no human means of escaping from the difficult circumstances, and remembrance of God is stolen away by inexplicable oblivion. When he began to drown, the Apostle Peter cried out to the Lord: let us too, from the midst of the constraining circumstances that surround us, compel ourselves to remember God, to turn to Him with heartfelt prayer for salvation. Salvation will not be slow to come, and everyone who sees it will hear in his conscience the gentle voice of rebuke: "O you of little faith, why did you doubt?" Temptations are necessary for us. They are permitted by divine providence, so that we, oppressed by them, may run to God, Whom we have forgotten, and come to know Him empirically. "Call upon Me in the day of thy trouble," God exhorts the person who is lamenting, "and I will deliver thee, and thou shalt glorify Me" (Ps 49:15). "Thou shalt glorify Me" means: "You will come to know Me through experience, with a living knowledge, and you will believe in Me with a living faith. With a dead knowledge, by the letter, it is as if I were nonexistent." The Lord gave His hand to the drowning Peter to save him; in order to extricate us from a difficult situation, the action of divine providence appears particularly clearly and palpably. To be shaken by tribulations is as nothing compared to the knowledge of God acquired through them. The torment of the tribulations is short-term; essential knowledge of God, combined with adoption of Him, is an eternal treasure, the pledge of all eternal good things.

We must act in exactly the same way when a storm arises in the soul, when the tranquility of the heart is disturbed and broken by sinful thoughts. These thoughts most often assume the appearance of righteousness, and attempt by any possible means to deceive the person; but they can be recognized by the confusion they produce, and by the fact that they take away the peace of the heart. A storm of the passions is terrible, more terrible than any external disaster. An internal disaster is more dangerous than an external one. During a visible storm the sun is darkened by clouds; in a storm of the heart, the reason is darkened and closed off by a dense cloud of thoughts. The exhortations of Holy Scripture and of the holy Fathers are forgotten; the boat of the soul is covered with the waves (Matt 8:24) of various different passionate sensations. Neither conversation with friends nor edifying reading has a beneficial effect. The soul, filled with troubled water, does not receive anything into it. Increased prayer remains the only means of salvation. Like the Apostle Peter, we must cry out to the Lord with our whole heart. "He shall call upon Me, and I will hear him; yea, I am with him in trouble, I will deliver him, and bring him to glory. With long life will I satisfy him, and show him my salvation" (Ps 90:15–16). What a comforting promise! What an abundance of comforting promises! God promises to listen to someone who has called upon Him. God, Who foresees the future, declares that through divine providence He is already with the person who has called upon Him. He then promises to rescue from tribulation the person who has called upon Him and bring him to glory by giving him the grace of God. The promises are crowned with one of blessed eternity and the appearance of salvation in the soul, through establishment within it of the heavenly kingdom, which is the pledge of blessed eternity. The Saviour of the world gave His hand to the drowning Peter to save him from drowning: He sends down on His servants the grace of God, touching their spirit with it, and saves those who are drowning and perishing in the storm of agitated passions.

When the Lord had calmed the storm, "then those who were in the boat came and worshiped Him, saying, 'Truly You are the Son of God.'" When the storm of the heart subsides because the Lord has been called upon, and the winds that aroused it—the demonic thoughts—abate, then the thoughts of the soul worship the Son of God in spirit, and they confess Him because they have received the news, in the treasury of the soul, that He is the Son of God and God, and the Saviour of the world.

External temptations bring knowledge of God through the appearance of His providence for us, they bring faith in the providence of God, they instill in our hearts the fear of God and reverence toward Him, as to One Who both sees us and is visible to us, and they incline a person to live according to the commandments of God, and to avoid the sin that provokes anger in Him. Internal temptations bring deeper knowledge. And those who undergo these temptations and the active learning and instruction that they bring are almost always those servants of God who have fully devoted themselves to serving Him, and practice prayer of the mind in silence, which reveals a person's soul to him. "They that go down to the sea" of the heart "in ships," that is, under the guidance of the Word of God and the tradition of the Church, not by means of their own willful theorizing and struggle, "that do business in great waters," in the thoughts and sensations of the heart, "these men have seen the works of the Lord, and His wonders in the deep" of the heart (Ps 106:23–24). In various most wise and good ways, God permits man to suffer an internal struggle: "He spake, and there stood up a stormy wind, and lifted up the waves thereof. They go up as high as the heavens, and they go down as far as the deep" (Ps 106:25–26). From the terrible turbulence of feelings produced by demonic thoughts—by this stormy spirit—the "soul" of the ascetics "melted away because of the peril. They were tossed to and fro; they staggered like a drunken man, and were at their wit's end" (Ps 106:27) because of the darkness produced by the storm, because of the invasion of many reflections, because of terrible confusion and perplexities that could not be solved by human reason. "So they cried unto the Lord in their trouble, and He delivered them out of their distress. And He commanded the storm, and it stood down into a calm, and the waves thereof grew still" (Ps 106:28–29). After an internal struggle, spiritual consolation is usually granted: "Then were they glad, because they were at rest, and He guided them unto the haven of His will" (Ps 106:30). Those who have been trained in internal battles acquire knowledge of the all-holy will of God, and gradually learn to remain within it. Knowledge of the will of God and obedience to it serve as a haven for the soul: in this haven the soul finds calm and the assurance of its salvation. Those who have secretly been taught the knowledge of good and evil by the Lord, from the sensations they have experienced within themselves of the effect of sin and of the effect of the grace that destroys it, "O let them give thanks unto the Lord" in their prayers, filled with thanksgiving and glorification, "for His mercy and for His wonderful works to the children of men," to their brothers, in conversations edifying to the soul. "Let them exalt Him in the congregation of the people, and praise Him in the seat of the elders!" (Ps 106:31–32).

"To those who love God," says the apostle, "all things work together for good" (Rom 8:28), not only internal tribulations and disasters, but also tribulations produced by the revolt and the storm of the passions. It is these that reveal to a person that he is falling, bringing him down from the heights of pride and conceit to a state of self-knowledge and humility, reveal his complete need of the Redeemer, and throw him down in self-denial at His feet.

Let us not be embarrassed when we see the passions rising up within ourselves, as those who lack self-knowledge are usually embarrassed. We are damaged by sin, and the passions have become natural to us, as the various symptoms of an illness are natural to it. When the passions rise up, we must immediately turn to God with prayer and weeping, firmly resisting the passions, and patiently awaiting help from God. The passions trouble not only those people who are in their power, but also those who have advanced in virtue. This happens with the permission of God, so that the very state of being virtuous may not serve in a weak person as a reason for vanity and pride.[119] Often, after a prolonged period of calm, a terrible storm rises up; those who thought they were in a safe haven suddenly find themselves in the open, storm-tossed sea. A person can only be said to be safely free from passion when his body is placed in the tomb, and his soul leaves this world that is full of delusion, temptations, and deception.

"Lord, save us! We are perishing!" (Matt 8:25) the disciples cried out to the Saviour of the world on a different voyage in the sea, to wake Him when a great tempest had arisen and the boat was covered by the waves while the Saviour slept. The sleep of the Saviour represents our forgetfulness of God. The forgetfulness is destroyed by temptation. When remembered and called upon for help, God "rebukes the winds and the sea." All-blessed and almighty, He brings "a great calm" (Matt 8:26) to everyone who remembers and calls upon Him for help in time of trouble. Amen.

30. On Justice, Mercy, and Faith

Sermon on the Tuesday of the Eleventh Week after Pentecost

"The weightier matters of the law: justice and mercy and faith" (Matt 23:23).

Justice is almost always violated by human mercy, and mercy is often precluded by justice. In the law of God, on the other hand, justice and mercy are in a wondrous union. This union constitutes a subject for spiritual contemplation for the mind that has been illumined with the grace of God. A mind admitted to such contemplation enters into a state of holy joy, and cries out with David: "Mercy and judgment shall be my song unto Thee, O Lord; I sing and understand in a blameless way" (Ps 100:1–2).

Why are human mercy and human justice at variance with one another, but mercy and justice that emanate from the Gospel are in an indissoluble union? Because human mercy and human justice are based on man's fallen reason, his fallen will, and his fallen spirit. This mercy and this justice bear the stamp of the fall; they have effects worthy of their character. Human mercy and justice are not true, pure or holy, and are defiled by sin. The "mercy and judgment" that are imparted to man by the teaching of the Gospel are based on faith in God, on living faith expressed by works and by a person's whole conduct. "Mercy and faith" are understood "in a blameless way," that is, they are comprehended only by someone leading a blameless, virtuous life.

"The weightier matters of the law [are] justice and mercy and faith," said the Saviour of the world to the blinded "righteous men," so as to distance them from their own destructive righteousness, from actions that followed their own understanding and their own will, and to bring them to the saving righteousness of God, to actions in accordance with the will and reason of God. Is it not necessary for us too, brothers, to take notice of the Lord's exhortation? Have we ever examined these "weightier matters of the law," the most important parts of the law, "justice and mercy and faith"? Have we not tried to manage our lives without being guided by the teaching to which the Saviour has attached so much significance? And has our activity perhaps for this very reason been a series of sins, and our conduct a constant, uninterrupted aberration?

A godly life must be based entirely on faith. "The just shall live by faith" (Heb 10:38), says the Scripture: "For the word of the Lord is true, and all His works are faithful" (Ps 32:4). "Without faith it is impossible to please [God]" (Heb 11:6). "Faith," says St Peter Damascene, "is the foundation of all blessings, the door to God's mysteries, unflagging defeat of our enemies, the most necessary of all the virtues, the wings of prayer and the dwelling of God within our soul."[120] Faith teaches us always to act in accordance with the commandments of the Gospel, and not with the inspirations of our fallen will and reason. Acting in accordance with the Gospel gradually liberates a person from being dominated by the passions. He ceases to be carried away and deluded: in his meekness, no longer disturbed either by anger or by lust, there appears the dominion of a mind restored in the power of divine grace. The Lord "will guide the meek unto judgment, He shall teach the meek His ways" (Ps 24:9). Those who lead a sinful life, possessed and deadened by their passions, do not receive this blessing from God: "The ungodly" in their spirit "shall not rise at the judgment, neither the sinners in the council of the righteous" (Ps 1:5); they will not receive spiritual reason, which is granted only to the servants of God and with which God crowns their ascetic effort.

"O Lord, the King"—the mind of Thy servant—"shall be glad in Thy strength, and in Thy salvation shall He greatly rejoice" (Ps 20:1), seeing himself victorious over the passions and restored to power, seeing the sensations of his heart obedient to him. Obedience of the mind to God entails obedience of the heart to the mind. When the mind is obedient to God, then the heart obeys the mind. This is what meekness consists of. What is meekness? It is humble devotion to God, combined with faith that is covered with the protection of divine grace: "Because the King putteth His trust in the Lord, and in the mercy of the Most High He shall not be provoked" (Ps 20:8). The king—the mind—does not turn aside from justice and wisdom as it did when enslaved to the passions; it is not carried away either by anger, or by unhealthy predilections or expressions of a love that ails through sin; it is not carried away by the flattery of vainglory, nor by suggestions of conceit and pride; it does not weaken when struck by sorrow and despondency. It studies the Gospel constantly and attentively, and is guided by it. By looking at itself in the right way and acting rightly within itself, it acquires the right attitude to humanity and begins to act in the right way toward other people.

Man was created good; a holy peace of the heart and continual goodness were his natural attributes. These were disrupted and impaired by the fall, which allowed various vicious passions to enter the soul. The passions are the cause of disturbance and turmoil. In the renewal of man by the Redeemer, in the curbing of our passions by His creative and almighty power, the mind regains power over the heart, to which peace and goodness return. They return to the heart like exiles after a long absence from their homeland, and they rejoice together and greet one another: "Mercy and truth are met together, justice and peace have kissed each other" (Ps 84:11). We see a marvelous union of mercy and righteousness in the way the God-Man acts, which is reflected in the behavior of the true disciples of Christ. The disruption of goodness by anger and of peace of the heart by various passionate sensations always brings the soul into an unhealthy state, in which the mind loses its dominion, prudence is impaired, and spiritual reason withdraws.

Justice acquired through faith, or spiritual reason, is clothed through this reason in "tender mercies, kindness, humility, meekness, longsuffering" (Col 3:12); a person who has it acquires God-pleasing rightness and righteousness, directing the powers of his soul and body according to the purpose appointed for them by the Creator, cultivating his salvation and eternal blessedness in his works, and these are works of faith, the inseparable companion of spiritual reason. "There is reason that precedes faith," says St Isaac the Syrian, "and there is reason born of faith. Reason that precedes faith is natural reason; reason born of faith is spiritual reason."[121] As long as faith acts, and a person is guided by the commandments of the Gospel, spiritual reason shines in him. When faith stops acting, a person abandons activities that follow the teaching of the Gospel, and begins to act in accordance with his own ideas and the suggestions of his heart. Reason then descends from the heights of a spiritual state to a carnal state, the feeling of goodness leaves the heart, the passions angered by their expulsion enter it, and peace is replaced by all kinds of turmoil. A person who has experienced these opposing states in his soul comes to know through experience the essential importance of this exhortation by the Lord, and of the union of faith with spiritual reason and mercy. "The weightier matters of the law [are] justice and mercy and faith." The renewal and salvation of mankind consist in the union of these virtues.

This teaching of the Lord, so edifying for every Christian, is particularly profitable and necessary for a Christian to whom divine providence has entrusted leadership of his brothers. Without possessing the above three virtues it is impossible to lead others in a God-pleasing, prudent, or helpful way. A leader without these virtues necessarily becomes the plaything of his passions, and also a tool of the passions by which those surrounding him are led, that they in turn try to satisfy by means of the leader. This results in countless calamities in society. Often the leader himself perishes from their impact; the society he leads always perishes or suffers terrible harm.

Powerful people of the earth, listen to the exhortation the Lord gave to the righteous, the wise, and the powerful: "The weightier matters of the law [are] justice and mercy and faith." Fathers of families, spiritual and civil leaders, teachers of the people, listen to the Lord's exhortation: "The weightier matters of the law [are] justice and mercy and faith." Listen to it and follow it. A leader has a duty, first and foremost, to restore within himself the rightful control ordained by God, in order to gain command of himself. Otherwise, will he be able to refrain from actions suggested by weaknesses and passions? Will he be able to refrain from actions that result from false notions? The consequence of such actions is turmoil in society. The consequence of such actions is atrocities committed both by individual people and by society as a whole, often on a vast scale. After gaining command of himself, a leader must gain command over the passions of secondary leaders subordinate to him, so as not to be led astray by their passions, false reasoning, flattery and slander, and turn from a leader into a slave, his power becoming a weapon. Only by the light of spiritual reason will he be able to discern in those around him slyness, deception, betrayal, evil intentions, slander, and self-interest. When a leader is carried away by the passion of a neighbor, he quickly loses a significant level of self-control, and adopts incorrect views, makes one-sided and wrong judgments, and sets himself on a false course that has corresponding consequences. And many leaders who have the best of hearts, the purest of intentions, and even the deepest piety, after losing justice and submitting to an evil and ill-intentioned influence, have committed crimes and become the cause of great disasters. There can be no mercy where there is no justice. In order to do works of mercy, a person must be just: only justice, which bestows upon everything its due importance, is capable of bestowing true mercy, and this mercy alone "triumphs" through God "over" human "judgment" (Jas 2:13). Acts resulting from the passions, even if they appear to be the greatest good works, in essence always have the significance of evil deeds: they crown vice, they trample on virtue and on personal and societal good. "Do not judge according to appearance," says the Lord, "but judge with righteous judgment" (John 7:24). Do not be carried away by sweet words or by a heavenly smile on someone's lips or by anything external. Do not judge with a carnal mind. Ensure that your reason is right and holy, and judge people by their fruits (Matt 7:16). "You judge according to the flesh" (John 8:15), due to your false reason, your sinfulness, and that is why you judge wrongly, to your detriment and that of your neighbor. "If I do judge," says the Lord, "My judgment is true" (John 8:16). When we judge, let us try to become tools of the judgment of God: then our judgment will be cleared of faults. The more faithfully we are guided by the commandments of the Gospel, the more our judgment will be cleared of faults. These commandments both teach a person right judgment and reveal shortcomings in his judgment. Justice that emanates from spiritual reason is filled with wisdom, peace, and goodness; it is not cruel; it does not flare up in anger with sinful people; it feels compassion for them and has mercy on them; it heals and curbs sins with firmness; it replaces pointless and inhuman punishments with more effective, wise measures.

"Give the King Thy judgment, O God," prayed the royal prophet, "and Thy righteousness unto the King's son, to judge Thy people according unto justice, and Thy poor with judgment. . . . He shall judge the simple folk, and shall save the children of the poor, and humble the slanderer" (Ps 71:1–2,4). "Judgment," or spiritual reason, is a gift of God. Let us strive for it with works of faith, let us ask it of God with the prayer of faith. A holy king asked God for spiritual reason for himself and for his son. This was an act worthy of imitation. Leaders of the world, ask God for this gift for yourselves and for your subordinates, and when you are given it, you will impart true good works to humanity. In the happiness of your neighbors, you will find your own happiness. Through justice you will curb the evil that tries to captivate, deceive, capture, and destroy you. Through justice you will be able to appreciate virtue and true merit, to bestow mercy on those worthy of it, to guard yourselves against a great moral offence: that of approving and strengthening the enemies of virtue by bestowing mercy that is reckless and destructive to humanity. Such mercy is a grave sin.

And every Christian can and should say for himself this prayer of the crowned prophet. He can take the word king to mean his own mind and the son of the king to mean the activity born in his mind. The people and the poor can signify the attributes of the soul given to man by God and impoverished due to the fall. The slanderer signifies false reason and the fallen angel that cooperates with it, the bearer and the source of false reason. They strive constantly to show virtues and vices in a distorted form. They contradict and counteract the Word of God. They slander the Word of God, and impudently endeavor to present the wisdom of God as foolishness (1 Cor 1:18–25). "Give the King Thy judgment, O God, and Thy righteousness unto the King's son," for "The weightier matters of the law [are] justice and mercy and faith." Amen.

31. Beneficial Instruction from the Word of God

Sermon on Avoiding Faults and Offenses Due to a Lack of Judgment

"The outcry against Sodom and Gomorrah has been completed, and their sins are exceedingly great. Therefore, I will go down now and see whether or not they are carrying out the outcry coming to Me concerning them" (Gen 18:20–21).

So many people are carried away by evil rumors and slander about their neighbors. Many very good, well-intentioned and even very clever people have committed great atrocities because they were deceived by evil rumors, believed slander, and carelessly became the tool of evil intentions. Why is this? It is because they have forgotten about the foundation of all virtues: God-pleasing justice.[122] It is natural that abandoning justice leads to reckless acts. The history of mankind shows irrefutably that the evil deeds of virtuous people were reckless acts or, to put it another way, acts that were not forestalled by justice.

So as to deter us from such acts, the holy Fathers[123] invite us to pay particular attention to the following words of God: "The outcry against Sodom and Gomorrah has been completed, and their sins are exceedingly great. Therefore, I will go down now and see whether or not they are carrying out the outcry coming to Me concerning them." Let us examine the meaning of these words of our Lord God, imprint them in our memories and be guided by them in our behavior, so as to avoid both the small faults and grave offences that are often committed solely due to lack of judgment.

The cities of Sodom and Gomorrah were situated in a fertile valley beneath the blessed skies of Palestine. Scripture compares the fertility of this valley with that of Egypt, and the exceptional beauty of its nature with that of paradise (Gen 13:10). The inhabitants, abounding in earthly good things, succumbed to the passion of gluttony. It is difficult for us to comprehend the level to which gluttony developed among ancient peoples who enjoyed physical strength and health beyond our understanding.[124] "The lawless action of ... Sodom" consisted in "fullness of bread and abundance of wine" (Ezek 16:49). From surfeit a carnal state usually develops, inseparable from a carnal mind, or the way of thinking of a person who "shall be compared unto the brute beasts, and is become like unto them" (Ps 48:13). The inherent, main, essential character of a carnal mind is pride, which acts as a gateway to all sins and vices. A proud person is alien to the worship of God, alien to the fear of God, to respect for the law of God and civil law, to respect for his neighbors and their benefit, well-being and even lives, alien to self-knowledge and to virtue, and an enemy and evil-doer to other people and to himself. He is capable of all iniquities as if he had some special right to commit them. A proud person has a hardened heart and a demonic mind. From surfeit a carnal state had developed in the Sodomites; pride was created in the soul of the carnal state.[125] From the combination of blind pride and a carnal state, the offspring intrinsic to them was born: insatiable, unbridled depravity. This depravity was not content with natural gratification: it desired the unnatural and strove for it in a frenzy. "The men of Sodom," says the Scripture, "were exceedingly wicked and sinful before God" (Gen 13:13). They were not cured of their sins despite powerful treatments. The Sodomites did not come to their senses and repent of their sinful life even after "twelve years" of enslavement to the people and king of another tribe (Gen 14:4), or after their army had been defeated and a great number of their citizens had been taken captive (Gen 14:10–12). Punishment from heaven was summoned for the unrepentant sinners who had been irrevocably captivated by sin. "The outcry against Sodom and Gomorrah has been completed," God proclaims to His beloved prophet, "and their sins are exceedingly great. Therefore, I will go down now and see whether or not they are carrying out the outcry coming to Me concerning them."

God, appearing to a man[126] in the form of a man so that the man was capable of hearing His words, also uses the human manner of speech, so that this speech, being easy to understand and to apply, can serve as edification for all people, even the simplest. The omniscient, all-seeing God Who is ever present says, "Therefore I will go down now and see." I will go and see whether the great iniquities of which rumor has reached Me are really being committed in Sodom and Gomorrah. These conceal the following thought: "I do not believe the rumor; I intend to assure myself with my own investigation, with my own discretion." These words contain guidance to us not to believe readily the words of people who slander someone, and not to rush to judge, chastise or punish our neighbor, or rush to strictness or cruelty, for the employment and benefit of executioners before seeing for ourselves and finding out reliably what the neighbor is accused of. It is an attribute of a weak and frivolous mind, and of a weak, base soul, to believe the words of slanderers hastily, to be angry with the slandered person and to rush at him with vengeance and punishments without finding out whether the slander is just. The anger of malicious people is often the beginning of a malicious rumor, and the credulity of thoughtless people causes the rumor to be spread. The malice contrives slander and passes it on to thoughtless and weak-minded people to be sown in human society, and sometimes an insignificant sin, a minor transgression, turns into the greatest addition of untruth to truth, because a story has been embellished with barbed mockery and malicious suggestions. In this way virtue is presented in human society as sin, and a deficiency the size of a twig is presented as a crime the size of a log. Evil is accustomed to act in this way in order to conceal itself: it throws a black cloak over the activity of its neighbor, hypocritically judging him in order to present its own activity as bright and shining. Soberness, caution, and the judgment commanded by God are all needed so that a lie is not accepted as the truth, existence is not given to the nonexistent, a minor thing is not turned into something enormous, and the forgivable into something unforgivable. An evil rumor must be verified using one's own judgment. To teach us this, God presents His own divine action as an example. "The outcry against Sodom and Gomorrah," He says, "has been completed, and their sins are exceedingly great. Therefore, I will go down now and see whether or not they are carrying out the outcry coming to Me concerning them." Being all-seeing, He knew all about the sins of the people of Sodom and Gomorrah, but took upon Himself an action that is more fitting to limited beings, so that we may act in accordance with our limitations, not carried away by an action appropriate to an unlimited being who cannot be mistaken in His hearing and vision and who is not susceptible to deception. After hearing the outcry against Sodom, God does not immediately stretch out His hands to punish, but precedes punishment with very thorough examination of the matter, although He already knows all the details about it. Abandonment of justice, which is the only foundation for right and truly good works, has been the cause of great evil. People who are devoted to vanity and have not dedicated their lives to piety, to the benefit of humanity, and to pleasing God continually fall into this sin. They do not even notice that their way of behaving is false due to its false origin. They do not know that the origin is false, because they do not know and do not want to know the law of God. They create falsehood as if it were truth and commit evil deeds thinking that they are doing great good, or, at least, works of justice. "The ways of undiscerning men are right in their own eyes" (Prov 12:17), says the Scripture.

We see an example of such action and such behavior in that of Potiphar, a courtier of the Pharaoh, toward the pure and virtuous Joseph. Potiphar's wife was seized with an unlawful passion toward Joseph, and since she was not able to satisfy it, she slandered the innocent and righteous man to her husband out of vengefulness. Without carrying out any questioning or investigation, Potiphar locked Joseph up in prison. Potiphar's action seemed to him so reasonable and proper, certainly from the habit of behaving in this way, that it did not even occur to him to verify it throughout the prolonged period of time in which Joseph languished in captivity until he was freed through God's providence (Gen 39:7–20).[127]

It is not surprising that a heathen who did not know the true God was subject to a sin that led to an evil deed: holy men have been subject to it when they forgot that judgment must come before actions against and punishment of people accused of something. Forgetting this, the Emperor Constantine, equal to the apostles, condemned to death his virtuous son Crispus, who was beloved by all, after he had been slandered by his stepmother, Fausta, just as Joseph was slandered by the Egyptian woman. The truth was revealed later. The emperor fell into deep sorrow, wept, and sobbed; he repented of his hasty act and, having executed an innocent person, felt himself compelled to subject the guilty person to execution. Fausta was killed. Two people lost their lives, one justly and the other unjustly: both these deaths were caused by abandonment of the justice commanded by God and by precipitous, hasty action in reaction to slander.[128]

In the life of St John the Merciful, Patriarch of Alexandria, we read the following edifying and at the same time terrible story: For several days, a certain monk walked around Alexandria in the company of a very beautiful young woman. Many people who saw this were scandalized, thinking that the monk had the girl with him for the purposes of sin, and reported him to the patriarch. The patriarch immediately gave orders for them both to be seized, subjected to severe corporal punishment, and imprisoned.[129] After nightfall, the monk appeared to the patriarch in a dream and showed him his back, wounded from merciless beating. "Does this please you, your Grace?" he said. "Is this how the apostle taught you to shepherd the flock of Christ 'not by compulsion but willingly' (1 Pet 5:2). Believe me, you have made a mistake, as a person." After saying this, the monk left him. The patriarch awoke and began to reflect on the dream; perceiving his sin, he sat on his bed grieving and regretting his thoughtless and hasty action. When morning came, he ordered the monk to be brought to him so that he could see him and find out whether he was the one who had appeared in his dream. The monk came with great difficulty because he hardly had the strength to move due to his serious injuries. When the patriarch saw him, he became as though dead and could not say a single word. Coming to himself, he asked the monk to remove his clothing, so that he could be sure that he was injured in the same way as he had seen him in the dream. The monk bent down with difficulty to take off his clothes. When he did this it became apparent that he was a eunuch, which had not been obvious from his appearance, because he was young. When the patriarch saw his mutilated body, he deeply regretted it, sent for the people who had slandered the monk and excluded them from the Church for three years, and he asked forgiveness of the monk, saying to him, "Brother, forgive me, for I did this in ignorance. I sinned before God and before you. Still, you ought not to have walked around the city so openly with the young woman, so that the laypeople were led astray: after all, you are dressed as a monk." Then the monk replied with great humility. "Believe me, your Grace, I will tell you the whole truth of the matter. Before this I was in Gaza, and as I was going to venerate the grave of the holy martyrs Cyrus and John, I met this young woman in the evening. She fell at my feet and begged me with tears to allow her to travel with me. I refused and wanted to leave her. But she followed me and said, 'I entreat you by the God of Abraham, who came to save sinners and is to judge the living and the dead, do not leave me.' Hearing this, I said to her, 'Why are you entreating me in this way, young woman?' She answered, sobbing, 'I am a Jew. I wish to abandon the evil faith of my fathers and to become a Christian: I implore you, father, do not abandon me, but save my soul that wishes to believe in Christ.' Hearing this, I was afraid of the judgment of God, and taking her with me, I taught her the holy faith. When we came to the grave of the holy martyrs, I baptized her in the church, and I am walking with her in simplicity of heart with the intention of accommodating her in a women's monastery." When the patriarch heard this, he sighed and said, "How many hidden servants God has! And we, cursed ones, do not know them." And before everyone he told of the vision he had seen in the night. He took one hundred gold coins and gave them to the monk; but the monk did not want to take a single one, saying, "If a monk believes that God takes care of him, he has no need of gold; but if he loves gold, he does not believe in the existence of God." After he had said this, the monk bowed down to the patriarch and went away. Having learned through bitter experience, the patriarch eschewed thoughtless judgment of his neighbors, and taught this to his flock.[130]

Amongst the afflictions produced in our souls by the fall are the failure to see our faults, the desire to hide them, and at the same time the longing to see, reveal, and punish the faults of our neighbours.[131] Because we do not have the means to reveal our neighbors' faults, or because they do not even have the faults we would like to see in them, we resort to fabrications, concealing, embellishing, and reinforcing them with brilliant, pointed words. Our own faults seem to us forgivable, negligible; we try to magnify the faults of our neighbors, and to present them as worthy of any censure, any punishment. This affliction in our souls is highly developed in those who do not heed themselves; but it also exists in people who pay attention to their own salvation. It is necessary to be vigilant with oneself in order to avoid being carried away by this affliction. St David fell into a grave sin, and for an extended period of time, as often happens with people who have fallen into the abyss of sin, he was unable to come to his senses and repent. The Lord commanded the prophet Nathaniel to expose David. The prophet portrayed the king's sin to him with a parable in which both the sin and the sinner were concealed, asking for a judgment and punishment for the sinner. David immediately pronounced a sentence that far exceeded the requirements of the law in severity (2 Kgs 12:1–14). Such is our fallen nature! We seek leniency and mercy for our own sin, but condemnation and punishment for the sins of our neighbor. Discretion and vigilance are necessary. We must be vigilant with ourselves. Do not judge according to your opinion and understanding, based on slander, hearsay and rumors, and on your own superficial observation, but imitate God, Who said, "The outcry against Sodom and Gomorrah has been completed, and their sins are exceedingly great. Therefore, I will go down now and see whether or not they are carrying out the outcry coming to Me concerning them." Assure yourself in as much detail as possible and only then decide to condemn, if you are required to do this by the law. For the law forbids us even simply to condemn our neighbor when we do this of our own will, without this being required by the law. Envy, hatred, and slander have presented to human society the greatest, most righteous people, even the God-Man Himself, as the greatest evildoers.

Judgment that is pleasing to God must precede all our actions that relate to our neighbors, so as to avoid condemning and accusing innocent and righteous people, and to prevent unjustifiably excessive measures being taken in response to sins. But this judgment must also anticipate all other our actions, both external and internal. The holy Fathers call such judgment "spiritual discernment," a fundamental virtue on which genuineness, and consequently the value of all the other virtues, depends.[132] A virtue can be false, and evil may take the guise of a virtue. Our natural goodness is mixed up with evil, and has been adulterated by it. Because of our corruptedness, we can trust neither the good thoughts that occur to us, nor the urges of our hearts that appear at first glance to be good. Both our limitations and our fallen state demand that we consider carefully before acting.

St John Cassian tells us the following excellent teaching of St Anthony the Great on spiritual discernment. Once the holy elders from the surrounding hermitages and monasteries visited this saint of God, and during a prolonged night of conversation, they considered what virtue guards a monk from self-deception and the traps of the devil. Some of the elders pointed to fasting and keeping vigil, because they refine the thoughts and, after gaining purity, a person can more easily approach God. Others named poverty and scorn of property, because by breaking off the bonds of the many different earthly cares, one's thoughts easily adopt God. Others preferred almsgiving, based on the words of the Lord: "Come, you blessed of My Father, inherit the kingdom prepared for you from the foundation of the world" (Matt 25:34), and similar. After hearing each person's opinion, St Anthony answered, "Everything you have said is both necessary and beneficial for people who seek God; but it is impossible to assign a decisive advantage to any of these virtues because we see many people who spend their lives in fasting and vigils, who have moved to the desert, have kept the strictest poverty, giving away all their possessions in alms and because of this finding themselves destitute, but have then unfortunately fallen away from virtue into sin and even lost their faith. What caused the turmoil in their souls? In my opinion it was none other than the fact that they did not have the gift of discernment. It is discernment that teaches a person to avoid excesses in all things and to walk along the 'king's highway' (Num 20:17). It does not allow him to be stolen away either from the right-hand side through excessive abstinence, or from the left-hand side through excessive indulgence of the body. It is like an eye and a lamp for the soul, according to the teaching of the Gospel, which says, 'The lamp of the body is the eye. If therefore your eye is good, your whole body will be full of light. But if your eye is bad, your whole body will be full of darkness' (Matt 6:22–23). And this is so. Discernment, considering all the thoughts and actions of a person, eliminates every thought and intention that is not pleasing to God, and removes temptation from us. This can be shown in Holy Scripture. Saul, the first king of the Israelites, did not have discernment. His thoughts became darkened, and he could not understand that obedience to God's commandment was more pleasing to Him than offering sacrifices on his own volition; he angered God through something with which he had meant to please Him. Saul would not have been subject to this if he had acquired the light of discernment within him. The apostle calls discernment 'the sun,' when he says 'do not let the sun go down on your wrath' (Eph 4:26). We could also call it the 'leader' of our souls, as Scripture says 'Those for whom there is no leadership fall like leaves' (Prov 11:12 LXX). Scripture also calls it counsel, without which we must do nothing. It is forbidden to drink even the spiritual wine that gladdens the heart of man without counsel: 'Do all things with counsel; drink wine with counsel' (Prov 31:4 LXX). Also: 'As an unfortified city whose walls are broken down, so is a man who does something without counsel' (Prov 25:31 LXX). Discernment combines wisdom, reason, and the spiritual sensation that distinguishes good from evil (Heb 5:14), without which neither our inner house is built, nor spiritual riches are gathered (Prov 24:3–4)." This clearly demonstrates that without the gift of discernment not a single virtue can either exist or remain steadfast to the end. The mother and the keeper of all virtues is discernment. The other fathers also agreed with the opinion of St Anthony the Great.[133]

Spiritual discernment is acquired through reading Holy Scripture, primarily the New Testament, and the holy Fathers, whose writings correspond to the particular way of life led by a Christian. Someone who lives in the world should read the Fathers who wrote guidance applicable to all Christians; a person living in a cenobitic monastery should read patristic instruction for cenobitic monastics; a Christian who lives in the desert should immerse himself in the writings of the holy hermits who lived in constant self-contemplation, and progressed from spiritual, grace-filled contemplation of themselves to spiritual, grace-filled contemplation of God. Of course, reading must be accompanied by the corresponding behavior: "But be doers of the word, and not hearers only, deceiving yourselves" (Jas 1:22). A person's way of life must be in keeping with his reading, so that his study can be realized through actions, and does not merely prompt fruitless dreaming that leads to a state of excitement and self-deception. "Thy Law is a lamp unto my feet, and a light unto my paths" (Ps 118:105), says Holy Scripture, calling action in general "feet," the personal actions of a Christian "paths," and spiritual discernment "light." While studying the law of God, and making our own efforts to fulfill it, we must beg with heartfelt humble prayer for grace-filled illumination from on high. Holy Scripture also teaches us this: "O estrange me not from Thy commandments" (Ps 118:10); "teach me Thy statutes" (Ps 118:12); "Open Thou mine eyes, that I may recognize the wondrous things of Thy Law" (Ps 118:18); "O hide not Thy commandments from me" (Ps 118:19).

It is beneficial to our salvation to follow the instruction given by Holy Scripture and the holy Fathers to precede all our actions with God-pleasing judgment, and to submit all our intentions to this judgment, all our thoughts, all the strivings of our hearts and our urges, and to regulate both our internal and our external lives in accordance with the word of God and with divine reason. Without this our behavior cannot be either prudent, or virtuous, or pleasing to God. Without this, we must constantly subject ourselves to deception from without and self-deception within ourselves. May the fear of God teach us soberness and caution, and may the study of the Word of God and a way of life that follows it give us spiritual discernment, which is the door to the chamber of virtues and the treasure-house of spiritual good things. The words of the Lord will not fail to be fulfilled for us: "For with what judgment you judge, you will be judged; and with the measure you use, it will be measured back to you" (Matt 7:2). Amen.

32. On Salvation

Sermon on the Twelfth Sunday after Pentecost

"Good Teacher," a certain young man asked our Lord Jesus Christ, "what good thing shall I do that I may have eternal life?" (Matt 19:16), that is, "What shall I do in order to be saved?" This is a very important question. It is a question that should occupy every person throughout his time on earth. Just as someone who is traveling on the high seas constantly imagines and recalls a quiet harbor, so we, tossed in the waves of the sea of life, must hold eternity constantly before the eyes of our minds, and in the arena of our temporal life we must arrange our destiny in eternity. What acquisition that we make on earth can remain our inalienable property forever? That is our salvation. If someone has spent his earthly life amassing riches, he will leave them behind when he passes to eternal life. If someone has spent his earthly life acquiring honor and glory, cruel death will take them from him. But if someone has spent his earthly life seeking salvation, that person will take his salvation with him into eternity, and will be consoled eternally with the acquisition he has made on earth.

Dear brothers! What should we do in order to be saved? We find a most satisfactory answer to this question in the Gospel. The Lord proclaimed that for those who do not believe in Christ to be saved, it is essential to acquire belief in Him; and for believers in Christ to be saved it is essential that they live according to His commandments. A person who does not believe in Christ will perish unto the ages, and a person who believes in Christ in word alone, and does not fulfill His most holy commandments, thus denying Him through his works, will also perish unto the ages. In other words, for salvation a living faith in Christ is needed.

When the Jews asked the Lord, "What shall we do, that we may work the works of God?" He answered them, "This is the work of God, that you believe in Him whom He sent" (John 6:29). A living faith in Christ is work, and the work of God is so extensive that salvation is fulfilled through it. Living faith is expressed with the whole life, the whole existence of a person: it encompasses his thoughts, the feelings of his heart, and all his actions. "He who believes" with such faith "has everlasting life" (John 6:47). "This is eternal life, that they may know You, the only true God, and Jesus Christ whom You have sent" (John 17:3). A living faith means seeing and knowing God (Heb 11:27). A living faith is a life completely dedicated to devoutness and dead to the world. A living faith is a gift of God. The holy Apostles asked the Lord for this great gift when they said to Him: "Increase our faith" (Luke 17:5). Only by means of living faith can a person give up the transient values of his fallen nature and become a disciple and follower of the Lord in reason and in actions that befit his renewed nature.

The spiritual mansion in which spiritual treasure is kept and from which it is taught abundantly is the true faith, the one, holy Orthodox Church. For this reason it is essential for salvation to belong to the Orthodox Church: "Let" someone who is insubordinate to the Church "be to you like a heathen and a tax collector" (Matt 18:17), the Lord said. In vain do some people consider a sin of the mind to be a minor, insignificant sin. To the extent that the spirit is above the body, so virtue in the spirit is loftier than virtue in the body; and as the spirit is superior to the body, so a sin accepted and committed in the spirit is graver and more destructive than a sin committed in the body. A sin in the body is obvious; a sin of the spirit is very often hardly noticeable, sometimes unnoticeable for people immersed in the cares of the world. That makes it all the more terrible, its blows all the more true, the wounds it inflicts more incurable. It was after being infected with a sin of thought that one radiant angel became a dark demon and, banished from the dwelling-places of heaven, descended to the nether regions. He enticed there a great number of angels and a great number of people who allowed their way of thinking to be infected with false notions. The Lord, after calling the fallen angel the father of lies, called him a murderer who did not stand in the truth (John 8:44). Lies are the source and the cause of eternal death; the truth, on the other hand, is the source and the cause of salvation, as defined by the Lord Himself (John 8:32). The holy Church keeps holy truth in its bosom. By belonging to it and obeying it, we can have the right way of thinking about God, about man, about good and evil, and therefore also about salvation. It is obvious that without the right way of thinking about salvation, it is impossible to possess salvation itself. The beginning of salvation is truth; the beginning of salvation is right thinking. It is a guarantee of destruction to deviate from the truth by way of a false thought. Any deviation from the teaching of holy truth and any acceptance of a false thought that opposes this teaching entail the terrible sin of blasphemy and renunciation of God. We see the empirical demonstration of this in the fall of the forefathers, which began with accepting a false thought; we see it in all heresies. Some heretics blasphemed God by striving to deny the divinity of our Lord Jesus Christ, or to distort the most holy dogma of His incarnation; others[134] blasphemed by ascribing divine qualities to man; some blasphemed God by calling the Holy Spirit a created being; others[135] blasphemed by rejecting the action of the Holy Spirit in the mysteries of the Church and calling them a human invention. Finally, some people blasphemed against God by neglecting to live according to the commandments of Christ, remaining silent about the dogmas of the faith, but at the same time mortifying the faith, which is essential to their lives in matters of faith. "Faith without works is dead" (Jas 2:20), said the apostle. According to the teaching of the apostle, before the end of the world, the very greatest disaster must befall those people who "did not receive the love of the truth, that they might be saved. And for this reason God will send them," that is, will permit, "strong delusion" in the form of the greatest transgressor, "that they should believe the lie, that they all may be condemned who did not believe the truth but had pleasure in unrighteousness" (2 Thess 2:10–12). By seeing the worst of all evildoers as a god, people expose and confess the merit of their reason and of the disposition of their hearts. Our way of thinking, or our reason, can be spiritual only when it abides fully in the truth, ascending to it through living faith in Christ.[136] To deviate from the truth is to fall from the spiritual heaven to a carnal mind, to false reason, to perdition.

Dear brothers! Let us offer to the Lord the most heartfelt prayer, as The Apostles did, that He may grant us the only means of salvation: living faith. After praying for this, let us demonstrate the sincerity of our wish to receive the priceless gift, through our own efforts to acquire it. "Let us turn away from evil, and do good" (Ps 33:14; Ps 36:27; 1 Pet 3:11). Let us force our hearts away from sin and acquire virtue in them. We are now standing in the holy church before the invisible God, and we have the opportunity to ask of Him anything that is necessary for our salvation: the time will come when we will stand before His face together with the whole of humanity, to give an account of our earthly life. Let us take care not to bring to God at that time only the vain name of a Christian without the works that God demands of us. He promised to give a terrifying response to hypocritical Christians, and He will give it. "Then I will declare to them, 'I never knew you; depart from Me, you who practice lawlessness!'" (Matt 7:23). Amen.

33. On the Reason People Turn Away from God

Homily on the Thirteenth Sunday after Pentecost

"He who believes in the Son has everlasting life; and he who does not believe the Son shall not see life, but the wrath of God abides on him" (John 3:36). This is what the infallible Word of God says.

This definition by the Word of God is fulfilled both for every individual person and in the context of whole peoples. It was fulfilled in a particularly clear way for the people of Israel, who were originally chosen by God but then became a people who were mainly rejected. It was in the midst of the people of Israel that the God-Man was made incarnate and accomplished the salvation of mankind; He did not turn to any other people with His divine preaching; He bestowed all His good works exclusively on the chosen people; but the chosen people rejected the God-Man. In vain, over the course of fifteen centuries, did the God-inspired lawgiver of Israel proclaim terrible punishments on the people if they disobeyed God. In vain did the royal prophet of Israel, for a whole millennium, advise Israel to accept the Redeemer given by God to mankind: "Choose chastening"—accept His Son[137]—"lest the Lord be angry, and so ye perish from the right way, when His wrath be suddenly kindled" (Ps 2:12). In vain were the writings of Moses read aloud every Sabbath day. In vain were the psalms of David sung at every service. In vain were the threats of the holy lawgiver and the advice of the holy king repeated: the Jews rejected the Saviour; they stretched out the hands of deicide toward God incarnate. They numbered the all-perfect God among the criminals, and sentenced him to a torturous death, like a common criminal, like the first among criminals.

After committing this terrible deed, to which there is none comparable among all evil deeds ever committed by men, the wrath of God was not slow to be kindled: it was kindled "suddenly," as the Holy Spirit had foretold. The punishments of people are usually the result of their own violation of the law of God, their own mistakes. This is what happened with the Jews. Wholly occupied with their earthly importance, given to them temporarily, and dreaming of remarkable earthly success, they rejected the Messiah for the sake of the mere vain dreams of this importance and progress. It is obvious that their notion of temporary importance and their dream of the greatest secular progress constituted a great, absurd fallacy. The Jews expected something that had been promised them in a spiritual sense to come in a material form that was temporal and humiliating for God, and fruitless for man. They, the chosen people, were predestined to be the object of attention and contemplation of all other peoples who had turned aside to foolish, ridiculous, and pitiful idolatry. The divine blessing expressed in the miraculous victories of the Israelites, against whom no other people could prevail, and in their earthly prosperity, enjoyed by no other people, were compelling evidence to the people of the world, who were immersed in sensuality and could only be influenced by the evidence of their senses, that the God worshiped by the Jews is the one true God. Experience showed that this was the very impression given to those peoples who looked sensibly and perceptively on the Jews (Jdt 5:5–24). The very time when God chose the Israelites as the people of God coincides with the time when other peoples were turning to idolatry. By contemplating the special providence and omnipotence of God that appeared clearly and tangibly in the context of the chosen people, all the peoples of the earth were being prepared for unqualified acceptance of the Redeemer, the God-Man, Who was to be born from among the chosen people as its Head and King, and at the same time the Head, King and Saviour of the whole of fallen humanity.

The God-Man, as all-perfect and all-powerful God, brought with Him to the unhappy world abundant blessing, a gift of incalculable worth and extent, worthy of the eternal and all-perfect God. The fruit of such a blessing from God could not be temporal and material good things, which, after being given and received, are necessarily taken away by death, and often before death through the vicissitudes of earthly life. The fruit of the divine blessing granted to humanity by the God-Man became the reconciliation of men with God (Luke 2:14), the adoption by human nature of divine nature (2 Pet 1:4), by means of the adoption by divine nature of human nature, of the created being by the Creator. The fruit of this blessing is the adoption of men by God: the Son of God, by assuming human nature, became the Son of Man, and made His brothers, the sons of men, sons of God. The fruit of this blessing is the inalienable, eternal blessedness of men, beyond comprehension, beyond all desire: instead of descending into the underground dungeons of hell to eternal torment, men, conceived in wickedness and born in sins, ascend to heaven, to paradise, and together with the cherubim and the seraphim they surround the Throne of God, on which is seated the Man, Who, being God, deigned to become man, in his ineffable love for humanity.[138] In comparison to these eternal, heavenly, divine gifts, what is the significance of transient, earthly good things, liable to decay? Less than none. Their significance is negative, and if someone gives them a positive meaning, he must expect to be deprived of eternal good things for their sake, and to undergo the same calamity as that of the Jews. The Jews were given temporal good things, like a shadow, a prototype of the true, eternal good things. They chose to remain in the shadow, and rejected that essential good gift, which cast a dense shadow over humanity, so as to attract humanity toward heaven. This is why the God-Man asks men to renounce transitory good things. Not only this, He also requires people to acknowledge that they are fallen and lost, that the earth is a place of temporary persecution and punishment, the threshold of the prisons of hell and eternal torment; He requires them to strive toward God and eternity, not paying attention to the earth, as if it were a temporary hostel, or prison, condemned to demolition; He asks them to submit eagerly to all tribulations of this transitory life, thus confessing through their works their fallen nature and their need for the Redeemer, giving glory to the divine justice that chastises them, and becoming worthy of the mercy of God. The Jews did not like this teaching. For people who sought and honored earthly prosperity, the word of the cross seemed like a temptation. They considered their position on earth to be precious, the only achievement that was worth any sacrifice. It was to preserve this position that they justified their behavior toward the One sent by God (John 11:49–50). They forgot about eternity and spiritual blessings. Pursuing the idea of earthly success, of ruling the whole world, as if this were what the Word of God had promised to the people of Israel, the Jews, in their blindness and delusion, rebelled against the powerful Romans, the rulers of the world at that time. The result of the uprising was war. The war ended with the defeat of the rebels, the capture and destruction of Jerusalem, the death of countless Jews, and the capture and dispersal across the face of the earth of those who survived the sword.[139]

Fifteen centuries before this, as we said above, the lawgiver of the Israelites and God-seer Moses prophesied a terrible punishment for them for breaking the covenant with God. Fifteen centuries before the event, the God-seer paints a vivid, terrible picture of it, with remarkable precision and detail, as clearly as if it were already happening before his eyes. When the Israelites were preparing to enter the Promised Land and to become a people and a nation, at that point, with the Promised Land in sight, the inspired lawgiver made a frightening prophesy to Israel about the lot that was in the end to befall them there: "The Lord," said Moses, "will bring a nation against you from afar, from the end of the earth, as swift as the eagle flies, a nation whose language you will not understand, a nation ruthless in appearance which does not respect the elderly, nor is merciful to the young" (Deut 28:49–50). Moses was correctly portraying the Romans, who did not yet exist at that time, but already existed in the predetermination of God; he correctly portrayed their military character, likening it to the swiftness, rapaciousness, and strength of an eagle, which was acknowledged by the Romans themselves, who crowned their flags with eagles. The "nation ruthless in appearance," this people that has not yet been born, Moses continues to forewarn Israel, "shall eat the offspring of your cattle and the produce of your land; so as not to leave you grain, wine, or olive oil, or the herds of your oxen, or the flocks of your sheep, until they destroy you and wipe you out in all your cities, until your high and fortified walls in which you trust come down throughout all your land; and He will afflict you in all your cities the Lord your God gave you" (Deut 28:51–52). The prophecy was fulfilled exactly: the Romans captured and destroyed the fortresses of the Jews, one after another, laid waste to the land, and then approached Jerusalem. Jerusalem was surrounded by a broad area of ancient olive groves. The Romans cut down the olive trees to build siege machines and for other needs of their camps, in this way turning magnificent country into empty desert. After a prolonged siege, they captured the city, burned down the famous temple, and destroyed the buildings and city walls, not leaving a single stone standing upon another. Moses describes the terrible distress of the besieged as follows: "You shall eat the offspring of your womb, the flesh of your sons and your daughter the Lord Your God gave you, in the distress and desperate straits in which your enemy shall distress you" (Deut 28:53). All this happened to Israel after it had fulfilled the extent of its transgressions with deicide. "The tender and delicate woman among you,"—Moses continues his horrifying prophecy—"who would not venture to set the sole of her foot on the ground because of her delicateness and sensitivity, will turn a grudging eye toward the husband in her bosom, and upon her son and daughter, and toward her placenta which came out from between her thighs and her child whom she might bear; for she will eat these secretly for lack of everything in the siege and desperate straits in which your enemy shall distress you in all your cities" (Deut

28:56–57). Flavius Josephus, a Jewish priest who described the war and took part in it, relates that a certain rich young woman named Maria, who had arrived in Jerusalem for the feast of the Passover, was unable to leave again, because the Romans had suddenly surrounded it from all sides. Some of the rebels who filled the city robbed her, taking even her food stores. Driven to extremity and despair, Maria killed her baby son, prepared a terrible food, and ate. The rebels, drawn by the smell of food, broke into her lodgings, drew their swords, and demanded that Maria give them the food she had prepared. "I have a kept a portion of my dish for you," Maria told them, offering them the leftovers. The rebels were horrified at the unexpected sight, ran out of Maria's lodgings and broadcast around the city what they had seen. The famine that afflicted the besieged city was followed by infectious diseases. More than one million Jews died a violent death during the siege; around one hundred thousand were taken captive. The captives were put in boats and taken to Egypt where, in the crowded markets of Alexandria, they were sold into slavery for the lowest price. With this act, too, the Romans were again fulfilling the prophecy of Moses. The lawgiver forewarns Israel, which has only just completed the difficult, forty-year journey across the Arabian Desert from Egypt to the land of Canaan: "Then the Lord will take you back to Egypt in ships, by the way of which I said to you, 'You shall never see it again.' There you shall be offered for sale to your enemies as male and female servants, but no one will buy you" (Deut 28:68). Two thousand five hundred captive Jews died in Caesarea from fire, from wild beasts, and from the gladiator's sword at a national festival given by Titus, the leader of the victors, after the capture of Jerusalem. At another, later festival, at Beirut, a large number of Jews were also killed. Their leaders, Symeon and John, accompanied by seven hundred of the most famous citizens, were led in triumph into Rome and condemned to death as insurgents. The rest of the Jews, dispersed throughout the known world of the time, were subject to strict surveillance, suspicions, oppressions, and persecutions. "Then the Lord your God," Moses continues his strange prophecy, "will scatter you among all the nations, from one end of the earth to the other ... But even among those nations He shall give you no rest, nor shall the sole of your foot have a resting place; but there the Lord will give you a trembling heart, failing eyes, and anguish of soul. . . . and you shall fear day and night, and you will not believe in your Life. In the morning you shall say, 'Oh, that it were evening!' And at evening you shall say, 'Oh, that it were morning!' because of the fear which terrifies your heart, and because of the sight your eyes see" (Deut 28:64–67). This prophecy was fulfilled with surprising accuracy in the numerous descendants of Jacob, scattered across the face of the earth, and is being fulfilled up to the present day. Peoples of the world have looked and still look upon the Jews with distrust; their situation constantly fluctuates depending upon the various views of them held by different governments; they have often been subjected to harsh persecutions, and not infrequently have perished by the thousand. Their land has been struck by the wrath of God. That was the Promised Land, a land of such plenty that Holy Scripture describes it as flowing with milk and honey. Millions of people lived there within a small area, not only providing themselves with luxurious foodstuffs but selling the surplus of their produce to neighboring peoples (3 Kgdms 5:9). Subsequently, the earth of the Promised Land changed, losing its blessed fertility. In the place where millions used to live, there are now tens of thousands, supporting themselves very meagerly. All travelers to Palestine attest to this unanimously. Let us listen again to the prophecy of Moses, let us listen again to the list of punishments intended for the chosen people who rejected their election by God. "[They and] the foreigner who comes from a far land," says Moses, "and [sees] the plagues of that land"—once the Promised Land—"and its diseases which the Lord sent upon it [will say], 'The whole land will be brimstone and burning salt; it will not be sown, nor will it bear, nor will any grass grow there ...' They and all the nations will say, 'Why has the Lord done so to this land? ...' Then they will say, 'Because they forsook the covenant of the Lord God of their fathers which He made with their fathers'" (Deut 29:22–25). The Israelites forsook God and turned to idolatry. Because of these temporary instances of turning away from God they underwent temporary punishments, the most prolonged of which was their seventy years of captivity in Babylon. By rejecting the Messiah and committing deicide they conclusively destroyed the covenant with God. They endure a terrible punishment for a terrible crime. They have borne the punishment over the course of two millennia, and they persist in implacable hostility toward the God-Man. This hostility maintains and seals their rejection.

The behavior of the Jews toward the Redeemer is worthy of bitter, inconsolable tears; their blindness, their stubbornness, and their bitterness deserve close attention. The causes of this bitterness and stubbornness are worth thorough examination. How low man has sunk! What darkness he is capable of, what delusion and sinful passion, what crimes he is capable of. The behavior of the Jews toward the Redeemer, who was one of their own people, without doubt also applies to the entire human race:[140] this is all the more reason why it deserves attention, deep reflection, and investigation. God incarnate performed the most astonishing signs before the eyes of the people: he healed incurable diseases, raised the dead, and commanded the waters, the winds, earth, and heaven—and the people did not believe in Him! They rejected Him; they saw in Him their enemy, an adversary of God and someone who trampled on the law of God. Where could such incredible blindness, such incomprehensible darkness, such senseless stubbornness, and bitterness come from? We reply that it comes from a wicked way of life. "The light has come into the world," says the Saviour of Himself, "and men loved darkness rather than light, because their deeds were evil. For everyone practicing evil hates the light and does not come to the light, lest his deeds should be exposed. But he who does the truth comes to the light, that his deeds may be clearly seen, that they have been done in God" (John 3:19–21). The Lord vouched for Himself to the Jews with powerful, compelling words, and they answered with abuse. He gave undeniable proof of His divinity, and in reply they took up stones to kill Him. He tried to persuade them to stop seeking glory among men, which makes it impossible to seek glory from the one God and makes people incapable of faith (John 5:44); He tried to persuade them to give alms and to renounce avarice, which makes it impossible to serve God: the pharisees responded by deriding the Lord; to their sin-loving hearts even the teaching about virtue seemed strange and harsh (Luke 16:13–14). "O Jerusalem, Jerusalem, the one who kills the prophets and stones those who are sent to her! How often I wanted to gather your children together, as a hen gathers her chicks under her wings, but you were not willing!" (Matt 23:37).

Among the many means the Lord used to make the Jews understand is the parable He told the chief priests and elders, which we heard in today's Gospel (Matt 21:33–44). In this parable, the Lord warned that a terrible punishment awaited the Jews for the deicide they planned. "There was a certain landowner who planted a vineyard and set a hedge around it, dug a winepress in it and built a tower. And he leased it to vinedressers and went into a far country" (Matt 21:33). The landowner is God, the Creator and Owner of the visible and invisible world: He is referred to as a man to illustrate His ineffable love for mankind, because of which He first created man in His image and likeness, and then Himself deigned to become man, without ceasing to be God. The vineyard is His Church, planted by Him amid humanity, and set about, as if by a hedge, with His Providence; the gates of hades do not prevail against it (Matt 16:18). The winepress signifies the sacrifices of the Old Testament, at which the blood of animals was shed, and the tower is the God-given law. God entrusted His Church to the people of Israel, primarily to its leaders, who at the time of Christ were the high priests. After arranging his affairs in this way, the Landowner "went [away]": this action represents the fact that the Church entrusted to the Israelites remained under their authority for a long time. "Now when vintage-time drew near, he sent his servants to the vinedressers, that they might receive its fruit. And the vinedressers took his servants, beat one, killed one, and stoned another. Again he sent other servants, more than the first, and they did likewise to them." The Lord calls the Prophets who were sent to Israel at various times the servants of the landowner. "Then last of all," continues the parable, "he sent his son to them, saying, 'They will respect my son.'" These words show that there is no comparison between the sending of the prophets and the sending of the Son. The sending of the Son is so far above that of the prophets that the Jews, who had not listened to the prophets, their brothers, and had killed them, ought to have shown absolute obedience to God incarnate. But "when the vinedressers saw the son, they said among themselves, 'This is the heir. Come, let us kill him and seize his inheritance.' So they took him and cast him out of the vineyard and killed him." With these words the Lord, Who sees men's hearts, reveals the hidden reason for the planned deicide: the high priests' fear of losing their power, their importance in the Church, and the earthly privileges that were connected with their power and importance. The Lord is telling the high priests directly how they will behave toward Him—and they were indeed soon to take the Lord out of the city and condemn Him to death. The parable remained unclear to them; after relating it, the Lord asked a question: "'Therefore, when the owner of the vineyard comes, what will he do to those vinedressers?'" They said to Him, "He will destroy those wicked men miserably, and lease his vineyard to other vinedressers who will render to him the fruits in their seasons." Then the Lord said openly to them that "the kingdom of God will be taken from you and given to a nation bearing the fruits of it." The people who replaced the Israelites, consisting of many peoples, are called Christians, and the new Israel, and the Church, which until then was called a vineyard, is called the Kingdom of God: the Old Testament Church contained only the prototype of salvation, but that of the New Testament teaches salvation itself.

Those of the Jews who believed in Christ, the "remnant according to the election of grace" (Rom 11:5), became members of the new Israel, consisting of the Jews who believed in the Lord, the leaders of whom were the twelve

Apostles. Until the redemption of mankind by our Lord Jesus Christ, the Jews were the chosen people and shunned and disdained communication with other peoples, as this was forbidden by Mosaic Law. As instructed by the law, they believed that the rest of humanity was rejected, and contact with them amounted to self-defilement. After the Lord had redeemed humanity, the superiority of the Jews to other peoples and the distinction between them were eradicated. The price of redemption for every human being is the Lord Jesus Christ. "For there is no distinction," says the apostle, "between Jew and Greek, for the same Lord over all is rich to all who call upon Him. For 'whoever calls on the name of the Lord shall be saved'" (Rom 10:12–13). "If you confess with your mouth the Lord Jesus and believe in your heart that God has raised Him from the dead, you will be saved. For with the heart one believes unto righteousness, and with the mouth confession is made unto salvation" (Rom 10:9–10). The cornerstone on which is erected the spiritual living building, the Kingdom of God, the Church of the New Testament, the people of God, the blessed, holy new Israel, this cornerstone is our Lord Jesus Christ. The royal prophet and ancestor of the God-Man in the flesh said, "The stone which the builders refused is become the head stone of the corner" (Ps 117:22). When the Lord had finished telling the parable, He reminded the Jewish high priests of this saying Psalmist: "Have you never read in the Scriptures: 'The stone which the builders rejected has become the chief cornerstone. This was the Lord's doing, and it is marvelous in our eyes? ...And whoever falls on this stone will be broken; but on whomever it falls, it will grind him to powder'" (Matt 21:42–44). The vinedressers—the chief priests and scribes—disregarded the Lord; but the wisdom of God arranged that the God-Man, through His voluntary death and resurrection, became before the eyes of His enemies and opponents the supremely firm, resolute and broad foundation of the New Testament Church, which formed in the midst of Jerusalem itself and from Jerusalem embraced the whole world. The "corner," according to the explanation of the teachers of the church, is a union of two different groups of people who were not previously united: the Jews and the gentiles. They were unified in Christ and formed the Church of which the foundation and the head is Christ (1 Cor 3:11; Eph 5:23). After they had believed in Christ, when they saw that the Roman army surrounded Jerusalem, then, as prophesied by the Lord (Luke 21:20), they came out of the city that was doomed to destruction. There was every opportunity for them to leave the city in this way because, after surrounding Jerusalem for the first time, the Romans retreated and left Judea; they soon returned, began a regular, sustained siege, and completed that punishment of the murderers of God that they themselves had called upon themselves and upon their descendants (Matt 27:25). The Jews who fell on the spiritual stone were destroyed, and the wrath of God fell on them and ground them to powder; this is represented by the destruction of their government, the death of countless numbers of their people, and the captivity and dispersal around the world of those who escaped a violent death (Matt 21:43; Luke 21:24). But these punishments at the time are as nothing compared to the eternal punishments of the enemies of God.

The holy Apostle Paul writing to formerly gentile Christians of the disastrous fall of the Jews says: "And if some of the branches were broken off, and you, being a wild olive tree, were grafted in among them, and with them became a partaker of the root and fatness of the olive tree, do not boast against the branches. But if you do boast, remember that you do not support the root, but the root supports you. You will say then, 'Branches were broken off that I might be grafted in.' Well said. Because of unbelief they were broken off, and you stand by faith. Do not be haughty, but fear. For if God did not spare the natural branches, He may not spare you either. Therefore consider the goodness and severity of God: on those who fell, severity; but toward you, goodness, if you continue in His goodness. Otherwise you also will be cut off" (Rom 11:17–22). Let us pay attention to this warning and to the terrible threat implied by it. The reason for the renunciation by the Jews of the Saviour was their immoral way of life, both personal and societal. They constantly contravened and defied the Law of God. Let us avoid this reason for turning away from God, lest we also turn away from Him. "Each time," says St Tikhon of Voronezh, "a sinner takes pleasure in a sin which has become a passion for him, he denies Christ in his heart; each time he commits a sin in deed, he makes a sacrifice to an idol." A constantly sinful life is a constant denial of Christ. Even if not spoken by the tongue or the lips, it has, alas, long been expressed. The lips and tongue cannot avoid revealing a secret withdrawal and denial within the heart. It is as if they unwittingly expressed it. Denial of Christ has been and still is expressed by various heretical teachings[141] which conceal this denial by inappropriately keeping the name of Christianity; it has been and still is expressed by various teachings that result from fallen human reason, presenting themselves as light and removing the true light, Christ; it has been and still is expressed not only by a depraved way of life, but also by a life that neglects the commandments of God. "The commandment of the Lord is bright, giving light unto the eyes" (Ps 18:9), and only with its help is it possible to behold the Redeemer; only whoever "works righteousness" is capable of receiving the Redeemer (Acts 10:35) and abiding in communion with Him (John 15:10).

The falling away of the new Israel from the Saviour until the end of times will develop extensively, as the Apostle prophesies: "the falling away comes first," and then, as a consequence and fruit of the falling away, "the man of sin is revealed, the son of perdition" (2 Thess 2:3), who dares to call himself the promised Messiah, demands for himself the worship of a god, and will receive it from those who have prepared themselves to receive the antichrist by falling away from Christ, either openly or secretly. The falling away will be so extensive that "because lawlessness will abound, the love of many will grow cold" (Matt 24:12). This means that sinful temptations and examples will multiply so much that they will entice a great number of people into a sinful way of life. Faith in Christ will hardly exist, as the Lord Himself proclaimed: "when the Son of Man comes, will He really find faith on the earth?" (Luke 18:8). Transitory, material occupations, and pleasures will attract all the attention of mankind. "As it was in the days of Noah, so it will be also in the days of the Son of Man: They ate, they drank, they married wives, they were given in marriage, until the day that Noah entered the ark, and the flood came and destroyed them all. Likewise as it was also in the days of Lot: They ate, they drank, they bought, they sold, they planted, they built" (Luke 17:26,28). Abundant earthly success and vast earthly enterprises, such as are obvious to everyone, have been set down by the Word of God as a sign of the last times and of the ripened sinfulness of humanity, that is to a great extent not obvious or comprehensible to a superficial or inexperienced eye. People never want to declare themselves to be followers of evil, even if they are drowning in evil; they always strive to show themselves as virtuous. The more they allow themselves to transgress, the more they are concerned to justify themselves in the eyes of other people (Luke 16:15); then they become even more hypocritical, and begin to proclaim their own perfection and virtue (John 9:28). Attachment to material things and to material success can easily seize a person completely, his mind and his heart, and steal all his time and all his effort: because of my fall, "My soul cleaveth to the dust" (Ps 118:25) from my youth, instead of being on high. Such attachment distracts a person from the Word of God, from thoughts of death and eternity; it distracts him from faith in God and knowledge of God, and destroys him by means of eternal death. "If anyone loves the world," the Holy Spirit of God proclaims to everyone without exception, that is, loves earthly life with its success and pleasure, "the love of the Father is not in him" (1 John 2:15). "Friendship with the world is enmity with God ... Whoever therefore wants to be a friend of the world makes himself an enemy of God" (Jas 4:4). "You cannot serve God and mammon" (Matt 6:24), that is, God and earthly success. Serving mammon, especially when all the strength of one's soul is sacrificed to this service, means falling away from serving God and is a true sign of falling into the deep, perpetual abyss of sin. Just as the ancient Israel sacrificed the spiritual virtue offered to it by the Redeemer to earthly benefit and to vain hopes of abundant earthly success, so the new Israel, according to the testimony of Holy Scripture, will reject the spiritual virtue it has already been granted by the Redeemer, for the sake of worldly success that will soon perish and is envisioned only in flattering dreams, and will disparage the Holy Spirit in its fallen, false reason (2 Thess 2). The ancient Israel was deceived by a dream of greater earthly progress, and the new Israel is deceived by a similar dream and a similar aspiration. Both transitory and eternal calamities befell the ancient Israel because it rejected the Redeemer: these adversities are a faint prefiguring of the terrible calamities that must be the punishment of the new Israel for its iniquity. It will undergo ferocious punishment, both transitory and eternal, it will not escape it, "if we neglect so great a salvation, which at the first began to be spoken by the Lord, and was confirmed to us by those who heard Him, God also bearing witness both with signs and wonders, with various miracles, and gifts of the Holy Spirit" (Heb 2:3–4).

What must we do, people ask at this point, to avoid falling away from the Redeemer and being subject to the wrath of God? "Therefore," the holy Apostle Paul answers this question, "we must give the more earnest heed to the things we have heard, lest we drift away" (Heb 2:1). This means that as we live we must pay particular attention to the New Testament into which God deigned to enter with us, uniting us with Him through the holy sacraments, proclaiming to us His most holy and perfect will in the Gospel, and crowning the faithful sons of the New Testament with the clear and tangible gift of the Holy Spirit. Let us be mindful of death and divine judgment, to which we will be subject as soon as we are parted from our bodies; let us be mindful of the blessed or the sorrowful eternity that must be our lot, depending on the judgment of God. When we constantly remember death and divine judgment, and blessed or calamitous eternity, the attitude of our hearts toward earthly life changes: we begin to regard ourselves as pilgrims on earth; a pledge of coldness and indifference toward earthly things appears in our hearts; all our attention is turned toward studying and keeping the commandments of the Gospel. Just as a traveler who is lost in the dense forest in the dark of the night tries to get back home by following the sound of a bell or a horn, so a true Christian, by paying attention to the teaching of Christ, makes an effort to leave the domain of false reason that is born in and sustained by life according to the flesh. "Thy statutes have been my songs in the place of my pilgrimage. I have remembered Thy Name, O Lord, in the night-season, and have kept Thy Law" (Ps 118:54–55)—this is how the holy prophet David, who made his confession to God both in the royal mansions and in the glory of an unvanquished hero, recognized that he was a wanderer on earth, and that the earth is the place of his pilgrimage, of his wandering and persecution. Do not think that with an attitude such as this we become weak people who are of little use to society. No: by holding this view, we fulfill our obligations to humanity with particular zeal, with self-sacrifice. This is natural, for then the sole goal of our activity is the benefit of humanity, and not the acquisition of earthly advantages. On the other hand, when we forget eternity and God, and live on earth only for the sake of earthly acquisitions, then unconsciously, without noticing or realizing it, in defiance of our conscience and our obligations, in defiance of the commands of the great God, we sacrifice the well-being of our neighbor, the benefit of mankind, and our own eternal blessedness, for the sake of our self-love and our self-deception. The Lord is long-suffering toward us (2 Pet 3:9): that is obvious. "Consider that the longsuffering of our Lord is salvation" (2 Pet 3:15), says the apostle, that is, know that the cause and the purpose of this long-suffering is the goodwill of God toward us, that we may not be carried away by a pervasive stream of evil, that we may work out our salvation guided by the Word of God. The majority of people, fed by the false and flattering teaching of the rejected spirits (1 Tim 4:1), and seized by the effect within them of this teaching, have scorned the Word of God, and neither know nor want to know it. It is necessary, most necessary, to pay attention to the Word of God, that is justified by the very events of a time and disposition hostile to it, "and never to fall away!" This attention is truly necessary, so that we may not be deprived irrevocably of the salvation that has not yet been taken away from men, through the wondrous mercy and long-suffering of our God, Who offers the possibility of being saved to the poor remnant of those who believe in Him. Amen.

34. On the Rich Man and Lazarus

Homily on the Twenty-second Sunday after Pentecost

Dear brothers! The world calls its amusements and enjoyments harmless. It is essential for each of us to know how God looks upon them and judges them. Each one of us, at an indeterminate time not known to him, will and must leave the arena of brief wandering on earth and enter the domain of eternity. There he must answer for how he has used the time allotted to him to acquire salvation: if he has used it well, he will ascend to the dwelling-place of eternal blessedness; if he has used it badly, he will descend to hades unto eternity. This is addressed in the Gospel we heard today (Luke 16:19–31). The judgment of God has been proclaimed in good time. Let us make haste to acquire the way of thinking taught by God, so that false, captivating notions do not deflect us from God-pleasing actions, and serve as the initial cause of great, eternal catastrophes. Let us not be careless in determining and deciding our eternal state. Let us concern ourselves with this most important matter with all possible attention. It demands and is worthy of it. Let us consider the judgment of God on carnal human amusements, a judgment pronounced in advance by way of warning and instruction; let us direct our actions in accordance with the will of our God, and His final pronouncement will not shock us with a sentence to eternal death when, at the sudden command of God, we leave this world behind and leave our bodies in it—only with our souls will we enter the world of spirits, to be numbered there either with the blessed spirits or with the rejected.

"There was a certain rich man," the parable in the Gospel recounts, "who was clothed in purple and fine linen and fared sumptuously every day" (Luke 16:19). The Gospel presents for pious and salutary contemplation two features in the life of the rich man: his luxury and his devotion to amusements. In contrast to this situation of a person who abounds in earthly blessings, is satiated with them, we are also shown the suffering of the poor and sick man who is languishing under the oppression of every privation. People in these situations that differ so much often live adjacent to one another, in reciprocal material and moral relationships. Here too, in close proximity, poverty is crowded together in the same place as opulence and prosperity. "But there was a certain beggar named Lazarus, full of sores, who was laid at [the] gate" of the rich man, "desiring to be fed with the crumbs which fell from the rich man's table." The rich man did not find time for the poor man. He was preoccupied with ensuring that nothing was wanting in his revelry and amusements, that the demands of exquisite taste and contemporary fashion or custom were satisfied, together with the vanity of the host, who needed to put on show to his guests both his wealth and what he regarded as his knowledge of the world, of decency, of life, so as to satisfy all the carnal desires of his guests, with all kinds of sensual pleasure. The rich man's servant also had no time for the poor man. All his attention was focused on quick and exact fulfillment of the instructions and orders of his master, who no doubt shone with brilliant inventiveness in his chosen field.

Alas, every earthly situation is taken away by death, wiped away as if it had never existed. "So it was that the beggar died," the Gospel account continues, "and was carried by the angels to Abraham's bosom. The rich man also died and was buried." Just "he was buried"! And that is how the journey ends of every great person on earth who has sacrificed his life for the earth. What a cold expression this is: "he was buried." A person who possessed transitory good things is accompanied to eternity with indifference by the heirs of those good things. Merely for the sake of decency, at the graveside ceremony, they assume the forced appearance of sorrow. They will soon appear at the luxurious feast that follows the burial, at the table where transient sorrow is drowned with cups of wine, and turns to joy. Soon even the memory of the departed will die. All the attention will soon be on the heirs, and there will be exclamations pronouncing them fortunate and worthy of envy. They will achieve happiness through the death of a person supposed to be close to their hearts. "He was buried": this is said not so much of the burial of the rich man's body in a shallow grave, as of the burial of his soul in a very deep grave, in the abyss of hades. The lot of the rich man beyond the grave is recounted in contrast to that of the beggar.

The parable in the Gospel does not end here. It goes on to relate events in the invisible world, the world that awaits us after our physical death. The rich man, "being in torments in Hades ... lifted up his eyes and saw Abraham afar off, and Lazarus in his bosom. Then he cried and said, 'Father

Abraham, have mercy on me, and send Lazarus that he may dip the tip of his finger in water and cool my tongue; for I am tormented in this flame.'" What a change in circumstances! Temporary well-being is replaced with eternal sorrow, and temporary suffering with eternal blessedness. Not long ago, the poor man lay half-naked and purulent at the gates of the rich man, and longed to relieve his hunger with the crumbs that fell from the table, not even with other more substantial leftovers, which the servant ate; not long ago, the rich man did not even want to glance at the poor man; he saw him only in passing, as if he did not see him; he turned his eyes away from him, loathing him as a disgrace. Now the poor man is full of joy and blessedness; now the rich man begs the poor man to wet the end of his finger and cool down his tongue, parched from the flames of hades. It turns out that the rich man knew very well the situation of the poor man: he even knew his name. Ignorance was not the reason why he ignored the poor man. "But Abraham said, 'Son, remember that in your lifetime you received your good things, and likewise Lazarus evil things; but now he is comforted and you are tormented. And besides all this, between us and you there is a great gulf fixed, so that those who want to pass from here to you cannot, nor can those from there pass to us.'" Abraham answers the prisoner of hades with mildness, humility, and love. He does not judge the man who has been judged by God and handed over to eternal torment; he does not turn away from speaking with him; he does not renounce his kinship in the flesh, but calls him his son; he does not denounce him but only reminds him of the way of life while still on earth that has served as a reason for eternal blessedness for the one and eternal torment for the other. Abraham speaks of the fact that circumstances beyond the grave cannot be changed, without adding any explanation: this is a divine institution that is not subject to human judgment, is accepted through faith, and is entirely clear for the one God.

Encouraged by this merciful response, the prisoner of hades asks the holy patriarch another question: "I beg you therefore, father, that you would send him to my father's house, for I have five brothers, that he may testify to them, lest they also come to this place of torment." This plea reveals inexperience in spiritual, ascetic life. An inexperienced person asks on behalf of other inexperienced people for a dangerous thing: the appearance of beings from the world of spirits, which God has closed to us, so as to protect us from being deluded by fallen and evil spirits who take on the appearance of angels of light and then very easily deceive and destroy people. The patriarch shows the unfortunate man the true path, the path of learning and following the law of God: he tells the man who has fallen into hades some information that could have saved him from going there, if he had acquired and made use of it in good time. "They have Moses and the prophets," says Abraham, "let them hear them." Knowledge acquired through the Word of God is truer than knowledge acquired even through true and holy visions. This can be seen in the second epistle of the holy Apostle Peter. After reminding his readers about the glorious Transfiguration of our Lord on Mount Tabor of which the apostle was a witness, he says, "And so we have the prophetic word confirmed, which you do well to heed as a light that shines in a dark place, until the day dawns and the morning star rises in your hearts" (2 Pet 1:19).

In his deep ignorance, the prisoner of hades does not understand the deep truth taught to him. He enters into a discussion with the patriarch, objecting: "'No, father Abraham; but if one goes to them from the dead, they will repent.' But he said to him, 'If they do not hear Moses and the prophets, neither will they be persuaded though one rise from the dead.'" To those who do not want to acquaint themselves as they should with the law of God, who waste their earthly life wholly in serving sin and the world; to those who study the law of God only according to the letter, scorn active study of it, or trample upon it with their behavior: to those people, the appearance of a blessed soul from the dwelling-places of paradise will not bring any benefit. Even resurrection from a sealed, guarded tomb will not resurrect a capacity for faith that has been destroyed by a sinful life and an evil disposition. The Lord rose from the dead, and what did the chief priests and elders of the Jews do? They bribed the Roman soldiers they had set on guard at the tomb, who had brought credible news of the resurrection, to cover up and tell lies about the resurrection of the Lord. What did the soldiers do, who had the honor, far exceeding their virtue, of seeing the angel descend from heaven like lightning and roll the stone away from the tomb, in which the body of the Lord was confined, striking them with terror, from which they fell to the ground and became as dead? They accepted pieces of silver and, under the influence of this, despite witnessing the awesome miracle, they covered it up with the darkness of lies (Matt 28:11–15). Neither the most wondrous signs, nor terrifying visions, nor the most delightful visions yield beneficial effects on the heart or direct it toward salvation if it is not guided on the way of salvation by the law of God. But if the heart is illumined by this lamp given from on High to guide all who wish to receive blessedness unto eternity (Ps 118:105), then it will acquire this blessedness without the help of visions and miracles. A great many experiences in the history of Christian ascetic struggle demonstrate this.

The basic cause of the eternal blessedness of a person lies in thorough studying of the law of God and living in accordance with it. The basic cause of eternal affliction of the soul lies in ignorance of the law of God, in living according to the inspirations and notions of false reason and the urges of the will, and in the damaged and distorted state resulting from the fall. It is obvious that the unhappy rich man had a wrong and false understanding of himself, and of his relationship to property, to humanity, in short, to everything. He acted in accordance with these notions, and perished. He did not acquire true knowledge of God, did not know what significance a person has, what the goal of his eternal existence or of his temporary presence on earth was, what his obligations were to God, to himself, to his neighbors, and to the world, visible and invisible. Darkened by ignorance, darkened by his fallen state, by the example of others, and by the customary practices of human society, he considered life to be the life of the body alone, and paid no attention to the life of the soul; he wanted to develop only the life of the body, offering it every possible enjoyment, using all the capabilities of the soul to serve it. That is how he acted with regard to his own soul, and that is how he acted with his neighbors: he despised them. The only ones he did not despise were those whom he used to implement his own will and who assisted it. He deemed his property to be his own possession in every way, and himself to have the right to use this property at will. Scripture judges the matter differently. It calls wealthy people merely managers of property that belongs to God and that they are entrusted with managing it for a time in accordance with the will of God.[142] The rich man used both his property and his earthly life solely to satisfy his flesh. He threw away into decay these temporary gifts of God, with which he could have acquired eternal gifts. He feasted and lived in luxury—not infrequently, not at the customary times, but every day, continually: he "fared sumptuously every day." He went from one pleasure to another, constantly amusing and dissipating himself, not allowing self-contemplation, so as to avoid subjecting himself to any upsetting sight; he did not revive any sad memory, or disturb a joyful disposition. In this way of life God, eternity, blessedness and suffering are forgotten, so completely that they seem to be nonexistent. And many people, intoxicated with living for the flesh, have not only forgotten about spiritual matters, but in their intoxication have begun to deny the existence of God, of the invisible world, of their own souls. Yes, they have ceased to feel the existence of these things. They would deny visible death itself, if it were possible to do so. They deny its meaning, calling it the destruction of man. Such an understanding is reconciled with and commends carnal living. Someone who has adopted this understanding can easily "fare sumptuously every day," entertain every whim, trample upon the most sacred obligations, and upon all virtues, provided that good impressions and decency are preserved in the eyes of the world. A person who spends his earthly life in this way, alienating himself from God, acquiring all the attributes that are not pleasing to God, willingly rejecting adoption by God, naturally departs at his demise to the land that is doomed to be the dwelling-place of those rejected by God: he goes there because he has rejected God. He descends to the prison of hades as a stranger to God, although he was not openly an evildoer.

The Gospel does not mention a single virtue of the poor man named Lazarus; it speaks only of his life full of suffering and of the fact that angels carried his soul to the part of paradise known as the bosom of Abraham. The holy Fathers even comment that Lazarus had sins on account of which God permitted him to suffer illness and poverty. The words said of him that he "received ... evil things" lead to this conclusion. A similar expression is used of the rich man, meaning that the property was granted to him by God, and was not his own, as many people wrongly think of their property. Where can we find the reason for the salvation and eternal blessedness granted to Lazarus? What was his virtue? The reason for his salvation and his virtue was repentance. It is clear that he, like the thief crucified on the right hand of the Lord (Luke 23:39–43), considered himself deserving of punishment, thanked and glorified God for the punishment in his lifetime, and prayed for mercy in eternity. As we have already mentioned, the patriarch, while conversing with the prisoner of hades, said nothing either about the sinfulness of this prisoner, or about the righteousness of Lazarus: he only presented the situation of each in eternity as a consequence of his situation on earth. It was too late, and it would have been redundant, to denounce the sinfulness of the one who had been handed over to eternal torment, or to proclaim to him the merits of the one who dwelt in paradise. This would only have caused further pain to the one struck with by eternal death, through which not existence but enjoyment of existence is taken away forever, and existence entails suffering as great as that of death. The holy patriarch pities the man punished by God; he not only does not dare to judge or even to add his judgment to that of God: he sympathizes with the man suffering eternal torment as with a member of his own body, a member of humanity (1 Cor 12:26), and says: "Son, remember that in your lifetime you received your good things, and likewise Lazarus evil things; but now he is comforted and you are tormented." This means: "God granted you great wealth, so that you might use it to help those in need and in poverty, as the law of God commands, and so work out your salvation; but you misused the gift of God, throwing it down into the stench of carnal pleasure, and because of this you have descended into the abyss, the flame of hades. Also, God sent Lazarus poverty and disease to cleanse him from his sins. He used these things, admitted his sinfulness, justified and confessed the justice of God, and repented. He was carried up by angels to the dwelling-places of paradise for eternal blessedness, because he had fulfilled the will of God." The Fathers rightly observe that this virtue of Lazarus, though omitted from the account, is apparent from the consequences: otherwise the angels would not have appeared to him and carried him to the eternal resting-place of the saints who have pleased God. St Niphon, Bishop of Constantia in Cyprus, a man of great holiness, when talking one day with some brothers about profit to the soul, remembered the following story: "There once lived in this city" (Constantinople, where the saint lived until he was made a bishop) "a slave to one of the nobles whose name was Vasily, a tailor by trade, wicked in disposition, dissolute and a buffoon, who wasted his time with games and carnal sins, despite the admonishments of his master. Through the wondrous care of the merciful God, his salvation was worked out in the following way. There came a great famine, and the nobles began to evict their slaves due to the lack of food. Vasily was also evicted by his master. He first sold his clothing to buy bread, then began to walk the streets half-naked, asking for alms. It was winter at the time, and he suffered greatly from the cold. Finally, he lay down exhausted on the street. One by one his toes fell off, and then his legs became paralyzed. Vasily patiently endured this, recognizing it to be a punishment for his sins; he continually repeated, 'Glory to God for everything.' In this way he spent two months in the street, without shelter, sighing and weeping for his sins. It happened that there passed along this street a certain lover of Christ whose name was Nicephorus. Seeing Vasily suffering, he ordered that he be brought to his house, where he gave him rest and food. After two weeks, on a Saturday, the sick Vasily suddenly said, 'Welcome, holy angels: wait a little while, and we will go.' They said, 'No, come quickly, because the Lord is calling you.' Vasily answered, 'Be patient a little longer, so that I can repay a debt: I borrowed ten copper coins from one of my friends, and I haven't paid it back yet; supposing the devil stopped me in the air because of that?' The angels agreed to wait. Vasily asked for the money and sent it to where it belonged, and then gave up his spirit to God."[143]

In the course of their earthly life, people are given various situations through what they see as unfathomable fate: some enjoy wealth, glory, power, and health; others are poor, so insignificant in human society that anyone can insult them; others spend their lives in sadness, passing from one tribulation to another, tormented by sickness, persecutions, and humiliations. None of these situations is accidental: they are apportioned by divine providence, like problems to be solved, like lessons to be learned, so that each person works out his salvation in the situation in which he has been placed, fulfilling the will of God. Those who bear a burden of tribulations must bear it with humility, in obedience to God, knowing that He has laid it upon them. If they are sinners, then the tribulations will serve as retribution for them within time. By acknowledging their sinfulness and bearing the tribulation cheerfully, they save themselves from retribution in eternity. If they are innocent, then the sorrow that is sent or permitted to them at the behest of God, with a most worthy divine purpose, prepares for them special blessedness and glory in eternity. If we complain about a tribulation sent down upon us, to God who sent it, this destroys its divine purpose, deprives us of salvation, and exposes us to eternal torment.

Those who are granted to have earthly goods at their disposal must take special care to guard themselves against misusing them. Glorious and powerful people of the earth, your function is to be benefactors to others, and through this philanthropy to do good to yourself. Abraham has a bosom in heaven, that is, an abode, in which he accepts people who are worthy of it and have suffered on earth. His place in heaven is similar to the one he chose for himself on earth. On earth he was a rich man. He gave hospitality to strangers, and helped the oppressed and needy. His blessed place in heaven is a consequence of his virtuous life on earth. You too, by leading such a life, will gain such abodes and such a place in eternity, which can then justifiably be deemed to belong to you. This place in heaven will never be taken away, whereas earthly ranks and advantages, earthly wealth, all earthly good things are granted only for temporary enjoyment. The Gospel calls earthly treasure "unrighteous" and "another man's", and that of heaven "true" and a man's property. "Therefore if you have not been faithful in the unrighteous mammon, who will commit to your trust the true riches? And if you have not been faithful in what is another man's, who will give you what is your own?" (Luke 16:11–12). Temporary riches are referred to as "unrighteous" because they are a consequence of the fall. We would need neither money, nor protection from the elements, which we try to make splendid, nor other means of relief that become items of luxury, if we had not been cast out of paradise down to earth, where we remain for a very short time, given to us by the mercy of God to restore the lost paradise. Temporary riches are called "another man's": even by themselves they are destroyed, and pass constantly from one person's hands to another's; they are not intrinsic to man, and they serve to reveal both his need to help himself, and his fallen condition. They are elusive; they never stay in one place or in one person's hands; they are always given for a more or less brief length of time, always equally brief in comparison with boundless eternity. Eternal property is referred to as "true" because it is the incorruptible, unchanging, ever-present property of the one who will one day receive it. It is also referred to as a person's "own" because the person has been created to possess and enjoy it; it is intrinsic to him. In order to receive a true treasure that is your own, inalienable, you must remain true to God in managing what has been entrusted to you for a time. Do not deceive yourselves: do not consider earthly property to be your own. Do not deceive yourselves: you do not have the right to do what you wish with this property, contrary to what you may believe. Do not deceive yourselves: do not consider it permissible to use this property for luxury and amusement. You have a duty to arrange your affairs in accordance with the commands of God, who entrusted you with the responsibility. If you use your property for luxury and amusement, you trample on the law of God, and you take away from your neighbors what God entrusted you to distribute among them. If you indulge in feasting and amusements, you destroy yourself. You enslave your spirit to your body; you stifle and deaden your soul; you forget God and eternity, and you lose your very faith. Cultivating within yourself only carnal feelings, reinforcing them with refined and excessive food, and constant carnal amusements, you will not be able to resist fornication, you will indulge in it insatiably. In this mortal sin you will conclusively bury your salvation. "Woe to you," proclaimed the Saviour, "who are rich," that is, who misuse your wealth, "for you have received your consolation. Woe to you who are full, for you shall hunger. Woe to you who laugh now, for you shall mourn and weep" (Luke 6:24–26). "Give alms; provide yourselves money bags which do not grow old, a treasure in the heavens that does not fail" (Luke 12:33). You can find pleasure in working on virtues. You need only to touch on them, and you will be met by that spiritual, holy pleasure, and carnal pleasures will seem disgusting to you. From the alms you give, a living faith will start to appear within you, through which you will see God and come to know Him through experience. It is inherent in mercy to produce faith, and in faith to produce mercy. Abstinence from satisfying carnal desires gives a pure mind, and the attitude of the mind toward the earth and all earthly matters changes: what it has thus far not seen is revealed to it, that the corruptible is corruptible and the transient is transient; from then on its thoughts begin to be raised up to eternity; it finds it essential to consider eternity in good time and to study its boundless scope. "Make friends for yourselves by unrighteous mammon" (Luke 16:9), exhorts the Gospel, by "unrighteous mammon" meaning material property and by "friends" meaning angels and those holy people who have already departed from here into eternity, and whose virtuous life and partaking in divine grace we should adopt during our earthly wanderings. "Make friends for yourselves by unrighteous mammon, that when you fail, they may receive you into an everlasting home" (Luke 16:9). You will certainly fail in the full sense of the word when, in the mystical action of death, you leave on earth everything belonging to the earth and taken from the earth, even your very bodies. May the celestial beings then "receive you into an everlasting home," into the dwelling-places of paradise. May the mercy of God honor us with these longed-for dwelling-places in return for obedience to His all-holy will. Amen.

35. An Explanation of the Lord's Prayer

Homily on the Tuesday of the Twenty-third Week after Pentecost

Prayer, which is the precious inheritance of all Christians, forms the main occupation of the holy hermits. It is their food, it is their book, it is their science, and it is their life. The great hermit, John the Forerunner of the Lord, was an active man of prayer; he was also a teacher of it. The holy Forerunner taught his disciples this great science that unites man with God, as we heard in today's Gospel (Luke 11:1–4; Matt 6:9–13).[144]

The disciples of the Lord wished to learn prayer from the Lord Himself. This is a profound, righteous desire. The true teacher of true prayer is God alone.[145] Holy human teachers give only basic notions about prayer, indicating the correct disposition in which grace-filled teaching about prayer can be communicated through thoughts and sensations that are spiritual and beyond nature. These thoughts and sensations come from the Holy Spirit and are communicated through Him. The Lord fulfilled this wise request of His disciples, essential for edification of the soul and for salvation: He taught them a prayer that God alone could teach, as will be shown by means of an explanation of this prayer, known as the Lord's Prayer, to distinguish it from the prayers written by holy people.

The Lord's Prayer begins with the appeal "Our Father." What holy person would have permitted himself and his brothers, sinful people, cast out, held in captivity by the devil and by eternal death, to appeal to God in this way? Not one, of course. Only God could permit this. Since He permitted this, which means that he granted it. The Son of God, made man, made men sons of God, and thus His brothers. He addresses God the Father by right of nature as "Our Father," and thus gives us the grace-filled right to turn to God as to a Father and to begin our prayer to Him with a wondrous, striking opening that no man would have dared to allow to enter his mind: "Our Father."

The opening of the Lord's Prayer is a gift from the Lord, a gift of infinite value, a gift from the Redeemer to the redeemed, from the Saviour to the saved. The requests that constitute the Lord's Prayer are requests for spiritual gifts obtained for humanity through the redemption. There is not a single word in the prayer about the carnal, transient needs of human beings. The One Who commanded us to seek only the kingdom of God and His righteousness, and promised to grant all necessary transitory things to those who seek this kingdom (Matt 6:33),[146] teaches prayer that is in keeping with this command and this promise.

Immediately after the appeal an indication is added of the place where the Father Who cannot be confined in any space, and is present everywhere, encompassing everything is: "Our Father in heaven." By indicating the Father's abode in heaven, the son who is praying ascends there. Forget every earthly thing: pay no attention to the earth, that refuge that is granted to you for the briefest of times; pay no attention to all the things pertaining to this refuge that will be taken from you within a very short time; turn all your concerns toward your home country, toward heaven, which was taken from you through the fall and returned through the redemption: bring your prayer to be granted eternal, spiritual, holy, divine good things that, in their ineffable virtue, exceed not only human comprehension, but even the comprehension of the angels. These good things are already prepared for you; they already await you. The justice of God, inseparable from His goodness, demands that your wish to receive treasures from heaven is expressed through your prayer and your way of life.

All servants of the Lord, without exception, are astonished and confused by the greatness of the Lord's Prayer. Divine munificence is spread by the right hand of God. Even a righteous person admits that he is unworthy of it, and it is not permissible for him to ask for it. All the more bewildered is a sinner who recognizes that he deserves only punishments. This bewilderment is resolved with an explanation that brings more confusion. The Lord's Prayer was given to mankind before their redemption had been conclusively accomplished: they are called sons, and are called to the rights of sons, before their adoption, before being reborn through baptism, before participating in the mystical supper, before being renewed by the Holy Spirit. The Lord's Prayer is given to sinners.[147] Where God acts, everything is possible and everything is incomprehensible.

The Lord's Prayer was given to sinners, and the first thing they are taught to ask of God the Father is that His "name be hallowed." This petition consists in recognition of sinfulness, and of fallenness. This petition consists in asking to be granted sincere repentance. "Hallowed be Your name" in the temple of my soul. I ask for this because I do not find it within myself. I find the opposite: I am pitifully enslaved to sin and to fallen spirits who have contrived sin and infected me with it, who have enslaved themselves and keep me enslaved by means of sin. In my soul there are bad, malodorous thoughts and feelings. I do not know whether they enter it from without, or whether they are born within it; I know that they appear unhindered and peremptorily, that I do not have the strength to expel them from myself or to throw them out. God becomes angry with these thoughts and feelings; they deter the most holy God; they blaspheme God; in their presence I remain a stranger to God. I need cleansing; I need repentance. My heavenly Father, grant me powerful repentance, to cleanse my internal temple from all impurities and stench, to make me able to accept adoption by You, to make me already a citizen of heaven during my earthly pilgrimage. Until now I have crawled upon the earth. May true knowledge of God come into my soul! May it sanctify my mind, my heart, all my activities: "Hallowed be Your name" in me (Matt 6:9). This is the meaning of this petition. We can desire repentance and purity; we can and must use all the means at our disposal to gain them; but acquiring them does not depend on us. It is a gift from God. We must first of all pray to the heavenly Father, that He may send down from His spiritual treasury the gift of repentance and cleanse us through it from the pollution of sin, and adorn us with blessed purity, that sees God (Matt 5:8), and is the only way to receive true knowledge of God. "Hallowed be Your name"!

"Your kingdom come." "The kingdom of God is within you" (Luke 17:21). What wonderful progression there is in the Lord's Prayer! This represents the progression, the gradation, the elevated and holy system of spiritual progress. After asking to be granted perfect knowledge of God, the Lord teaches the person adopted by God to ask for the kingdom of God to descend into his soul. He commands him to ask for this kingdom with a humble but powerful prayer of faith. It is impossible for a believer not to receive it. It has been promised by the Word of God: "He who has My commandments and keeps them, it is he who loves Me"; in whom My name is hallowed, "it is he who loves Me. And he who loves Me will be loved by My Father" (John 14:21). "If anyone loves Me, he will keep My word; and My Father will love him, and We will come to him and make Our home with him" (John 14:23). "Your kingdom come." What a wonderful petition! And what a wonderful desire is aroused by the petition. A bold prayer is inspired by a desire that is beyond nature. And this prayer is answered. Experiences that serve as evidence show that it has been answered. To what else can we ascribe the great signs accomplished by the saints of God, than that God was present and acted within them? To what else can we ascribe their ability to prophesy, to reveal the secrets within the depths of hearts and minds, than that God—from Whom there are no secrets—was present within them and spoke through them, looking at the distant future as if at the present? The saints themselves bear witness to this. The Apostle Paul wrote of himself to the Galatians: "it is no longer I who live, but Christ lives in me" (Gal 2:20). He wrote to the Corinthians: "you seek a proof of Christ speaking in me" (2 Cor 13:3). When the Apostles Peter and John healed the man who had been lame since birth at the Beautiful Gate of the temple in Jerusalem, and the astonished people crowded around the apostles, they said to them: "Men of Israel, why do you marvel at this? Or why look so intently at us, as though by our own power or godliness we had made this man walk? The God of Abraham, Isaac, and Jacob, the God of our fathers, glorified His Servant Jesus" (Acts 3:12–13). In the book of the Acts of the Apostles, we read of a shocking event. The Christians of Jerusalem, to fulfill the Lord's commandment, were selling their property and contributing the proceeds toward the common use of the Church, in which for this reason there was not a single beggar. A certain Ananias and his wife, Sapphira, did the same, selling an estate that belonged to them, but by mutual agreement they kept a part of the proceeds. Ananias brought the money in the customary way, as if it were the full amount, and laid it at the feet of the apostles, intending to deceive the bearers of the Spirit. Then St Peter said to him: "Ananias, why has Satan filled your heart to lie to the Holy Spirit and keep back part of the price of the land for yourself? While it remained, was it not your own? And after it was sold, was it not in your own control? Why have you conceived this thing in your heart? You have not lied to men but to God." After hearing these words, Ananias fell down dead. The same fate befell Sapphira, who had wanted to support the action of her husband and had taken part in his sin before the Holy Spirit that dwelled within the apostles (Acts 5:1–10). Throughout the centuries of Christianity, experiences have been written in the records of church history that reveal in the saints of God actions that go beyond human nature and belong not to it but to God, who dwells and reigns within holy people. St Macarius of Egypt says: "In those in whom the grace of the Divine Spirit has shone, dwelling within the depths of their minds, the Lord becomes like a soul." And again this great father among Fathers says: "The action and the power of the Holy Spirit are present within a renewed person."[148]

A person who feels the kingdom of God within him becomes a stranger to the world that is hostile to God. This person may wish, in true love for his neighbors, that the kingdom of God also be revealed within each of them. He may blamelessly wish that the visible kingdom of God would begin on earth, that sin be swallowed up from the face of the earth, and that Truth reign. St John the Theologian was in this condition when he appealed in prayer to the Lord, Who was conversing with him in his spiritual rapture and had promised to come soon to settle conclusively the fate of the world: "Surely I am coming quickly" (Rev 22:20): "The earth is filled with iniquities, it has need of purification and renewal." A person who is not adequately prepared and sees the temple of his soul still pitifully empty, uninhabited by God, asks for the opposite. He asks to be given time to complete his ascetic struggle, like the gardener who begged his master after he had ordered him to cut down the barren, strange fig-tree: "Sir, let it alone this year also, until I dig around it"—separating it from the passions that deplete its strength—"and fertilize it" with humility and repentance (Luke 13:8).

"Your will be done on earth as it is heaven." "Heaven" refers to the inhabitants of heaven, who fulfill the will of God perfectly and tirelessly. They do not even mix their own will with that of God. They do not even have a separate will. Their will has become one with that of God. In them is fulfilled what the Saviour of the world asked of God the Father for his disciples and for all His followers: "I do not pray for these"—the disciples—"alone, but also for those who will believe in Me through their word; that they all may be one, as You, Father, are in Me, and I in You; that they also may be one in Us ... that they may be one just as We are one: I in them, and You in Me; that they may be made perfect in one" (John 17:20–23). "Your will be done on earth as it is heaven." The "earth" means Christians. None of us will sin if, uttering this petition, we use the word "earth" to mean our hearts, not separating our bodies from them.[149] The direction taken by the powers of the heart will be followed by the powers of the body, and the urge of the body is transformed, in conformity with the attraction of the heart, from carnal and bestial to spiritual, holy, and angelic. Complete union of the human will with the will of God is a state of perfection that only a reason-endowed creature of God can attain. Angels possess this perfection. Our Saviour wills that we too, weak and unfortunate humans, taken from the earth, wandering on earth for a short time, after which we descend into the earth, attain what the holiest of heavenly spirits possess. He commands us to seek perfection that is still incomprehensible to us. A person who feels within him the kingdom of God learns not to be satisfied with this; he learns not to give in to carelessness and inaction; he learns to strive for abundant development within himself of divine dominion. May the will of God act exclusively within the whole essence of the person, in all his constituent parts, in his spirit, soul and body, uniting through himself and within himself their will that was separate. Only through the will of God can the human will poisoned by sin be healed; only in and by means of the will of God can the desires of a person's constituent parts, that have taken different, opposite directions from each other,[150] pass from difference to agreement, and unite in a single desire; only the human will that is enlivened by the will of God can drag itself up from the earth and be raised to heaven. "Brethren, I do not count myself to have apprehended; but one thing I do, forgetting those things which are behind and reaching forward to those things which are ahead, I press toward the goal for the prize of the upward call of God in Christ Jesus. Therefore let us, as many as are mature, have this mind" (Phil 3:13–15).

"Give us this day our daily bread." It is not of perishable food (John 6:27) that is spoken here. "Therefore do not worry, saying, 'What shall we eat?' or 'What shall we drink?' or 'What shall we wear?'" (Matt 6:31); this means food that gives everlasting life and exists eternally, the new food that the Son of God incarnate gave to men, the bread of life that came down from heaven, the bread of God that can feed and give everlasting life to the whole world. The word "daily"[151] means that this bread is superior in quality to everything that exists.[152] Its greatness and its holiness are boundless and incomprehensible; the sanctification and the benefit acquired by tasting it are unfathomable and inexplicable. The bread that is given by the Son of God is His most holy flesh, that He gave "for the life of the world" (John 6:51). The wondrous food is united with an equally wondrous drink. Just as the flesh of the God-Man is given as food to believers, His blood is given as drink. The God-Man was no different from other people, while being a perfect man; but He was at the same time perfect God: in appearance everyone saw and felt Him to be a human being, but in His actions they recognized God. In a similar way, He willed to cover His most holy Body and His most holy Blood with material bread and wine: they look and taste like bread and wine, but in them we take and eat the Body and Blood of the Lord. There are no words, no means by which to express the state into which communicants in the Body and Blood of the God-Man are brought. He Himself represented their state in this way: "He who eats My flesh and drinks My blood abides in Me, and I in him" (John 6:56). The state depicted and explained by these words is incomprehensible and inexplicable: they express heights that are unattainable for the human mind and are known only to God: "no one knows who the Son is except the Father" (Luke 10:22), and whoever is united with the Son. These heights are completely unfathomable both to this person's neighbors and to himself, and can be comprehended only by God.

It was due to its virtue and its action that the Lord called His flesh the only true food, and His Blood the only true drink for man renewed through redemption (John 6:55). The normal food of the sons of the old Adam, common to them and to dumb animals, that needs to be digested and cannot eradicate death, is "food which perishes" (John 6:27), and was not worthy of being called food, when the "daily bread," the "bread of heaven," the bread that abolishes death, that gives everlasting life (John 6:58), had appeared. "Give us day by day our daily bread"—this is how the Evangelist Luke writes the petition (Luke 11:3). Implied within this petition is a command that places upon Christians an obligation, so often neglected now, to receive the holy Mysteries daily. "By saying 'day by day,' the Lord was indicating that without this bread we are unable to pass a single day of spiritual life. And by saying 'this day,' He meant that it must be eaten every day, and that it is not enough to have been given it on the previous day if it is not given to us again today. Our daily need for it demands that we make this petition more frequently, and offer it at any time: there is no day on which it is not essential for us to make firm the heart of our internal man by partaking in the daily bread."[153]

"And forgive us our debts, as we forgive our debtors." Having given sinners, in His boundless mercy, the most sublime, priceless good things, the Lord demands of us mercy toward our neighbors. The mystery of redemption is based on mercy. The redemption is the appearance of the mercy of God toward fallen mankind, and can be accepted only with a disposition of soul that is entirely inclined toward mercy to fallen mankind. We cannot accept the redemption given to us by God without being merciful toward ourselves and toward other people, without acknowledging our sinfulness, our fallenness, our perdition—without acknowledging the sinfulness, fallenness and perdition of all humanity—and our shared unqualified need for the mercy of God. We need to forgive our neighbors their sins toward us, their debts: if we do not do this, we will never acquire a disposition that is capable of accepting redemption. Hardening of the heart is like firmly locked iron gates. It will not allow the divine gift to enter our hearts. To explain this characteristic of redemption and the reason for the condition implicit in the petition, the Lord says: "For if you forgive men their trespasses, your heavenly Father will also forgive you. But if you do not forgive men their trespasses, neither will your Father forgive your trespasses" (Matt 6:14–15). A Christian should pay particular attention to the ailment of the soul that is resentment, and evict it when it first appears, not allowing it to take root under any pretext, however justified the pretext may initially appear. If we allow resentment to act, it will devastate our soul, make all our efforts and virtues fruitless, and deprive us of the mercy of God. Forgiving the trespasses of our neighbors is a sign that the Spirit of God has entered us, reigns within us, and governs and controls our will. Until this happens, we need to exert particular effort to fight the passion of resentment. God will help us secretly in our struggle against this passion, not helping us openly so that our intention may be clearly expressed. Resentment is based on pride. Pride is hidden even within those blessed with grace and chosen by God.[154] It is essential even for them to keep watch against this internal poison and against the destruction of the soul that is born from it. By forgiving our brothers their debts, we attract the grace of God upon ourselves: let us keep it within us by always forgiving our neighbors their debts.

"And do not lead us into temptation, but deliver us from the evil one." Let us explain the second half of the petition first. What is meant by temptations here is those truly unfortunate instances and adversities when from our own willful striving toward sin we surrender ourselves to the power of the devil, and are ruined, as happened to Judas Iscariot. "Satan entered him," the Scripture says of him (John 13:27). The above petition is not teaching us to reject tribulations that are necessary for our salvation and that protect us from our passions and demons.[155] "I take pleasure," says the apostle of the great tribulations he underwent, "in infirmities, in reproaches, in needs, in persecutions, in distresses, for Christ's sake. For when I am weak, then I am strong" (2 Cor 12:12). Divine providence permitted these tribulations to the apostle, as he himself explains, so as to protect him from being "exalted above measure" (2 Cor 12:7). Tribulations are a gift from God to His followers for the whole time of their wandering on earth. "In the world you will have tribulation" (John 16:33), He said to the apostles, and with them to all Christians: "If you were of the world, the world would love its own. Yet because you are not of the world, but I chose you out of the world, therefore the world hates you" (John 15:19). "And you will be hated by all for My name's sake. By your patience possess your souls" (Luke 21:17,19). Together with the dogmas of the Christian faith, the holy Apostle Paul preached to the world that "we must through many tribulations enter the kingdom of God" (Acts 14:22). In his epistle to the Hebrews, the apostle says that all those who please God have undergone punishment and lessons from the Lord, while those who have not undergone them will be rejected by God as if foreign to Him (Heb 12:8).

"Do not lead us into temptation, but deliver us from the evil one." In other words, not only do not allow the passions—through which we submit to the devil—to possess us, but deliver us from the captivity with the devil in which we find ourselves because of our fallenness. Do not allow us to be carried away by our sinful will, through which we deceive and destroy ourselves. Do not allow us to be misled by false thoughts and teachings. Do not allow us to be vanquished by love of money, ambition, or lust for power. Do not allow us to become enslaved by sensuality or gluttony at times when we abound in earthly good things, or by pusillanimity and grumbling when we are surrounded by deprivations. Do not allow us to sin. Do not allow us to be seized with pride when we are leading a virtuous life, or to be swallowed up by hopelessness and despair in the face of stumbling-blocks.

The beginning of the Lord's Prayer, which permits mankind to address God as a father, explains the reason for the exalted petitions that constitute the prayer. A son may ask of the father anything that he possesses. And we, in the Lord's Prayer, ask God to grant us Himself as our inalienable property, to dwell within us, to establish His kingdom within us, so that we, through this, may reside within Him, and reign through Him over all. The end of the Lord's Prayer corresponds to the beginning. The immensity of what is asked in the petitions is founded upon the boundless goodness of God toward mankind. Our conviction that the petitions will be heard and answered establishes the omnipotence of God. "For Thine is the kingdom and the power and the glory forever. Amen." The Lord's Prayer is sealed with these words of faith. They recognize and confess one essential, all-embracing power: the power of God. By confessing this, a Christian makes himself free, as the Lord proclaimed to the blind Pilate who was boasting of his power over Him: "You could have no power at all over Me unless it had been given you from above" (John 19:11). Spiritual freedom is the property of the perfect Christian. The apostle says of this freedom: "where the Spirit of the Lord is, there is liberty" (2 Cor 3:17).[156] When the omnipotence of God is revealed before the eyes of a mind that has been cleansed through repentance and enlightened through grace, then the power both of angels and of men descends into insignificance (Rom 8:35–39); then a person who believes and prays confesses the great truth "for" to the one God belongs "the kingdom and the power and the glory forever."

The Lord's Prayer does not eliminate the need for prolonged time spent in prayer. An example of prolonged and, indeed, nighttime prayer, so necessary and useful to us, is set by the Lord Himself (Luke 11:1; 9:18; 6:12). The Lord's Prayer does not make other prayers accepted and appointed by the holy Church unnecessary or superfluous: it constitutes their essence; it serves as a rule for them, it teaches us that in our other prayers we must also ask God only for spiritual good things. All prayers written by the holy Fathers, used in the holy Church, satisfy this holy requirement: the source of them all is the Holy Spirit, Who speaks abundantly in the Lord's Prayer. It is not pleasing to our Redeemer, Who redeemed us with the price of His priceless Blood unto blessed eternity, that we trouble Him about something perishable and temporary.[157] If necessity forces us to approach the greatness of God with a request relating to our temporal need, then we do this cautiously and reverently, without passion or excitement, not in complicated words but in a few humble words, finishing the prayer by offering ourselves and our petition to the will of God. We must not be verbose and oratorical in prayer; we must not ask for the earthly good things and privileges that are the only things filling the prayers of heathens and of carnal people who resemble heathens, and are concerned only with the worldly and the transient, forgetting any care for the eternal. "When you pray, do not use vain repetitions as the heathen do," the Lord commanded us, when he instituted and gave us the Lord's Prayer: "For they think that they will be heard for their many words. Therefore do not be like them. For your Father knows the things you have need of before you ask Him" (Matt 6:7–8). "Seek first the kingdom of God and His righteousness," that divine righteousness that enters into this kingdom, "and all these things"—all the necessities of earthly life—"shall be added to you" (Matt 6:33). Amen.

36. On Love for God

Sermon on the Twenty-fifth Sunday after Pentecost

"You shall love the Lord your God with all your heart, with all your soul, with all your strength, and with all your mind" (Luke 10:27).

Dear brothers! It is characteristic of love to remember and think about one's beloved; it is characteristic of love to direct one's heart and soul often toward the beloved. It is characteristic of perfect love to remember and to think about the beloved person constantly, and to be constantly attracted to this person. God wants us to love Him with such perfect love as this. This is natural. God is perfect, and he should be loved with a perfect love.

When we consider ourselves dispassionately, we do not find such love for God, or even the capacity for it, within ourselves. What does this mean? It means that our capacity for love, like other capabilities, has been damaged by the fall into sin. And it means that we must cultivate love for God within ourselves, to the extent that the commandment of God demands it of us.

The holy Apostle Paul says that the love of God has been poured out in our hearts by the Holy Spirit (Rom 5:5). The apostle says this of perfect love. Exactly the same thing must also be said of the other virtues. Faith, humility, meekness, patience, and courage can only reach perfection within us when our hearts are renewed by the Holy Spirit. We show our desire to acquire virtues by cultivating them as far as possible and by praying fervently to receive them.[158]

The means of cultivating love for God is demonstrated within the very commandment about it: "You shall love the Lord your God with all your heart, with all your soul, with all your strength, and with all your mind."

It is obvious that in order to direct our heart, soul, and mind toward God, we must first of all abandon a sinful way of life. "Shun evil," the Holy Spirit teaches each one of us, "and do good" (Ps 33:15); turn away from evil, and only then will you become capable of cultivating virtues within you. It is impossible to serve both God and sin. A person who serves sin takes upon himself the poison of sin that impregnates and defiles him. For this reason, he cannot be adopted by God. If a pure heart is necessary in order to see God (Matt 5:8), how much more necessary it is in order to be united with Him. Divine love, in accordance with the goodwill of the good God, unites man, His reason-endowed creation, with Him, and "he who is joined to the Lord is one spirit with Him" (1 Cor 6:17).

To serve God coldly and superficially, while at the same time serving the passions, to confess God only with one's lips, and not through one's actions and through the inner life of one's heart, merely performing certain external rituals and following certain ecclesiastical rules, is recognized to be empty, soul-destroying hypocrisy. The Saviour of the world rebuked as "hypocrites" those who neglected the commandments of God and instead preferred to keep the traditions of their forefathers with meticulous exactness: "Hypocrites! Well did Isaiah prophesy about you, saying: 'These people draw near to Me with their mouth, and honor Me with their lips, but their heart is far from Me. And in vain they worship Me, teaching as doctrines the commandments of men,'" (Matt 15:7–9). The regulations of the church are very useful and necessary, both for each individual Christian and for Christian society, because they provide order and rules of behavior. Order and rules contribute to a devout way of life. But the commandments must form the very soul of every Christian and every Christian society. The Saviour of the world attributed due importance and value both to the traditions of the forefathers and to the commandments of God. "These"—that is, the traditions of the Fathers, "you ought to have done", He said, "without leaving the others"—that is, the commandments of God—"undone" (Matt 23:23). When a person keeps the regulations of the holy Church it becomes easy for him to keep the commandments, and a life led in accordance with the commandments protects the exact observation of ecclesiastical regulations from vainglory, hypocrisy, and a carnal mind. The law of God is "spiritual" (Rom 7:14); the commandments of the Gospel "are spirit, and they are life" (John 6:63). But because humans consist of both soul and body, external rites and regulations proved necessary. They are combined with the spirit of the Law. A person who is content with keeping only the regulations and rituals of the church, and who pays little or no attention to the commandments of the Gospel, brings the Law down from the heights of spiritual meaning and removes from it the spiritual benefit it gives him, all its essence, and perishes in and because of his own carnal mind (Rom 8:6).

"You shall love the Lord your God with all your heart [and] with all your soul." We must direct our whole will toward God. Just as we take care to fulfill the wishes of the people we love, and therefore try to find out their wishes and to learn their inclinations, so we must also act in relation to God. We must take pains to familiarize ourselves thoroughly with the will of God. This will has been revealed to us in the law of God, which is the Gospel. "Blessed is the man," says the Prophet, "that hath not walked in the counsel of the ungodly, nor stood in the way of sinners, and hath not sat in the seat of the scornful. But his delight is in the Law of the Lord, and in His Law will he exercise himself day and night" (Ps 1:1–2). "And do not be conformed to this world," instructs the apostle, "but be transformed by the renewing of your mind, that you may prove what is that good and acceptable and perfect will of God" (Rom 12:2). Having found out the will of God, we must fulfill it, because that is what love demands. Love is not content to find out the will of those it loves: it longs to fulfill it. In order to fulfill the will of the beloved, it devotes itself to finding it out; after finding it out, it devotes itself to fulfilling it. Learning and fulfilling the will of God is recognized by God Himself as a true sign of love for God. "He who has My commandments and keeps them, it is he who loves Me. ... If anyone loves Me, he will keep My word. ... He who does not love Me does not keep My words" (John 14:21, 23–24).

"You shall love the Lord your God with all your heart"—this is not enough: "You shall love the Lord your God with all your soul." Eradicate all division within yourself. Let your whole inner being be united and focused completely toward God. Preserve this focus from hypocrisy and hesitation; keep it from being distracted by any predilection, however insignificant it may seem. Just one insignificant predilection can keep a Christian shackled to the earth, and take from him any spiritual progress. Oh, how feeble we are! How our fall has perverted and blinded us! We see that all our brothers, one by one, each in his turn, are called to eternity by God's command, which can be neither resisted nor opposed. When they leave the earth, this lodging-place, this prison, this place of exile, they all inevitably leave behind everything that belongs to the earth. We see this; we know for sure that our turn will also come; but we spend our life as if we had never seen people dying, and had never heard of the existence of death; as if we, unlike others, were destined to remain on earth forever. We bind ourselves to countless attachment; our love is wasted on many different objects, but we neither concern ourselves with nor even think about attaining love toward God, and being adopted by Him. What terrible self-deception! When we leave here with our souls bare and enter the other world, then our only hope, our only consolation can be that we have been adopted by God in the course of our earthly lives. If we attain this adoption here, we will take it there with us. There it will serve as a pledge for us, a reason to receive eternal, ineffable good things. What does God not grant to those who have made themselves His own? What can He give to those who, not hearing the call of His voice, have willfully alienated themselves from Him, have made themselves incapable of being in His presence, incapable of receiving His precious and eternal gifts? Eternal blessedness is spiritual, divine. This blessedness can only be inherited by someone who has previously broken off his relationship with sin, and has entered holy intercourse with God. Conversely, a person who has acquired a hostile disposition toward God and all that is pleasing to Him must by necessity be rejected from before the face of God, and cast down to the place where all enemies of God are sent.

"You shall love the Lord your God with all your strength." Not only should all the efforts of our souls be directed toward God: our very bodies should participate in this endeavor. The body is capable of this. The desire for God was originally natural to our bodies, which were created with it. This desire for God is spiritual and holy: the body was also spiritual and holy. Because of the fall, it was infected not only with corpulence and corruption but also with animal desires. The Redeemer restored to it the capacity for spiritual desire, and His true followers have made use of this gift by banishing passionate desires from their bodies and attaining holy desire. Divine love is intrinsic to our bodies. After they have been freed from the ailment of sinfulness that is unnatural and hostile to them, even while wandering on earth they are already drawn continually to God, in accordance with their nature and with the action of the Holy Spirit upon purified nature; they are drawn to God with all their strength, uniting their strength with that of the soul. At the general resurrection, the sanctified bodies, receiving within them the sanctified souls, will be caught up through the power of divine love and of the Holy Spirit to the dwelling-places of paradise (1 Thess 4:17); they will be caught up to heaven, where our Lord Jesus Christ went up with His holy flesh as a forerunner to humans. The apostle says, "I beseech you therefore, brethren, by the mercies of God, that you present your bodies a living sacrifice, holy, acceptable to God" (Rom 12:1). "For this corruptible" body "must put on incorruption, and this mortal must put on immortality" (1 Cor 15:53). "It is sown a natural body, it is raised a spiritual body" (1 Cor 15:44).

"You shall love the Lord your God with all your mind." This last part of the commandment is kept through constant remembrance of God. Constant remembrance of God seems impossible for minds that are unfamiliar with true service of God, and forcing ourselves to remember God in this way seems to be a heavy burden, an intolerable effort. But the Gospel commandment says "Love the Lord God" with all your thoughts, "with all your mind" (Mark 12:30; Matt 22:37); it commands us to keep our minds continually directed toward God, and to keep the thought of God constantly present in them. The "commandments" of God "are not burdensome," as that zealous keeper of the commandments, the beloved disciple of the Lord, bears witness (1 John 5:3). If the commandments of God are not burdensome, then the commandment telling the servant of God to be inseparably with God in mind and thought is not burdensome either. It seems burdensome only because we do not have the habit of it, or the slightest experience of it. It is not burdensome: it is longed for. "I foresaw the Lord always before me, for He is on my right hand, that I should not be moved" (Ps 15:8), says the Prophet. To possess living and constant remembrance of God is to see God. When God is forgotten by a person, it is as if He does not exist for that person and is hidden from him. When He is constantly remembered, it is as if He has come to life, appears, and becomes "present everywhere" and almighty, accompanying the person. The soul changes when a spiritual feeling is revealed within it, through which the presence of God is felt, and the invisible is made visible. The soul is clothed in unassailable spiritual weapons, in unwavering courage, in faith, in endurance, in tireless vigil. The life of the person begins to pass before the gaze of the unsleeping eye of God that steadily watches and sees everything we do and everything that befalls us. By living and acting before the eyes of God, the person is particularly well protected from sins, and applies himself with particular zeal to keeping God's commandments; he regards ephemeral, transient blessings coolly, he endures the vicissitudes of earthly life easily. When the time comes for his soul to be parted from his body and enter eternity, there appears to him a consciousness filled with joy and consolation that his earthly life has passed not in oblivion, nor in self-deception and attachment to vanity and sins, nor in forgetfulness of God, but in constant remembrance of Him, and in fulfillment of His most holy will, under His holy guidance.

The beginning of constant remembrance of God consists in close study of His law, and attentive reading of the Gospel, the whole New Testament, and the holy Fathers of the Orthodox Church. It is impossible not to remember frequently within the course of a day something to which one has paid especial attention for an hour. Fulfillment of the commandments of the Gospel constitutes remembrance of God in itself. The spiritual consolation and enlightenment that result from keeping the commandments stimulate and warm the heart toward profound remembrance of God. A life that is completely dedicated to keeping the commandments consists of constant remembrance of God. One very important aid to unceasing remembrance of God is faithfully to keep our personal prayer rule in our cell and to participate in communal worship in church as often as possible. The time of prayer is intrinsically a time of special remembrance of God, of union with Him. The prayerful disposition a person receives in church and when following his personal prayer rule continues to accompany him and to act within him during all his activities, bringing the mind and the heart to remembrance of God. Finally, another excellent means of remembering God is to turn to Him in prayer before any undertaking, and to ask for His blessing, His edification, His help, and His mercy. The Lord Himself asked this mental effort of us when He told His disciples: "Without Me you can do nothing" (John 15:5). The greatest saints of God would call on the Lord for help before every action, before every conversation, and passed on this very important, holy, powerful, though invisible practice as a precious treasure to their disciples and to all Christians. When we are alone, we can call upon God both in mind and aloud; when we are with our neighbors, we must communicate with God in mind only. "There is nothing quicker than the mind," says St Barsanuphius the Great: "raise it up to God"[159] every time you are in need. Experience will quickly show a watchful struggler how important this effort is, and how close God is to us, how He continually takes care of us, and how true and almighty is He Who said: "Because he hath set his hope upon Me, therefore will I deliver him; I will shelter him, because he hath known My name. He shall call upon Me, and I will hear him" (Ps 90:14–15).

These are the blessed actions that cultivate love for God. In the writings of the holy fathers[160] we find the teaching, based on Holy Scripture (1 John 2–5), that love for God is acquired through love for the image of God: for human beings. What a blessed teaching! And what a true teaching! This teaching is one and the same as the teaching that love for God is acquired by keeping the commandments of the Gospel: because true love for our neighbor consists in keeping these commandments in respect to him, and not at all in satisfying his whims, or in actions toward him that follow the urges of the fallen heart, and the considerations and understanding of false reason. For the most part, keeping the commandments of the Gospel with regard to other people is incomprehensible and unpleasant for them. They seek and demand that their will be done and their passions be satisfied. This is what they call love, and this is the love, filled with hypocrisy, slyness, and deceptiveness, that the sons of the world bring to those who require it in the form of earthly, material success. Scripture calls this false love, this distortion of love, this hatred concealed with a mask of love, "pleasing men." To please men is to destroy not only love for God but even remembrance of God. "God hath scattered the bones of the man-pleasers" (Ps 52:6)—all the power of the soul, without which no virtue can be steadfast. "For if I still pleased men, I would not be a bondservant of Christ" (Gal 1:10), says the apostle.

We see the level of our love for God with particular clarity in prayer, which serves as an expression of this love and in patristic writings is rightly called the mirror of spiritual progress.[161] When we are subject to constant distraction in prayer, this is a sign that our heart is in captivity to earthly passions and cares that do not allow it to be directed wholly toward God, and to remain close to Him. Attentive prayer serves as a sign that the heart has broken off the threads of the passions, and therefore is turning freely toward God, becoming attached to Him, and being adopted by Him. To progress from distracted prayer to attentive prayer, or from love for the world to love for God, takes much time, much labor, much effort, and much assistance. It requires the help of fasting, of chastity and purity, of voluntary poverty, of faith, of humility, of mercy, of divine grace. It is with the combined action of all these forms of help that the heart breaks away from love for the world, and a person who is released from the invisible chains of the fall and of sin focuses all his being toward God. Having come to know the heights and the blessedness of this state, he seeks to attain it more often. The love of God demonstrates to him through experience its presence within him, and he shows his love toward God with constant attentive prayer that is not interrupted by thoughts of the objects and affairs of the transient world. The first spiritual manifestation of love for God is revealed in the sensation of the fear of God, which in Holy Scripture is called "the beginning of wisdom" (Prov 1:7). What is the wisdom of God, if not divine love? It is natural for the fear of God to be the beginning of love and the first fruit of attentive prayer. What other feeling could a person burdened with countless sins and infirmities have, when he feels that he is in the presence of God and stands before Him face to face, if not a feeling of fear and of the deepest reverence? If we were invited to the palace of an earthly king, showing us special favor, the first feeling to overcome us in his presence would be one of fear. This would be inspired both by the greatness of the royal rank and the splendor of the surroundings, and by the negligibility of our significance before the king. Gradually, through the graciousness of our reception, the fear would begin to lessen, giving way to feelings of pleasure and love. This is what happens in our relationship with God. When a blessed purity appears in a soul that sees God, the soul is initially overcome with fear. The fear of God, which is an action of divine grace, possesses its own particular spiritual sweetness. In the process of gradual adoption by God, this sweetness increases, and is eventually transformed into love, which is the most abundant action of that same divine grace. When a person makes all the effort he can, this is crowned with a gift from God. If he does not first labor, by way of proof of his good intentions, the gift is not sent down from on high. If no gift is sent down, the labor is in vain: it is stolen and damaged either because it has been done carelessly and hypocritically, or because vainglory and man-pleasing have contaminated it.

May the ineffable mercy of God grant us to act in the right, God-pleasing way to attain divine love, and may it crown us with the gift of love in return for sincere desire for it and the proper pursuit of it. Love for anything that the transient world presents as an object of love must without fail be broken off, in accordance with the will of God, which determines that we must in due course be separated from these objects. A person who has acquired love toward God has acquired God, Who, when He makes Himself the object of love and the inheritance of a person here on earth, remains with that person unto eternity. Amen.

37. On Love for One's Neighbor

Second Sermon on the Twenty-fifth Sunday after Pentecost

"You shall love ... your neighbor as yourself" (Luke 10:27).

Dear brothers! This is the commandment of our Lord God that today's Gospel proclaims to us. The Gospel adds that the whole of divine law comprises love for God and love for our neighbor, because love is the virtue that constitutes the fullness of all the other virtues. "Love ... is the bond of perfection" (Col 3:14), according to the apostle's definition.

It is obvious that in order to love our neighbor as ourselves, we must first of all love ourselves, and do so in the right way.

Do we love ourselves? Disregarding the strangeness of this question, which is new and intriguing only from the excessiveness in it, it must be said that it is very rare for a person to love himself. The majority of people hate themselves and seek to do as much harm to themselves as possible. If one were to measure the harm done to a person throughout his life, one would find that his worst enemy had not done him as much harm as he had done himself. Each one of you, if you examine your conscience dispassionately, will find this to be a justified observation. But what is the reason for this? What causes us to harm ourselves almost continually, while constantly and insatiably desiring good for ourselves? The reason is that we have replaced true love for ourselves with self-love, which inspires us to strive for indiscriminate fulfillment of our desires, of our fallen will, guided by false reason and an evil conscience (Heb 10:22).[162] We are carried away by greed, by ambition, by vengefulness, by resentment, and by all sinful whims. We flatter and delude ourselves, thinking that we are satisfying true love for ourselves, whereas in fact we are satisfying only our insatiable self-love. In striving to satisfy our self-love, we harm and destroy ourselves.

True love for ourselves consists in keeping the life-creating commandments of Christ: "This is love, that we walk according to His commandments"

(2 John 1:6), says St John the Theologian. If you do not get angry and do not harbor resentment, you love yourself. If you do not curse and you do not lie, you love yourself. If you do not offend others, you do not steal, and you do not seek revenge, if you are patient with your neighbor, gentle and forgiving, you love yourself. If you bless those who curse you, do good to those who hate you, pray for those who cause you misfortunes and persecute you, you love yourself, for you are a child of the Heavenly Father, Whose sun shines on the evil and the good, Who sends down His rain on the just and on the unjust. If you offer to God painstaking and heartfelt prayers from a broken and humbled heart, you love yourself. If you are temperate, not vainglorious, and sober, you love yourself. If you transfer your property from earth to Heaven by giving alms to your destitute brethren, and making your perishable property imperishable, and your ephemeral property eternal and inalienable, you love yourself. If you are merciful to the extent that you sympathize with all the infirmities and deficiencies of your neighbor, and refrain from judging and humiliating him, you love yourself. When you forbid yourself from judging and condemning your neighbor, which you in any case have no right to do, the righteous and merciful God removes the just judgment and revokes the just condemnation that you deserved from your many sins. A person who wants to love himself in the right way, not to flatter himself or be carried away by self-love, that is, by his fallen will, guided by false reason, must carefully study the commandments of the Gospel, which comprise spiritual reason, and lead someone who keeps them to feel like a new person. While and after studying the Gospel commandments, it is essential to monitor the desires and urges of our hearts with great vigilance and sobriety. With strict vigilance it becomes possible for us to analyze these desires and urges. From habit and from the fear of God, this analysis becomes a natural exercise. We must reject not only every desire and urge that is clearly against the commandments of the Gospel, but all desires and urges that disturb the peace of the heart. Everything that flows from divine will is accompanied by a holy peace, as the holy Fathers teach from their own experience; conversely, everything that is accompanied by agitation has its origin in sin, however good it may seem to be in outward appearance.[163]

A person who has learned to love himself in the right way can love his neighbor in a way that pleases God. The children of the world, who suffer from and are enslaved by self-love, express love for their neighbor by fulfilling all his desires indiscriminately. Disciples of the Gospel express love for their neighbor by fulfilling the relevant holy commandments of the Lord with regard to him; they recognize that satisfying human desires and whims is soul-destroying people-pleasing, and they fear it as much as they fear and avoid self-love. Self-love is a distortion of love in relation to oneself, and man-pleasing is a distortion of love in relation to one's neighbor. A person who loves himself destroys himself, and a man-pleaser destroys both himself and his neighbor. Self-love is pitiful self-deception; people-pleasing attempts to make the neighbor an accomplice in this self-deception.

Do not think, brothers, that love acquires from self-denial a severity that is uncharacteristic of it, or that keeping the commandments of the Gospel exactly causes it to lose its warmth or become cold and mechanical. No! The Gospel commandments drive out from the heart the carnal fire, which is extinguished very quickly in the face of any resistance, sometimes the very least; but they kindle a spiritual fire that cannot be extinguished by human misdeeds or even by the powers of the fallen angels (Rom 8:38). The holy Protomartyr Stephen burned with this blessed fire. Cast out of the city by his murderers, stoned by them, he prayed. There followed deadly blows, and from their ferocity Stephen fell half-dead onto his knees, but at the moment of his separation from life, the fire of love for his neighbor burned even brighter within him, and he cried out "with a loud voice," saying of his murderers, "'Lord, do not charge them with this sin'" (Acts 7:60). With these words the protomartyr gave up his spirit to the Lord. The last impulse of his heart was one of love for his neighbors; his last words and his last act were a prayer for his murderers.

The invisible struggle against self-love and people-pleasing initially entails hard work and intensive effort. Our hearts, as the hearts of our forefathers have done ever since our progenitor fell into sin, "always resist the Holy Spirit" (Acts 7:51). They do not admit that they have fallen, they bitterly defend their wretched state as if it were one of complete satisfaction, complete triumph. But for every victory over self-love and people-pleasing, the heart is rewarded with spiritual consolation; after tasting this consolation, it enters the battle with greater courage and more easily gains victories over itself and its inner fallenness. More frequent victories attract more frequent visitation and consolation by grace; then the person begins to trample with zeal upon self-pleasing and self-will, striving from the path of the commandments for the perfection of the Gospel, confessing and silently crying out to the Lord: "I ran the way of Thy commandments, when Thou didst enlarge my heart" (Ps 118:32).

Brothers! Let us courageously enter the fight against self-love under the guidance of the Gospel, which represents the good, acceptable and perfect will of God (Rom 12:2), and in which the new Adam, Christ, mystically abides, and imparts affinity with Himself to all His children who truly desire it. Let us learn to love ourselves in the right, holy way: then we will be able to keep, in relation to our neighbor, the most holy commandment of our great God: "You shall love your neighbor as yourself". Amen.

38. On Covetousness

Sermon on the Twenty-sixth Sunday after Pentecost

Dear brothers! One day, during the time when our Lord Jesus Christ was wandering on the earth, a certain unknown man brought Him a complaint against his brother regarding a disagreement between them about the distribution of their inheritance. The kingdom of the Lord, however, "is not of this world" (John 18:36). The Lord answered the man who had asked for His judgment on an earthly matter with gentleness and humility: "Man, who made Me a judge or an arbitrator over you?" (Luke 12:14). It was not for the sake of earthly matters that God the Word incarnate was sent down to earth. So, guiding the contending brothers to the right attitude to themselves, to earthly life and to its blessings, the Lord added, "Take heed and beware of covetousness, for one's life does not consist in the abundance of the things he possesses" (Luke 12:15), that is, the length of one's life on earth does not depend on one's property. The passion of covetousness is evil. The Lord commands us to be vigilant against it, so that it may not steal imperceptibly into our souls. The passion of covetousness is destructive. The Lord commands us to beware of it. This passion, striving to find itself a way into the soul, usually sets before a person the image of a long life, a painful old age, and various vicissitudes and chances that could befall him, against which accumulated property is presented as the only remedy. The Lord, in order to strike the passion of covetousness at its very inception, in the underlying thoughts on which it relies and is based, shows that these thoughts are wholly wrong and false, and that the length of a person's earthly life, with its vicissitudes, has no connection with excess property that he has accumulated. A long life and happiness spring not from abundant property, but from the blessing of God. When the mercy of God departs from a person, irresistible and terrible misfortunes approach him, and strike him in all his abundance and all his power. Wealth looks with coldness upon its supposed possessor when the hands of God chastise him, and it responds without sympathy to the final anguished looks that he throws as he is parted against his will from his perishable property.

In the parable He told the two brothers after warning them to beware of covetousness, the Lord presents vividly the falsity of the thoughts and dreams that delude a person when he clings to wealth with all his soul and places his hope in it. "The ground of a certain rich man yielded plentifully"—the parable begins—"and he thought within himself." The rich man's first reaction to an abundant harvest was that he applied himself to special reflection. This almost always happens with people who become rich unexpectedly, or who suddenly receive a substantial increase in their wealth. Reflecting to himself, the rich man said, "What shall I do?" St Theophylact of Ochrid and Bulgaria rightly observes that excessive wealth is similar to poverty. A person possessing either the one or the other, being in a difficult situation, cries out: "What shall I do?" The reason for the difficulty in the case of poverty is insufficient means to meet physical needs, and in the case of wealth, an excess of means. "What shall I do," the rich man asks himself, "since I have no room to store my crops?" ("I have nowhere to put the riches I have acquired.") Eventually, he devised a solution, and, as if rejoicing in his resourcefulness, he said joyfully and decisively, "I will do this: I will pull down my barns and build greater, and there I will store all my crops and my goods. And I will say to my soul, 'Soul, you have many goods laid up for many years; take your ease; eat, drink, and be merry.'" The spiritually blind rich man did not think of God, of eternity, of his destitute brothers: he thought only of himself, and he thought in a way that was disastrous for him, because he forgot the purpose of his soul and condemned it, in his dreaming, to certain subjugation to the body. He did not think of God, Who, being his Benefactor, was calling upon him, in his turn, to offer good works. He did not think of eternity where it is essential to send a portion of one's property in advance, in the form of almsgiving, so as not to end up in poverty there, unworthy of the heavenly mansion. With what a false dream the rich man deluded himself! He said that his property was enough for a long time, meaning by this that his life would continue at least for that long, or even longer. He based his arrangements on this vain, shaky dream. This state of self-delusion is common to all who love wealth and who love the world. Their earthly life seems eternal to them. The thought of death is completely alien to them, like the thought of an event that could never have any connection to them. What are the assumptions that the blinded rich man bases on his enrichment? As people say in the world, he "wants to live well." What does "living well" mean in this context? It means eating and drinking well and in large quantities, giving oneself over to amusements and entertainments, committing adultery, living in luxury, being vainglorious, and satisfying all one's lusts and whims. If we look carefully at the world, we will find that the Gospel parable of the rich man can serve as a mirror for us all: we are not all constantly captivated by the dreams of the rich man, but we are all occasionally carried away by them to a greater or lesser extent.

While the rich man was dreaming with delight of the sinful life that he believed lay before him, the judgment of God was suddenly uttered against him: "Fool! This night your soul will be required of you; then whose will those things be which you have provided?" What happened to the rich man happens to everyone who forgets God and gives himself up wholly to serving sin. At the point when such a person reaches the pinnacle of his desires and is arranging his situation in the best way, God sends death, or permits some other vicissitude, and even the most stable earthly prosperity falls apart. The Lord also expressed this in the words with which He concluded the parable: "So is he who lays up treasure for himself, and is not rich toward God." Such is the fruit of the love of money, covetousness and in general of intensive striving to acquire property, under the exclusive influence of self-love. The Lord called the self-loving rich man a "fool," because this man, blinded by self-love, acting in self-delusion as if only for his own benefit, in fact acted against himself, lowering himself from the great dignity of a person created for eternity, who ought to act on earth in preparation for heaven, and always to prioritize the mastery of the soul over the body. To become rich in God means to live a God-pleasing life. Activity on earth that is guided by the commandments of the Gospel acquires incorruptible riches for the soul: knowledge of God and of oneself, faith, humble-mindedness, love for God and for one's neighbor. Such activity manages earthly property in the right way, as a gift from God, and thus transforms corruptible property into incorruptible, and a person's treasures are transferred from earth to heaven. By transferring his perishable property to heaven, through almsgiving, a Christian imperceptibly transfers his heart to heaven, as the Lord Himself bears witness: "For where your treasure is, there your heart will be also" (Luke 12:34). Such a Christian will dwell in heaven in his thoughts, in his attractions, in his feelings, just as the Apostle, who proclaimed of himself while he still lived on earth: "our citizenship is in heaven" (Phil 3:20) dwelt there. Amen.

39. On the Kingdom of God

Sermon on the Monday of the Twenty-sixth Week

Certain carnal people, who were tethered with all their souls to earthly life, who knew the law of God superficially, to the letter (2 Cor 3:6), as they were taught at school, who were alien to the law of God in spirit, in their hearts, in life, in their affairs—in a word, the pharisees—asked the Lord "when the kingdom of God would come" (Luke 17:20). Of course, the question was not asked with sincerity of heart, or for a good purpose: it was asked flippantly, out of curiosity, to see what answer He would give. The cunning and wicked pharisees hoped that the Lord would give them a pretext to accuse Him easily. Having created for themselves an understanding of the Messiah as a magnificent king and a great conqueror, when they saw Him in the form of a poor wanderer, with nowhere to lay His head, the pharisees put the question, concealing their mockery with it, and expressed through it their carnal mind, alien and hostile to the reason of God (Rom 8:7).

The Lord gave an answer that suits everyone, including carnal people who are tethered to the earth and who lead a sinful life amidst constant worldly cares and material enjoyment. The God-Man gave this answer to the pharisees: "The kingdom of God does not come with observation," that is, the kingdom of God will not come in a way that our physical eyes can perceive, "nor will they say, 'See here!' or 'See there!' For indeed, the kingdom of God is within you" (Luke 17:20–21). This means that it is necessary to abandon a carnal and sinful way of life, and then, through repentance and by living in accordance with the commandments of the Gospel, to purify and adorn the temple of one's soul; when this has been accomplished, the Holy Spirit will visit it and complete the final cleansing and furnishing. God descends into such a temple, and establishes in it His invisible, spiritual but at the same time wholly tangible and knowable kingdom. A person who has embraced the kingdom of God within himself can have a clear understanding of the second coming of the God-Man.

He can recognize and avoid or resist the antichrist. On the other hand, a person who has not accepted the kingdom of God within himself will not recognize the antichrist; he will inevitably, without realizing it, become a follower of his; he will not recognize the impending end of the world and the approaching dread second coming of Christ; it will find him unprepared. There is no human teaching, no teaching in word or in words that is sufficient to edify a person who demands instruction within the soul, that is, from God Himself. A person who has acquired the kingdom of God within himself has the Holy Spirit as his guide Who teaches "all truth" (John 16:13) to the person guided by Him, and does not allow him to be deceived by a lie that clothes itself in the appearance of truth in order to deceive him more easily. A certain blessed monk was right to say, when talking of the antichrist: "Many will believe in the antichrist and will glorify him as if he were a mighty god. Those who have God always within them and are illumined in their hearts will see the truth through their pure faith, and will recognize him. To all who possess the knowledge and the wisdom of God, the coming of the tormentor will be known. For those whose minds are always on the things of this life and who love the world, it will be impossible to understand, for they are tethered to the things of this life. Even if they hear the word, they will not believe, but will loathe the one who preaches it."[164] They will consider someone who preaches the word to be mad, or worthy of scorn or pity. Humanity, darkened with its carnal mind, will not believe in the second coming of the Lord. "Scoffers will come in the last days, walking according to their own lusts, and saying, 'Where is the promise of His coming? For since the fathers fell asleep, all things continue as they were from the beginning of creation'" (2 Pet 3:3–4).

After the pharisees had gone away from the Lord, He said to His disciples that one sign of the end of the world and the imminent second coming of the Lord would be exceptional material development: people would forget God, they would forget heaven, they would forget eternity and, in their delusion, as if they were to remain eternally on earth, they would turn all their attention to it, and to acquiring for themselves the greatest possible and most reliable prosperity. What could be more insane than this tendency? Does not death, that will befall and constantly befalls all people, bear witness that we are created for eternity, that we are wanderers on earth for the briefest of times, and that, for this reason, our cares relating to eternity must be our main and greatest concern, and those concerning the earth must be very moderate? In spite of all the recklessness of this tendency, it will appear on earth, in an inevitable fulfillment of the divine prophecy. If it has appeared, then, being hostile to the Word of God, it serves for us as one of the clearest proofs of the truth of the Word of God. "As it was in the days of Noah," proclaims the Lord, "so it will be also in the days of the Son of Man." The days of the Son of Man refer to the time preceding His coming, which will end when He comes—at the beginning of the eternal, never-ending day, the end of time and of times. Time will end with the ending of the phenomena with which it is marked: when day, and night, and morning, and evening, and weeks, and months, and years, and centuries are all replaced with a single eternal day, there will no longer be any time. "As it was in the days of Noah, so it will be also in the days of the Son of Man: They ate, they drank, they married wives, they were given in marriage, until the day that Noah entered the ark, and the flood came and destroyed them all. Likewise as it was also in the days of Lot: They ate, they drank, they bought, they sold, they planted, they built" (Luke 17:26–28). Holy Scripture recounts that the contemporaries of Noah and the fellow citizens of Lot indulged in unbounded depravity. Depravity is born from turning away from God, from striving exclusively toward earthly pursuits and material progress. When can a person who is constantly and solely occupied with worldly affairs and material progress think of God or cultivate his salvation? But everyone who scorns the knowledge of God and care for his salvation, who is occupied entirely with arranging his temporary situation in the flesh and for the flesh, without understanding or perceiving it, develops his fallen nature; it is as if he made his immaterial soul somehow material; he becomes darkened and alien to God; he becomes wholly sin, wholly flesh; he is rejected by God as someone who has completely destroyed within himself the purpose for which he was called by the Creator into existence from nonexistence. "My Spirit shall not remain with these people forever, for they are flesh," the Lord says of the contemporaries of Noah (Gen 6:3). General depravity together with the abundant material progress that arises from it will be a sign of the end of the age and the impending dread judgment of Christ. Not only love of pleasure will prevail then, but depravity in the wider sense of the word will become the treasure of humanity in the last times of its existence on earth. "For men will be lovers of themselves, lovers of money, boasters, proud, blasphemers, disobedient to parents, unthankful, unholy, unloving, unforgiving, slanderers, without self-control, brutal, despisers of good, traitors, headstrong, haughty, lovers of pleasure rather than lovers of God, having a form of godliness but denying its power" (2 Tim 3:2–5). Sin will reach its peak, and although it will become more terrible, although its dominion will become stronger, the mask of godliness will be preserved. Who will understand that this superficially flourishing godliness has lost all its essence, all its power? The essence and the power of the religion of the Jews had been destroyed in the time of Christ, and the people could not understand this, not even the scribes and the Levites and the Jewish high priests were able to understand, being filled with pride in their learning and knowledge. But this learning and this knowledge consisted solely in studying the Law of God according to the letter that kills (2 Cor 3:6), alongside a way of life that went against the commandments of God. Such a life deadens faith. Humanity will not see its disastrous situation in moral and spiritual terms; on the contrary, it will trumpet its success, blinded by success in material progress for time and for the earth, and rejecting Christian progress for the spirit, for eternity, for God. When the world proclaims and extols its success, and the establishment of the greatest prosperity and of undisturbed "'Peace and safety!' then sudden destruction [will come] upon them" (1 Thess 5:3), then the end of the world will suddenly come, which it, in its darkened state, in the thrill of earthly progress, will not expect at all. Because of the blindness of the world, "the day of the Lord so comes as a thief in the night" (1 Thess 5:2). Indicating this blindness, the Lord called the time of His coming "night" (Luke 17:34). Why, in the eyes of God, should this world continue to exist when it, that is, humanity, completely rejects the purpose for which God granted it to wander the earth, when it chooses for this wandering a willful purpose that is devoid of meaning? This purpose is already being chosen! With this purpose in mind, a person's brief life on earth is taken for eternity, and he exhausts all the strength of his soul and body not in preparing himself for eternity but in sacrifice to an impossible, absurd dream; it is exhausted in order to arrange the highest possible degree of carnal prosperity and pleasure in the earthly lodging-place, in our prison, as if in the most lasting eternal dwelling-place. This false dream cruelly deceives its followers. It is like an inhuman tyrant with them, like a wicked demon. It is a demon! Nothing can be more evil than it, nothing can be more insidious or deceitful. It is the mockery of humans by fallen spirits. This disastrous dream deludes people along the entire path of their earthly life. It betrays them at the end of their lives, it consigns them to reality, it leaves them with nothing. They enter eternity totally unprepared for it, totally unacquainted with it. Moreover, they enter it having adopted an attitude that is completely hostile to its spiritual good things, and to their own happiness there. Where is the place beyond the bounds of time for such tares? There is not and cannot be any other place for them than in the depths of hades: there they must be hidden from the view of the world.

The monks of the monastery of Solovki recount the reply given by St Zosimas to his disciples when they asked him how to recognize the antichrist when he came. The saint replied: "When you hear that Christ has arrived or appeared on earth, then you will know that this is the antichrist." This reply is exactly right! The world, or humanity, will not recognize the antichrist: it will deem him to be Christ, and he will be proclaimed as Christ. Consequently, when a rumor spreads that Christ has come, this will be a sure sign that the antichrist has come, and has begun his foreordained and permitted ministry. The reply of St Zosimas is based on the words of the Saviour. The Saviour of the world, when acquainting His disciples with the signs that would herald His second coming, said, "Then if anyone says to you, 'Look, here is the Christ!' or 'There!' do not believe it. . . . Therefore if they say to you, 'Look, He is in the desert!' do not go out; or 'Look, He is in the inner rooms!'" (i.e., in some private part of the house), "do not believe it. For as the lightning comes from the east and flashes to the west, so also will the coming of the Son of Man be" (Matt 24:23–27). It will not be necessary and it will be impossible for people to pass on to each other the news of the coming of the Son of God. He will appear suddenly; He will appear in His omnipotence, to all people and to the whole earth at the same time. The objection of learned people that it is impossible for the Son of God to appear to all of humanity at the same time, due to the natural spherical construction of the earth, is groundless. If the almighty God derived both the earth and the whole universe from nothing at His almighty and most wise command, without needing to consult any scientists beforehand, then it is surely possible on the same grounds, due to His boundless might and wisdom, to appear to all of humanity at the same time, although the means of realizing this is impossible, as it must be, for all the scientists of the world. "The Lord will come from heaven," says St John Damascene, "in the same way that the holy apostles saw Him going up into heaven (Acts 1:11); perfect God and perfect man will come with glory and with power. Let no-one expect Him from the earth, but let everyone expect Him from heaven, as He Himself confirmed."[165]

The Lord concluded the teaching about the end of the world and His second coming with the following warning: "Take heed to yourselves, lest your hearts be weighed down with carousing, drunkenness, and cares of this life, and that Day come on you unexpectedly. For it will come as a snare on all those who dwell on the face of the whole earth" (Luke 21:34–35).

With these words, this testament, this counsel, this commandment, the Lord forbids carnal life and excess in earthly pursuits, which together turn a person from a spiritual into a carnal and material person, make him forget eternity and God, and lead him to fall into all kinds of sin. All the passions can easily enter a heart that is not protected and stamped with the remembrance and the fear of God; spiritual darkness and ignorance of God enter it. For people who have been intoxicated and clouded by a carnal, sinful life, the coming of the Lord will be like a trap. This trap will catch the whole of mankind. It will be impossible for anyone to run away or escape from it. Knowing this, let us always be sober. By running to God with more frequent, constant prayers that are filled with contrition and weeping, by acquiring and keeping the kingdom of God within ourselves through a way of life that follows the will of God, we will be able, through the grace and power of God, to save ourselves from the trap of the sin and from the plots of the ruler of this world. We will be able, with good hope and the spiritual knowledge that we will find mercy and salvation, to stand before the impartial Judge Who will pronounce judgment and decide our lot unto eternity. Amen.

40. Jesus Teaches the People

Sermon on the Twenty-seventh Sunday after Pentecost

"He was teaching in one of the synagogues on the Sabbath" (Luke 13:10).

Dear brothers! It is comforting to hear that our Lord Jesus Christ was teaching the people on the Sabbath day (Luke 13:10–17), which was the equivalent in the Old Testament Church of the day of resurrection, or Sunday, in the Church of the New Testament. We who are now gathered here in the holy church, in the name of our Lord Jesus Christ, eighteen centuries after he departed the earth, are doing the same thing. We cannot see our Lord with our bodily eyes, but we gaze upon Him and see Him with the eyes of faith. We hear His teaching, proclaimed through the holy Gospel; the events that accompanied His wandering on earth, described with holy simplicity and exceptional clarity by the apostles, appear vividly, as if they were happening in front of us; we are in constant communion with the Lord by means of the holy Mysteries; we can intensify and develop this communion by constantly meditating upon Him, by acting in accordance with His most holy commandments, and by calling upon Him constantly in prayer. To be clear: our Lord Jesus Christ is among us. It is only to those who deny His presence that He does not exist. This is not a product of an overheated imagination. It is not a captivating dream. The Lord Himself says to His disciples, "Lo, I am with you always, even to the end of the age" (Matt 28:20). Whoever does not see the Lord among us is not a disciple of Christ.

There is no benefit in seeing the Lord with our bodily eyes when our mind is blind, when faith—that power of spiritual vision—is not active. Conversely, when faith is active, then the heavens open, and we see the Son at the right hand of the Father, "everywhere present" in His divinity, "filling all things" and "indescribable."[166] Nothing hinders us from acquiring faith. Let us acquire it, and we will see God. Let us cease to be content with weak literal knowledge of God; let us stretch out our weakened hands to do works of faith; let us acquire an active, living faith: only through this faith does the Lord appear.

The eyes of the body are insensitive and blind when the mind is blind. Our Lord Jesus Christ worked astonishing wonders during His time on earth to prove His divinity: these signs were so obvious, so tangible, that the divinity of God incarnate ought to have become manifest and clear to the most limited, the most sensual people. But the people looked intently, and saw nothing. With surprise and disbelief, but also complaining about his contemporaries and with pain on their behalf, the Evangelist says, "although He had done so many signs before them, they did not believe in Him" (John 12:37). He goes on to reveal the reason for this blindness: the darkening of their minds, the hardening of their hearts, born of a sinful life that sharpens and strengthens the sensual eyes that are of no use for the purpose of coming to know the Truth (John 12:40; 3:19–20).

The event related in today's Gospel is shocking. After teaching the people, the Lord sealed His teaching by healing a woman who had been tormented by the burden of a serious long-term disease. People who had not understood the teaching could understand the miracle. Those who have not come to know God from His "words of eternal life," as Peter did (John 6:68), can at least recognize a God-pleasing man by a sign worked through him, as did Nicodemus (John 3:2), or the blind man who was healed (John 9:33). The sight seen by the people that day was most pitiful, edifying and startling. The fallen angel, through whom human nature submitted to and participated in the fall, bound a certain woman with a strange and most trying ailment. The woman's body was contorted such that she was bent over for eighteen years, unable to straighten her limbs or get any relief from her constrained and unnatural posture. The Lord said to this woman: "'Woman, you are loosed from your infirmity.' And He laid His hands on her, and immediately she was made straight, and glorified God" (Luke 13:12–13).

Just as the woman, having so easily shaken off the burden that had oppressed her, was joyfully glorifying God; just as the crowd of people was justifiably expressing joy at the obvious action of divine grace, clearly being revealed as the salvation of a suffering woman from an oppressive and exhausting affliction; just at that moment the ruler of the synagogue was overcome with indignation. He saw no miracle or healing. He did not see the Redeemer and Saviour of mankind or the action of the Holy Spirit. He did not even see a God-pleasing man. His mind's eye was distorted by some inexplicable power from hades. In the action of God, he saw an offence against the law of God. In a spirit of fault-finding, he saw labor and work in the labor-free healing of the sick woman, and in his self-deception used a divine commandment—that labor and work should be done on the other six days of the week but was forbidden on the Sabbath day—against the healing. The essence of the matter lay in the fact that the ruler of the synagogue was a pharisee, at least in the disposition of his soul, and when he saw what he thought was a person, a servant of God, bolstering his powerful words with a miracle, he became inflamed with envy. The envy was born out of pride and vainglory: the ruler wanted to take precedence in the opinion of the people for his earthly justice. This precedence was taken from him effortlessly by the appearance of Heavenly Justice; the ruler, in order to keep his false precedence, rose up against Heavenly Justice and tried to degrade it; so as to hide how nefarious his behavior was under the guise of justice, he presented himself as an upholder of the law.

The Lord, Who sees into people's hearts, exposed the pharisee, calling his behavior hypocrisy. While trying to satisfy his passions and working solely for sin, a hypocrite wishes to preserve an appearance of virtue in the eyes of other people. A central position is held among our passions by vainglory, which seeks to enjoy human praise. It is not concerned with whether this praise is justified or unjustified, or whether or not the route toward receiving it is right: receiving praise, by whatever means, is the whole purpose of the vainglorious hypocrite. He forgets God: a hypocrite is incapable either of faith or of knowledge of God. "How can you believe," says the Lord to the Jews, of whom a significant proportion or the majority were infected with phariseeism, "who receive honor from one another, and do not seek the honor that comes from the only God?" (John 5:44).

The ruler of the synagogue of the Jews referred to in today's Gospel showed how a hypocrite is unable to believe in Christ, to receive the Redeemer. This vainglorious soul, thirsting for praise and for human honor, deeming himself worthy of them, could not endure that the miracle worked before everyone attracted involuntary praise and astonishment from the people. This soul was seething with envy. It was impossible to deny the miracle: this soul strove to degrade it, to disparage it, accusing God's miracle of breaking the law of God. The hypocrite resolutely attacked God, resolutely blasphemed against the Holy Spirit. If the worker of the miracle had been a grace-filled person, then the pharisee would have been disparaging and blaspheming against the grace of the Spirit. But since the worker of the miracle was the God-Man, the pharisee was entering into clear opposition with God. A person cannot perform a true miracle on his own: it is performed by the goodwill and the work of the all-holy God, and for this reason it cannot possibly be against the will of God and the law of God. The pharisee's accusation and disparagement of the sign of God served only to reveal how his mind was darkened and his heart hardened, as a result of his sinful life.

The impudent, terrible deed of the pharisee, who had the audacity to censure the action of the Saviour in His very presence, is worthy of our particular attention, and we should weep for it with bitter and inconsolable tears. We should weep for it because it arose from the fallenness and rejection that is common to us all. We should pay particular attention to it so that, by considering all its gravity and fearing it as a terrible and most grave act, we may avoid it. Christ also acts now, in our times! And the Holy Spirit also performs saving signs in the Christian mysteries now! And God also has blasphemers, opponents, and enemies among the people of our day.

Every kind of sinful life comprises defiance of and opposition to God; every kind of sinfulness is an offence against the law of God and a rejection of God's will. "Whoever commits sin," says the apostle, "also commits lawlessness, and sin is lawlessness" (1 John 3:4). Hypocrisy is the type of sinfulness that particularly opposes knowledge of Christ and Christianity. The beginning of turning to Christ consists in knowledge of one's own sinfulness and fallenness. When a person looks at himself in this way, he recognizes his need for the Redeemer and approaches Christ through humility, faith, and repentance. But a hypocrite, afflicted with passions that are insufficiently perceptible to people—vainglory, arrogance, love of money, envy, slyness, malice—and concealing them with hypocrisy and pretense, is incapable, just as Satan is incapable, of acknowledging himself to be a sinner. Both virtues and passions become natural through habit. Thus hypocrisy, too, becomes like a natural attribute from force of habit. A person who is possessed by it does not see hypocrisy as a soul-destroying vice, and he does works of hypocrisy as if they were works of justice. The soul of a hypocrite is infected with blindness. This is why the Lord called the pharisees fools and "blind" (Matt 23:16–26). A hypocrite is that unfortunate person who is in his own opinion a righteous man, but is rejected by God: "I did not come to call the righteous, but sinners, to repentance" (Matt 9:13). Here the pharisees are called righteous not because they really were righteous, but because they believed themselves to be, meticulously fulfilling the ritual rules of God's law and flouting its essence, which consists in a person aligning his mind, his heart, and his entire being with the will of God. In order that they might be reconciled with God, the Lord granted human beings the virtue of repentance. How could this spiritual gift be received by those who were completely satisfied with themselves, and expected in the promised Messiah someone who was primarily a worldly conqueror, who would repay their carnal, absurd righteousness filled with arrogance and malice with abundant worldly rewards? In their darkened state and their bitterness, the pharisees even boasted of their inability to know and accept the Redeemer: "Have any of the rulers or the Pharisees believed in Him?" (John 7:48), they said. The Lord also indicated that they were incapable of truly knowing God: "Assuredly, I say to you that tax collectors and harlots enter the kingdom of God before you" (Matt 21:31). An obvious sinner, one who has fallen into deadly sins and attracted the contempt and loathing of other people, is more capable of repentance than a supposedly righteous person who is irreproachable in terms of visible behavior, but in the depths of his soul is satisfied with himself. Phariseeism is a terrible affliction of the human spirit, similar to the affliction of the fallen angel, who keeps his fallenness for himself, as if it were a treasure. "Beware," the Lord told His disciples, "of the leaven of the Pharisees, which is hypocrisy" (Luke 12:1). Hypocrisy is referred to as leaven because when it steals into a person's soul, it penetrates all the thoughts, all the feelings, all the works of the person, it becomes his character, so that we might say it becomes his soul.

A person who wishes to protect himself from hypocrisy must first of all do all his good deeds in secret, as the Lord commanded (Matt 6:1–6); then he must refrain from condemning his neighbor. Condemning one's neighbor is a sign of hypocrisy, as the holy Gospel instructs us (Matt 7:5). In order not to condemn our neighbor, we must avoid making any judgment about him. This is why, when the Gospel forbids us to condemn our neighbor, we are also forbidden to judge him. "Judge not, and you shall not be judged. Condemn not, and you shall not be condemned" (Luke 6:37). People first allow themselves to judge the affairs of their neighbor, then they unwittingly fall into condemnation. Let us not sow the seeds of weeds, and then weeds will not grow. Let us forbid ourselves from judging our neighbors unnecessarily, and then condemnation will not follow. People will ask here what the connection is between condemnation and hypocrisy. The connection is obvious. A person who condemns and disparages his neighbor unwittingly presents himself as righteous, perhaps without expressing this in so many words, or even without realizing it. We are all sinners, and so any presentation of ourselves as righteous, whether direct or indirect, is hypocrisy.

When we gather for friendly conversation, it is often, if not always, the case that most of this conversation consists in gossip about one's neighbors, in mocking them, and in slander, disparagement, and defamation. A stream of sharp words pours out; laughter rings out as a sign of approval. In this unfortunate period of forgetfulness and self-deception, our souls share in demonic attributes, and are fed with the poison of hypocrisy. On this subject the Holy Gospel, seeking our salvation, also attacks sin: "for every idle word men may speak, they will give account of it in the day of judgment. For by your words you will be justified, and by your words you will be condemned" (Matt 12:36–37). Brothers, let us look closely at the origins of sins, let us guard ourselves from sinful beginnings, and we will avoid sinful development. The seeds of sin, such as, for example, idle talk, appear to be negligible: they are sown imperceptibly in the field of the soul. But when these seeds sprout, especially when the shoots grow stronger and thicker, then sin overtakes the whole person and it becomes extremely difficult to destroy it.

"Whoever forbids gossip to pass his lips," says a certain great holy Father, "guards his heart from the passions. Whoever guards his heart from the passions sees God at every hour. Whoever focuses within himself the eyes of his mind sees within himself the spiritual dawn."[167] What will we see, brothers, in the chamber of our souls, when they are illumined by divine light? We will see the countless multitude of our sins. We will see and feel within ourselves the fall of our progenitor, of which Holy Scripture tells us;[168] we will see and feel within ourselves the need for the Redeemer. Having recognized our Lord Jesus Christ as the Redeemer, we will confess Him; having recognized and confessed Him, we will see Him, and we will worship Him with the veneration that befits God our Creator and our Saviour. Amen.

41. The Parable of the Great Supper

Sermon on the Twenty-eighth Sunday after Pentecost

"A certain man gave a great supper and invited many" (Luke 14:16).

Dear brothers! Today's Gospel (Luke 14:16–24) tells us of a certain man who gave a magnificent feast, to which he invited many guests. It goes on to relate a strange circumstance: it was not the people who were originally invited who took part in the meal, but completely different people. The luxurious banquet was given in the evening, and for this reason it is known as the "great supper." The evening is what we call the last hours of the day before the night.

The story of the Great Supper is a vivid parable with which our Lord Jesus Christ represents the "kingdom" of God prepared by the Heavenly Father "from the foundation of the world" (Matt 25:34) for His chosen ones—and also shows how mankind received the good news of this kingdom after being called to it.

Death lies before all of us, without exception; we must all enter eternity through the gates of death and remain in eternity forever. Life on earth is the threshold to eternity. It is like a crowded and stifling front room before the most magnificent and spacious halls. In eternity, the Kingdom of God is prepared for us; outside it, there is eternal sorrow, affliction that never ends—inconsolable weeping and sobbing that will never be quieted. If there were to be an event tomorrow, in a week's time, or in one month's time, that decided our fate on earth either for good or for bad, would we not make every possible arrangement, every effort, take every precaution, so that the event had a favorable outcome for us? Let us turn our attention to our fate in eternity. Let us rise from the sleep of despondency and forgetfulness in which we are immersed; let us reject the blindness and self-deception that make a person think his life on earth is endless. Let us believe the most credible truth. Let us believe that inevitable death lies before us all. Just as it is true that we will die, so it is essential that we concern ourselves with our lot in the world beyond the grave. With this aim, let us consider our Lord's parable of the Great Supper.

Who was the provider of the supper? Holy Scripture calls him "a certain man," that is, an unknown, unspecified man. It is obvious that this is God. He has replaced Himself in the parable with His image—man. But just as people have forgotten God, and lost true knowledge and proper understanding of Him, so God, calling Himself a man, also calls Himself an unknown man: "A certain man gave a great supper and invited many." The large number of people invited signifies that all of humanity, without exception, is destined for eternal blessedness. Brothers! We are all called! No-one is forgotten. No-one has either cause or the right to give way to mourning and despondency.

When the time came for the longed-for meal, the Provider of the feast sent His Servant to inform the guests. Both the time of the feast and the lonely figure of the Servant are deeply significant. In the Greek text of the Gospel, written by St Luke, the definite article "τόν" has been placed before the word for "servant" (δοῦλον), which gives it a special, unique, and specific significance. Here the Lord Jesus Christ calls Himself exclusively the Servant of God.[169] He, equal in divinity to the Father and the Spirit, is the only true Servant of God in terms of His humanity. He alone has fully and perfectly fulfilled the will of God and is free from all sin. Other holy people are only comparatively holy (Rom 4:2); human holiness is the least possible degree of sinfulness, in line with human possibilities. The sole Servant of God is presented in the parable as the only agent of human salvation: the prophets, the apostles, and the teachers of the church were only servants and instruments of the Word: "All things were made through Him, and without Him nothing was made that was made" (John 1:3). The time when the guests were invited was the evening. This means that our Lord Jesus Christ came down to earth in the last hours of the life of the visible world. Eighteen centuries have passed since the time of that most joyful occasion; the life of the world has not yet ended: "But ... with the Lord one day is as a thousand years, and a thousand years as one day" (2 Pet 3:8). The evening of God is extended and prolonged so that all those invited arrive in time to meet at His Supper, and that none of the chosen be deprived of it.

This is how the parable represents the way God views people; let us now look at how it represents the behavior of people toward God. As if they had conspired together, all the guests make their excuses and decline to attend the supper. What kind of plot is this, what kind of unanimous opposition to God? This is the action of the fall that is common to everyone; this is evidence of people's good disposition toward their fallen state and willingness to remain in it; it is a sign of the mortification through sin of the soul, powerless and unwilling to rouse itself from mortal sleep, even when called by the voice of the Son of God. By way of excuse for their unwillingness to come to the supper, the invitees put forward their worldly commitments. One ascribed such importance to his learned, official occupations that he considered himself justified in disdaining God; another had given himself up to family cares and forgot God; a third, finally, was carried away by the passions, immersed himself in crude carnal pleasures and became completely alien to God. It is not only obvious sin that takes our spiritual treasure from us: it is any earthly concern, any earthly situation, when our souls are completely given over to and confined by it.

When the people who had been invited refused to attend the supper, the Provider sent that same Servant to gather the maimed, the beggars, the lame and the blind from the streets and alleyways of the town, the roads and the crossroads, and to persuade them to come to the supper.

The Gospel calls those who have been invited the Jews, as they were called to Christianity in advance through the law and the prophets; the homeless beggars and cripples who roam the streets and the lanes, the wanderers who toil on the road or have stopped at the crossroads to choose which path to take, represent the gentiles who are outside the house, outside the Church, beyond knowledge of God; their various physical defects should be understood in terms of the soul. The Jews who were chosen refused decisively; the gentiles who were called after them were persuaded with difficulty to come to the supper. Many centuries, countless sacrifices, and whole rivers of blood were needed for the Word of God to persuade them to adopt Christianity.

The people invited should be understood to be certain Christians who are renowned, learned, and successful in this world. The advantages God has given them over other people, and the easy access to knowledge of God and service of God that accompanies these advantages, express, without doubt, the fact that God has called them to salvation and higher blessedness ... Alas, this is a lamentable sight. Those who have been invited remain like stones, paying no attention to Him Who calls them. It seems that only those afflicted with tribulations, illnesses, poverty, deprivations, only the maimed and the beggars in the worldly sense are capable of hearing God. It is "the foolish things of the world," as the apostle expresses it, the weak, the base, the despised people of the world (1 Cor 1:27–28), who show obedience to God. And these despised people must, under the guidance of the Word of God, with His powerful aid, undergo the hardest battle with their fallen state in order to submit to God and to acquire salvation. It is characteristic that the parable shows how the wondrous Servant had to persuade and convince the beggars, the blind, the lame, and the crippled to come to the supper. We have become accustomed to and come to love our fallen state, and it is difficult for us to be parted from it. Our own nature has become incapable of goodness, and without the Saviour it cannot do any true, perfect good: "Without Me," He says, "you can do nothing" (John 15:5). Our own goodness is contaminated by evil. It cannot be otherwise, because its source, fallen human nature, consists of a mixture of good and evil, and it inevitably produces corresponding actions.

The Lord concluded the parable with a terrible judgment. Seeing with His all-seeing eye how little attention people would pay to Him both in the present and in the future, He said, "many are called, but few are chosen" (Matt 22:14).[170] The merciful God calls all to salvation, but very few obey Him. We are all numbered among those who are called through the inexpressible love of God for us, but very few of us are among the chosen, because being included among the chosen is left to our own will. Amen.

42. On Giving Thanks and Glorifying God

Sermon on the Twenty-ninth Sunday after Pentecost

The account in today's Gospel (Luke 17:12–19) of the ten lepers healed by our Lord Jesus Christ is appointed by the holy Church to be read on all occasions when we communally give thanks to God for a blessing or blessings He has granted us. Of the ten lepers healed by the Saviour, only one thought to bring thanks to Him. Nine who had received the blessing and had seen wrought upon themselves the wondrous sign of the mercy and omnipotence of God, did not ascribe any spiritual value either to their sudden healing from an incurable disease or to the One at Whose command the healing took place.

The Lord condemned the act of the ungrateful, embittered people, dead in mind and in heart. When one of the lepers, after receiving healing, returned to the Lord, glorifying Him in a loud voice, falling at the feet of the Saviour and thanking and glorifying Him, the Lord said, "Were there not ten cleansed? But where are the nine? Were there not any found who returned to give glory to God?" These words have a deep meaning. The God-Man, in His humanity, was not seeking to be glorified by men: He wanted God to be honored by them in the proper way, for their own good. Those who were well-disposed toward the true worship of God found Him, concealed by His humanity, found the Saviour and, in Him, their salvation. Those who rejected the Saviour were those who had first rejected God in their souls. The Lord said to the Jews who hated and blasphemed against Him: "If God were your Father, you would love Me, for I proceeded forth ... from God. He who is of God hears God's words;" "therefore you do not hear, because you are not of God" (John 8:42,47).

Gratitude is a rare virtue among men. Unfortunately, we hear again and again among us a triumphant exclamation, accompanied by laughter: "I got this or that out of someone!" This exclamation expresses a terrible depravity of the soul. What does it mean? It signifies that a good deed has been extracted from someone by flattery, pretense or other similar means, that the person who has submitted to deception and has done the good deed incurs ridicule in return for his good act. In some physical ailments an inexplicable willfulness can be observed. This willfulness also exists in ailments of the soul. Good deeds often provoke in the beneficiary a feeling of implacable, furious hatred toward the benefactor. This strange reaction is encountered so often that there is a folk proverb to express it: "Don't give any food or drink and you will gain no enemies." The poison of sin with which we are permeated is strong: people infected with it are capable of hating not only their fellow humans who are their benefactors, but even God. They have shown this many times and in numerous different ways.

Enmity toward God is expressed by disregard for His commandments and by living according to one's own will and one's own mind. The Saviour says, "He who does not love Me does not keep My words" (John 14:24). Why do we disregard the commandments of God? Why do we forget God? Why do we not know Him? Because we do not think either about God or about ourselves, we live our lives carelessly, occupying ourselves only with vain things. Visible creation proclaims the almighty, all-good, all-wise God; we also proclaim Him ourselves. We received existence and all the capabilities of the soul and body, all the means toward material existence and the development of our spirit, without our desire or knowledge. We do not make anything from nothing. We make everything from resources prepared for us. The very capacity to make things was put into our nature, not acquired by us. We are equipped from without and within ourselves with reasons to think about God and to thank Him. Holy Scripture and the writings of the holy Fathers reveal to us the great number and significance of the blessings God has given to humanity, prompting us to thank God. Giving thanks to God has its own special attribute: it brings forth and strengthens faith, and brings us closer to God. Ingratitude and forgetfulness of God destroy faith and distance us from God. The apostle says that those who truly believe in Christ are "rooted and built up in Him and established in the faith, as you have been taught, abounding in it with thanksgiving" (Col 2:7).

In order to gain substantial benefit to our soul by thanking God, He has commanded us to practice thanking Him and to cultivate within ourselves a feeling of gratitude toward Him. "In everything give thanks," says the apostle, "for this is the will of God in Christ Jesus for you" (1 Thess 5:18).

When the holy apostle says that the will of God proclaimed by him to give thanks for everything is the will of God "in Christ Jesus," what he is expressing is this: The New Testament commandment to give thanks is secret, spiritual, and divine. It flows out from the mystery of the incarnation of Christ, and is based on this mystery. The God-Man spent His earthly life in deprivations and tribulations. In this way He blessed the deprivations and tribulations of those who truly believed in Him, elevating earthly deprivations and tribulations far above earthly well-being. He had no part in the latter. The commandment to give thanks is alien to the carnal mind: it can be understood only by spiritual reason and is fulfilled in the light of it. Even if a person with a carnal mind sometimes gives thanks, then it is only for material blessings; in case of temptation he is brought into confusion, he grumbles and blasphemes. But God's commandment is to give thanks for everything, even for tribulations. We are commanded to give thanks for our tribulations because in this way we can share in the sufferings of Christ; we are commanded to give thanks for our blessings and our well-being, as for God's condescension to our weakness. "Jesus also, that He might sanctify the people with His own blood, suffered outside the gate. Therefore let us go forth to Him, outside the camp,"—outside the customs of this world—"bearing His reproach. For here we have no continuing city, but we seek the one to come" (Heb 13:12–14). "For to you it has been granted on behalf of Christ, not only to believe in Him, but also to suffer for His sake" (Phil 1:29). A gift is naturally followed by thanks. If tribulations in Christ are a gift of God, given by Him to a true Christian, then the true Christian is obliged to show his Christianity by giving thanks for sorrows, and he must confess and accept the gift of God by giving thanks for it. Faith is strengthened through thanksgiving, and the deep mysteries of Christianity are revealed; through the action of the grace-filled peace and spiritual consolation that are the immediate consequence of thanksgiving, a deep and clear knowledge of God is brought to the soul. "The lips of one who constantly gives thanks," says a great Father, "will receive blessing from God; divine grace is implanted in the heart that abides in thanksgiving. Grace is preceded by humility: punishment is preceded by conceit. A heart that constantly strives to give thanks to God attracts grace to itself; a complaining thought that constantly moves within the heart invites temptation into the soul."[171] "Thanks given by a person who receives a gift encourages the Giver to give even more gifts, greater than the first. Gifts only remain without increase when no thanks is given for them. The portion of a foolish person is small in his eyes."[172] All the Fathers of the Orthodox Church reason in a similar way. They exhort us to thank God for everything that happens in our lives, whether pleasant or distressing.[173] Faith teaches us that everything that happens to us happens in accordance with the all-good and all-wise providence of God and to our own advantage.[174] In this way, faith guides us toward giving thanks to God, and faith in turn is deepened through thanksgiving. From conviction of the mind we begin to give thanks; giving thanks inspires the conviction of the heart.

A broad arena of thanksgiving and glorification is opened up before the Christian who leads a righteous life and keeps the commandments of the Gospel without allowing himself to be dazzled by vain attachments and cares, and looks constantly toward the haven of eternity. Everything transient passes in its turn. The future becomes present, the present becomes the past. Everything that has been has passed, and will not return; everything that is in the future will come for the shortest time, and will then become a thing of the past.

Only a person who lives his earthly life as a pilgrim, in his way of thinking, in the sensation of his heart, and in the activity arising from them, can ceaselessly glorify and thank God. King David was granted this sensation by the Holy Spirit, and, embraced and enraptured by glorification and thanksgiving, he sent them up to God from the depths of his soul. "Bless the Lord, O my soul," says the inspired David, "and all that is within me bless His holy Name. Bless the Lord, O my soul, and forget not all His benefits" (Ps 102:1–2). "I will give thanks to Thee, O Lord, with my whole heart; I will speak of all Thy marvellous works" (Ps 9:1). "I will exalt Thee, O my God, my King, and I will bless Thy name for ever, yea, for ever and ever. Every day will I bless Thee, and I will praise Thy name for ever, yea, for ever and ever" (Ps 144:1–2). As a reason to glorify God, David expounds His infinite greatness: "Great is the Lord, and highly to be praised, and of His greatness there is no end" (Ps 144:3). David sees the greatness of God in His works: "O Lord my God, Thou art become exceeding glorious ... Wrapping Thyself with light, as it were a garment, and spreading out the heavens like a curtain ... Whoso layeth the earth on its foundations" (Ps 103:1,2,5, etc). The visible creation can justly be called the clothing of God. When clothed in it, the invisible God can be seen: "In ... majesty hast Thou clothed Thyself" (Ps 103:1). The natural world that is visible to us is indeed magnificent. It preaches the existence of God, it preaches His omnipotence, His wisdom, and His goodness. All creatures, from the greatest to the very smallest, have their own laws; to discover a fraction of these laws constitutes glory to the human mind, which is obliged to admit that their discovery is negligible compared to what has not been discovered. The tiniest proportion has been discovered of what is possible given human limitations; an infinite number of things remain undiscovered; an infinite number of these hidden things are impossible for humans to discover. The human mind, which has measured and calculated the paths of the planets in the vast heavens, stands in amazement before a tiny blade of grass, trampled carelessly beneath our feet. It cannot explain what the life of this blade of grass consists in, what juices it draws with its stalk from the earth, how and by what means these juices decompose, giving to different plants different appearances, different smells, colors, and tastes. What is a sunbeam? What is electricity? It is possible to ask an infinite number of similar questions. We see an action; the action attests to the existence of rules; the rules are hidden from the human mind because they are beyond understanding. The discovery of a rule, the discovery of the existence of rules that are beyond comprehension, constituting trouble and glory for the human mind, is clear evidence that they have been produced and established by the most sublime Mind. This Mind is unfathomable, because what it produces—nature—is unfathomable. "How great are Thy works, O Lord! In wisdom hast Thou made them all" (Ps 103:24); only in madness and folly can it be declared that the created world, which exists in accordance with the wisest laws, is the product of chance, or of mindlessness. The works of the Mind are slandered by godless people in their madness, who boast of their own cleverness when they discover one of those rules that they had ascribed to mindless chance. What can be more senseless than slander that contradicts itself?

The greatness of the works of God, observed in visible nature, leads to glorification of God: "Generation and generation shall praise Thy works, and declare Thy power. They shall speak of the glorious majesty of Thy holiness, and tell of Thy wondrous works; And of the might of Thy terrifying acts shall they speak, and tell of Thy greatness" (Ps 144:4–6). "What may be known of God is manifest in them, for God has shown it to them. For since the creation of the world His invisible attributes are clearly seen, being understood by the things that are made, even His eternal power and Godhead, so that they are without excuse" (Rom 1:19–20) to all those who have not come to know and do not recognize God from contemplation of visible creation. Visible nature is there to serve us. We are served by the celestial bodies, the air and numerous other gases, the earth, the sea, rivers, animals, plants, metals, minerals. O wanderer of the earth! Look at nature, at this lodging-place, this hostel where you are being accommodated for the briefest time, while you are on this earth—look at it with purity of mind, formed from a virtuous life that is far from that of an animal—look at the abundance of good things with which you are surrounded. When you look around you in this way, your soul will naturally be filled with thanksgiving to God. This has happened with everyone who has observed nature with a disposition acquired through a Christian way of life. The prophet foretold of them: "The memory of the abundance of Thy kindness shall they gush forth, and exult in Thy righteousness. The Lord is merciful and gracious, long-suffering, and of great kindness. The Lord is good unto all, and His mercies are upon all His works. Let all Thy works praise Thee, O Lord, and let Thy saints bless Thee" (Ps 144:7–10).

It is granted to all people to see God clearly in nature, and to venerate, glorify, and give thanks to Him. Very few, however, have seen Him; those who have seen Him are those who have not deprived themselves of the capacity to see, by leading a dissipated, sensual life and by accepting false thoughts, and who have not, under the influence of these harmful guides, taken the wrong path, toward false activity, decisively hostile to God, and rejecting Him in various ways. In His infinite goodness, God has also appeared to humanity in a different, far closer way, so that we may draw nearer to Him, be adopted by Him, be united with Him, and attain in Him our salvation and blessedness, liberating ourselves from the perdition and eternal tribulation into which we have descended through our voluntary fall. God has appeared to mankind not in splendid robes—in the visible natural world—although he remained in this imperial purple, while being higher than anything He could be enveloped in. He appeared in the humble form of a man, taking humanity upon Himself together with all our weaknesses, all the consequences of our fall, with the exception of the sin that caused it. God appeared clothed in humanity, He appeared in the country of our exile, spent His life there, like an outcast, in deprivations, in sorrows, in persecutions. He ended this life with a violent death on the wood of the cross. With His life and His death, the God-Man confessed the justice of God, through which humans were thrown out of paradise down to earth. He confessed the culpability of human beings before God, because this was the essential and sole condition for reconciliation between them and God. All who wish to be true Christians must confess this guilt, first by recognizing it in their hearts, then with their lips and in words, and finally through their actions or their life. Everyone must take up his cross and follow Christ (Matt 16:24): without this no-one can be a disciple of Christ.

A Christian marvels at the greatness of divine goodness that he sees in the incarnation of God the Word, and in His salvation of mankind. When contemplating this, he is inspired to glorify and give abundant thanks to God, and a fervent zeal is kindled in him to live in accordance with the commandments of the Gospel, and to follow Christ on the narrow and difficult way (Matt 7:13–14). When the Christian enters the narrow way, then he perceives the disastrous deception that prevails on the broad way. When he tastes the spiritual consolation with which the Saviour feeds those traveling by the difficult way, as He fed the Israelites with manna in the wilderness (Exod 16:4–22), then he abhors the carnal and sinful pleasure in which Egypt so abounded. The Christian ineffably glorifies and gives thanks to God among the deprivations and sorrows with which the providence of God distances him from becoming sympathetic toward and enslaved by sin, and thanks to which he is numbered among the followers of Christ. No-one has lifted up such voices of praise to God for their earthly well-being, as those raised by the holy martyrs for the trials and tortures they endured, through which God granted them to seal their confession of Christ and enter into the closest union with Him. Never was such glorification and thanksgiving to God heard from magnificent halls, or from luxurious feasts, as was heard from the wretched huts of monastics, from among their deprivations and sorrows, or from the table of fasters who had eaten their meager meal of bread to strengthen the body in order to serve the soul, guarding themselves from surfeit that enslaves the soul to the body. Through a carnal mind and a carnal way of life, a person forgets God and forgets His blessings, and the great work of redemption is hidden as if behind a thick curtain: all this is revealed to those who "have crucified the flesh with its passions and desires" (Gal 5:24). From the cross we are capable of confessing and glorifying God; amidst earthly well-being we are capable of denying Him.

Brothers! Let us cultivate the invisible effort to give thanks to God. This effort reminds us of God, Whom we have forgotten; it reveals to us the greatness of God that has been hidden from us, and it reveals the ineffable and innumerable blessings He has bestowed upon people in general and each person in particular. This effort places within us a living faith in God; it gives us God, Who is not with us, Who has been taken away from us by our coldness toward Him and our negligence. Evil thoughts defile and destroy a man (Matt 15:18–19): holy thoughts sanctify him and animate him. "Dishonest reasoning separates people from God" (WSol 1:3): holy thoughts bring people to Him. From them arise God-pleasing words and deeds. The wise leper was brought by a holy thought before the face of the Saviour, praised and gave thanks to Him, and heard from Him the good news of his salvation: "Your faith has made you well" (Luke 17:19). We too can draw near to God through God-pleasing thoughts, among which a place of honor belongs to thanksgiving to and glorification of God; we can please Him with the holy words and deeds commanded by Him, and through them acquire a living faith in God, and thus gain our salvation. Amen.

43. On Signs and Miracles

Homily on the Monday of the Twenty-ninth Week after Pentecost

The Holy Gospel recounted to us today how the pharisees, not content with the miracles the Lord had already performed, demanded a special miracle: "a sign from heaven" (Mark 8:11). The demand for a sign of this kind, corresponding to some strange understanding about signs and miracles, was repeated more than once, as the Lord bears witness: "[Why does] this generation seek a sign?" (Mark 8:12). The Sadducees, whose beliefs differed greatly from those of the pharisees, made the same demand (Matt 16:1). The desire for "a sign from heaven" was also expressed occasionally by the people. Thus after the Lord had miraculously multiplied the five loaves to feed a crowd of people numbering five thousand men, in addition to their wives and children, the witnesses of this miracle, who had participated in the meal, said to the Lord: "What sign will You perform then, that we may see it and believe You? What work will You do? Our fathers ate the manna in the desert; as it is written, 'He gave them bread from heaven to eat'" (John 6:30–31). The multiplying of the bread by the hands of the Saviour did not seem to them sufficiently wondrous: it was performed quietly, with the holy humility that permeated all the actions of the God-Man, whereas they needed to see something impressive. They needed the sky to be covered with thick clouds, thunder to rumble and lightning to flash, and loaves of bread to fall from the air. This was the kind of miracle the Jewish high priests and leaders demanded of the God-Man, when He deigned to be lifted up upon the cross. "The chief priests also, mocking with the scribes and elders, said, 'He saved others; Himself He cannot save. If He is the King of Israel, let Him now come down from the cross, and we will believe Him'" (Matt 27:41–42). They recognized the miracles worked by the Lord as miracles, and at the same time mocked Him; in mocking Him, they rejected these miracles; in rejecting the miracles granted through God's mercy, they demanded a miracle of their own invention and in keeping with their own judgment, a wonder that, if it had been worked, would have destroyed the purpose for which the God-Man had come to earth, with the result that the redemption of mankind would not have taken place. One of those who wished to see a miracle worked by the Lord, with which they intended to amuse themselves by satisfying their curiosity, frivolity, and folly, was Herod. He needed a sign as a pleasant way to pass the time; when he did not receive what he wanted, he showered the Lord with mockery, and in that way entertained himself for a moment (Luke 23:8–11). What is the significance of the general demand for the God-Man to work miracles, a demand that originated from such diverse people, and was combined with disregard for the amazing miracles He had already performed? It is an expression of the understanding of miracles held by people with a carnal mind.

What is a carnal mind? It is a way of thinking about God and all spiritual matters that man has taken from his fallenness, and not from the Word of God. The characteristic enmity and opposition toward God with which a carnal mind is infected and filled is expressed with particular clarity in the demand that the God-Man work miracles that are in line with the understanding of false reason, while disregarding, rejecting, and condemning the true miracles worked by Him in His inexpressible goodness, as the One Who has "the power of God and the wisdom of God" (1 Cor 1:24).

Part One

It was a grave sin to ask the God-Man for miracles based on the principles of a carnal mind. When He heard this impudent, blasphemous demand, He "sighed deeply in His spirit, and said, 'Why does this generation seek a sign? Assuredly, I say to you, no sign shall be given to this generation.' And He left them, and ... departed" (Mark 8:12–13).

There is joy in heaven from one repentant sinner: thus, conversely, the angels in heaven are grieved when a man falls into sin and a sinner refuses to repent (Luke 15:10). In grace-filled contemplation of the infinite goodness of God toward humanity, and of His holy will that all men be saved, St Macarius the Great had no reservations in saying that the most holy God, while free from passion, is enveloped in weeping from the perdition of men.[175] Weeping that is beyond our understanding is not alien to the Spirit of God, and the Spirit of God dwelling within a person "makes intercession" for him "with groanings which cannot be uttered" (Rom 8:26). Such groaning was prompted in the Son of God by the proud and foolish demand for a miracle. He sighed deeply in His spirit, and said, "Why does this generation seek a sign?" This question was God's response to the hostile demand for a sign. What deep sorrow can be heard from God in this response! It sounds like bewilderment at the absurdity and impudence of the request. It shows a loss of hope for the salvation of the people who made a request that was contrary to the Spirit Who grants salvation. The Lord abandons those who have adopted a carnal mind and stubbornly keep it, ailing incurably from it: He commits them to themselves, to perdition, which they have chosen and voluntarily kept. "And He left them, and departed." Exactly: "To be carnally minded is death" (Rom 8:6). Just as it is characteristic of a corpse not to feel that it is dead, it is characteristic of a person with a carnal mind not to understand or to feel his perdition. Because he is not aware of his perdition, he does not recognize his need to be revived, and, on the basis of a false awareness of life, he has rejected and continues to reject the true life that is God.

Can a "sign from heaven" have a particular authenticity? Of course, those who asked for such a sign did so because they ascribed this authenticity to it. Is it possible to conclude that a sign from heaven is definitely a sign from God? Divine Scripture shows the contrary. Even the expression "sign from heaven" is very imprecise. Most people, both in those times and now, being unfamiliar with science, associate with "heaven," or the sky, everything that happens in the air and the space above it. Thus the sun, the moon, and the stars are seen as being in heaven, while they are in space; rain, thunder, and lightning are seen as phenomena from heaven (Jas 5:18), while they occur in the air, in the atmosphere of the earth, and thus belong on earth. Holy Scripture tells us that, by the action of the devil, "The fire of God fell from heaven and burned up the sheep and the servants" of the righteous Job (Job 1:16). It is obvious that this fire formed in the air, just as lightning forms in it. Simon the sorcerer, who believed that the power of Satan acting within him was "the great power of God," astonished the blind people with miracles (Acts 8:10). Simon particularly impressed the idol-worshiping Romans when, at a great gathering of them, he declared himself a god and expressed his intention of ascending to heaven, and then suddenly began rising into the air; St Symeon the Translator recounts this, having taken it from the manuscripts of ancient Christian writers.[176] The absence in a person of true knowledge of God is a terrible calamity, because without this knowledge, the works of the devil are taken for the works of God. Before the second coming of Christ, when Christianity, spiritual knowledge, and reasoning among people will become extremely scarce, "false christs and false prophets will rise and show great signs and wonders to deceive, if possible, even the elect" (Matt 24:24). In particular, the antichrist himself will perform abundant miracles, to impress and satisfy carnal minds and ignorance: he will give them the "sign from heaven" that they seek and thirst for. His "coming," says the holy Apostle Paul, will occur "according to the working of Satan, with all power, signs, and lying wonders, and with all unrighteous deception among those who perish, because they did not receive the love of the truth, that they might be saved" (2 Thess 2:9–10). Ignorant and carnal-minded people, seeing these miracles, will not stop at all to reflect; they will immediately accept the miracles because of the affinity of their spirit with the one who worked them, and in their blindness they will recognize and confess the action of Satan to be a great manifestation of the power of God. The antichrist will be accepted very hastily and thoughtlessly.[177] People will not understand that his miracles have no good or reasonable purpose and no particular meaning, that they are devoid of truth and filled with lies, that they are a monstrous and malicious theatrical show that is devoid of meaning and attempts to astonish people, to bring them to confusion and forgetfulness, to seduce, deceive and distract them with fascination for a luxurious, empty, foolish effect.

It is not strange that the miracles of the antichrist should be accepted unquestioningly and with enthusiasm by people who have turned away from Christianity, enemies of the truth and of God: they have prepared themselves for open, active acceptance of the messenger and tool of Satan, of his teaching and of all his actions, by entering at the right time into communion in spirit with Satan. It is worthy of close attention and deep sorrow that the miracles and acts of the antichrist will cause difficulty even to the chosen people of God. The reasons for the strong influence of the antichrist on people will lie in the infernal guile and hypocrisy with which he skillfully conceals the most terrible evil, in his unrestrained and shameless impudence, in the close cooperation of the fallen spirits, and finally in the ability to work wonders, which, although false, are still impressive. Human imagination is powerless to conceive of how evil the antichrist will be; it is not possible for a human heart, even a depraved one, to believe that evil can reach the level that it will reach in the antichrist. He will trumpet about himself as his forebears and precursors did. He will call himself a preacher and a restorer of true knowledge of God. Those Christians who do not understand will see in him a representative and upholder of true religion, and will join him. He will proclaim himself to be the promised Messiah. Those with a carnal mind will exclaim in meeting him; seeing his glory, his power, his genius, his great progress from a worldly viewpoint, they will proclaim him god and become his fellow workers.[178] The antichrist will present himself as meek, merciful, and filled with love and with every virtue. He will be recognized as such, and people who recognize fallen human "truth" as the truth, and have not renounced it in favor of the truth of the Gospel, will submit to him because of his great virtue.[179] The antichrist will offer to arrange great earthly well-being and prosperity for humanity, he will offer honors, wealth, splendor, carnal comforts, and pleasures. Those who seek earthly things will accept the antichrist and declare him their master (John 5:43). The antichrist will present to humanity, like an artful theater show, the sight of amazing miracles that cannot be explained by the science of the time; he will inspire fear with the threat and the wonder of his miracles, and will use them to satisfy reckless curiosity and coarse ignorance, to satisfy vainglory and human pride, carnal-mindedness and superstition, and will cause bewilderment in human learning: all those who are guided by the light of their fallen nature and alienated from guidance by the light of God will be enticed into obedience to the seducer (Rev 13:8). The signs of the antichrist will appear principally in the layer of the air,[180] where Satan rules (Eph 2:2; 6:12). The signs will act mainly upon the sense of sight, captivating and deceiving it.[181] St John the Theologian, contemplating in Revelation the events that will precede the end of the world, says that the antichrist will perform great works, "so that he even makes fire come down from heaven on the earth in the sight of men" (Rev 13:13). Scripture points to this sign as to the highest of the signs of the antichrist, and the location of this sign is the air: it will be an awe-inspiring and terrible sight. The signs of the antichrist will supplement the actions of his cunning behavior, and convince the majority of people to follow him. The opponents of the antichrist will be regarded as troublemakers and as enemies of the common good and of good order. They will be subjected to both hidden and open persecution, to torture and torment. Evil spirits, sent out throughout the world, will promote a very high opinion of the antichrist among people, a general delight and an irresistible attraction to him.[182] Scripture has depicted the final persecution of Christianity and the cruelty of the oppressor with many characteristics. One decisive and definite characteristic is the name given by Scripture to this terrible person: he is called a "beast" (Rev 13:1), just as the fallen angel is called a "serpent" (Gen 3:1) and a "dragon" (Rev 12:3). These names truly represent the character of the two enemies of God. The latter acts more in secret, whereas the former acts more openly; but to the beast, which resembles all beasts,[183] combining within itself various different forms of ferocity, "the dragon gave ... his power, his throne, and great authority" (Rev 13:2). There will be a terrible trial for the saints of God: the evil, the hypocrisy, the miracles of the persecutor will try to deceive and captivate them; the subtle and invented persecutions and constraints hidden with cunning inventiveness, and the unlimited power of the torturer, will put them in a very difficult position; their small number will make them seem negligible in the face of the rest of humanity, and particular weakness will be attached to their opinion; general scorn, hatred, slander, oppressions, and violent death will be their lot. Only with the help of divine grace, and with its guidance, will the elect of God be able resist His enemy, and to confess the Lord Jesus before him and before men.

The conclusion we can draw from all the above is that when the pharisees and the Sadducees demanded "signs from heaven" of the Lord, they were demanding miracles with the character of the miracles of the antichrist. The fact that they were demanding this kind of miracle explains the Lord's response to their demand. On one occasion, when a demand of this type was made of Him, the God-Man expressed deep bitterness, refused with more than resolution, did not even want to remain in the presence of those who had permitted themselves to demand this, and left them. Another time, he gave them the following alarming reply: "A wicked and adulterous generation seeks after a sign, and no sign shall be given to it except the sign of the prophet Jonah" (Matt 16:1–4; 12:38–42). All those asking for a sign are called a generation because of the affinity between them in spirit; they are called an adulterous generation because they had entered into communion with Satan in spirit, by breaking off communion with God; they are called a wicked generation because, although they recognized the miracles of the God-Man, they pretended not to; although they disparaged and blasphemed against the miracles of God, they asked for miracles corresponding to their unhappy disposition, their spirit. The request for "signs from heaven" was not so much a request for a miracle, as a mockery of the miracles of the God-Man and the expression of an ignorant and distorted understanding of miracles. The sign of the prophet Jonah, as explained by the Saviour Himself (Matt 12:40), signifies the signs accompanying His death and resurrection. That was the occasion when God's "sign from heaven" was given. On that day the sun, seeing the Lord crucified, darkened at mid-day; there came a general deep darkness that lasted three hours; the veil of the temple at Jerusalem was torn in two of its own accord, from the very top to the bottom; the earth quaked; rocks split, graves were opened; many saints were raised and appeared to many in the holy city (Luke 23:45; Matt 27:45, 51–53). At the resurrection of the Lord, there was another earthquake. The radiant angel came down from heaven to the grave of the Lord, as a witness to the resurrection, and struck down with fear the guards who had been placed at the tomb by those who had been looking for "signs from heaven." The guards reported the resurrection of the Lord to the council of the Jews. This council, after receiving a "sign from heaven," expressed the same disparagement and hatred toward it, as it had toward all the preceding miracles of the God-Man, and bribed the guards to join them in concealing God's miracle with the darkness of lies (Matt 28:2–4; 11–15).

Let us now consider the miracles performed by our Lord Jesus Christ. They were a gift of God to humanity. The gift was given not to pay a debt, but solely in goodwill and mercy. Men ought to have received this gift with the greatest reverence and gratitude, because the Giver of the gift proclaimed Himself God, after clothing Himself in humanity to save men, and the gift was His testimony of this. The gift had indisputable value. But just as it was left to men's free will to accept salvation, it was also given to men to consider the miracles of Christ, to consider their credibility and quality, to draw conclusions about the One who performed them on the basis of them, so that recognition and acceptance of the Redeemer might be the result of free, positive conviction, and not of a hasty, careless, forced enthusiasm. The miracles of Christ were completely certain. We can say of them all what the Lord said to the Apostle Thomas: "Reach your finger here, and look at My hands; and reach your hand here, and put it into My side. Do not be unbelieving, but believing" (John 20:27). The miracles of Christ were tangible; they were clear to the most simple people; there was nothing mysterious about them; anyone could easily examine them; there was no place for doubt or perplexity about whether they were miracles or only appeared to be. The dead rose again, lepers were healed, people born blind received their sight, mute people began to speak; food was multiplied instantaneously for those who needed it; the waves of the sea and the winds subsided at a single word of command, and those whose lives had been at risk from the storm were saved; the nets of the fishermen who had labored long and in vain were suddenly filled with fish, obedient to the wordless voice of their Lord. The miracles of the God-Man had many witnesses, the majority of whom were hostile to Him, inattentive, or sought only physical help from Him. The miracles were undeniable. The most bitter enemies of the Lord did not deny them: they only attempted to disparage them with blasphemous misinterpretations and every means suggested to them by cunning and spite (Matt 12:24; John 9:24). In the miracles of the Lord there was no vanity, no theatrical effect; not one single miracle was worked for show; all of them were covered with the protection of divine humility. They constitute a chain of blessings for suffering humanity. At the same time, they clearly expressed the power of the Creator over material creation and over created spirits, they expressed and showed the power of God, who had assumed human nature and appeared as a man among men.

One of the miracles of the Lord, which possesses a mystical significance, was not accompanied by any visible good work toward a particular person. It signified a blessing that was ready to be poured out over all of humanity. The miracle was the withering of the fig tree that had no fruit and was rich only in leaves (Mark 11:13–14; 20–21). This tree is mentioned in Scripture (Gen 3:7) as one of the trees of paradise during the account of the fall into sin of the first parents. It provided Adam and Eve with leaves to cover their nakedness, which they had not noticed until they fell into sin, and which sin then revealed to them. It is possible that the fruit of the fig tree in paradise was the forbidden fruit. The Lord did not find fruit on the fig tree: He looked for it there out of season, He permitted His body to desire food at the wrong time. This shows the wrongness of the desire of the first parents, which, like all human weaknesses, the Lord carried within Himself and destroyed through Himself. Not finding fruit, the Lord rejected the leaves also, and destroyed the very life of the tree: a different tree, the tree of the cross, was already being prepared as a tool for the salvation of men. The tree that was the instrument of the perdition of men withers at the command of the Saviour of mankind. This mystical miracle was performed in the presence of just a few close disciples of the mystical teaching, the holy apostles. It was performed just before the God-Man entered into the struggle of His redemptive sufferings for mankind, just before He ascended the cross.

The miracles of the Lord had a holy meaning, a holy purpose. While they were great blessings in themselves, in the context of the divine view they served only as testimony and confirmation of an incomparably higher blessing. By assuming human nature, the Lord brought men an eternal, spiritual, priceless gift: salvation, healing from sin, resurrection from eternal death. The word of the Lord and His way of life revealed this gift in the most satisfactory way: in life the Lord was sinless, all-holy (John 8:46); His word was filled with power (Mark 1:42). But men had fallen deep into the darkness and gloom of the carnal mind; their hearts and minds had been blinded. It was necessary to condescend to the sick state of men; it was necessary to give the clearest possible witness to their bodily sensations; it was necessary to communicate, through these physical feelings, knowledge of life to the minds and hearts that had died a death peculiar to them, an eternal death. The miracles of God are given as an aid to the word of God. In order for men to understand and accept the spiritual gift perceived only with the eyes of the soul, the Lord united to the spiritual, eternal gift another, comparable gift, a temporal, physical one: the healing of physical human illnesses. Sin is the cause of all illnesses in a person, both of soul and of body, and is the cause of both temporal and eternal death. In showing His power over the consequences of sin in human bodies, the Lord also showed His power over sin in general. A person with a carnal mind sees neither illnesses of the soul nor eternal death; but he sees and recognizes bodily illnesses and the death of the body, and they affect and trouble him greatly. When He healed the sick with a single word, a single command, raised the dead, and commanded unclean spirits, the Lord showed His power, the power of God over people, over sin, over fallen spirits, and He showed it clearly for physical sensations, for carnal-mindedness itself. A person with a carnal mind, seeing and feeling this power, was able and, logically, was obliged to recognize the power of the Lord over sin not only in the connection of sin with the body, but also in its connection with the soul, and to recognize the Lord's power over the soul itself, especially as certain miracles of the Lord, as for example in raising the dead, showed His unlimited power over both the body and the soul. The body was revived; the soul was summoned back into it, after departing from this world to the world of spirits, and was reunited with the body from which it had parted forever. Thus signs were given to man within himself, not somewhere outside him; man was given evidence of his salvation within himself, not far away from him. Testimony of the eternal salvation of the soul and the body was given through the temporal salvation of the body from bodily illnesses and physical death. When the miracles of the Lord are viewed in the right way, with reverence, they prove to be filled with divine reason; the demand for "a sign from heaven" proves to be senseless. It is rare for the power of the Lord to manifest itself beyond people, over objects of material nature, but there have been such cases. They provide testimony that the power of the Lord over all of nature is a boundless power, the power of God. These miracles supplement the miracles that constitute blessings for humanity itself, so that the significance that men were intended to ascribe to the Redeemer of men was defined as precisely as possible. Just as the purpose of the Lord's coming on earth was to save mankind, so the cares of the

Lord were focused on man, on His most refined work of creation, on His image, on His spiritual temple. The land of our exile and our wandering full of suffering is the earth, and the whole of material creation, despite its enormous size, has not attracted His attention. Even if certain miracles are performed in the material world, this is done to satisfy human needs.

This was the significance and the purpose of the miracles worked by the Lord and also by His apostles. The Lord proclaimed this; the apostles proclaimed it. On one occasion, a great number of people were gathered in the house where the Lord was. The house was full, and the crowd was pressing against the doors; it was already impossible to enter the building. A paralytic was then brought there, who could not get up from his bed. When the people who had brought him saw how crowded and packed the house was, they carried the sick man up onto the roof; then they made an opening in the ceiling and lowered him down on his bed before the Lord. Seeing this act of faith, the merciful Lord said to the paralytic, "Son, your sins are forgiven you" (Mark 2:5). Some of the scribes were sitting there. As they knew the letter of the law but were filled with envy and hatred toward the God-Man, the thought immediately came to them that blasphemy had been spoken. "Who," they thought, "can forgive sins but God alone?" The Lord, Who knows men's hearts, perceived their thoughts and said to them: "Why do you reason about these things in your hearts? Which is easier, to say to the paralytic, 'Your sins are forgiven you,' or to say, 'Arise, take up your bed and walk'?" A hypocrite or a fraud can also say "Your sins are forgiven you," though without demonstrating it. "But that you may know that the Son of Man has power on earth to forgive sins"—He said to the paralytic, "I say to you, arise, take up your bed, and go to your house." The paralytic was immediately healed and regained his strength: he took up his bed and went out in front of everyone (Mark 2:2–12). This miracle is filled with divine wisdom and goodness. First of all, the Lord grants the suffering person an essential spiritual gift, invisible to physical eyes: forgiveness of sins. This gift prompted in the scribes the involuntary confession that such a gift can only be given by God. With His response to the reasonings of their hearts, the Lord gives them new evidence that He is God. Finally, the spiritual gift and the spiritual testimony are sealed with the material gift and testimony: the immediate and full healing of the sick man. The holy Evangelist Mark concludes his Gospel by saying that after the Ascension of the Lord, the apostles "preached [the word] everywhere, the Lord working with them and confirming the word through the accompanying signs" (Mark 16:20). This same thought is expressed by all the apostles in the prayer with which they turned to God after the threats of the Sanhedrin forbidding them to teach and act in the name of Jesus: "Grant to Your servants," they said, "that with all boldness they may speak Your word, by stretching out Your hand to heal, and that signs and wonders may be done through the name of Your holy Servant Jesus" (Acts 4:29–30). The signs of God were given to support the word of God. The signs testified to the power and meaning of the word (Luke 4:36). The essential agent is the word. No signs are needed where the word is accepted, because the virtue pertaining to the word has been understood. Signs are a condescension to human weakness.

The word works in one way, and signs work in another. The word acts directly upon the mind and the heart; signs act on the mind and the heart by means of physical sensations. The consequences of the effect of the word are stronger, and more definite, than the consequences of the effect of signs. When the word and signs work together, the effect of signs remains somehow unnoticed because of the powerful effect of the word. This can clearly be seen in the accounts of the Gospel. Signs had an effect on Nicodemus, and he recognized in the Lord merely "a teacher come from God" (John 3:2). The word acted upon the apostle Peter and he confessed the Lord to be the Christ, the Son of God. "You have the words of eternal life," he said to the God-Man: "Also we have come to believe and know that You are the Christ, the Son of the living God" (John 6:68–69). St Peter witnessed many of the Lord's miracles. Shortly before he made this confession, the five loaves of bread had been multiplied miraculously and had fed a large crowd of people to satiety. But in his confession the Apostle said nothing of the miracles. He spoke only of the power and the action of the word. The same thing happened with the two disciples who conversed with the Lord without recognizing Him on the road to Emmaus, and recognized Him after their arrival, inside the house, at the breaking of the bread. They had hardly had time to recognize the Lord, when He became invisible. They said nothing of this amazing wonder, but gave all their attention to the action of the word. "Did not our heart burn within us," they said to each other, "while He talked with us on the road, and while He opened the Scriptures to us?" (Luke 24:32).

The God-Man blessed all those who had not seen signs and had believed (John 20:29). He expressed sympathy with those who were not satisfied with the word and needed miracles. "Unless you people see signs and wonders, you will by no means believe" (John 4:48), He said to the nobleman at Capernaum. Indeed, those who abandon the word and seek to be convinced by miracles are worthy of pity. Their need and demand for miracles reveals a particular prevalence of a carnal mind, gross ignorance, a life sacrificed to corruption and sin, indifference toward studying the law of God and in God-pleasing virtues, an inability in the soul to feel the presence of the Holy Spirit and His action in the word. Signs were intended mainly to persuade sensual people, occupied with the cares of the world, and bring them to the faith. People who are immersed in the cares of life, their souls constantly pinned down to the earth and to its affairs, have little capacity to value the virtue of the word. The merciful Word drew them toward the salvation given to them by the word through visible signs which, by offering a material means of persuading them, and acting via their sensations, brought their weak souls to the omnipotent, saving Word. Those who believed because of signs constituted the lowest category of believers in Christ. When they were offered spiritual, sublime, all-holy teaching, many of them interpreted it according to their own understanding (John 6:60). They did not want to ask God for explanations of God's word, and they condemned the word that was "spirit and life" (John 6:63), thus revealing their superficial faith and the superficial pledge of their hearts, and "many of His disciples," who had seen many signs, "went back and walked with Him no more" (John 6:66).

Neither the word nor the signs of the God-Man had a beneficial effect on the Jewish high priests, scribes, pharisees, and Sadducees, although, with the exception of the latter, they knew the law of God to the letter. They were alien to God and hostile to Him, and not only because they were infected with the sin common to all of humanity, but because they made themselves so, they confirmed and sealed that disposition within themselves from their own will, from conceit, from their wish to live and succeed in a way of life that is forbidden by the Gospel. They could not hear the Son of God speaking to them; they did not listen to His word as they should, they did not heed Him; they only perceived those words that seemed to them convenient for misinterpretation, in order to use them to accuse the Lord. This is how hatred is usually inclined toward the words of its object. "Why do you not understand My speech?" said the Saviour to His enemies, who had stubbornly and bitterly rejected the salvation He offered. Why do you not understand My teaching? Why do you not accept My healing word? "Because you are not able to listen to My word" (John 8:43): it is unbearable for you. Since you are born of and work for lies, "because I tell the truth, you do not believe Me" (John 8:45). "He who is of God hears God's words; therefore you do not hear, because you are not of God" (John 8:47). "If I do not do the works of My Father, do not believe Me;

but if I do, though you do not believe Me, believe the works, that you may know and believe that the Father is in Me, and I in Him" (John 10:37–38).

In vain were these words that, as God's truth, in themselves constituted full attestation (John 8:14); in vain were the miracles, which also constituted full attestation, and were so tangible and visible, that the enemies of the God-Man, despite all their desire and efforts to deny them, could not avoid acknowledging them (John 9:24). The means that had an effect upon the people who hated the law of God or who knew very little of it, and spent their lives in earthly occupations and vanities, but did not voluntarily reject the law of God, these means had no effect on those who had a thorough knowledge of the letter of the law of God, but rejected it in their lives and in their will (John 5:46–47; 7:19). Everything that could be done for the salvation of men was done through the ineffable mercy of God. "If I had not come and spoken to them," the Saviour points out, "they would have no sin, but now they have no excuse for their sin. . . . If I had not done among them the works which no one else did, they would have no sin; but now they have seen and also hated both Me and My Father" (John 15:22–24). Christianity has been preached with such certainty that there is no justification for those who do not know it. The only reason for ignorance is people's will. Just as the sun shines down from the heavens, so Christianity shines. If a person has voluntarily closed his eyes, let him ascribe the fact that he cannot see and his ignorance to his own will, but not to the absence of light. The reason why men reject the God-Man lies in the men, just as the reason for accepting the antichrist lies within them. "I have come in My Father's name," the Lord testified to the Jews, "and you do not receive Me; if another comes in his own name, him you will receive" (John 5:43). He presents them here at the same time both as people who reject Him and as people who accept the antichrist, although the antichrist is mentioned as one who is to come in the future. Rejecting Christ in line with the disposition of their spirit, they at the same time and due to the same disposition accepted the antichrist: they were numbered among those who accepted the antichrist, although they ended their earthly wanderings many centuries before his coming. This is because they carried out his greatest work: deicide. No comparable atrocity is left for the antichrist to carry out himself when he comes. Just as their spirit had adopted a hostile attitude toward Christ, so it was in a state of communion with the antichrist, while separated from him by a vast expanse of time, now approaching the second millennium since they lived. "Every spirit," says St John the Theologian, "that does not confess that Jesus Christ has come in the flesh is not of God. And this is the spirit of the Antichrist, which you have heard was coming, and is now already in the world" in spirit (1 John 4:3). Those who are with the antichrist in spirit deny Christ; they have accepted the antichrist in spirit, they have entered into communion with him, and they have submitted and bowed down to him in spirit, recognizing him as their god. "For this reason God will send," that is, will permit, "them strong delusion, that they should believe the lie, that they all may be condemned who did not believe the truth but had pleasure in unrighteousness" (2 Thess 2:11–12). God is righteous in whatever He permits. What He permits is satisfaction for the human spirit, and at the same time rebuke and judgment. The antichrist will come at his foreordained time. His coming will be preceded by a general deviation from the Christian faith in the majority of people. By withdrawing from Christ, mankind will prepare itself to accept the antichrist and will take him into its spirit. In the very disposition of the human spirit there will arise a desire for, an invitation to the antichrist, a sympathy with him, just as a seriously sick person might thirst for a deadly drink. They will invite him. A voice will call out in human society expressing an urgent need for the genius of geniuses, to advance material development and progress to the highest possible level, and establish on earth such happiness that paradise and heaven appear superfluous. The antichrist will be the logical, just, natural consequence of the general moral and spiritual tendency of men.

The miracles of God incarnate constituted the greatest material blessings that humanity could possibly imagine. What blessing could be greater than the return of life to a corpse? What blessing could be more precious than the healing of an incurable disease that deprives the sufferer of life even during his life, and makes his life more like prolonged death? However, despite their benevolent character, their holiness, the spiritual significance of the miracles of Christ, they were only temporal gifts. In the precise meaning, they were in fact signs. They were signs of the eternal salvation given by the word. Those raised from the dead by the God-Man died again in their time: they were given only an extension of their earthly life, but life was not returned to them forever. Those whom the God-Man healed became ill again and also died: their health was returned to them only for a time, not forever. The temporary and material blessings were poured out as a sign of the eternal, spiritual blessings. The visible gifts were handed out to people who were in thrall to sensuality, so that they might believe in and accept the invisible gifts. The signs extracted them from the abyss of ignorance and sensuality, and brought them to the faith: faith brought them knowledge of eternal good things and inspired in them a desire to acquire them. It was with the help of miraculous signs that the apostles spread Christianity quickly around the world: the signs were clear and strong testimony of Christianity, both for educated peoples and for those living in ignorance and barbarity. When faith had been planted everywhere, and the word was also planted, then the signs were also taken away, as they had fulfilled their function. They stopped taking effect to a great extent and everywhere, and were performed only rarely by chosen saints of God. St John Chrysostom, a Father and writer of the fourth and fifth centuries, says that in his time the gift of signs was already dying out, although there were still sign-bearing men in places, especially among monastics.[184] Over time, the number of sign-bearing men has continually decreased. The holy Fathers have prophesied that there will be no sign-bearing men in the last times.[185]

> Why, some ask, are there no signs now? Pay particular attention to my answer to this, because I hear this question from many people, often and always. Why then did everyone who was baptized in the old days begin speaking in foreign languages, but this does not happen any more? ... Because the grace of miracles has been taken away from men? God does this not to dishonour us but in fact to offer us greater honour. In what way? I will explain. The people of those times were more feeble-minded, as they had only just been drawn away from idols; their minds were dull, they were absorbed in material things, and devoted to them, and could not imagine that immaterial gifts existed, nor did they know the importance of spiritual grace, all of which is accepted only through faith. This is the reason for the signs. Of the spiritual gifts, some are invisible, and are accepted simply by faith, and others are combined with a sign, subject to the senses, to awaken faith in unbelievers. For example, the forgiveness of sins is a spiritual, invisible gift. We do not see how our sins are forgiven with our bodily eyes. The soul is cleansed, but this process is invisible to the eyes of our body. And thus the cleansing of sins is a spiritual gift that cannot be revealed to the eyes of the body; however, the sudden ability to speak in foreign languages, while among to the actions of the Spirit, also serves at the same time as a sign that is subject to the senses, and therefore can easily be perceived by unbelievers: an

> invisible action accomplished within the soul becomes manifest and is revealed through the external language we hear. For this same reason Paul says, 'But the manifestation of the Spirit is given to each one for the profit of all' (1 Cor 12:7). And thus I have no need of signs. Why is this? Because I have learned to believe in the grace of God without them. An unbeliever needs evidence; but I, a believer, have no need of evidence, or of signs; although I do not speak in foreign tongues, I know that I am cleansed of sin. In those days people did not believe unless they were given signs. They were given signs as evidence for the faith they were adopting. And thus signs were given not to believers but to unbelievers, that they might believe; Paul also says this: '[signs are] not to those who believe but to unbelievers' (1 Cor 14:22).[186]

If signs were essential, they would have remained. What remained was the word, which the signs helped to establish. It spread, it reigned, and it embraced the whole world. It has been explained most wisely by the Fathers of the Church, so that it has become particularly easy to access and adopt it. It is vital; it is essential; it accomplishes the salvation of men; it transmits to us eternal good things; it acquires the kingdom of heaven for us; in it are concealed the most lofty spiritual signs of God (Ps 118:18). "But the word of the Lord endures forever. Now this is the word which by the gospel was preached to you" (1 Pet 1:25). In the word of the Lord is life, as He, the Word, is life (John 1:4). It raises dead people to eternal life, giving them its own all-holy life: the hearers and doers of the word exist "having been born again, not of corruptible seed but incorruptible, through the word of God which lives and abides forever" (1 Pet 1:23). To become acquainted with the meaning of the word, it is necessary to keep it. When a person keeps the commandments of the Gospel, they immediately begin to transfigure, to transform, to renew the person, to change his way of thinking, the feelings of his heart, even his body: "For the word of God is living and powerful, and sharper than any two-edged sword, piercing even to the division of soul and spirit, and of joints and marrow, and is a discerner of the thoughts and intents of the heart" (Heb 4:12). The word of God contains within it the proof of its own existence. Like the signs of healing, it acts within the person himself, and through this action it testifies about itself. It is the highest sign. It is a spiritual sign that, when it is given to a person, satisfies all the requirements for his salvation, and renders unnecessary any help from material signs. A Christian who does not know about this attribute of the word reveals himself to be cold toward the word, ignorant of the word of God or knowing only the cold letter of the word.

Part Two

The eagerness encountered in contemporary Christian society to see miracles and even to work them must not be ignored. This desire needs to be examined carefully. The desire to work miracles is much censured by the holy Fathers: it reveals self-deception living in and possessing the soul, based on conceit and vainglory. The great teacher of monks St Isaac the Syrian reasons as follows on this subject:

> The Lord is at all times a close defender of His saints; but He does not needlessly display His power in an obvious way, with a deed or a sensual sign, so that His protection may not become ordinary to us, and so that we may not lose the proper reverence toward Him, to our detriment. This is how He acts in taking care of the saints: He allows them in every circumstance to show ascetic effort corresponding to their strength, and to labour in prayer; at the same time He shows them that His secret care for them does not stop for a single hour. But if the circumstance becomes more difficult than they can manage, if they become exhausted and are no longer in a position to act due to the weakness of their nature, then He does what is necessary to help them, in the greatness of His power, as necessary and as He knows. He strengthens them, as far as possible, in secret, placing within them the strength to overcome their tribulation. He resolves their difficult trial by means of the knowledge that He grants from Himself, and when they comprehend His providence, He prompts them to give glory, which is beneficial in every way. When the circumstance requires visible help, then, if necessary, He gives it. His means and forms of help are most wise. They help in scarcity, in case of need, and they do not act without a reason. A person who dares to pray to God to accomplish anything unusual without need for it, who wants miracles and signs to be worked with his own hands, is being tempted in his mind by the mocking of the devil, and shows himself to be vainglorious and ailing in his conscience. It is fitting to ask for help from God in tribulation, but to put God to the test without need is disastrous. Anyone who desires such a thing is in

> truth not righteous. We find examples in the lives of the saints when the Lord, while expressing his lack of favour, fulfilled wishes of this type. A person who wants and desires this wilfully, without being compelled to it, falls away from a state of guarding himself, and is inclined to turn aside from knowledge of the truth. If a person who asks for this is heard, the evil one takes up a position within him, as in one who walks without reverence before God, with impudence, and causes him to fall into greater blunders. Truly righteous men not only do not desire to be miracle-workers, but when they are given the gift of working miracles, they refuse it. They do not want this either before the eyes of men, or even within themselves, in the secret depths of their hearts. A certain holy Father, by reason of his purity, received through the grace of God the gift of foreseeing who was to visit him; but he asked God to take this gift from him, and even asked his friends to pray for the same thing. If certain of the saints accepted gifts, they did this because of need, or out of their simplicity; others accepted them as directed by the Divine Spirit acting within them, and never by chance or without reason ... Truly righteous men constantly think that they are unworthy of God. The fact that they deem themselves cursed, undeserving of God's care, bears witness to their truth.[187]

From these holy thoughts we can draw the conclusion that those who want to perform signs want this from carnal fervor, carried away by passions they do not understand, although it may seem to them that they are motivated by zeal for the work of God. Those who want to see signs are in the same state of self-deception and fervor. It is always forbidden to put God to the test, violating our reverence toward Him; we are permitted to ask for help from God in extreme need, when we have no means of our own at our disposal to escape the situation; but we must leave it to God to choose the means of help and give ourselves up to His will and mercy. The Lord always sends down help that is beneficial to our souls, and the exact help that we need, and through this very help He gives us a holy taste of humility. The help does not come with external brilliance, as our carnal minds would have liked it, so that the soul is not harmed by satisfaction of its vainglory. And in the work of God, in the very service of the Church, we must constantly call upon the blessing and help of God, and we must believe that it is only divine, spiritual means that can be beneficial for faith and piety, and never the means suggested by the carnal mind.

death and the judgment of God). If my body were healthy, then remembrance of this time would be completely alien to me. When the body is healthy, it is more inclined to prompt actions that are hostile to God. Afflictions serve as a means to keep the commandments of God."[198] When illnesses and other afflictions befell them, the holy Fathers endeavored first of all to show the endurance that was within their own control—they would resort to self-reproach and self-condemnation in order to strengthen their hearts and force them to be patient;[199] they would remember death and divine judgment, the eternal torments that weaken the importance and the sensation of earthly afflictions (Matt 10:28–31); they would raise their thoughts to divine providence, reminding themselves of the promise of the Son of God that He would remain always with His followers and protect them, and in this way they encouraged their hearts to be of good cheer and have courage (Matt 28:20); they compelled themselves to give glory and thanks to God for their affliction, and to acknowledge their sinfulness, asking God to punish them for it and teach them in His justice and goodness. In addition to their own efforts to acquire patience, they increased their diligent prayers to God to be given the spiritual gift of patience, inseparable from the other spiritual gift of grace-filled humility, which serves together with it as a true guarantee of salvation and eternal blessedness. The great wonderworking Fathers did not give the healing that was so easy for them to their disciples who were subjected to illness through the providence of God, so as not to deprive them of the spiritual progress that illness would certainly bring them when endured in accordance with the spiritual tradition of the Church. St Selidos, the abbot of a Gaza community and a disciple of Barsanuphius the Great, who kept silence in the same monastery, was ill for a long time. Certain of the older brothers asked the great saint to heal the abbot. St Barsanuphius replied: "Some of the saints gathered here could pray to God for the health of my son, as I also told him, so that he did not have a single day of illness; but then he would not receive the fruits of patience. This illness is very beneficial to him for patience and thanksgiving."[200] Explaining the need for an ascetic of Christ to undergo tribulations, St Isaac the Syrian says: "Temptation is beneficial to every human being. If it is beneficial to Paul, then 'every mouth may be stopped, and all the world may become guilty before God' (Rom 3:19). Ascetics undergo temptation so as to increase their riches; weak people so as guard themselves from what is harmful to them; those who are sleeping, so that they may wake up; those who stand far away, so as to draw nearer to God; and the friends of God, so as to become even closer to

Him. An untaught son does not undertake to manage the wealth of his father, because he will not do this properly. For this reason God first tests and wearies us, then gives a gift. Glory to the Master Who gives us the enjoyment of health by means of bitter medicine. There is no-one who has not lamented during his period of learning. There is no-one to whom the time when he was drinking the cup of temptations did not seem bitter. But without these temptations it is impossible to attain strength of soul. Besides this, even the means to endure is not our own. How could a vessel of clay carry water if it were not first strengthened by divine fire? If we ask God humbly for patience, with reverence and with constant desire for it, we will receive everything in Jesus Christ our Lord."[201]

Part Three

Before the second coming of Christ "there will be signs in the sun, in the moon, and in the stars," and the sea will roar and be troubled (Luke 21:25). How can we distinguish these signs from those that the antichrist will also make in the sun, the moon, the stars, and the air? The signs of Christ will be true, and in this they will differ completely from those of the antichrist, which will consist of phenomena that deceive the senses. The signs of the antichrist will be performed by him and his apostles, whereas the signs in the sun, the moon, and stars that herald the coming of Christ will be done of themselves, without mediation. The heavenly bodies will fulfill the purpose for which they began shining in the heavens, at the command of the Creator (Gen 1:14). They already fulfilled this purpose at the birth of Christ, through the wondrous star (Matt 2:2); they fulfilled it at the crucifixion of the God-Man, when the sun was covered in darkness in the middle of the day (Matt 27:45). The holy Evangelist Matthew says that, after the tribulation caused by the reign of the antichrist has passed, the coming of Christ will follow immediately, and at that point "the sun will be darkened, and the moon will not give its light; the stars will fall from heaven" (Matt 24:29). These heavenly bodies will stay in place, according to St Theophylact of Ochrid and Bulgaria; but they will darken and will seem to the human eye to have disappeared from the firmament of heaven due to the abundance of heavenly light illumining the earth to prepare it to receive the Lord in His glory.

The teaching on miracles and signs that we have presented is, we dare to say, the teaching of the holy Orthodox Church and her holy Fathers. There is an obvious need for a precise exposition of this teaching that is as thorough as possible. True signs have been aids to true knowledge of God and of the salvation it gives; false signs have been aids to confusion and the resulting perdition. In particular, the effect of signs performed by the antichrist will be broad and powerful, and will entice all of unhappy humanity to recognize the messenger of Satan as a god. It is edifying, consoling, and salutary to contemplate with reverence the miracles performed by our Lord Jesus Christ. What holy simplicity is in them! How easy they have made it for all of humanity to know God! What goodness, what humility, what undeniable strength of persuasion they contain! Contemplation of the miracles of Christ leads us to the Word That is God. In order to resume communion with fallen humanity, God was well pleased for His Word to be clothed in human nature, to appear, circulate among us, interact closely with us and, adopting us unto Himself, take us up to heaven. Having clothed Himself in humanity, the Word remains the Word of God, and acts as the Word in accordance with His divine virtue. He sits at the right hand of the Father in His human form, and remains everywhere as God. He is written on paper, He is clothed in sound, but being "spirit and life" (John 6:63), He enters minds and hearts, he transforms those who are united with Him in spirit, attracting even the body to a spiritual way of life. By contemplating the miracles of Christ we come to knowledge of that great meaning contained within the Word of God, "the one thing needed" (Luke 10:42) for our salvation, the Word that serves and accomplishes salvation. Knowledge of the Word of God from Holy Scripture, spoken and also explained by the Holy Spirit, combined with the knowledge drawn from actions that are guided by the Word of God, and illumined by the knowledge taught through divine grace, gives the Christian purity of mind and heart. In this purity, spiritual reason shines forth like the sun in a clear, cloudless sky. When day breaks after the darkness of the night, the form of perceptible objects changes: some of them, invisible until now, become visible; others, that were vaguely visible, blurring in with other objects, become distinguishable from them and are revealed distinctly. This happens not because the objects have changed, but because the relationship between them and human vision changes when the darkness of night is replaced by the light of day. Exactly the same thing happens with the relationship between the human mind and spiritual objects, when the mind is illumined by spiritual knowledge that comes from the Holy Spirit. Only in the light of spiritual reason can the soul perceive the holy path that leads to God. Only in the light of spiritual reason can the mind and heart proceed invisibly without sin toward God. Only in the light of spiritual reason can we avoid delusion and ruinous mazes and abysses. Wherever that light is absent, truth cannot be seen; wherever that light is absent, there is no God-pleasing virtue that is salutary for man and leads him to the dwelling-places of paradise.[202] It is in the light of spiritual reason that we must view signs and miracles, so as to avoid those calamities into which we may be drawn if we view the former with a carnal mind. We have seen the character of the miracles of the God-Man; we have seen what their purpose was. After serving this purpose, signs ceased to be worked everywhere, leaving the essential worker, the Word, Who remains and will remain the worker until the end of the world, as He proclaimed of Himself: "Lo, I am with you always, even to the end of the age" (Matt 28:20). After signs, accompanied by the seed of Christianity preached by the Apostles and other saints equal to them, had ceased to be performed everywhere, they were still performed in certain places by chosen vessels of the Holy Spirit. In the course of time, as Christianity gradually weakened and morality deteriorated, sign-bearing men became fewer.[203] Finally they disappeared almost completely. Meanwhile, people who have lost their reverence and respect for everything holy, who have lost their humility, which deems itself unworthy not only of working signs but even of seeing them, thirst for miracles more than ever before. People fed by conceit, arrogance, and ignorance strive indiscriminately, precipitately toward everything miraculous; they do not refuse to be participants in the working of miracles themselves, and they decide to do this without thinking about it. This tendency is more dangerous than ever before. We are gradually approaching the time when the sight of many startling false miracles must be revealed, to carry away to their ruin those unhappy students of the carnal mind, who will be seduced and deceived by these miracles.

The renewal of the soul by the Word of God produces a living faith in Christ. We might say that living faith sees Christ (Heb 11:27). Under its gaze, Christianity becomes visible, after remaining hidden; having been unattainable, it is clear and understandable, no longer hidden by the thick, impenetrable curtain of dead faith. Living faith is spiritual reason.[204] It has no need of signs, being completely satisfied with the signs of Christ and the greatest of His signs, the crown of signs, His word. The desire to see signs is an indication of unbelief, and signs were given to unbelievers in order to turn them into believers. Let us attach ourselves to the Word of God with all our souls, let us unite ourselves with Him in one spirit, and the signs of the antichrist will not even attract our attention. Disregarding and loathing them, we will avert our eyes from them as from a demonic sight, from the deeds of the frenzied enemies of God, from an outrage against God, or from deadly poison and infection. Let us remember the following especially important comment, originating in the experiences of ascetic struggle: all diabolical phenomena have the characteristic that even the smallest degree of attention toward them is dangerous; from attention alone, without any sympathy toward the phenomenon, it is possible to be stamped with the most harmful impression and subjected to great temptation.

Humble-mindedness is inseparable from spiritual reason. St Isaac the Syrian says: "Only he who has humility can be recognized as being perceptive; he who does not have humility can never acquire perception."[205] Living faith reveals God to the eyes of the soul: the Word of God unites the soul with God. Someone who sees and experiences God in this way sees his own insignificance, becomes filled with ineffable reverence toward God, toward all His works, and toward all His teaching, and acquires humble-mindedness. A humble-minded person does not dare even to be curious about what happens against the will of God and what has been condemned by the Word of God: the signs of the antichrist will be alien to the humble-minded person, as they will have no pertinence to him.

To see its own insignificance and weakness, and to see God, His greatness, omnipotence and infinite goodness, kindles in the soul a desire to hasten to God in prayer. All the hope of such a soul is focused on God, and there is therefore no reason for it to be distracted in prayer. It prays, uniting all its efforts together, and hastening toward God with all its being; it takes refuge in prayer as often as possible; it prays constantly. When great tribulations come in the times of the antichrist, all those who truly believe in God will cry out in intensified prayer to Him.[206] They will cry out for help, for assistance, for divine grace to be sent down to strengthen and guide them. Even if people are true to God, their own strength is not enough to resist the combined forces of the rejected angels and of people who will be acting in a frenzy and with despair, sensing their imminent destruction (Rev 12:12). Divine grace, enlightening the chosen ones of God, will make ineffective the delusions of the deceiver, remove the terror from his threats and make his miracles pitiful; it will grant them to confess with courage the salvation of mankind by the Saviour, and to expose the false messiah, come to destroy mankind; it will lead them up to the scaffold as if to a royal throne, to a wedding feast. The feeling of love for God is sweeter than the feeling of life.[207] Just as the torments of death constitute the beginning of eternal torments for a sinner,[208] so torments for Christ and forced death for His sake constitute the beginning of the eternal joys of paradise. We see this clearly in the action of divine grace in connection with the martyrs of the first centuries of Christianity: it was initially left to them to reveal their intention, but after they had suffered the initial tortures, help came down to them from on high, making them long for torture and death for the sake of Christ. When telling of the tribulations that are to precede the second coming, the Lord commanded His disciples to be vigilant and to pray: "Take heed, watch and pray," He told them, "for you do not know when the time is" (Mark 13:33). Prayer is always necessary and beneficial for a person: it keeps him in communion with God and under His protection; it protects him from arrogance, from being deceived by vainglory and pride, both his own, growing out of his fallen nature, and brought into his intentions and dreams from the realm of the fallen spirits. In times of tribulations and dangers, visible and invisible, prayer is especially necessary: because it expresses rejection of arrogance and hope in God, it draws God's help to us. The omnipotent God becomes an agent of the person at prayer in his difficult circumstances, and leads His servant out of them by His wondrous providence.

Knowledge of God, living faith, grace-filled humble-mindedness, pure prayer—all these belong to spiritual reason; they are its component parts. Thus, conversely, ignorance of God, unbelief, blindness of the spirit, pride, arrogance, and conceit belong to the carnal mind. The carnal mind, not knowing God, not accepting or understanding the means provided by God to receive knowledge of Him, puts together for itself a false, soul-destroying means of acquiring knowledge of God, corresponding to its disposition: it asks for "signs from heaven." Amen.

44. On Salvation and Perfection

Sermon on the Thirtieth Sunday after Pentecost

"But if you want to enter into life, keep the commandments" (Matt 19:17), said our Lord Jesus Christ to a certain young man who, as we heard in today's Gospel, asked the Lord: "Good Teacher, what shall I do to inherit eternal life?" (Luke 18:18)—that is, what good works should I do in order to be saved? When the young man again asked which commandments he must keep, the Lord pointed him, a Jew who believed in the true God, to the commandments relating to one's neighbor. The young man answered that he had kept all these commandments, and again asked: "What do I still lack?" The Lord said: "If you want to be perfect, go, sell what you have and give to the poor, and you will have treasure in heaven; and come, follow Me, take up the cross" (Matt 19:20–21; Mark 10:21).

We learn from the Lord's answers to the young man that He has prepared two blessed states for those who believe in Him: the state of salvation and the state of Christian perfection.[209] It can be seen very clearly from these replies of the Lord that the blessed state of salvation is attainable for all Christians, but perfection can be attained only by those Christians who simultaneously give away their property to the poor and, renouncing all ties with the world, follow Christ, taking up the cross, that is, submitting themselves with zeal and love to all deprivations, all dishonor and all tribulations permitted to them, as befits true members of Christ who have rejected all justifications presented by the carnal mind that is so hostile to Christ and to carrying one's cross.

Brothers! Let us, first of all, examine what the conditions for salvation are, since salvation is something that all Christians long for and can attain. We mentioned above that the Lord was preaching His most holy teaching to a Jew who believed in the true God, and that is why He did not mention faith, of which He spoke in other situations, but listed only the commandments concerning how we relate to our neighbor. It is essential for someone who wishes to be saved to believe in God, the Creator and Redeemer.

"This is eternal life, that they may know You, the only true God, and Jesus Christ whom You have sent" (John 17:3). "He who believes in the Son has everlasting life; and he who does not believe the Son shall not see life"—that is, he will not receive salvation—"but the wrath of God abides on him" (John 3:36). It is essential for someone who wishes to be saved to belong to the Orthodox Church, the only true Church, and to obey her statutes. The Lord likened one who refused to listen to the Church to a heathen, alien to God (Matt 18:17). Each one of us, when reciting the Creed, confesses that he believes in One, Holy, Catholic and Apostolic Church, and therefore that apart from this Church there is no other, let alone other Churches, although various human social organizations have called themselves churches. It is essential for someone who wishes to be saved to be baptized in the bosom of the Orthodox Church in the name of the Father, the Son, and the Holy Spirit, as the Lord Himself said: "He who believes and is baptized will be saved; but he who does not believe will be condemned" (Mark 16:16). It should be noted that in the Greek language, in which the apostles wrote the whole New Testament,[210] the word *baptism* (βάπτισμα) in its literal sense means "immersion." Wherever the words *baptism*, *baptize*, *was baptized* are used in the New Testament, we should understand immersion, immerse, was immersed. This is why immersing crockery in water, the way it is normally washed—"the washing of pitchers and cups," is called "baptism" in the Greek—and Slavonic—texts of the Gospel (Mark 7:8). All over the world, the holy sacrament of baptism took place by immersion for the first twelve centuries after the Nativity of Christ. From the twelfth century onwards, people began in the West to pour the water over the person being baptized instead of using immersion; as a result, in some Western societies, immersion has been replaced with sprinkling.

It is essential for a person who wishes to be saved to repent of his sins and be purified through confession, as Holy Scripture testifies: "If we say that we have no sin, we deceive ourselves, and the truth is not in us. If we confess our sins, He is faithful and just to forgive us our sins and to cleanse us from all unrighteousness" (1 John 1:8–9).

Through the sacrament of repentance, the purity acquired at baptism is maintained and renewed, as is the union with Christ given to us through holy baptism. "You are baptized in a second baptism through the Christian sacrament" says the priest, as ordained by the holy Church, when serving the sacrament of repentance on the Christian repenting before him. The sacrament of repentance has been changed in the West, and rejected by the Protestants. It is essential for a person who wishes to be saved to receive communion in the holy Mysteries of Christ, the most-holy Body and Blood of Christ. "Most assuredly, I say to you, unless you eat the flesh of the Son of Man and drink His blood, you have no life in you. Whoever eats My flesh and drinks My blood has eternal life" (John 6:53–54). The great mystery of the transformation of bread and wine into the body and blood of Christ is accomplished through the invocation and the inspiration of the Holy Spirit during the prayers that precede and follow this mystery and combine to make up the Divine Liturgy. Without the Divine Liturgy, served by an Orthodox bishop or priest, the bread that is offered cannot be transformed into the body of Christ, and the wine that is offered cannot become the blood of Christ. All the ancient Liturgies in the world are exactly the same in their essential components: in all of them, the Holy Spirit is invoked for the transformation, and the images that are offered, that is, the bread and wine, are blessed by the priest. In recent times the invocation of the Holy Spirit has been excluded from the Roman Liturgy, and the Protestants have rejected the Liturgy altogether. Thus, for those who wish to be saved, it is essential first of all to believe in God in the right way, to belong to the Orthodox Church, and in her bosom to be baptized, to be anointed, to be cleansed from sins through repentance and to receive communion in the holy Mysteries of Christ. It is also essential, as the Lord said to the young man, to keep the commandments of God. The Lord initially indicated the commandments that forbid flagrant, deadly sins. He repeated what Moses had already told ancient Israel: "'You shall not murder,' 'You shall not commit adultery,' 'You shall not steal,' 'You shall not bear false witness'"; then He commanded him to honour his father and mother, and finally, to love his neighbor as himself (Matt 19:18–20). Why did the Lord say nothing about love for God? Because love for God is included in love for one's neighbor, and whoever cultivates love for his neighbor within himself at the same time acquires within his heart a priceless spiritual treasure—love for God: "If we love one another," said St John the Theologian, "God abides in us, and His love has been perfected in us" (1 John 4:12).

What does it mean to inherit salvation, to be saved? It means to familiarize oneself with the Redeemer, to remain in this state for the whole of one's earthly life, and after death, because of this familiarity with the Redeemer, to be borne in soul to the dwelling-places of the blessed spirits, and with them to delight in holy joy, in expectation of the general resurrection of the dead; then, at the general resurrection, to be reunited with the body, which the Lord will revive and make incorruptible, and with the body to inherit double, eternal blessedness. Our Lord Jesus Christ is Life and the Source of life: we make ourselves participants in this life through belief in the teaching of Christ, through baptism in the name of the Father, of the Son, and of the Holy Spirit, sealed by anointing the baptized person with holy myrrh. Anointing with myrrh takes the place of the laying on of hands by the apostles on the newly baptized. The apostles sealed baptism by laying their hands on the newly baptized and bringing down the Holy Spirit (Acts 19:6). We maintain and renew our familiarity with the Lord by offering repentance for the sins into which we fall through our weakness, by receiving communion in His body and blood, and by living in accordance with His most holy commandments. A person who neglects to keep the commandments of God does not heal himself constantly through repentance, and does not maintain familiarity with Christ by communion in His body and blood, cannot avoid becoming estranged from Christ, and cannot avoid losing salvation. "If you keep My commandments, you will abide in My love. If anyone does not abide in Me, he is cast out as a branch and is withered; and they gather them and throw them into the fire, and they are burned" (John 15:10,6).

What does Christian perfection mean? Faced with this question, it is better to keep silence than to answer—it is better to weep than to be eloquent. What can a poor man say of magnificent royal mansions to which access is forbidden him because of his rags, because he stinks and is destitute, because he is completely unable to present a decent appearance in the royal mansion. If this poor man happened to look at the exterior of the royal house, or even to see it often, then the sight would only double his distress, and his destitution would seem more burdensome, the more splendid and the richer the unattainable objects that reached his eye. Such a beggar would be right to decline to entertain vain dreams of mansions inaccessible to him, and to concern himself with finding the means to earn his daily bread and with earning it. For us too, brothers, who are bound by worldly cares and duties, it is much better to concern ourselves with our salvation, and carefully to keep God's commandments, than to dream and philosophize about Christian perfection. Such dreams, such philosophizing, are almost always a mistake, because only a spiritual person can discuss a spiritual, that is, a perfect Christian, and understand and appraise him (1 Cor 2:15). Whom has the world recognized as holy? Whom has it blessed and extolled in praise? The false prophet, the false teacher, the hypocrites (Luke 6:26). How did it react to true saints of God? It rejected them, showered them with abuse and slander, persecuted them, as if they were enemies of human society, and subjected them to the fiercest persecutions and tribulations (Luke 6:22–23; Matt 23:34). Let us see, brothers, the path toward Christian perfection as it has been indicated to us by the Lord, the very path that is unreachable and unattainable to us. The Lord commands someone who wishes to move toward attaining perfection not to give alms gradually, as is required of someone who wishes to be saved, but to sell all his property in one go, and to distribute all the proceeds among the poor, again in one go, and with great haste, and in this way to break all his links and connections with the world, and follow Christ, taking up his cross. What does it mean to take up one's cross and follow Christ? Taking up one's cross means to embrace with faith and love all the privations, all the persecutions, all the tribulations and abuse from the world, just as Christ bore them; to take up one's cross means to crucify the flesh with its passions and desires, to live in the flesh but not for the flesh, to put to death the deeds of the body through the Spirit, to live in the Spirit, and to be guided by the Spirit (Gal 5:24–25; Rom 8:12–13). And what does Christian perfection mean? It means the perceptible and clear renewal of a Christian through the Holy Spirit that can only be accomplished in one who has died to sin and to the world on the cross of Christ. A person who is renewed by the Spirit becomes a God-bearer, a temple of God and a Priest who serves in this Temple and worships God in Spirit and in Truth. The Apostles and all other saints of God were honored to varying degrees with such perfection (Col 1:28; Phil 3:15).[211]

Blessed are the chosen of God who are called by God to perfection! But those to whom the merciful God grants salvation are also truly happy. To this happiness, brothers, we are all called, without exception. The Lord has shown us the path to salvation with all clarity. Whoever has not until now taken any care for his salvation can do so from now on. For as long as our earthly life continues, repentance, and therefore also salvation, is entirely possible for us. Let us stop being despondent, let us stop being in a state of negligence, that death may not steal up on us unexpectedly, "as a thief in the night" (1 Thess 5:2), and take from us the possibility of acquiring from God the gift of salvation that is so necessary to us for eternity. "Be ready, for the Son of Man is coming at an hour you do not expect" (Matt 24:44), "to give to every one according to his work" (Rev 22:12). "Blessed are those who do His commandments, that they may have the right to the tree of life, and may enter through the gates into the city. But outside are dogs and sorcerers and sexually immoral and murderers and idolaters, and whoever loves and practices a lie" (Rev 22:14–15). Amen.

45. The Mystical Significance of the Blind Man Receiving His Sight

Sermon on the Thirty-first Sunday after Pentecost

The holy Fathers ascribe a mystical interpretation to the event described in today's Gospel. In the blind man who attracted the attention and the mercy of the God-Man with his intensive pleading and cries, they see the image of a sinner who prays persistently with lamenting and by means of such prayer receives forgiveness of sins and renewal of his soul through divine grace.[212] We are all sinners; we are all in great need of God's mercy. Let us examine attentively how a sinner is granted the mercy of God by means of prayer.

Our Lord Jesus Christ, the Gospel tells us, was coming out of the city of Jericho. Behind Him followed His disciples and a large crowd of people. By the road sat a blind man who was begging passers-by for alms. Hearing the noise of the crowd, he was curious about the reason for it. He was told that Jesus was passing by and that his presence had attracted the throng. Then the blind man began to cry out in a loud voice: "Jesus, Son of David, have mercy on me!" Those who were walking in front of the Lord tried to stop the blind man, commanding him to be quiet; but he cried out all the more: "Son of David, have mercy on me!" The Lord stopped and commanded that he be brought to Him. The blind man was called. He threw off his outer garment and stood before the Lord. The Lord asked him: "What do you want from Me?" The blind man answered, "Lord, I want You to give me my sight." The Lord said, "Receive your sight; your faith has made you well." The blind man immediately received his sight and followed Jesus, glorifying God (Luke 18:35–43; Mark 10:46–52).

In the spiritual regard, all sinners should be deemed blind men: they are just that—blind. Holy Scripture calls them blind (Matt 15:14); and their very deeds demonstrate their blindness. The eyesight of sinners is so distorted and damaged by sin that it ought justly to be deemed and called blindness. This blindness is of the spirit. It is all the more dangerous in that it usually believes and declares itself to be the most satisfactory, strong eyesight. The blind sinner sees neither God, nor eternity, nor himself, nor the purpose for which mankind was created, nor death, which awaits him and every other human being, and cannot be avoided either by him or by anyone else. Unhappy man! He is guided by his blindness, he works toward his own ruin, he concerns himself only with the vain and the temporal. He pursues only phantoms and the death that he has forgotten comes and snatches him away from the field of his activities presenting him before the judgment of God about which he never thought and for which he is totally unprepared. For a blind sinner to recognize and confess his blindness and to abandon the activities done under its guidance serves as the beginning of a return to sight.

Jericho was located in a valley cut through by the River Jordan. The other cities of Israel were generally in mountainous terrain. The low-lying position of Jericho represents our state of fallenness. The mystical blind man had come out of Jericho. He had stopped participating in the activities with which its citizens were occupied: he had stopped committing overt sins of the body; he had sat on the path of the Saviour and of salvation, he had begun to ask passers-by for alms and to eat meagerly, from charity. The passers-by represent the living vessels of the Holy Spirit whom God has sent into the world, to lead it to salvation, throughout the course of the life of the world.[213] They also represent the instruction of the shepherds of the Church and the ascetics of godliness, temporarily wandering on earth like all other people: they guide the sinner at the start of his conversion; they feed his hungry soul with knowledge gained through faith by hearing (Rom 10:17). The blind man, although he had come out of the city, could not walk far away from it due to his blindness. He sat down near the city gates; the rumors of the city reached his ears, troubled his heart, brought his mind into confusion. In the same way, a spiritually blind sinner, when he abandons his grave sins, cannot dissolve the bonds with the sin that both lives within him and acts upon him from within. So even after his conversion he remains close to sin and in sin; sinful thoughts, dreams, sensations do not cease to trouble his mind and his heart. Those who accompany and assist Christ—the prophets, the apostles, and the holy fathers—tell the blind person how close the Saviour is to him, because he, in his darkened state, cannot possibly imagine that God is near him. He imagines God to be far away, as if He did not even exist. When the blind man is taught by the word of God that God, Who is present everywhere, is closer to him than anything in the visible and invisible world, he takes heart, and begins to make an effort in prayer. He has begun the struggle; but his mind is stamped with a carnal disposition and, being material, because it has assimilated material impressions, it cannot pray spiritually; his heart is constantly distracted from prayer by various predilections with which it has been infected. The prayer of the blind man is awkward, materialistic, mixed up with carnal and sinful thoughts and dreams, defiled by them; it cannot raise itself from the ground, it crawls along the ground, it keeps falling down, it hardly makes the effort to lift itself up from the ground. The blind man does not have enough understanding of God, because this understanding is not characteristic of a carnal state; the blind man's prayerful struggle to pray is still a physical struggle. "Blind," says St Mark the Ascetic, "is he who cries out and says, 'Son of David, have mercy on me' (Mark 10:48). He still prays bodily, he has not yet acquired spiritual reason." He sits alone at the gates of Jericho.

In the arena of prayerful struggle, an ascetic encounters many different obstacles. The effects and the power of these obstacles are based on the blindness of the struggler. When the blind man was begging passers-by for alms, he was in a sitting position. And when he uttered his first cries, he was still sitting down. There is no true spiritual progress, there is no spiritual movement in a person who occupies himself with studying the "letter" (2 Cor 3:6) of the word of God and with bodily prayer. He continues to be under the influence of sinful intentions and sensations and of a carnal mind; he continues to be on the earth; it is impossible and unnatural for him to go up to heaven. He struggles to pray. He compels himself to struggle, dragging himself toward the effort to pray, but it seems alien to him, like his worst enemy, like a merciless murderer. This feeling of a carnal person toward prayer is characteristic: prayer kills, it slaughters our "old man" (Eph 4:22), and the old man fears this and wants to escape it, resisting it with all its strength. Around the blind man who is struggling stand the fallen spirits. They have not withdrawn from him, because he has not been released from them after submitting to them through his former sinful life before he turned to God. They try to keep him in thrall to them; they forbid him to pray; they threaten him, they confuse him, they apply every possible means to compel him to be silent. They bring him unbelief, suggesting to him that his prayer will not be heard. They bring him lack of hope, reminding him of the many sins he has committed, vividly presenting them to his imagination and his feelings, provoking enjoyment of them in soul and body. They plunder and destroy his prayer, introducing various cares into his thoughts and suggesting that he needs to deal with them immediately. They produce a coldness, a despondency, in the struggling man's soul, that he might see the fruitlessness of his struggle and abandon it. They ridicule the struggle, they mock it, saying that it is fruitless and futile, because they tremble before its consequences. The ascetic of prayer, devoted to the struggle to pray, far from the pursuits of human society, will hear the infernal sound of demonic voices. He will see his captivity, his chains and his prison. "Thou hast made us the rebuke of our neighbors," says the great man of prayer, "a scoff and derision of them that are round about us. All day long my confusion is before me, and my face is covered with shame, at the voice of the slanderer and blasphemer, at the face of the enemy and avenger" (Ps 43:14,16,17).

Here faith is needed: "Your faith has made you well," the Lord said to the blind man after healing him. Faith is needed for constancy in the struggle to pray; constancy, patience, and long-suffering are needed. We need to reject false shame and persevere, so that the struggle may yield its wonderful fruit. First of all, increased physical effort is necessary: we need to kneel, to tire the body and subdue the soul; we need to stand for prolonged periods and to keep vigil all night; we need prayer with the lips and the voice, prayer combined with weeping and crying out, when we are alone in our secluded cells, and we can cry and groan freely; we need secret prayer with secret weeping of the heart when we are in the company of others. The blind man was forbidden to cry out, and he cried out even more; he was ordered to be quiet, and he called out even more loudly. We must also do the same: we must overcome and trample upon all obstacles to prayer; we must pay no attention to them and pray yet more ardently and fervently. If during your morning prayer rule your prayer was plundered by intrusive thoughts and daydreams, and belonged not to yourself but to the force of the passions that have seized you, do not weaken, do not fall into despondency. Stand with renewed zeal at your evening prayer rule, trying to heed your prayers and gathering your distracted thoughts like the leader of the Israelites, who said to his warriors: "Be of good courage, and let us be strong for our people and for the cities of our God. And may the Lord do what is good in His sight" (2 Kgs 10:12). In the struggle to pray, it is essential to deny ourselves, to leave our progress to the will of our God, Who grants grace-filled prayer at a time known to Him to a person who demonstrates his will to possess it through his own efforts and actions (1 Kgs 2:9). "I [do not] count my life dear to myself" (Acts 20:24), says the apostle; it is those who are puffed up with pride and conceit who consider themselves worthy of grace. If after one year our progress in prayer, despite constant practice of it, turns out to be meager and insignificant, then the following year let us use all the strength at our disposal so that our progress may bear fruit.

If ten years have passed, if decades have passed, and we have not yet seen the desired fruit, then let us try to remain faithful to the struggle for the rest of our lives. The treasure acquired through ascetic effort is eternal; it is of great price, and it is by no means strange that the providence of God permits us to make an effort toward it even if it corresponds only a very little to the value of what we eventually acquire.

The main condition for progress in prayer is always to pray with the greatest reverence and attention. This means not only abandoning a sinful way of life, but also moving away from the "city," that is, rejecting all concerns and cares during the time of prayer. We achieve this when we place everything that affects us into the Lord's hands. The holy Church invites us to such devotion to God. She often reminds us of it, saying "let us entrust ourselves and one another and our whole life to Christ our God."[214] It is an aid to attentive prayer to remember that God is present everywhere and sees everything: if God is present in every place, then He is also present in the place where we are praying. If He sees everything, then He also sees the disposition of our hearts, the attitude of our minds. When we stand in prayer, we stand before the face of God, at the judgment of God; we have the opportunity to beg for God's mercy with our prayerful cries and groans. Remembering the uncertainty of the hour of our death also stirs us to zealous and fervent prayers. We will by no means do wrong if, every time we pray, we do so as if in the last hour of our lives, as if at the hour of death. When the mind pays attention to the prayer, the heart also heeds it, expressing and demonstrating this with a feeling of repentance. In order to achieve a state of attentiveness, the holy Fathers recommend praying unhurriedly, as if enclosing the mind with the words of the prayer, so that not a single word escapes attention. A word that has escaped is a word that is lost. A prayer that has escaped attention is a lost prayer.

A mind that has not acquired the habit of attentiveness learns it with difficulty. This should not lead a struggler for prayer into despondency and alarm. "Instability," says St John of the Ladder, "is intrinsic to the mind"[215] of fallen man, the mind that is corrupted by sin. "When your mind," St John continues to instruct the struggler in prayer, "is distracted because of its youth, bring it back to the words of the prayer. Acquire for yourself this invisible struggle, and persevere in it. If you act in this way, then He who sets the bounds of the sea will come to you and command your mind: 'This far you may come' in your prayer, 'but no farther, and here your proud waves must stop!' (Job 38:11). Let your thoughts be concentrated within you. Persistent labor to attain attentiveness is active testimony before God of our sincere desire to possess it, but it is impossible for a person to bind his spirit in his own strength: this needs the command of the highest Spirit, of that Spirit that is the Master and Creator of our spirit."[216] This work is done by the Spirit of God. This is that Messenger sent by the Son of God to the blind man who sat and cried out, Who called him to Jesus (John 16:7,14). The Spirit of God proclaims the Son of God (John 16:7–14). The Spirit that visits the servant of Christ guides him "into all truth" (John 16:13), and also guides him to attentive prayer. Attentiveness of the mind during prayer is the complete striving of the mind for the Truth, its correct state and activity; distraction, on the other hand, is a state of self-deception. It is a sign that the mind is being led astray by false teaching, by thoughts and daydreams that are brought to it by demons and that arise from the ailing sin of our nature. A state of deep, constant attentiveness at prayer results from the touch of divine grace on our soul. Grace-filled attentiveness granted to a person at prayer is the original spiritual gift of God.[217]

Having heard the invitation and been reinvigorated and gladdened by it, the blind man rose to his feet, took off his outer clothing, and came to stand before the Lord. "The mind," say the Fathers, "once it is united with the soul" by means of grace-filled attentiveness, "is filled with indescribable delight."[218] That is when the spiritual progress of a struggler in prayer begins; that is when with strength and purity of prayer he strives toward God with all his being; that is when all extraneous thoughts and fantasies recede and disappear, as King David says: "Away from me, all ye that work iniquity, for the Lord hath heard the voice of my weeping. The Lord hath heard my petition; the Lord will receive my prayer. Let all mine enemies"—rejected spirits—"be confounded and sore vexed; let them be turned back, and put to shame suddenly" (Ps 6:9–11). The removal of outer clothing represents the abandonment of the many various external ways of prayer: they are replaced by prayer in the inner chamber of the soul that embraces and unites all the individual spiritual works. Being a broad activity, it absorbs and combines within itself the whole life of the struggler. "There are many types of virtue," says St Nilus of Sora, "but they are individual; prayer of the heart is the source of all good things: the soul is watered by it just as a garden is watered by abundant waters."[219] Pure prayer is standing before the face of God. A person standing before God asks to be given sight and receives grace-filled enlightenment of the mind and the heart. He acquires true knowledge of God and service of God: he no longer returns to his former state of immobility, to the gates of the town, but, joining the other disciples of the Lord Jesus Christ, follows Him. He has all the opportunity and the necessary ability to follow Him in this way. "Whoever prays with the lips," says St Symeon the New Theologian, "but has not yet acquired spiritual knowledge, and cannot pray with the mind: he is like the blind man who cried out: 'Son of David, have mercy on me!' But he who has acquired spiritual knowledge, and prays with the mind, the eyes of whose soul have been opened, is like that same blind man after he had been healed, who, seeing the Lord, no longer called Him the son of David but confessed Him to be the Son of God, and worshipped Him as befits God."[220]

Faith is the foundation of prayer. A person who believes in God as one should believe will without fail turn to God in prayer and will not abandon his prayer until he receives the things that God has promised, until he is adopted by God, united with God. "Faith," says St John of the Ladder, "is a state of the soul that is alien to doubt, that is unwavering in the face of all obstacles. A person confesses himself to be a believer if he not only confesses God as omnipotent, but also believes that he will receive everything from Him. Faith is the mother of silence"[221] both in the cell and in the heart. Whoever believes that God constantly provides for him, and places all his hope in Him, comforts his heart with hope, and with the help of hope eliminates all cares from himself and gives himself up with his whole heart to learning the will of God, revealed to mankind in Holy Scripture, and yet more abundantly through the struggle for prayer. Through faith in God, the struggler endures and overcomes all obstacles arising from his fallen nature and raised by the spirits of evil, obstacles that endeavor to disturb his prayer and take from him the means to commune with God. "Many a time have they fought against me from my youth up. The plowers plowed upon my back; they made long furrows" (Ps 128:2–3). But I, strengthened and guided by faith, "unto Thee," my Lord, "have I" constantly "lifted up mine eyes," my mind and my heart. "Behold, even as the eyes of servants are upon the hand of their masters, and as the eyes of a maid are upon the hand of her mistress, even so are our eyes upon the Lord our God, until He have pity upon us" (Ps 122:1–2). Amen.

46. On Zacchaeus

Sermon on the Thirty-second Sunday after Pentecost

"The Son of Man has come to seek and to save that which was lost" (Luke 19:10).

Dear brothers! These words filled with mercy that we heard in today's Gospel were said by God incarnate of a sinner. The righteous judgment of God had called this sinner lost, but through the power and grace of redemption, he was sought, found, and numbered among the saved.

The sinner, Zacchaeus, was a tax collector, to be precise, a chief tax collector. He possessed substantial wealth, as the Gospel mentions, hinting in this way at the means by which his wealth was acquired. Tax collectors collected taxes from the people. Money is tempting! The shine of gold and silver charm the eyes of the descendant of Adam, eyes that are infected with sinfulness, and wherever there is money, it is rare that misuse of it does not creep in. Most tax collectors fell into covetousness. When covetousness turns into a passion, it allows itself any violence, any oppression of the sinner's neighbor. The passions of slyness and hypocrisy come to the aid of the passion of covetousness. This combination disposes a person toward fault-finding, and becoming attached, under the pretext of essential compliance with laws, to all the minutiae that contrive culpability of innocent people, endeavoring through such behavior to give an appearance of fairness to inhuman acts of oppression and cruelty toward the person's neighbors. Because this is the way in which they tended to act, tax collectors were regarded with fear by the people in general, and with contempt by honorable people. Zacchaeus was a chief tax collector: his abuses were more extensive than those of his subordinates. Not without reason is it mentioned that he was rich! He became rich through wrongdoing. His sin was covetousness; the sickness of his soul was greed and the mercilessness and lack of sympathy for others produced by it. Because of his grave sins, because of the culpable disposition of his soul, Zacchaeus is referred to as lost. It is not the careless, often erroneous judgment of men that calls him lost: God referred to him in this way. Zacchaeus had become a confirmed sinner: to acquire wealth by means of abuse, a person must act consistently in this way for a prolonged period of time.

The cause of the sinful life of Zacchaeus is the same that causes many to lead a sinful life even now: it lies in following an accepted practice of behavior and in ignorance of or only the most superficial knowledge of the law of God. Tax collectors usually fell into the vice of avarice: Zacchaeus too had been carried away by it. The majority of the population of Judea in the time of Christ were occupied almost solely with their earthly situation, striving toward material improvement and earthly success. At that time the law of God was almost always studied according to the letter; divine services were directed mostly toward satisfying prescribed ritual; virtues were accomplished superficially, coldly, more for the sake of public opinion. Zacchaeus was also content with this. He lived as everyone lived. Even today, one can often hear people saying, "I live just like everyone else." What a vain justification this is, and what a deceptive consolation! The Word of God proclaims and commands otherwise. "Enter," it says, "by the narrow gate; for wide is the gate and broad is the way that leads to destruction, and there are many who go in by it. Because narrow is the gate and difficult is the way which leads to life, and there are few who find it" (Matt 7:13–14). The narrow gate is the careful, thorough study of the law of God both in Scripture and in life; the difficult way is behavior that is completely in keeping with the commandments of the Gospel.

At the time when Zacchaeus was living his life according to the custom of a world hostile to God, and had secured for himself what was, according to the wisdom and the expression of the world, a prosperous situation, not without importance and brilliance, but from the spiritual viewpoint was a lost sinner, doomed to eternal torment in the prisons of hades, at that time the Saviour of the world was wandering on the earth, in the land of the twelve tribes of Israel. Zacchaeus was seized with the desire to see the Lord, and demonstrated the sincerity of his desire through his actions. His wish was granted by the Lord, Who sees into men's hearts, and He deigned to visit Zacchaeus in his house. The sinner was filled with joy when he saw the Lord coming toward him, and he was disgusted by his own sins. His heart was torn away from love for the fruits of a sinful life, for transient wealth. Standing before the Lord who sees into men's hearts, Zacchaeus said: "Look, Lord, I give half of my goods to the poor; and if I have taken anything from anyone by false accusation, I restore fourfold" (Luke 19:8).

This promise contains acknowledgment of sin, repentance, and correction, combined with great self-denial. Zacchaeus confesses to covetousness, and resolves to make amends for oppressing his neighbors by means of abundant compensation; he confesses to greed, and resolves to purify and sanctify his property and his heart with generous almsgiving. The repentance of Zacchaeus is accepted immediately by the Lord. Of that sinner, who a few moments previously had been among the rejected and the lost, the Lord proclaims: "Today salvation has come to this house, because he also is a son of Abraham" (Luke 19:9). Zacchaeus was a descendant of Abraham in the flesh; but in the judgment of God he is only adopted by Abraham through virtue. The word "house" can be understood to mean the soul of Zacchaeus, into which salvation entered in the wake of the repentance that had purified it from sin; this word of the Lord could also be applied to the household of Zacchaeus which, following the example of its head, as often happens, with similar self-denial, entered the path to true knowledge of God and to a God-pleasing way of life.

Everyone who saw the Lord visiting the house of Zacchaeus complained, deeming it inappropriate and humiliating to visit such a sinner, as Zacchaeus was generally viewed. It was incomprehensible, and it remains incomprehensible to the carnal mind, how the mystery of redemption heals all human sins, great and small, with unique power and ease, extricates sinners from any fatal abyss, however deep it may be. Such a wondrous act demands of a person faith in the Redeemer and sincere repentance. Those who complained did so because they did not understand; they did not understand because a work of God was being accomplished before their eyes which was incomprehensible for a human mind not enlightened by grace. Explaining the incomprehensible and revealing the boundless power of redemption, the Lord said: "the Son of Man has come to seek and to save that which was lost" (Luke 19:10). Having assumed human nature without being sought or called upon by men, God Himself, in His inexpressible goodness, came "to seek and to save" the human race that was lost because it had alienated and distanced itself from God; He came "to seek and to save" every person who has been carried away to his perdition through sin, if only this person does not reject the God who seeks and desires to save him.

The Holy Gospel can be compared to a mirror. Each one of us, if he wants, will see in it the state of his soul and the almighty healing that is offered by God, the almighty physician. God the Son calls Himself "the Son of Man" because He has assumed nature and circulated among people without being different from them in appearance in any way. This is a consequence of eternal divine love, of inexpressible divine humility. The "Son of Man"—let us say in line with human custom—had the right to forgive people all their sins, because He had offered Himself, the all-perfect God, as a sacrifice for mankind, and had destroyed all human sins, whether insignificant or grave, through the inconceivably boundless price of the redemptive value. The judgment of the "Son of Man" over men, as we see in the Gospel, is completely different to that of people over their neighbors. The judgment of people is based on their own justice that has been damaged by sin and is rejected by God. The Saviour has justified all sinners who have accepted redemption through repentance and faith, even if they were condemned by men; on the other hand, He has condemned all those who rejected redemption by rejecting repentance and faith, even if men deemed them to be righteous, worthy of respect and of reward.

In the mirror of today's Gospel we have seen a sinner, carried away by the passion of avarice, who had acted through this passion with wrongful extortion and offences of many different kinds against his neighbors; we have seen this sinner judged by men and justified by God for his faith and his true repentance. What a consoling, encouraging sight! And to this day the Saviour, according to His true promise, remains among us; and to this day He heals souls infected by sins; and to this day His divine announcement still applies: "the Son of Man has come to seek and to save that which was lost." Amen.

47. On Prayer

Sermon on the Saturday of the Thirty-second Week after Pentecost

Dear brothers! In order to progress in the struggle for prayer, so as to taste the sweet fruit of prayer at the right time, through the inexpressible mercy of God, which consists in the renewal of the whole person by the Holy Spirit, it is necessary to pray constantly, and to endure courageously those difficulties and tribulations that accompany the struggle for prayer. This is what the Lord commanded us to do, as we heard in today's Gospel: "Men always ought to pray and not lose heart" (Luke 18:1), that is, not become despondent. People generally become despondent after setbacks, and so the Lord commands us not be despondent if we do not notice the desired progress after engaging in prayerful struggle for a prolonged period of time; if our minds, instead of praying attentively, are diverted by various vain thoughts and daydreams; if our hearts, instead of being filled with devoutness, which is almost always accompanied by consoling tears, are cold and hard; if at the time of prayer obscene and turbulent passions suddenly flare up within us, and impure recollections are brought to us; if our prayer is visited by its worst enemies, the demons. All obstacles encountered in the arena of prayer can be overcome by constancy in prayer.

The Lord deigned to teach us about the benefit and the fruit of constant prayer, as well as many other of His teachings, by means of a parable. A parable is imprinted particularly easily in the memory, together with the teaching it conveys.

"There was in a certain city a judge," said the Lord, to explain the necessity of remaining constantly and patiently in prayer, "who did not fear God nor regard man. Now there was a widow in that city; and she came to him, saying, 'Get justice for me,'—that is, protect me—'from my adversary.' And he would not for a while; but afterward he said within himself, 'Though I do not fear God nor regard man, yet because this widow troubles me I will avenge her, lest by her continual coming she weary me.'" (Luke 18:1–5).

The ruler here is shown to have reached a high level of sinfulness. Many people who lead a depraved life have lost the fear of God; but although they sin without fear of the all-seeing God, Who seems to them, in their blindness and in the hardness of their hearts, to be invisible or even nonexistent, they are ashamed to sin openly before men, and try in every possible way to conceal their transgressions from others, and to inspire in others the best possible opinion of themselves. The ruler had lost both the fear of God and human shame: nothing bound him to any actions; he could be guided by his own will alone. Such a desperate sinner does the judge appear to be at first glance; but on further examination it turns out that, in a mysterious sense, many characteristics ascribed to the judge apply to God.[222] First, God cannot fear Himself, and secondly, He does not regard a human face: all people are equal before Him, all are creation, all are His servants, all have equal need of His mercy, and are fully in His power. He is called unrighteous, that is, unjust, because "He hath not dealt with us after our sins, nor rewarded us according to our wickednesses. For He knoweth whereof we are made; He remembereth that we are but dust" (Ps 102:10,14). In the spiritual joy of seeing the inexpressible love of God for mankind, St Isaac the Syrian exclaims: "Do not dare to call God just, because His justice over you cannot be seen. Although the prophet calls Him just and right, His Son proclaimed that He is more than good and merciful: He is good to the 'unthankful and evil' (Luke 6:35). How can we call Him just, when we read the parable about the payment of the workers? 'My friend, I am not offending you, but I want to give this person who arrived last (who has barely started working) the same wage that I agreed to give you (who have endured the hardship of the whole hot day). Do I not have authority over my own affairs? Is your eye envious because I am good?' (Matt 20:1–15). Again, how can we call God just if we read the story of the prodigal son, who wasted all his wealth in dissipation? Merely because of the compunction expressed by the son, the father ran out to meet him, embraced him and gave him his former dignity. None other than the Son of God Himself bore witness to this of God; there is no room for doubt about it. Where is the justice of God, when Christ died for us while we were His enemies?"[223]

In the parable the widow represents a human soul separated from God by sin and recognizing and feeling this separation. The city signifies the world, as the creation of God. Very few people in this city confess their spiritual widowhood; the majority remain without remembrance of death and of God's judgment, completely immersed in transient cares and pleasures. So few of them consider eternity and prepare themselves for it that in the whole city only one such person is mentioned. The state of widowhood is a state of loneliness and helplessness, a state inseparable from sorrow, and a state of constant mourning. It is into this state that those who have sensed their spiritual widowhood, those who have been deprived through sin of communion with the Holy Spirit, those who thirst for and endeavor to renew this communion through repentance, those who are dead to God because their communion with Him has been broken off, and those who are dead to the world because of its lack of compassion, come, bring themselves, and are brought by God. This state of the soul is essential to progress in prayerful effort: God heeds only the prayers of widows, that is, only the prayers of the poor in spirit, who are filled with the recognition of their own sinfulness, their weakness, their fallenness, and free from conceit, which consists in believing oneself to possess merit, virtues, and righteousness. Conceit is self-deception. Those who deem themselves to possess merit, virtues, and righteousness are called "the rich" in Holy Scripture. "The rich" are those who in fact possess no riches, but, deceiving themselves, think that they do, and try to present themselves as rich before men. The vainglorious, proud notions from which conceit is composed destroy within a person that spiritual throne on which the Holy Spirit sits, and they remove the only condition for attracting the mercy of God toward a person. On the other hand, the throne for the Holy Spirit within a person is founded on humble notions, and the condition, the guarantee for receiving the mercy of God comes into being. Conceit by itself destroys the possibility of progress in prayer, and for this reason Scripture says: "He has scattered the proud in the imagination of their hearts. He has put down the mighty from their thrones, and exalted the lowly. He has filled the hungry with good things, and the rich He has sent away empty" (Luke 1:51–53). The prayer of proud people is destroyed by distraction. They do not have control over themselves: neither their thoughts nor their feelings obey them. Their minds cannot focus on the introspection from which the feeling of repentance and reverence is born. A person who sows his seeds on rocky ground does not reap any fruit: in the same way, a person who prays without devoutness, coldly and superficially, goes away on completing his prayer devoid of spiritual fruit, and without being admitted to communion with God. God receives only the humble to commune with Him.

The struggle for prayer presents itself very differently to those who only dream about it, who are content with the most meager practice of it, and to those who have devoted themselves painstakingly to prayerful struggle, and have come to know it through experience. The former believe that this effort is very easy, that it depends completely on a person's will, and that they can achieve it any time when they think to begin it. They suppose that as soon as they abandon their worldly preoccupations and begin keeping silence, they will encounter the most abundant spiritual joy. "We will constantly converse with God," they think and say! And they sometimes even imagine themselves being granted various elevated spiritual gifts, such as that of discernment, of prophecy, of wonderworking, or of healing. This is how the ignorant dream and wander, unwittingly guided by the passion of vainglory. Experience shows and proves otherwise.

A person who undertakes true prayerful struggle is guided within himself by God Himself, with wisdom that is unattainable for those who are not dedicated to its mysteries. "Prayer"—said St John of the Ladder—"contains within it its own Teacher, God, Who teaches a person to comprehend (prayer), Who 'gives a prayer to the one praying, [Who] blesses [him] with righteous years'" (1 Kgs 2:9).[224] After divine wisdom has been dispensed, a person beginning prayerful struggle is initially granted to taste consolation from prayer.[225] Thus a successfully chosen medicine for a chronic illness, after touching its surface, gives immediate relief following the initial doses. When used for a further period of time, this same medicine, beginning to penetrate the whole body, agitates the illness, and while gradually expelling it, increases the pain, and sometimes brings the patient into torment. In the face of such symptoms, an inexperienced patient may easily doubt the efficacy of the medicine, but expert physicians see in these very symptoms confirmation of its beneficial nature. Exactly the same thing happens with prayer. When a Christian devotes himself to it constantly and painstakingly, then it gradually begins to reveal within him his passions, the existence of which he has hitherto been unaware. It reveals to him with startling depiction the fallenness and the captivity of human nature. When he conceives the idea of arising from his fallenness and being freed from captivity, then those spirits that have enslaved him will come and will persistently rise up against the prayer that is trying to acquire spiritual freedom for him. This serves as proof of the effectiveness of the prayer, as that same great teacher of monks said: "We infer the benefit of prayer from the opposition from the demons that we encounter when we accomplish it, and we infer its fruit from our defeat of the enemy."[226] Divine providence very often keeps ascetics in involuntary contemplation of their fallenness and in the fight against their passions and evil spirits for a very long time, for their essential benefit. Seeing the passions that constantly arise within him, seeing how sinful thoughts and daydreams brought by the spirits constantly prevail over him, the struggler gains the poverty of spirit preached by the Gospel (Matt 5:3), dies to the world, becomes a true widow in the spiritual sense and, from the strong feeling of widowhood, orphanhood, loneliness, homelessness, begins, by means of constant prayer combined with weeping, to put particularly insistent pressure on the Judge Who neither fears God nor is ashamed before men—to weary the One Who is unwearying. And although this Judge, being God, does not fear God, "because" the soul that has become a widow in relation to Him through sin and the fall "troubles" Him, He will "get justice from her adversary"—that is, from her body and from her enemies, the spirits.[227] How is this justice, this protection accomplished? By bestowing the Holy Spirit on the struggler who is wearied by effort in prayer: "So I say to you, ask, and it will be given to you; seek, and you will find; knock, and it will be opened to you. For everyone who asks receives, and he who seeks finds, and to him who knocks it will be opened ... [the] heavenly Father [will] give the Holy Spirit to those who ask Him" (Luke 11:9–13). The Lord confirms this to us. But in order to receive the gift, we have been commanded to ask, to seek, to knock persistently on the spiritual doors of the mercy of God.

It is not helpful to us, it is even harmful, to acquire spiritual riches quickly and easily:[228] if we receive them easily, we will not be able to keep them; they may become a cause of vainglory in us, of disdain for and condemnation of our neighbors, which leads the struggler to the serious falls that usually follow pride, and serve as a punishment and a lesson for those who are carried away by this most destructive passion that brought the fallen angels down from heaven. This is the reason why God allows strugglers in prayer to weary themselves for a long time in an unresolved battle against the passions and the spirits, between hope and hopelessness, between frequent victories and defeats. "With rebukes hast Thou chastened man for sin," says a great laborer in prayer, "and hast brushed his life away like a spider's web" (Ps 38:12). During this difficult time, strugglers acquire thorough empirical knowledge of the various kinds of passion and of demonic intrigues, and they acquire a thorough knowledge of the commandments of the Gospel, through prolonged and painstaking study. In this difficult time, strugglers prepare themselves thoroughly to receive and to keep divine grace. The Gospel parable concludes with the following words: "And shall God not avenge His own elect, who cry out day and night to Him, though He bears long with them? I tell you that He will avenge them speedily" (Luke 18:7–8). Here God's "bearing long" means the prolonged struggle against sin that is permitted to God's elect by none other than God Himself. The avenging, or defense, is described as being brought "speedily," because even during the struggle, God constantly supports His elect; after the struggle is over and the person has been renewed by the Holy Spirit, such joy streams into him that he quickly forgets all the torment of the struggle, which then seems to him to have lasted for a very short time. "We were satisfied with Thy mercy in the morning, O Lord, and we rejoiced and were glad"—this is how people make their confession to the Lord when they have been assured that their prayer has been heard, and have seen in their souls the appearance of the spiritual morning after the darkness of the night—"We were glad all our days; for the days wherein Thou didst humble us, the years wherein we saw adversity" (Ps 89:14–15). But the struggle is so hard that the cry of prayer of the elect becomes ever louder; it does not cease either by day or by night; the pauses between prayers disappear, and the servants of God begin to trouble God with unceasing prayer and weeping produced by that humble understanding of themselves that comes from seeing their sinfulness. "I go mourning all the day long," says the holy prophet David, "for my loins are filled with sores, and there is no healing in my flesh. I was bitter"—due to my passions and the evil spirits—"and utterly humbled" (Ps 37:7–9). "How long, O Lord, wilt Thou forget me? For ever? How long wilt Thou turn Thy face from me?" How long will You be patient? How long will You not avenge my adversaries? "How long shall I seek counsel in my soul, with anguish in my heart day and night? How long shall mine enemies triumph over me?" (Ps 12:2–3). "Mine enemies compass my soul round about. Like as a lion that is greedy of his prey, and as it were a lion's whelp, lurking in secret places. Arise, O Lord, disappoint them, and trip them up; deliver my soul from the ungodly" (Ps 16:9,12–13). "My God, I have put my trust in Thee: O let me never be confounded, neither let mine enemies laugh me to scorn. For all they that wait on Thee shall not be ashamed" (Ps 24:1,2).

When the Lord had concluded the parable with the promise to "avenge speedily" all who "cry out day and night to Him" in prayer, He then said, "Nevertheless, when the Son of Man comes, will He really find faith on the earth?" Why did He say these words? According to the interpretation of the Fathers, it was for the following reason.[229] When the Lord was listing the signs that will precede His second coming, He gave a teaching on prayer that will be especially needed in those difficult and calamitous times, just as He said the following another time for the same reason: "Watch therefore, and pray always that you may be counted worthy to escape all these things that will come to pass, and to stand before the Son of Man" (Luke

21:36). "Nevertheless, when the Son of Man comes, will He really find faith on the earth?" This means: will He find true believers, who prove their faith with works, especially with true, real prayer, the struggle for which is based on faith and which is accomplished by leaning constantly on faith? This question is tantamount to the following:[230] when the Son of God comes down to earth, He will find hardly anyone, at most a few people, with true faith and the progress in prayer that depends on it. And that is when this progress will be especially needed! "The end of all things is at hand," says the Apostle Peter: "therefore be serious and watchful in your prayers" (1 Pet 4:7). There will be neither progress in prayer, nor true labor in prayer; all people will occupy themselves with material progress and with converting the earth, which is condemned to be burned up (2 Pet 3:10), into their own paradise, thinking in their self-deception that temporal life is eternal, and they will reject and deride concerns about preparation for eternity. For those whose thoughts are completely directed toward the earth and occupied with the earth, there is no God. A person who ascends toward God with pure and frequent prayer acquires living faith in God, through which he sees Him, and will fly, as if on wings, through all the vagaries and tribulations of earthly life. He will see "justice from his adversary" and will rejoice not only in forgiveness of his sins but also in being purified from sinful passions. The holy Fathers call this state holiness, blessed freedom from passion, Christian perfection. In this state he will be counted worthy "to escape all these" tribulations "that will come to pass, and to stand before the Son of Man" (Luke 21:36), when he is called before Him by death and by the trumpet that will gather the living and the dead to judgment before the Son of God. Amen.

48. On Bodily and Spiritual Struggles

Sermon on the Gospel from St Luke: Read on All the Feasts of the Mother of God

During His wanderings on earth, the place of our exile and our sufferings, the Saviour of the world once visited two righteous women, sisters by birth Martha and Mary, who lived in a village near Jerusalem called Bethany. They had their own house there. They had a brother, Lazarus, who was counted worthy to be called a friend of the God-Man and of His Apostles (John 11:11). It is clear from the Gospel that the Lord visited the house of this pious family more than once. During one of these visits, He raised Lazarus from the dead after he had lain in the grave for four days.

During the Lord's visit to this house that we remember today, the holy Evangelist Luke tells us that Martha was occupied with serving the beloved Guest, but Martha sat at His feet, listening to His words. Martha, caring only that the best possible food was offered, asked the Lord to tell Mary to help her. But the Lord replied: "Martha, Martha, you are worried and troubled about many things. But one thing is needed, and Mary has chosen that good part, which will not be taken away from her" (Luke 10:41–42). According to the interpretation of the holy Fathers, Martha mystically represents the pious bodily effort, and Mary the spiritual.[231] This account of the Lord's visit to the two sisters is appointed by the Church to be read on all feasts of the Mother of God. For these two reasons, it is especially important and informative to examine the events and the teachings it contains.

Martha was the older sister and is presented by the Evangelist as the mistress of the house. She receives the Saviour into the home, she is in charge of providing hospitality, she prepares the food, clears the table, brings the dishes. Her service is uninterrupted activity. And bodily labor takes precedence in the ascetic life of every disciple of Christ. "Bodily work," says St Isaac the Syrian, "precedes spiritual, just as the creation of Adam's body preceded the creation of his soul (Gen 2:7). A person who has not acquired bodily work cannot have spiritual work: the latter is born of the former, just as the ear of corn is born of the naked seed of grain."[232] Bodily work or ascesis consists in fulfilling the commandments of the Gospel in body. This includes material almsgiving, giving hospitality, participation in the various needs and sufferings of humanity. It includes bodily chastity, and abstinence from anger, from luxury, from amusements and distractions, from mockery and gossip, and from all words that express malice and impurity of heart. It also includes fasting, vigils, psalmody, kneeling, standing in prayer, both in church and in one's cell. It includes monastic obediences and other external ascetic effort. Bodily ascesis demands constant activity of the body: a person undertaking it moves from one physical good work to another, and sometimes combines several good works at the same time. This physical ascesis gradually purifies the soul from passions and acquaints it with the spirit of the Gospel. When a person fulfills the commandments of the Gospel in deed, they gradually convey to him the deep meaning and the deep feeling contained within them, and communicate to him the Truth, the Spirit and the Life. Bodily ascesis has its limit and its end. This consists in the definitive transition of the struggler to spiritual ascesis. Gradual transition concludes with a decisive transition. The service of Martha ended when she had finished offering hospitality to the Lord.

"Mary ... sat at Jesus' feet and heard His word" (Luke 10:39). The position taken by Mary represents the state of a soul that has been favored with entering the spiritual struggle. This is a state both of stillness and of humility, as St Barsanuphius the Great said: "With internal labour, combined with sickness of the heart (with lamenting of the heart), true silence of the heart is produced; from such silence humility is born; humility makes a person the habitation of God."[233] A person who has acquired service of God in spirit abandons external works. He abandons cares about other means of pleasing God, or applies them with moderation and rarely, in cases of particular need. In his spirit he sits at the feet of the Saviour, hears only His word, recognizes himself to be a creation of God, and not made by himself (Ps 99:3). He recognizes that he is the one who is being cultivated, and God is the vine-dresser (John 15:1), and he devotes himself completely to the will and guidance of the Saviour. It is clear that a soul attains such a state through more or less prolonged bodily ascesis. Mary would not have been able to sit at the feet of the Lord and give all her attention to His teaching if Martha had not taken upon herself all the trouble connected with welcoming Him. Serving and worshiping God in spirit and in truth (John 4:23) are that "good part," that blessed state that, beginning during our earthly life, does not end, as bodily struggles do, when we complete our earthly course. The "good part" remains the inalienable property of the soul unto eternity, and in eternity it reaches its full development. The "good part" is never taken away from the soul that attains it, and remains forever its property.

Bodily effort is often concealed by a very serious failing. This failing consists in the struggler practicing the ascetic struggle recklessly, placing excessive value on the struggle, and accomplishing feats of bodily asceticism for their own sake, wrongly confining to them all his life, all his efforts to please God. This kind of mistaken assessment is always accompanied by disparagement of spiritual struggle, and an urge to dissuade others from practicing it. This occurred with Martha. She considered the behavior of Mary to be wrong and deficient, and her own to be more valuable and more worthy of respect. The merciful Lord, without denying the service of Martha, condescended to observe to her that there was much that was superfluous and vain in her service and that the action of Mary was fundamental. With this comment, the Lord purified Martha's effort of arrogance, and taught her to offer physical service with humility. Yes, bodily ascesis that is not yet illumined with spiritual knowledge always contains much that is vain and superfluous. A person who labors in bodily effort, even for the sake of God, does so from within the "old man" (Eph 4:22); in his fields, weeds grow together with the wheat; he cannot be free from the influence of the way of thinking and the activities of the carnal mind. It is essential for all of us to pay due attention to this teaching of the Lord, and to undertake with great humility our good works that are done in body, like servants obliged to fulfill the will of their Master, but unable to fulfill it as they should because of their weakness and the harm caused to them by sin. It is very useful for a person engaged in bodily ascesis to know that there is another form of struggle, one that is incomparably higher, the struggle of the soul, one that is rich in divine grace. "A person who does not possess work of the soul," says St Isaac the Syrian, "deprives himself of the gifts of the Spirit,"[234] whatever his ascetic achievements of the body may be. This great teacher of monastics likens bodily works, when not accompanied with works of the mind within the internal chamber of the soul, to a barren womb or shriveled breasts, because bodily work cannot approach knowledge of God.[235] This can be seen with Martha. She was so preoccupied with her work, so convinced of its importance, that she did not ask the Lord what He would like her to do, but offered her own viewpoint and her own direction, and asked for them to be followed.

Why does the holy Church appoint this Gospel extract to be read at all feasts of the Mother of God? Because the Mother of God brought to the God-Man both the highest bodily service and the highest service of the spirit, keeping "all these things in her heart" (Luke 2:51), observing everything that occurred with Him from infancy and everything that was concerned with Him "and pondered them in her heart" (Luke 2:19). To explain this, the account is supplemented by an incident from the following chapter of St Luke's Gospel, when a certain woman who had heard His teaching cried out to the Lord: "Blessed is the womb that bore You, and the breasts which nursed You" (Luke 11:27), to which the Lord replied: "More than that, blessed are those who hear the word of God and keep it" (Luke 11:28). This is the divine response to human judgment! Human judgment deemed the Mother of God to be blessed solely for giving birth to the God-Man, whereas He Himself elevates her far higher by calling especially blessed those who hear the word of God and keep it. The Mother of God possessed this blessing more than all other people, listening to the words of the Lord and keeping them with a degree of sympathy that no other person has ever had. Here the superiority of spiritual over bodily service, in contrast to human judgment, is again emphasized.

The merciful Lord calls all people to serve Him. Serving the Lord, together with crucifixion of the "old man" and rejection of his carnal and sinful desires and intentions, involves its own labor; but this labor also has its consolation from a clear conscience and from divine grace. The "yoke" of Christ "is easy," and His "burden is light" (Matt 11:30). Those who wish to begin serving the Lord, with the aim of receiving Him in the house of their soul and offering Him the hospitality He has asked for, must start with bodily struggle, by keeping the commandments of the Gospel by means of bodily actions. The soul is joined with the body from creation, and depends on it due to the fall. It is infected with sinful ailments and passions due to bodily actions; but passions are also destroyed within it, and good habits, virtues, are introduced into it, by means of bodily actions. A person who allows himself to act under the influence of anger becomes enslaved to this passion due to the habit that develops through actions; a person who allows himself to act on the impulses of greed becomes infected with the passions of love of money, of covetousness, of miserliness. All passions enter the soul in a similar way, based on the external activity of the person. This is why bodily effort is needed: it is essential in order to expel the passions through actions that are opposite to their demands; it is essential in order to sow the seed of virtues in the heart, as directed by the Gospel. Prudent bodily struggle, based on and illumined by the word of God, to a significant degree frees a person from sin and makes him a friend of virtue and a servant of Christ. Bodily struggle of this kind quickly prompts spiritual struggle that is capable of achieving salvation.

Bodily ascesis, whether calm or agitated, is harmful if it does not have the spiritual understanding required by the word of God, which must be the soul of the bodily ascesis. Otherwise, it leads to conceit, to contempt and condemnation of other people, and to self-deception, it develops a person's inner pharisee,[236] alienates him from God, and unites him with Satan.

When the grace of God falls abundantly on the struggler, this then reveals within him the abundant possibilities of ascesis of the soul, which leads toward Christian perfection. Then the sinfulness of the soul, until now hidden from it, is revealed. Then the veil is lifted from its eyes and boundless, majestic eternity, hidden until now, stands before it. Then the hour of death that had stood at some distant time approaches, and stands before the very soul, before its eyes. Then earthly life, that has until now seemed eternal, is reduced to the smallest dimensions: the past life of the soul is like a dream from the previous night. The remainder of its life merges into a single last hour before death. Then there emerge from the depths of the soul groans that it has never known before, and mourning that it has never felt before, and prayer that it has never spoken before. The prayer and the mourning rise up from the very depths of the soul. They are uttered by the mind and the heart with silent lips. They are spoken toward heaven. They throw the person who is praying at the feet of the Saviour, and they keep him there. The soul, confessing its sinfulness and the endless greatness of God, enters perfection, is brought to perfection by the right hand of the all-good God Who both created man, and is still creating him. "Bless the Lord, O my soul, and forget not all His benefits; Who forgiveth all thine iniquities, and healeth all thy diseases; Who redeemeth thy life from corruption, and crowneth thee with mercy and compassion; Who satisfieth thy desire with good things; thy"—eternal—"youth shall be renewed like the eagle's" (Ps 102:2–5) by the almighty Saviour, Who renewed our nature in Himself and still renews us. Amen.

49. How Deceptive Earthly Life Is!

Homily at the Opening of a Women's Monastery

This exhortation was given at the convent dedicated to St John the Forerunner near Stavropol in the Caucasus.

"Come out from among them and be separate, says the Lord. Do not touch what is unclean, and I will receive you. I will be a Father to you, and you shall be My sons and daughters, says the Lord Almighty" (2 Cor 6:17–18). To whom is this appeal by God aimed?—Toward those who have learned and believed that the purpose given by God to man at creation, and returned to him by the redemption, consists in men becoming sons and daughters of God. From what does God order people who wish to become sons and daughters of God to separate themselves? From the society of people who are captivated by the cares of life, by earthly progress and earthly pleasures, and who pay no attention to the higher, spiritual purpose of mankind.

How deceptive earthly life is! How terrible our fall! We see with our own eyes that all our brothers, without exception, die, after wandering on earth for a period of time that, whether longer or shorter, is brief compared to the infinity of eternity; we see that they leave here both their riches and all transitory property, and their very bodies. We see this; we know that we too must inevitably die, but we lead our earthly lives as if we were to remain on earth forever; we expend all our efforts, in soul and body, in search of earthly good things that are taken away on our deaths; we give in to sinful desires and impulses, we thirst for plentiful enjoyment of the sin that destroys us, we trample upon the commandments of God, we disregard His threats and His promises. It is natural that in the face of such behavior in human society, God should command His elect: "Come out from among them and be separate, says the Lord. Do not touch what is unclean, and I will receive you. I will be a Father to you, and you shall be My sons and daughters."

Many righteous men of the Old Testament chose to withdraw from the world and to live as wanderers in the desert, while enduring various deficiencies and deprivations. "They," says the apostle, "were stoned, they were sawn in two, were tempted, were slain with the sword. They wandered about in sheepskins and goatskins, being destitute, afflicted, tormented—of whom the world was not worthy. They wandered in deserts and mountains, in dens and caves of the earth" (Heb 11:37–38). They confessed with their very lives that men are "strangers and pilgrims on the earth" (Heb 11:13), just as sons of the world confess their self-deception through their very lives. St John the Forerunner of the Lord lived in the deserts from childhood (Luke 1:80) and, after receiving a command from God in the desert, came out into the country around the Jordan to announce to mankind the coming of the Redeemer, and to exhort the people to prepare themselves to receive Him through repentance and humility (Luke 3:23). Our Lord Jesus Christ began His great ministry by withdrawing to the desert, by fasting and by defeating the devil there, showing us that the desert is the most convenient place to live an ascetic life and to prepare oneself to serve God. During the time of His ministry, the Lord often withdrew to the desert to pray, not needing this Himself, as perfect God, but showing us, weak people, that the best place for undistracted and intensive prayer is a secluded wilderness. From the very beginnings of Christianity, the early Christians at once began to leave the noisy cities, and live on their outskirts, in the suburbs and surrounding areas. The Christians of the crowded city of Alexandria, in particular, did this; their secluded dwellings were called monasteries, and the people were called monks, that is, solitaries (from the Greek word μόνος—alone). The suburb of Alexandria and its environs were filled with the cells of Christians living solitary lives. As a result, when temptations in the world multiplied, at the command of God, pious monks moved deeper into the desert, and founded various forms of monastic life. St Pachomius the Great, on the instruction of an angel, founded communities for men and for women—the kind of monastic life adopted by the newly founded monastery of nuns opened and blessed by us today on the blessing of the Holy Synod, by order of our most pious Sovereign Lord, the Emperor Alexander Nikolayevich.[237] But all types of monastic life, which vary only externally, have the same goal, that is, to remove us in our weakness from the delusions and impressions of the world, to ascribe the proper value to both temporal and eternal life, and to use the former to achieve the latter. "The children of God," says St Isaac the Syrian, "differ from others in that they live in tribulations, and the world shines with enjoyment and rest. God was not well pleased for those He loved to rest while they were in the body; He wanted them to remain in tribulations while they were in this world, to be in a burdensome situation, in labours, in poverty, in nakedness, in isolation, in need, in sickness, in humiliations, in offences, in brokenness of heart, troubled in body, far from relatives, with a sorrowful way of thinking and a particular way of looking at the whole of creation, in a habitation unlike ordinary human habitation, secluded and silent, far from human sight, and devoid of all earthly amusement. They weep, while the world laughs, they mourn, while the world amuses itself; they fast, while the world enjoys itself."[238]

When the eye of someone looking at the world from the viewpoint of Christian piety falls on proudly magnificent palaces, erected by men for the purpose of abundant earthly amusement, in order to triumph in and enjoy their fallenness, in order to develop this fallenness, to seal and strengthen it, and to make it their inalienable property: then the heart of that observer is filled with inexpressible sadness and horror. The heart is filled with quiet consolation, on the other hand, when the eye meets the sight of the humble habitation of monks, their miserable cells, more like tents than buildings, wretched cells that testify that this is the camp of the spiritual Israel, wandering in the desert of earthly life, striving for the promised land—for Heaven. "How lovely are your tents, O Jacob! Your dwellings, O Israel! Like valleys that stretch out, like gardens by the riverside, like aloes planted by the Lord, like cedars beside the waters. ... Blessed is he who blesses you" (Num 24:5–6,9). Blessed are the inhabitants of these dwellings, blessed are the residents of this camp! For he "hath not walked in the counsel of the ungodly, nor stood in the way of sinners, and hath not sat in the seat of the scornful. But his delight is in the Law of the Lord, and in His Law will he exercise himself day and night" (Ps 1:1–2). "Bless the Lord, O my soul!" (Ps 102:1) "Praise the Lord, O my soul!" (Ps 145:1). "Blessed be the Lord, for He hath marvelously showed His mercy in a strong city" (Ps 30:22). "For He hath marvelously showed His mercy." This means that the Lord has performed great mercy in granting a Dwelling-place that is protected from the temptations of the world both by its location and by its walls and by its customs and by its very clothing—a Dwelling-place for His daughters who have desired to withdraw and estrange themselves from the world in order to serve God unceasingly. "Thou shalt hide them in the secret place of Thy presence from the provoking of all men; Thou shalt shelter them from the strife of tongues" (Ps 30:21).

Let us send from here, from the wilderness of the distant Caucasus, the heartfelt voice of deep gratitude to our pious Sovereign, the Emperor Alexander Nikolayevich, who has given us a new refuge in the wide expanse of the blessed Orthodox land of Russia for maidens and widows who offer themselves to Christ as a living sacrifice (Rom 12:1). May the divine blessing promised to the person who gave a cup of cold water to a disciple of Christ (Matt 10:42) come upon the one anointed by God for quenching the spiritual, pious thirst of many souls. Let us express reverent gratitude to the Holy Synod that has given the blessing for a monastic community in the lands of the Caucasus, where the local inhabitants have long forgotten not only monasticism, but also Christianity, which arrived thanks to the victorious Russian arms and is now followed by monasticism. Let us also offer due gratitude to the founder of this monastery, the first Bishop of the Caucasus; may his prayers and his blessing help the community to succeed and both to develop spiritually and to flourish materially. May all who have helped the monastery to be founded and built in the name of the Lord have the blessing of God: may rewards be prepared for them in heaven a hundredfold by our God, before Whom not even the smallest act of almsgiving or aid is forgotten. "Bless the Lord, O my soul, and all that is within me bless His holy Name" (Ps 102:1).

You too are blessed, the virgins and widows who have gathered in the wilderness to become familiar with God. You have chosen the good part, if until the end of your life on earth you have as your purpose to please God unceasingly. Make yourselves worthy of being called by God! You have been called by the heavenly Father to be His daughters: use all your effort to make yourselves daughters of God. Do not be burdened by your subordination and your humble situation, for our Lord Jesus Christ also "made Himself of no reputation, taking the form of a bondservant, and coming in the likeness of men. And being found in appearance as a man, He humbled Himself and became obedient to the point of death, even the death of the cross" (Phil 2:7–8). Do not be burdened by your prolonged prayers, your vigils and fasting: "those who are Christ's have crucified the flesh with its passions and desires" (Gal 5:24), as the apostle says. Do not be burdened by bodily ailments and other sufferings and deprivations that the Lord permits for your purification: "For whom the Lord loves He chastens, and scourges every son whom He receives" (Heb 12:6). The servants of God, although they apparently undergo many different tribulations and sufferings, "For though in man's view they were punished, their hope is full of immortality. Though chastened in a few things, great kindness will be shown them, for God tested them and found them worthy of Himself. He tested them like gold in a furnace and accepted them as a whole burnt offering" (WSol 3: 4–6). Do not be burdened by the abuse and insults to which you may be subjected by the world: "If the world hates you," the Saviour says by way of consolation to His disciples and followers, "you know that it hated Me before it hated you. If you were of the world, the world would love its own. Yet because you are not of the world, but I chose you out of the world, therefore the world hates you" (John 15:18–19). "Blessed are you when they revile and persecute you, and say all kinds of evil against you falsely for My sake. Rejoice and be exceedingly glad, for great is your reward in heaven" (Matt 5:11–12). On the basis of this testimony from Holy Scripture and of many other similar examples, the holy Fathers recognize that the tribulations permitted to a Christian by divine providence serve as a most reliable sign of God's mercy toward him and God's care for him. This is how St John of Karpathos consoles a suffering monk: "Your heavenly Father, who in His infinite love afflicts and oppresses you with various trials, warns you, O monk, 'Know this well, you pitiful monk, that as I said by My Prophet, I will be your chastiser (Hos 5:2). I will meet you on the road in Egypt, testing you with afflictions. I will block your evil ways with the thorns of My Providence, pricking and obstructing you with unexpected misfortunes, so that you cannot fulfill the desires of your foolish heart. I will shut up the sea of your passions with the gates of My mercy (Job 38:8); like a wild beast I will devour you with thoughts of guilt, condemnation and remorse, as you perceive things of which you were ignorant. All these tribulations are a great gift of grace from God.'"[239] "The way of God is a daily cross," says St Isaac the Syrian: "No-one has ascended to heaven by living in luxury ... It will be known that a person falls under the special providence of God from the fact that God constantly sends him tribulations."[240] The holy Apostle Paul bears witness that all without exception of those who please God have partaken of chastisement and instruction through tribulations permitted by divine providence: "If you are without chastening, of which all have become partakers, then you are illegitimate and not sons" (Heb 12:8). A son of the world and of this age, living in what is regarded as immutable happiness, drowning in constant pleasures, entertained by constant amusements—alas! such a person is forgotten, rejected by God. His constant happiness and satisfaction is a sign of the greatest eternal calamity: estrangement from God.

Daughters of the heavenly Father, I bring you my best wishes on the occasion of the granting of monastic rights and the naming of your monastery. I give you my best wishes for the arena of monastic struggles and rewards in heaven that is opening up before you. At the same time I give you my best wishes for the arena of many different tribulations: the path of monasticism is one of tribulations, and the reason for heavenly rewards is earthly tribulations. God does not call us to Himself with the promise of earthly happiness, but with a promise of sufferings. Paul had only just been chosen as apostle to the gentiles when countless sufferings were foretold to him (Acts 9:16). After undergoing many sufferings and seeing the spiritual fruit that is born of tribulations, the apostle calls other Christians to the same struggle. "Therefore we also," he says, "since we are surrounded by so great a cloud of witnesses, let us lay aside every weight, and the sin which so easily ensnares us, and let us run with endurance the race that is set before us, looking unto Jesus, the author and finisher of our faith, who for the joy that was set before Him endured the cross, despising the shame, and has sat down at the right hand of the throne of God" (Heb 12:1–2). "Now no chastening seems to be joyful for the present, but painful; nevertheless, afterward it yields the peaceable fruit of righteousness to those who have been trained by it. Therefore strengthen the hands which hang down, and the feeble knees" (Heb 12:11–12) and "count it all joy," that is, rejoice with great joy, "when you fall into various trials" (Jas 1:2): "We must through many tribulations enter the kingdom of God" (Acts 14:22). Amen.

50. On Salvation

Sermon to the People during a Visit in the Diocese

Dear brothers! The ineffable mercy of God has made me, the unworthy, your shepherd; this has given me the opportunity to visit you, to join my poor prayer with your prayers and to speak with you. But what shall we speak about? Let us speak about our salvation.

We are all wanderers on earth for a short time only. Each one of us will stay here for as long as appointed by God, and then, inevitably, will die. Our homes, our gardens, our fields, our property, even our bodies will be taken from us by death. Our soul, and only our soul, together with its works, good and bad, will enter eternity, and in eternity it will either constantly rejoice and be glad, or it will continuously be in torment, weeping and groaning. Let us talk about how to be saved, how to please God, how to save ourselves from the bitterness of hades, and how to inherit the sweetness of paradise.

Brothers! Prepare yourselves to listen closely to my words, so that you understand and remember them. Because I rarely have the opportunity to speak with you, I would like to give you the most necessary lesson. "O Lord, open Thou my lips, and my mouth shall show forth Thy praise" (Ps 50:17).

Whoever wishes to be saved must belong to the one, holy Orthodox Church, and be her faithful child, obeying her statutes in everything. If someone does not obey the Church, if someone has left the Church, if someone is a schismatic, then however many prostrations he may make, however much he may fast, however much he may pray, it is impossible for him to be saved. The Lord compared a person who does not obey the Church to an idolater: "if [someone] refuses even to hear the church, let him be to you like a heathen and a tax collector" (Matt 18:17). In the Old Testament, when Saul willfully made a sacrifice that went against the commandments of the Lord, the Prophet Samuel told him: "You have rendered it vain because you did not keep my commandments which the Lord commanded you" (1 Kgs 13:12). "If only the desired whole burnt offerings and desired sacrifices were equal to the Lord, as compared to one who heeds the voice of the Lord! Behold! Hearing is better than a good sacrifice and obedience than the fat of rams. That sin is one and the same as divination. Idols bring grief and pain" (1 Kgs 15:22–23). In the New Testament, the beloved disciple of the Lord testified that the Lord only accepts our prayer when it is asked according to His will (1 John 5:14). The prayers of those who oppose God in their actions are not accepted; they are rejected by God (Matt 7:21–23). Schismatics and heretics are foreign to humility, just as the devil is foreign to humility, and they are therefore foreign to salvation, just as the devil is. The devil once appeared to St Macarius and said: "Macarius! You fast a great deal, but I do not eat at all; you hardly sleep, but I do not sleep at all; with one thing only you defeat me: with your humility."[241] Schismatics keep prolonged and strict fasts, spend whole nights in prayer, make many prostrations, but alas, they labor in vain, because they do not want to humble themselves. Without humility it is impossible to be a disciple of Christ. The Lord said: "Take My yoke upon you and learn from Me, for I am gentle and lowly in heart, and you will find rest for your souls" (Matt 11:29). Whoever has not humbled himself is not a disciple of Christ, and has not submitted to Christ. True humility comes from obedience, says St John of the Ladder,[242] just as the Lord revealed His humility in that He "became obedient to the point of death, even the death of the cross" (Phil 2:8). Without obedience to the Church, there is no humility; without humility there is no salvation: "I humbled myself, and He saved me" (Ps 114:5). In addition to this, heresy and schism contain within themselves blasphemy against the Holy Spirit, which is a mortal sin for which God does not forgive a person either in this age or in the age to come, if he remains in this sin (Matt 12:31–32). Even a martyr's blood cannot purify a person from this sin, according to the teaching of St John Chrysostom. This sin is purified only when the person renounces his heresy, abandons the schism, and rejoins the holy Church.

Whoever wants to be saved must pray to God, even a little at a time, but often. On weekdays, pray to God at home: in the morning after rising from sleep; at night before going to sleep; before the midday and evening meals. Do not even eat breakfast or your evening meal without remembering God, and making the sign of the cross. On feast-days and Sundays, we must take part in communal church worship. Go to matins, to the vigil service, to Divine Liturgy and to vespers. It is a great good fortune when it is given to a sinful man to visit the church of God. He can pray to God to forgive him his sins and to grant him salvation. David was a glorious and rich king, and at the same time a prophet, but he asked one thing of the Lord: "One thing have I desired of the Lord, which I will require; even that I may dwell in the house of the Lord all the days of my life, to behold the fair beauty of the Lord, and to visit His holy temple" (Ps 26:4). David recognized the opportunity given to him of going to the temple as a most particular mercy of God: "As for me, by the multitude of Thy mercy I will come into Thine house; in Thy fear will I worship toward Thy holy temple" (Ps 5:8). In general, prayer is a very great virtue, the means of unifying man with God. The Holy Fathers call prayer the mother of all virtues,[243] because it allows us to request of the merciful Lord all other virtues, all good things, transient and eternal, as the Lord bears witness: "Ask, and it will be given to you; seek, and you will find; knock, and it will be opened to you." To the commandment that we should pray, the Lord also adds a promise to hear our prayer: "For everyone who asks receives, and he who seeks finds, and to him who knocks it will be opened ....Your Father who is in heaven [will] give good things to those who ask Him" (Matt 7:7–8,11). Prayer must be said with faith; it must be founded on a good and forgiving attitude. The soul is to the body what faith is to prayer. Just as the body is dead and incapable of movement without the soul, prayer is dead and powerless and ineffective without faith. Goodness is to prayer what foundations are to a house. Just as a house cannot stand without foundations, but must fall, so prayer, if it is not founded on goodness, cannot ascend to God, but is mired in carnal-mindedness and destroyed by it. The Lord says: "whatever things you ask when you pray, believe that you receive them, and you will have them. And whenever you stand praying, if you have anything against anyone, forgive him, that your Father in heaven may also forgive you your trespasses" (Mark 11:24–25). Prayer not only acquires transient and eternal good things, it not only brings the blessing of God upon us, but it also protects us from misfortunes and saves us from great tribulations. It brought the prophet Jonah out from the belly of the whale; it saved King Hezekiah from the death that had already been proclaimed to him. "Pray that you may not enter into temptation" (Luke 22:40), the Lord said. On the other hand, a person who neglects prayer is subject to many different misfortunes, and may lose salvation itself.

Whoever wants to be saved must give alms, in spirit and in body, as far as is within his means. Almsgiving of the soul consists in forgiving one's neighbors their sins, that is, insults and offences they have brought against us. Bodily almsgiving consists in helping our neighbor as far as we can afford with bread, clothing, money, and hospitality. The Lord said: "Blessed are the merciful, for they shall obtain mercy" (Matt 5:7), that is, they will be saved. On the other hand, judgment without mercy awaits the unmerciful (Jas 2:13), that is, the unmerciful cannot be saved.

Someone who wants to be saved must offer to God thorough repentance for his sins, both in his daily prayers, and, in particular, before his spiritual father in the sacrament of confession. The God-inspired prophet proclaims: "I have acknowledged my transgression and my sin have I not hid; I said, against myself will I confess my transgression unto the Lord, and so Thou forgavest the irreverence of my heart" (Ps 31:5). Consider closely the order of the words spoken by the Holy Spirit: first a person recognizes his sins, which is accomplished by devout self-examination; then he rejects the justifications with which a guilty conscience usually attempts to excuse its sin; finally, the repentant person becomes his own accuser, and tells the Lord, before the confessor as witness, all his sins, without any self-love. Then he receives forgiveness from God for his transgressions. The apostle says: "If we confess our sins, He is faithful and just to forgive us our sins and to cleanse us from all unrighteousness." For this reason, "if anyone sins, we have an Advocate with the Father, Jesus Christ the righteous. And He Himself is the propitiation for our sins, and not for ours only but also for the whole world" (1 John 1:9; 2:1–2). We have an all-powerful Advocate, the Lord Jesus Christ. We have all-powerful propitiation from our sins in Him. Having destroyed our sins by means of confession through such an advocate and such propitiation as this, we receive without doubt the joyful guarantee of our salvation. After purifying ourselves through confession before a spiritual father, we should receive communion, with fear of God, faith and love, in the most-holy Body and the most-holy Blood of Christ. Holy Communion is essential for our salvation. The Lord said, "Most assuredly, I say to you, unless you eat the flesh of the Son of Man and drink His blood, you have no life in you," that is, you do not have salvation. "Whoever eats My flesh and drinks My blood has eternal life," that is, he has salvation (John 6:53–54). We should receive communion at least four times a year, in each of the four fasting periods. If, regrettably and unfortunately, the cares of our lives do not even allow this, then we should without fail receive communion once a year.

Whoever wants to be saved must graciously endure all tribulations permitted to him during his brief sojourn on earth. If the harvest fails, or if the ripened wheat is destroyed by locusts, or by hail; if our animals die, if there is a fire, if we or a family member fall ill, or a close relative dies, or if we have to endure persecution and insults from a powerful person: all this we must endure nobly, without grumbling, and especially without blasphemy. The Lord told us, "By your patience [you will] possess your souls" (Luke 21:19); "he who endures to the end shall be saved" (Matt 24:13). This means that the one who is saved is not one who endures one tribulation patiently, but gives in to grief and grumbling about other tribulations; the one who is saved is the one who endures all tribulations, all misfortunes permitted to him throughout his earthly life, to the very end, until the day and the hour of his death. Noble endurance of tribulations means active, living recognition of one's sinfulness. Noble endurance of tribulations means active, living knowledge and confession of the Redeemer. Noble endurance of tribulations means following our Lord Jesus Christ. "Christ ... suffered for us," said the holy Apostle Peter, "leaving us an example, that you should follow His steps" (1 Pet 2:21). No voluntary struggle, no voluntary deprivation or suffering can bring such benefit to the soul as is brought by involuntary tribulations sent by God. No voluntary struggle is completely without more or less obvious conceit and vainglory; but the struggle to which a soul is elevated by a tribulation sent by God is free from these subtle and disastrous passions. This struggle brings abundant humility and true repentance to the soul. Tribulations sent by God are a true sign that a person has been chosen by God and is loved by Him. "As many as I love," the Lord bore witness, "I rebuke and chasten" (Rev 3:19). This is why the apostle comforts the sorrowing and suffering with these words: "My son, do not despise the chastening of the Lord, nor be discouraged when you are rebuked by Him; for whom the Lord loves He chastens, and scourges every son whom He receives. If you endure chastening, God deals with you as with sons" (Heb 12:5–7). This is the benefit of earthly tribulations, when they are endured with good humor. They are a gift from God (Phil 1:29). They are a sign of adoption by God! In order to learn patient and good-humored endurance of tribulations, we should meet every approaching trouble with the words of the blessed thief: "[I] receive the due reward of [my] deeds; Lord, remember me when You come into Your kingdom" (Luke 23:41,42). It is also helpful to remember and to repeat the words of the much-suffering Job. "If we accepted good things from the Lord's hand, shall we not endure evil things?" (Job 2:15 LXX [2:10]). "As it seemed good to the Lord, so also it came to pass. Blessed be the name of the Lord" (Job 1:21). All the saints inherited the Heavenly Kingdom by enduring many sorrows and deaths![244] All the saints glorified and thanked God for the temptations and disasters sent to them, through which they were purified, like gold in a crucible, and became capable of eternal blessedness. Good-humored endurance of tribulations sent by God is crucifixion on one's own cross. A person who confesses his own sinfulness becomes a confessor of the Redeemer, and from his cross he ascends to heaven for eternal enjoyment of the heavenly joys earned by earthly tribulations.

Someone who wishes to be saved must read sacred books. "Blessed is the man that hath not walked in the counsel of the ungodly, nor stood in the way of sinners, and hath not sat in the seat of the scornful. But his delight is in the Law of the Lord, and in His Law will he exercise himself day and night" (Ps 1:1–2). Our minds, darkened by sin, cannot possibly be satisfied in terms of salvation with their own feeble, wavering, deceptive thoughts: they must borrow divine thoughts by attentively reading or carefully listening to the Word of God, and be guided by them. We must study the Word of God very reverently and very frequently, so that it may be our guide in the work of salvation, because our own thoughts can easily distract us from the way of salvation by taking untruth for truth. Our own thoughts are so damaged through sin that they even contradict and counteract the Word of God. It is a great misfortune to believe them. On the other hand, it is a great thing when someone holds firmly on to the Word of God, as a blind man holds on to the hand of his guide. The holy Fathers called reading and listening to the Word of God the king of all virtues.[245] The Word of God reveals to us all the sinful passions living and acting within our damaged nature, it reveals all their tricks, and it unveils malice when it conceals itself in the guise of a virtue to deceive us. The Word of God uncovers the plots and intentions of our enemy, the devil, and teaches us how we must repel this evil adversary that longs for our perdition. The Word of God constantly calls us to repentance, telling us of the infinite mercy of God toward fallen mankind, suffering under the yoke of sin; it teaches us how to offer repentance, how to make this repentance effective and fruitful. The Word of God unveils to us all the vicissitudes and vanity of this world; it paints us a picture of the ruinous consequences of being deluded by the world and by sin; it reveals to us the great majesty of eternity with its rewards for a pious earthly life and with its terrible punishments for transgressions committed on earth. The Word of God gives us the most thorough and precise teaching about the virtues and the means of acquiring them and of becoming pleasing to God. In short, the Word of God teaches us salvation.

Whoever is a true child of the Orthodox Church, whoever daily, or even better, hourly, remembers God and asks Him for mercy and help in every place in His dominion, whoever conscientiously attends the church of God on Sundays and feast-days, and prays at home every morning and evening, whoever is merciful to the poor and to strangers, whoever offers repentance for his sins and receives communion in the holy Mysteries of Christ, whoever endures patiently the tribulations sent to him by God, whoever studies carefully the Word of God: that person possesses the precious guarantee of salvation. He still has one struggle ahead of him: he must without fail protect his treasure, his salvation, from sins, especially from mortal sins.

What is a mortal sin? A mortal sin is one that kills with eternal death the soul of a person who has committed it. If a person dies in mortal sin without due repentance, then demons steal away his soul and take it down to the dark and stifling abysses underground, to hades, to eternal torment. The following are mortal sins: heresy, schism, apostasy from the Christian faith, blasphemy, magic and sorcery, murder and suicide, fornication, adultery, unnatural sins of fornication, intoxication, sacrilege, robbery, theft, and any cruel offence against one's neighbor. Of the mortal sins, only for suicide is there no repentance; the other mortal sins, through the ineffable mercy of God toward our humanity, can be healed through repentance. Repentance for a mortal sin consists in confessing it to one's spiritual father, accepting his chiding, and not falling into this sin again. But so many people, having fallen into a mortal sin, have had no opportunity to repent of it. One person became intoxicated with wine, and in this state his soul was parted from his body; another went out stealing and robbing, and the wrath of God fell on him in the very act. Beware, brothers, of deadly sins. I repeat: mortal sins kill the soul. If someone dies in mortal sin, without managing to repent of it, his soul goes to hades. It has no hope of salvation.

What are non-mortal sins? These are sins in thought, word, and deed, in knowledge, and in ignorance, that do not kill the soul, but wound it to a greater or lesser extent. Even the saints are not without these sins; but the saints are vigilant, and when they notice a sin into which their human weakness has been enticed, they immediately heal it by means of repentance. If the soul is parted from the body at a time when the person has not managed to wash away his non-mortal sins through repentance, then the soul is not taken down into hades because of them; on its way to heaven, in the air, it is spared the torture of evil spirits, with the cooperation of which humans commit sins, and is allowed to redeem sins by means of good works. If a person's soul should have enough good works, in particular if the person gave alms generously during its earthly life, then the sins are redeemed through this almsgiving and other good works; the gates of heaven are opened to it and it enters into heaven unto eternal rest and joy. But it can happen that a soul has so many lesser sins and so few virtues that it goes down to hades due to the great number of non-mortal sins. The holy Fathers compare a mortal sin to a heavy rock, and a lesser sin to a tiny grain of sand. If a single large stone is tied around a person's neck, and he is thrown into the depths, he will drown: in the same way, a single mortal sin is enough to drown a soul in the abysses of hades. A few grains of sand weigh hardly anything: in the same way, in the saints of God, a non-mortal sin, greatly lessened in gravity and size through constant self-observation and continual repentance, has hardly any influence on their eternal lot. But this same non-mortal sin in souls that are dedicated to earthly cares, in particular earthly amusements, acquires an extraordinary heaviness and, like a mortal sin, drags the cursed soul down into hades. For example, if someone has said an amusing and even indecent word, and then repented of it, his sin is easily forgiven; but if someone constantly says amusing, blasphemous, and even shameful words, he may easily be subjected to eternal torment in hades for his idle talk and foul language. A great number of non-mortal sins can bring the same ruin to the soul as that brought by one mortal sin. In the same way, a bag filled with fine sand and tied around a person's neck can drown him just as easily as a very heavy stone.

The root of all sins, says the Apostle Paul, is the love of money, and after this, in the opinion of the holy Fathers, comes gluttony, of which the strongest expression is drunkenness. For love of money, Judas committed the most terrible crime of all those committed in human history: he betrayed the Lord. For love of money, countless atrocities are committed: the laws of God and of the state are broken, justice is trampled upon, injustice is covered up, the poor are oppressed, the taker of bribes is enriched, to his own ruin. The heart of a lover of money is closed to mercy, and he deprives himself of the mercy of God, and of salvation, which is given only to the merciful. Of what transgressions is a person who is dedicated to drunkenness not capable? He is heated up by wine, as if by the fire of Gehenna, he raves like a madman, he is possessed, as if in a frenzy. He is ready to commit adultery; he is ready for quarrels, for fights, for robbery, for murder. Any atrocity seems easy to a person who is possessed by drunkenness. Despite this, his evil deeds cannot be compared with those of a lover of money whose wicked deeds are deliberate, concealed by the appearance of truth, shrewd, imbued, and filled with satanic cunning, and not infrequently cause significant repercussions, turmoil and undermine the welfare of whole peoples. Not without reason does the holy Gospel say that "Satan entered" Judas, the lover of money, to assist and guide him in his diabolical intentions (John 13:27).

Beloved brothers! In my short talk with you I have outlined, as far as my poor understanding allows, the path of salvation, the means of salvation, and the way to keep the salvation acquired through virtue from being spoiled by evil.

Save yourselves, brothers, save yourselves! The earthly life of each one of us is very brief—we do not realize how quickly it passes. We do not realize how death creeps up on each one of us. At the terrible hour of death, every moment of gluttony and drunkenness, every instance of adultery and fornication will appear to us to be a stinking, deep pit and abyss. How we will begin to regret that we have fallen into this pit! Then we will know that the enjoyment of every passion is the most unfortunate, the saddest deception. Blessed is he who acquires salvation through his prayers, through his almsgiving, through his repentance. Such a man will enter into the joy of his Lord (Matt 25:21); such a man will enter into the paradise of sweetness, where the rivers of divine grace flow, where the eternal feast of salvation is celebrated.

Conversely, the soul that wallowed in sin during its earthly life will be dragged down into hades by cruel demons. O brothers! The torments are indescribable that await sinners in the prisons of the underworld. There is eternal darkness there and at the same time unquenchable fire; there is gnashing of teeth, and the worm that does not die. There is crying and groaning, people begging for mercy, but there is no-one to hear or pay attention even to the most convincing and pitiful entreaties. There people ask for help and salvation, but there is no-one to help or to save them. "It is impossible to convey in words," says St Cyril of Alexandria, "it is impossible to picture or imagine the adversities and sufferings undergone by a soul that is taken down into the abyss of hades. No human mouth has the power to explain the terror and trembling that overcomes the prisoners of hades; there are no human lips that could express their torment and their lamenting."[246]

Brothers, let us try to avoid the cruel torments of hades and to inherit the Kingdom of Heaven by living a virtuous life. Whoever among you has so far lived virtuously, may he continue that way of life. Whoever has so far permitted himself to lead a sinful life, may he offer repentance, and from now on may he lead a virtuous life. "'As I live,' says the Lord God, 'I have no pleasure in the death of the wicked, but that the wicked turn from his way and live'" (Ezek 33:11).

51. Homily on the Necessity of Rejecting Conceit in Order to Attain Fruitful Repentance

"Therefore bear fruits worthy of repentance, and do not begin to say to yourselves, 'We have Abraham as our father'" (Luke 3:8; Matt 3:8–9).

These words belong to St John the Forerunner of the Lord, the greatest of the prophets.[247] The Old Testament ended with him and the New Testament began with him, and he thus serves as a link between the two. The ministry of John was foretold by the prophets of the Old Testament; his works and his teaching are described by the apostles in the Gospel. "The beginning of the gospel of Jesus Christ, the Son of God" is dedicated to the account of John. "As it is written in the Prophets: 'Behold, I send My messenger before Your face, Who will prepare Your way before You. The voice of one crying in the wilderness: "Prepare the way of the Lord; make His paths straight." John came baptizing in the wilderness and preaching a baptism of repentance for the remission of sins'" (Mark 1:1–4). The ministry of John consisted in preparing the way for the Lord, Who was to appear very soon, clothed in humanity, and in making straight the paths for Him. What kind of way is this? What are these paths? This way is people's way of thinking; these paths are the feelings and intentions of people's hearts. In order to receive the Lord, it is necessary to have the right way of thinking; in order to receive the Lord, it is necessary to have both the will of the heart to do so, and humble sensations. This is how the Archangel Gabriel explained the ministry of the Forerunner to his father, the righteous Zacharias, when he announced his conception and birth: "He [the Forerunner] will turn many of the children of Israel to the Lord their God. He will also go before Him in the spirit and power of Elijah, 'to turn the hearts of the fathers to the children,' and the disobedient to the wisdom of the just, to make ready a people prepared for the Lord" (Luke 1:16–17).

"Repent," the holy Forerunner proclaimed to mankind, recognize that you are sinners, that you are fallen and lost beings, that you are in the jaws of eternal death, that you need to be saved. "Repent, for the kingdom of heaven is at hand!" that is, the blessed time has come and God Himself will appear very soon among us, and although He will appear with the humble appearance of a man, He will have the almighty power of God. He will destroy the dominion of death, He will retrieve from the fatal abyss and grant eternal blessedness to those people who direct their minds and hearts toward receiving Him, and who prepare themselves to do so by rejecting a sinful way of life, recognizing that they are lost and have need of salvation and of the Saviour, and resolving to follow and obey the God-Man. A person who does not recognize his own sinfulness, his fallenness, his perdition cannot receive Christ, cannot believe in Christ, cannot be a Christian. What can Christ do for someone who is already rational and virtuous, who is satisfied with himself, who considers himself to be worthy of all earthly and heavenly rewards? What can Christ do for someone who, without having proper understanding about God and man, does not want to think about eternity, but is completely absorbed in earthly cares and pleasures, as if he were to remain on earth forever? John chose the wilderness as the place of his preaching. Far away from the usual pursuits, from perishable objects of attachment and of passion, it is easier for people to raise their thoughts to God, to eternity; it is easier to hear spiritual teaching about God-pleasing virtues, the gateway to which is true repentance. The wilderness mystically represents the moral state of humanity, which has given itself up to vanity, losing its fundamental inheritance and dignity.

Now that I too have come to the wilderness for my salvation, I cannot find any more fitting words for my first address to its inhabitants who have settled here with the same aim, more fitting for me and for my new brothers, than the words and exhortations of the holy Forerunner. Having come to the wilderness for repentance, for which the salvation of God is granted, let us bear "fruits worthy of repentance" (Matt 3:8).

It is not enough to choose a place to live that is suitable for repentance; it is not enough to leave behind one's property, relations, and friends, to renounce close and frequent intercourse with the world: this is not enough. These things are only aids to repentance; these are actions that must precede repentance. Repentance is the field where the spiritual treasure of salvation is concealed; in order to buy the field, it is necessary to sell all one's property (Matt 13:44). After selling one's property, that is leaving behind material things and breaking off links with the world, it is necessary to bear "fruits worthy of repentance," so that repentance may be real and achieve its aim. So that repentance may be real, and bring us salvation and eternal blessedness, we must acquire it within ourselves, in our souls; our very spirits must grieve and submit to the God-pleasing sorrow that arises from recognizing and feeling our own sinfulness; we must expel any form of conceit from within ourselves. Repentance is impossible in the presence of conceit. One single wrong thought about oneself can bring conceit into the soul, feed, support, and strengthen conceit within it, and make it incapable of repentance. Conceit is a level of pride that is abominable to God! Conceit is that foolish, blind, and destructive passion that cast down the radiant angel from heaven, and made him a dark demon. Conceit is that deadly poison that the ancient serpent injected into human nature. Conceit is a sickness of the spirit that is not noticed by a person who is heedless of his salvation, but is so powerful and significant that it places a person among the rejected spirits that are hostile to God. A person infected with conceit is not capable of being adopted by God. Adoption by God requires total rejection of conceit.

The Archangel Gabriel gave a very apt explanation of the mission of the Forerunner, who was equal to the angels. As quoted above, he said that the holy Forerunner would "turn many of the children of Israel to the Lord their God." This means the holy Forerunner would bring to remembrance of God many of the Israelites who had forgotten about Him, and would bring close to God many Israelites who had become strangers to Him. The Archangel further said that the holy Forerunner would "turn the hearts," that is, the feelings and the pledges of the heart, "of the fathers to the children, and the disobedient to the wisdom of the just." Who are these fathers, and who are these just? The fathers are Abraham, the forefather of the Israelites, and all their holy ancestors, holy judges, kings, and prophets. We must understand the name of the just to mean all who were pleasing to God in the Old Testament, some of whom did not belong to the people of Israel. So, what were the feelings and pledges of the heart, the way of thinking of the Old Testament people who pleased God? The pledge of their hearts was humility, and their corresponding way of thinking was humble-mindedness. The holy patriarch Abraham, pouring out his heart in prayer, said: "I ... am but dust and ashes" (Gen 18:27). And when did he say this? When he stood face to face with God, when he heard the revelation of terrible mysteries, when he received the great promise, when God called him His true servant, worthy of divine revelations. The righteous, long-suffering Job, who was made worthy to see God, called himself "dust and ashes"; he so disparaged himself, he felt his own insignificance so strongly, that it was as if he "wasted away," as if he depreciated himself unto eternity, as if he ceased to exist (Job 42:6).[248] The renowned king, the famous warrior and commander, the God-inspired prophet David was a stranger to conceit; in his many holy hymns, he never once indicated his merit or virtue. He spoke everywhere of himself with the greatest humility; he ascribed his elevation to the throne and all his successes solely to the mercy of God. He openly proclaimed that humility was the reason for his salvation (Ps 114:5). Who is not moved by the deeply humble words of David, by his sincere confession of his sins, by his confession of the extraordinary greatness and mercy of God? The holy, inspired psalmist depicted faithfully and vividly both the personal sinfulness of a man and the general sinfulness of humanity, the depths of its fallenness, the burdensome captivity beneath the yoke of the ruler of the world, the fallen angel. It is as if he were measuring the depth of his fall, weighing the weight of the chains that bind him. "Have mercy upon me, O God," David cries out, "after Thy great goodness" (Ps 50:2). "Have mercy upon me, O Lord, for I am weak; O Lord, heal me, for my bones are vexed. Turn Thee, O Lord, and deliver my soul; O save me, for Thy mercy's sake" (Ps 6:3,5). David asks for mercy, recognizes that he is lost: he seeks a reason for mercy only in the mercifulness of God and in his own disastrous situation, in his weakness and inability to help himself. He does not see himself as above any other person, on the contrary, he deems himself unworthy to be called a man, and the most sinful of men: "I am a worm, and no man," he says, "a very scorn of men, and the out-cast of the people" (Ps 21:7). "I was conceived in wickedness, and in sins did my mother bear me" (Ps 50:7), David confesses, recognizing his own participation in the fall that is common to all of humanity, and on the state of his own soul he expresses himself as follows: "The waters are come in, even unto my soul. I was stuck fast in the deep mire, where no ground is; I am come into deep waters, and a tempest hath run over me" (Ps 68:2–3). "My wickednesses are gone over my head; like a sore burden have they become too heavy for me. My wounds stink, and are corrupt, because of my foolishness" (Ps 37:5–6). Mourning over his enslavement to demons and entreating God to save him from it, David says: "Have mercy upon me, O God, for man hath trodden me down; fighting all day, he hath pressed me sore. Mine enemies have trodden on me all day long. They had a loathing unto my words all day; all their thoughts were for evil against me" (Ps 55:1–3,6). "They [are] increased that trouble me. Many are they that rise against me. Many one there be that say of my soul, there is no salvation for him in his God. Arise, O Lord; save me, O my God" (Ps 3:1–2,8). The holy prophet Isaiah, who was made worthy to see the Lord, to sit on the high, exalted throne surrounded by the faces of the heavenly Powers, exclaimed: "Woe is me, for I am undone! Because I am a man of unclean lips, and I dwell in the midst of a people of unclean lips; for my eyes have seen the King, the Lord of hosts" (Isa 6:5). Having seen God, the prophet deemed himself unworthy of God both because of his own sinfulness and because of the sinfulness of all humanity, in which each person necessarily participates, being conceived and born in it.

Such was the disposition of soul of the righteous men of the Old Testament, of the fathers in the flesh of Old-Testament Israel, of the fathers in spirit of the New Testament Israel, the Christians. It was thanks to this disposition that they became capable, after several centuries, of receiving faith in the promised Messiah, and went to their rest in the hope of receiving salvation through Him, "not having received the promises, but having seen them afar off were assured of them [and] embraced them" (Heb 11:13). Such was the disposition that was required of the people who were contemporaries of the God-Man, so as to receive Him. Such is the disposition that is also required now, to receive and be united with Christ. We must, yes, we must reject conceit. We must recognize our sinfulness, our fallenness, our perdition. We must repent, that is, show contrition for the sins we have committed, and abandon our sinful way of life in order to acquire true knowledge of God and to serve Him.

The holy Forerunner, whose mission was to make the Israelites who were his contemporaries return to the way of thinking and the feelings of their blessed forefathers, among whom was Abraham, began his teaching with the following particularly important instruction: "Do not begin to say to yourselves, 'We have Abraham as our father'" (Luke 3:8). What does this mean? The great John wishes his hearers to follow the way of thinking and the feelings of Abraham, and at the same time demands of them: "Do not begin to say to yourselves, 'We have Abraham as our father.'" These words from the preacher of repentance have the lamentable meaning that the descendants of Abraham, not possessing either his way of thinking or his feelings, or his righteous deeds, were too much occupied with their descent in the flesh from Abraham; they were vain about it, and because of it they scorned other peoples. In this regard, the Israelites were following a general custom of the world hostile to God. The founder of the kingdom of Babylon, Nimrod, was the leader of a gang of robbers; the founder of the state of Rome, Romulus, was another robber chieftain; the patriarchs of other peoples, the founders of other states were people who were similar in virtue to Nimrod and Romulus. On the other hand, Abraham, the patriarch of the Israelites was a holy man, called a friend of God; their lawgiver, Moses, was another holy man, a great wonderworker; many other holy men sprang up from their midst; the Messiah Himself, the God-Man, was to be born into a family of the people of Israel. Unfortunately, the majority of Israelites, descendants in the flesh from Abraham and the prophets, in no way resembled these forefathers in either behavior or character; from the moral perspective, the Israelites were more similar to those of their forefathers who stained their hands with the blood of the prophets, and stoned those sent to them by God (Matt 23:37). The high opinion they had of themselves because they were descended from Abraham had infected the whole people with pride, and had made them incapable of repentance, of turning to God, of accepting the Messiah promised to them. It was with astute insight that the great John the Forerunner directed the first words of his preaching against the main ailment of the people: destructive conceit. "Do not begin to say to yourselves"—reject the secret thought that is deeply rooted within your hearts—"'We have Abraham as our father.'" Reject your foolish carnal-mindedness, hostile to God, that does not submit to God and is incapable of doing so. Reject your carnal mind that is already an eternal death for you, and seals eternal death in you if you remain within it (Rom 8:6). Know that Abraham pleased God with his faith (Rom 4:3), that Abraham served God in spirit and in truth, and therefore the descendants of Abraham are spiritual, and consist of all people who have acquired true faith in God, without being part of a particular ethnicity in the flesh, "that he" (Abraham) "might be the father of all those who believe, though they are uncircumcised ... and the father of circumcision to those who not only are of the circumcision, but who also walk in the steps of the faith which our father Abraham had while still uncircumcised" (Rom 4:11–12). In vain do you, drunk with conceit and pride, and with the carnal mind that comes from the fallen angel, scorn and disparage other peoples! If they are so strange to true understanding of God and so dead in their hearts that they can truly be called stones, then "I say to you that God is able to raise up children to Abraham from these stones" (Matt 3:9). "Do not begin to say to yourselves, 'We have Abraham as our father,'" because with such a high opinion of yourselves, you destroy any spiritual affinity, no, any proximity and relationship between yourselves and Abraham.

John rightly fought against conceit, which is born of the worldly way of thinking of the "old man" (Eph 4:22), and he justly used the strongest expressions against it, for his words were justified in the most grievous way. It was from conceit that the Jewish people rejected the Messiah, and in committing deicide they exceeded the sins of their forefathers, who had killed and stoned the prophets and messengers of God. While acting against the Messiah, they had constantly on their lips the names of Abraham and Moses who were true followers of the Messiah. "We are Moses' disciples," they said, trying cunningly to justify their rejection of the God-Man. "We know that God spoke to Moses; as for this fellow," the Lord Jesus Christ, "we do not know where He is from" (John 9:28–29). They said this at the same moment when there stood before their eyes the man born blind who had been healed by the Lord, when they, as it were, felt the Lord's miracle, while they knew of the ancient miracles of Moses only from Scripture. The Lord exhorted the Jews who had met before Him to accept His teaching and through this to inherit spiritual freedom from sin, or salvation and eternal joy. But pride and conceit prevented the Jews from accepting the exhortation of God. They answered the Lord abruptly: "We are Abraham's descendants, and have never been in bondage to anyone" (John 8:33). Blinded by pride and conceit, the unhappy people lied, not seeing their miserable state, their bondage not only in the spiritual sense, but also in the physical, civic context. At various times, the Jews were enslaved both by the Egyptians and many different Canaanite peoples, and by the Babylonians and the Assyrians. Moreover, at the time when they were so shamelessly proclaiming their freedom, they were fully enslaved by the Romans. An insurrection by the Jews, blinded by conceit and arrogance, against these powerful rulers of the known world, was the cause of the definitive death of the Jewish people as a civil entity.[249]

The holy Evangelist Luke writes that the great John the Forerunner, when exhorting the Israelites to reject conceit and the regrettable arrogance about their descent in the flesh from Abraham, called the multitudes a "brood of vipers" (Luke 3:7). The Evangelist Matthew writes that John called the Sadducees and the Pharisees a "brood of vipers" (Matt 3:7). The Saviour of the world Himself called the scribes and the Pharisees "serpents, brood of vipers" who would be unable to escape the condemnation of hell (Matt 23:33). This means that the epithet "brood of vipers" was not simply a strong expression: it was a definition of the judgment of God, spoken by the Son and Word of God Himself, and spoken through John by the Holy Spirit of God. It was the fallen angel, Satan, who was called a serpent and a viper here. Those infected with conceit, calling themselves sons and kinsmen of Abraham, were called children of the tribe of Satan, deemed to be such by God Himself. "You are of your father the devil," the Lord proclaimed to the Jews, when they, possessed by pride, dared, before the face of the Lord, to call themselves not only children of Abraham but children of God; "you do the deeds of your father, and the desires of your father you want to do" (John 8:41,44). You have attained both the behavior and the disposition of Satan. And your will is in agreement with the will of Satan, and your way of thinking is taken from him in all its fullness. While being sons of Abraham in the flesh, and dreaming that you are sons of God, you have made yourselves sons of the devil in spirit and in disposition, his messengers and his co-heirs.

Why were the Pharisees, whom the Lord had included in the category of serpents, or snakes, that is, rejected spirits, also called a brood of vipers, which is a particular type of snake? A viper is a very small, hardly noticeable snake, blind, but armed with very strong, deadly poison. In the same way, pride is an ailment of the soul that is hardly noticeable, often appears to people to be the deepest humility, and is often taken by people to be holiness and dispassion, although in fact it destroys the soul, making it incapable of any virtue. A viper is blind: pride is also blind. A person darkened by it does not see or know God, is deprived of good vision of himself and of mankind. The very door to virtues—repentance—is closed to him, firmly locked by pride. "Tax collectors and harlots," whose sins were so obvious and grave, turned out to be more capable of accepting repentance and through it of rejoicing in the Heavenly Kingdom, than the Jewish high priests and priests who had been infected with conceit (Matt 21:31).

Why did John the Forerunner call the multitudes "a brood of vipers," especially the Sadducees and the Pharisees? (Luke 3:7). Because most of the Sadducees and Pharisees were infected with the disease of carnal-mindedness and of conceit, and most of them gloried in being descendants of Abraham and having kinship with the prophets; as leaders and teachers of the people, they passed on their ailment to them. The Sadducees[250] were small in number; they consisted of distinguished laymen and the most distinguished and wealthiest of the priesthood (Acts 5:17). They did not believe in the life to come and did not think about it, as usually happens with people who are satiated with an abundance of worldly good things; they did not concern themselves with studying the Faith, because they were drowning in earthly cares and pleasures, like the rich man described in the Gospel (Luke 16:19–31), who is believed to have been one of them. The Pharisees consisted of most of the priesthood (John 1:19,24) and those laypeople who engaged with particular zeal in studying the law of God, such as the holy Apostle Paul. But the Pharisees pursued knowledge of God without self-denial; they did it not for the sake of Heaven, but for the sake of their earthly position, with the goal of receiving earthly advantages; for this reason, from the very study of the law of God, of its letter, that kills the spirit with eternal death, by studying the Law of God for human glory, in order to arrange their material situation within human society, they fell into the abyss and darkness of the carnal mind that is hostile to God.[251] In this way the Pharisees arrived at the same disposition of soul as the Sadducees, one that was incapable of accepting the Messiah, incapable of offering the fruits of repentance. The former, by not concerning themselves with the law of God and being ignorant of it due to their devotion to the world, the latter, having studied the law of God and knowing it to the letter, but with the aim of being loved by the world, became equally carnal people, enemies of God, children of the devil. Possessed by pride in their father, they boasted of rejecting the Messiah: "Have any of the rulers or the Pharisees believed in Him?" they said (John 7:48). After speaking these terrible words about the incarnate God, they followed them up with equally terrible words about their neighbors, words that expressed the content of their hearts, their diabolical pride, their contempt and hatred for mankind that developed from their false study and understanding of theology: "This crowd that does not know the law," they said, "is accursed" (John 7:49). Yes, such a way of thinking, such a disposition of the heart turns people into a brood of vipers, children of the devil and devils. They are incapable of repentance, they are incapable of adoption by God, incapable of inheriting salvation and the blessedness that the all-merciful God grants freely to people who recognize their sinfulness and heal it with true repentance. The fate of unfortunate proud people who are filled with conceit and carnal-mindedness is eternal death, death of the soul. This consists in decisive estrangement from God, and in being filled with hatred toward God and humanity, that same hatred that infected Satan and that he passes on to everyone who comes into communion with him. The fate of these unfortunate people after they are separated from their bodies, and then after they are reunited with their resurrected bodies, is eternal imprisonment in the dungeons of hell, eternal torment in the tortures of hell. "Serpents, brood of vipers!" the Lord said to them, "How can you escape the condemnation of hell?" (Matt 23:33). This means that, for self-aggrandizing people who extol their own ego, it is not possible to avoid condemnation at the dread judgment of God, if they do not concern themselves with curing themselves of conceit by means of repentance and self-denial.

The holy Apostle Paul, although he belonged by descent to the people of Israel, to the tribe of Benjamin, although he was a Jew of Jewish descent, a Pharisee by virtue of having studied the law, although he was chaste according to the contemporary Judaic interpretation of the law (Phil 3:5), rejected all these carnal and temporal advantages for the sake of the superior advantage acquired through Christ, a spiritual, eternal, essential, divine advantage. St Paul rejected advantages in the flesh as obstacles to gaining Christ: and they do present the greatest of obstacles. "What things were gain to me, these I have counted loss for Christ. Yet indeed I also count all things loss for the excellence of the knowledge of Christ Jesus my Lord" (Phil 3:7–8). This is the true fulfillment of the teaching of the great John the Forerunner, or rather of the Holy Spirit, the preaching of repentance. Paul, rejecting carnal-mindedness and conceit, recognizing them as disastrous for the soul, and as the cause of inability truly to know and to serve God, offered the greatest fruit of repentance. From a Pharisee and a persecutor of the Church of God, he became a true servant of God and one of His apostles.

Everyone who paid due attention to the preaching of the great John the Forerunner, to the voice of God that thundered from his lips, submitted to the blessed yoke of repentance. Among the number of his disciples, that is, those who accepted his teaching, were many people from the lower classes (John 1:35), even many people of depraved behavior, who abandoned their sinful way of life (Matt 21:32), and became capable of believing in the Saviour and following Him. But the Sadducees and the Pharisees rejected his preaching of repentance, and afterwards they also rejected the Saviour (Matt 21:32). A very few of them, Nicodemus (John 3:1–21;7:50;19:39), Joseph of Arimathea (Mark 15:43; Luke 23:50–51), Gamaliel (Acts 5:34–39; 22:3), followed to a certain extent the self-denial of the great Paul, and became followers of Christ, at first secretly, and later openly.

To this day, the voice that cries in the wilderness, calling all to repentance, has not fallen silent. John's lips were closed by a martyr's death (Matt 14:3–12), but he does not cease to cry out from the Gospel. In order to hear him, a good will is required. Without a good will, people "seeing they do not see, and hearing they do not hear, nor do they understand" (Matt 13:13), and those who have "heard the word with a noble and good heart, keep it and bear fruit with patience" (Luke 8:15). Let us accept the preaching of repentance with a good will. Having accepted it, let us not lose it to forgetfulness because we are distracted, or lured by passions; let us keep it in our memories, in our hearts, let us "bear fruits worthy of repentance." First of all, let us reject conceit and carnal-mindedness, which try to persuade us to be proud of our distinguished descent from a noble or priest's family, of our distinguished or wealthy relations, of our own nobility or wealth, or of various mental or physical talents, or of our learning or erudition. All these advantages given to a person for a time mean nothing compared to an advantage given for eternity. Our eternal, essential, spiritual advantage consists in the fact that we are Christians. The price at which this advantage was acquired by us is incalculable. "You are not your own," the apostle tells us, "for you were bought at a price" greater than any other price: the most precious blood of Christ. "Therefore glorify God in your body and in your spirit, which are God's" (1 Cor 6:19–20). Just as the same price is paid for each one of us, so the spiritual advantage is the same for each one of us. "There is neither Greek nor Jew, circumcised nor uncircumcised, barbarian, Scythian, slave nor free, but Christ is all and in all" (Col 3:11). "It is a great thing for me," said St Peter Damascene, "to be called a monk and a Christian. As Thou hast said, Lord, to one of Thy servants, 'It is no light thing for you to be called by My name' (Isa 49:6). This is more to me than all the kingdoms of heaven or of earth. Let me always be called by Thy most sweet name."[252] This advantage demands that we have a reverential attitude toward it, so that we may have a reverential attitude toward ourselves, as toward vessels containing an incalculable and priceless treasure, as toward the temples of divinity. We must protect ourselves closely from every evil, as from humiliating filth; we must disdain all advantages of the flesh, as worthless in comparison with our spiritual worth, and incompatible with it. This is how the holy pride of a renewed nature should be, as St Isaiah the Solitary said:[253] may it protect this nature from spiritual degradation. The wonderful, natural attribute of contempt for sin has changed in our fallen nature into contempt for our neighbors, into corrupted conceit, self-love and pride.

Before concluding our talk, let us return again to the preaching of John, let us refresh our memories of its content, so that we may be not only hearers but doers, and "bear fruits worthy of repentance." The holy prophet Isaiah, who foretold the ministry of the Forerunner seven centuries beforehand, outlined the content of his teaching as follows: "The voice of one crying in the wilderness: 'Prepare the way of the Lord; make straight the paths of our God. Every valley shall be filled, and every mountain and hill humbled; the crooked places shall be made straight, and the rough places into plains. The glory of the Lord shall be revealed, and all flesh shall see the salvation of God. Behold your God. Behold, the Lord is coming with strength, and His arm is with authority'" (Isa 40:3–5,9–10). We have already seen that the way of the Lord and His paths within human souls are what Holy Scripture calls the corresponding ways of thinking and feelings in a person's heart. In order to acquire these, we must fill all the valleys, that is, we must make embankments in all the low-lying, impassable places so that the Lord can walk easily there: we must abandon drunkenness, gluttony, fornication, pleasures of the flesh, so-called innocent games and amusements—in short, everything that constitutes carnal and sinful life, and relegates a person to the dignity of unreasoning cattle and beasts—and we must replace these sins with the corresponding virtues: abstinence, temperance, and soberness. A sinful and carnal life obstructs the Lord's way into the human heart. Furthermore, we must humble, that is, level out, every mountain and hill, that is, smooth out from our souls conceit and pride in all their forms, both the apparently significant and the most trifling. Finally, we must reject all false and self-willed understanding of the Faith, those crooked and rough paths, fully submitting ourselves to the teaching of God, preserved intact by the one Eastern Orthodox Church. Then all bends will be straightened, all unevenness will be smoothed out: the way of the Lord will be made completely free for every person to receive salvation, which will enter the soul together with the Lord. Amen.

52. On the Mother of God

Exposition of the Teaching of the Orthodox Church

The Mother of God, the Ever-Virgin Mary, is the highest of all created reason-endowed beings, incomparably higher than the highest angels, the cherubim and the seraphim, incomparably higher than all holy people.[254] She is the Lady and Queen of all creation, on earth and in heaven. She is Ever-Virgin, that is, she was a Virgin before giving birth to the God-Man, while giving birth to Him, and after giving birth to Him. The name Mary was given to her at the command of God, and it means "Lady."[255]

To comprehend the merit of the Mother of God, to the extent in which it is confessed by the Orthodox Church, we must have as our guide an exact and thorough understanding of an unfathomable action of the almighty God: the incarnation of God the Word.

The pre-eternal Son—the Son of God—through His creative power made flesh for Himself in the womb of the Virgin: He was conceived and was born as the God-Man. The son according to the Divine nature also became a son according to human nature. Jesus Christ was born of the Virgin, one Person in two complete and undivided natures, divine and human. The divine nature, although infinite, did not erase the human nature, and the human nature, although finite, did not in the least constrain the infinite character of the divine nature. This marvelous union, accepted with faith and born through it of spiritual understanding, but unattainable to the reason of the flesh and of the soul,[256] took place through divine omnipotence.

The Lord incarnate had everything that belongs to a person: spirit, soul, and body. The word spirit signifies the reasoning part of a person: his mind, his thoughts, the rational feelings of his heart, alien to animals, but common to both humans and angels. Essentially, the soul expresses itself in life force; desire or will is intrinsic to the soul, as is energy, or natural anger that does not turn into rage. We also see these characteristics in animals. The human spirit of Christ engaged in prayer and in explanation of the words of God in human words; the soul of Christ expressed joy, sorrow, anger, and torment; the body of Christ was conceived, was born, was fed, grew, worked, felt hunger and thirst, slept, suffered, was crucified and buried, and rose from the dead. Due to the inseparable union of the two natures in all situations, whenever it appeared that the human nature was in some way acting alone, the divine nature was working together with it, undivided and inseparable, although also unmingled, acting in accordance with God's will. In this way, although He was conceived as a human in the womb of the Virgin, at His very conception He was also already God; although He was born human of the Virgin, at the same time He was also born God; He grew up, ate food, became weary on the road, was bound and arrested in the Garden of Gethsemane, was struck on the cheek, was struck on the head with a reed, was crowned with thorns, and was crucified as a man, but at the same time also as God. In the same way, the Apostles were witnesses, disciples, and messengers of God;[257] Judas Iscariot betrayed God;[258] the Jewish high priest and Pilate committed deicide;[259] the Ever-Virgin Mary is the Mother of God. Due to the indivisibility of natures in a single Person, what happened in relation to one nature necessarily also applied to the other.

At the conception of the God-Man, one half of Him was taken from humanity, from the Virgin; the male sperm that usually fertilizes a woman's womb was superfluous. The reason for this is clear. The human race was given the capacity to reproduce immediately after creation (Gen 1:28). This capacity, together with all other capacities, was defiled by sin at its very root, in the forefathers; consequently, the very act of reproduction passes on to people the poison of sin, as the prophet David, inspired by the Holy Spirit, confessed on behalf of the whole of humanity: "I was conceived in wickedness" (Ps 50:7). A manner of conception that passes on sinfulness together with life could not be used to conceive the God-Man, Who was foreordained to be a redemptive Sacrifice for humanity. The Sacrifice in return for human sinfulness had to be free of sin, completely pure. Not only that: the value of this Sacrifice had to be immeasurable, so that it could redeem humanity, that was guilty before the eternal God, and therefore irredeemable at any limited price, however great. Human nature made the God-Man capable of being a Sacrifice, but divine nature gave this Sacrifice an immeasurable price.

In order to assume humanity, God the Word replaced the action of male sperm with the creative force of God. "The Son of God," says St John Damascene, "formed Himself from the purest virgin blood as the firstfruits of our nature, a fruit animated by a logical and rational soul, but formed not from seed but through creation."[260] The Virgin was prepared for worthy conception.

The Virgin, whose conception the angel announced to her parents, who were praying and bewailing their infertility, who was made as the fruit of tearful prayers and fasting, who was the daughter of righteous people, who was dedicated by them to God from birth, and who dedicated herself by the disposition of her spirit wholly to serving God—the Virgin was in herself already a most pure vessel. The purity of the Virgin was so unaffected by sensual feelings that her mind, constantly directed toward and fixed on God, did not even descend to thoughts of marriage. She bore witness of this to the archangel who brought her the good news of her conception and prospective birth of a Son (Luke 1:34). A pure vessel, prepared by God through holy people and holy angels, a pure vessel prepared by her own disposition, was purified yet more through the Holy Spirit to receive the most holy, immaterial seed, the Word. When the Virgin asked the Archangel how she was to conceive and give birth despite being without a man, he explained it to her in this way: "The Holy Spirit will come upon you, and the power of the Highest will overshadow you" (Luke 1:35). The power means the Word. The Word of God is at the same time both the Power of God and the Wisdom of God (1 Cor 1:24): "All things were made through Him"—the Word—"and without Him nothing was made that was made" (John 1:3). The Holy Spirit came down upon the pure Virgin, and purified her yet more. Pure from the condition of her own body and spirit, she became most pure from the all-powerful creative action produced within her of the Spirit of God that gives life to, purifies, renews, changes, and transforms Its vessels. The pure Virgin became the most-pure Virgin, devoid of any impurity in thought or feeling; she became pure through grace, a bearer of the Spirit, divine. It was into such a vessel, renewed and adorned by God, acquiring from the action of the Holy Spirit within it the capacity and virtue to receive God the Word, that God the Word descended, became both seed and fruit, and was made man.[261] "The Holy Spirit," says St John Damascene, "came down upon her, purified her, and granted her the capacity to receive within her the divinity of the Word, and to give birth to it. Then the Son of God, like a divine seed, overshadowed her."[262]

The all-pure Virgin offered her most pure blood as a gift from the whole human race to the Seed and Word, to conceive the God-Man.

By conceiving and giving birth to God and man in a one person, the Virgin became truly the Mother of God, because God was born by her, although

He was at the same time man. "How," exclaims St John Damascene, "can she who gave birth to God made flesh not be the Birthgiver of God?"[263] The Virgin, becoming the Mother of God, already naturally became the Mistress, Queen, and Lady of all reason-endowed creation, on earth and in heaven, while at the same time remaining a creature and servant of her Son and God. In giving birth to the One who sacrificed Himself for all of humanity, she also gave birth to Him for herself, since she also belonged to humanity. Her Son is God, Creator, Lord, Redeemer, and Saviour.[264]

When God pronounced the judgment in paradise on the fallen first two people, He also made a promise that the Seed of woman would bruise the head of the serpent (Gen 3:15). The promise makes no mention of the seed of man; the destruction of the rule of sin over humanity is ascribed exclusively to the Seed of the woman. As the time of the Redeemer's appearance on earth came nearer, the prophecy about the manner of His appearance was spoken more clearly. The prophet Isaiah prophesied the incarnation seven centuries before it occurred: "The Lord Himself will give you a sign, behold, the virgin shall conceive and bear a Son, and you shall call His name Immanuel" (Isa 7:14). This was indeed a wondrous sign, a sign from God that could not even have entered a person's thoughts! It was a preternatural sign devised and given by the Lord and Creator of human nature Himself, who changed the laws of nature by making the Virgin a Mother, and Himself, the Lord and Creator of all visible and invisible creation, the Fruit of her womb. Carried away by pride, Adam dreamed in paradise of becoming God. He attempted to steal divinity away from God by force, to change the infinite into the finite by means of the treachery and effort of a weak created being. In the attempt to bring to fruition an insolent, senseless intention, the created being was lost. He had not comprehended the infinite goodness of God, capable of granting His creature not only the advantage of the angelic and human natures, but also His divinity, to the extent that it is capable of receiving such a gift. The scheme and the act of the first-created people were vain, as well as deadly: God Himself was to grant His divinity to humans who desire it, by becoming incarnate of the Virgin, taking on the appearance of a servant (Phil 2:7) and a created being, partaking in the nature of reason-endowed creatures, so as to make them capable of partaking in the divine nature.[265] Accept the gift that is given without envy! Accept the gift that is given with inexpressible goodness; accept what cannot be stolen either by cunning or by destructive force. Accept the great honor with the same pride with which you wanted by your own efforts and ruthless cunning to steal and take for your own the sacred and unapproachable divine nature. Do not refuse God Himself, who deigned to take flesh and be born of the Virgin, for the sake of the dignity of animals and devils from the dignity of gods that brought you to earth to the vale of the tears of your exile.

The God-Man possessed human nature that was wholly pure, but limited. It was subject not only to the limitations with which man was created, but also to those that appeared to a much greater extent in the nature of man after his fall.[266] The God-Man did not possess any sin, was in no way implicated in it, even in its mildest forms: His natural attributes were not changed, as is the case with us, into passions;[267] these attributes were in their natural state within Him, in constant subordination to the spirit, directed by the spirit, and the spirit was constantly directed by the divine nature united with the human nature. The God-Man possessed the capacity to grieve and to sorrow; but sorrow never possessed Him, as happens with us, but was constantly directed by the spirit. The Lord grieved at the death of Lazarus, and shed tears at his grave (John 11:33,35,38). The Lord wept for Jerusalem foretelling its destruction for rejecting the Messiah (Luke 19:41). In the garden of Gethsemane, the Lord permitted within Himself such torment in anticipation of His death that the state of His soul is referred to in the Gospel as "agony" and sorrow "even to death." It was accompanied by a bodily strain so full of suffering that the body exuded sweat that fell to the ground like drops of blood (Matt 26:38–39); (Luke 22:43–44). But even in this intense struggle, the great sorrow submitted to the spirit which expressing at the same time both the extent of the sorrow and its power over it, said: "O My Father, if it is possible, let this cup pass from Me; nevertheless, not as I will, but as You will" (Matt 26:39). The God-Man possessed attribute of anger; but the anger functioned within Him as a holy power of the soul, as character, as energy, always preserving the human dignity, never showing any passion. The Lord expressed His indignation to those who did not allow the children to come near to Him (Mark 10:14); He was moved by anger toward the embittered and blind Pharisees, who dared to criticize an obvious miracle of God (Mark 3:5). Remarkable, striking restraint in anger, while making use of its power, can be observed in those terrible denunciations the Lord pronounced over the Jews (Matt 23:1–33; John 5:19–47; 7:14–24; 8:12–59; 12:37–50). A great spiritual sight is presented by the human attributes of Christ at the time of His sufferings for humanity: the Lord, throughout these sufferings, remained always true to Himself; not for one moment did He display the excitement, the enthusiasm that usually inspire earthly heroes; not for one moment did the verbosity or the oratory of such heroes appear in Him; not for one moment did any changeability appear in Him; the same unwavering strength acted constantly within Him, without weakening and without tension; this strength constantly expressed both its might and its submission to the holy power that directed it. If someone carefully studies the character of Jesus Christ in the Gospel, he will confess Jesus to be God from this character alone, just as the Apostle Peter confesses Him to be God from His word of life alone (John 6:68). There was never another such character among people, always entirely free and open, always the same, never carried away, never changing either in response to reproach or in response to praise, or even in the face of murderers and death. The God-Man was entirely free of one of the attributes of our fallen nature: He was quite free, not in body, but in the feelings of His soul and body, of that attribute that was never felt before the fall, but was felt immediately after it and then developed and became natural to fallen nature. Adam, created free from passion from the dust, and Eve, made free from passion from Adam's rib, were free from passion, in keeping with the passionless way in which they came into being. They were passionless and innocent to such an extent that despite their very close association and constant contact with one another, they did not need clothing, not even noticing their nakedness, despite the fact that they constantly saw it (Gen 2:25). The God-Man was conceived through the action of the Holy Spirit. The Word made Himself flesh in the womb of the most pure Virgin. God made His flesh divine in its very conception, capable only of spiritual[268] and divine sensations. Although the attributes of the flesh of the God-Man were human, they were all at the same time deified, as they belonged to a single Person who is both God and man. For the same reason, the human characteristics of the God-Man were at the same time both natural and beyond nature in relation to human nature. The holiness of the flesh of God the Lord was infinitely greater than the holiness in which the flesh of the created being Adam was created. It is obvious that the disease imparted by the fall of man to all people through the humiliating conception in the manner of beasts and cattle, a conception in sin, could have no place here, because the very means of conception had no place, that is, the means by which the disease of sin is transmitted had no place. Conversely, just as the conception was divine, so all its consequences were divine.

The God-Man, as the redemptive Sacrifice, took upon Himself all human weaknesses—the consequences of the fall—except for sin, so that, in redeeming mankind, He might save it from the burden of these weaknesses, and show it in a renewed state. The God-Man perceived and bore our weaknesses voluntarily, and He was not subordinated to them through the necessity of nature: while He was perfect man, He was also perfect God, the Creator of human nature and the absolute Master of this nature. For this reason He showed His humanity in a way that was pleasing to Him. Sometimes He presented His humanity with the weaknesses of fallen nature: He became exhausted, He thirsted, He rested in sleep, He was seized and bound in the garden of Gethsemane, He endured beating and mocking, was crucified and buried. Sometimes He presented His humanity within the laws of nature with which it was originally created: He walked on water; He rode into Jerusalem on an unridden colt on which no other person had sat. This power was originally the inheritance of Adam.[269] Sometimes the Lord showed His human nature in the state of glory and majesty that He gave to it by combining within Himself, in one Person, divinity and humanity, and which human nature did not have even immediately after its creation, in the state of innocence and immortality. He showed this majesty and glory through wondrous signs. Most of all He showed it to certain of His disciples at His transfiguration, to the degree that they were able to see it,[270] and not to its full extent. The divinity of the God-Man is united without mingling, but fully, with His humanity: the divinity of the God-Man is united with His human spirit, with His soul, with His body. When the soul of Christ was separated from the body of Christ through death, the divinity of Christ remained unseparated both from His soul and from His body. The holy Church proclaims: "In the tomb with the body and in hell with the soul as God, in paradise with the thief and on the throne with the Father and the Spirit, wast Thou O boundless Christ, the Indescribable One, filling all things."[271]

The body of the God-Man possessed exceptional proportions and beauty, as His forefather the holy prophet David sang prophetically of Him: "Thou art fairer than the sons of men" (Ps 44:3). But the bodily beauty of the Lord did not produce the effects on the female sex usually produced in it by male beauty. May that filthy and blasphemous thought, sometimes accepted and expressed by heretics, be rejected and cursed.[272] On the contrary, the body of Christ healed all passions, whether of the soul or of the body. It imparted to others the quality with which it was imbued. It gave abundant divine grace to everyone who looked at it, to everyone who touched it, man or woman. "Power went out from Him," the Gospel bears witness, "and healed them all" (Luke 6:19). "As many as touched Him were made well" (Mark 6:56). This is that divine body of which the Lord Himself bore witness: "Whoever eats My flesh and drinks My blood has eternal life, and I will raise him up at the last day. He who eats My flesh and drinks My blood abides in Me, and I in him" (John 6:54,56). Let every devout Orthodox Christian imagine the inconceivable greatness of the Mother of God, who carried such a body, first within her womb, and then in her arms, and was for a long time in a very close relationship with Him. It is not wrong to recognize and call divine the greatness of the Mother of God, on the basis of the divinity of the body of Christ.

The body of Christ was buried in a small man-made cave hewn from the rock, that is, from a hillside made of solid rock. The cave was so narrow that it is called a tomb in the Gospel. The entrance to it was so low that it was necessary to crawl into the cave, bent double. After the body of Christ had been taken into the tomb, a rock of considerable size was rolled up against the entrance (Matt 27:60). The Jewish high priests, afraid that the Lord might rise again, as He had foretold, and assuming that the body of Christ was subject to the same laws of nature that usually govern human bodies, sealed the stone that blocked the entrance onto the outside of the cave; in addition to this they placed a guard at the entrance. In this way, according to human understanding, all obstacles had been arranged so as to prevent resurrection. All measures had been taken so that, in the event of resurrection, the Risen One would immediately be destroyed, in a violent death. But the divine body rose from the dead, unaffected by both natural obstacles and human precautions. It penetrated through the thick, solid, and hard material of the cave: the stone remained in place, the seal unbroken; the cave had no fissure that would allow the risen body to pass through; the guards who had been set to watch and to apply force were not made worthy either of sensing the resurrection or of seeing the risen Lord. It was after the resurrection of Christ that the angel came down, broke the seal, rolled away the stone and proclaimed the resurrection that had been accomplished; the guards, merely from seeing the angel, fell to the ground like dead men (Matt 28:2,4). After the resurrection, the divine body passed through a locked door to the assembled apostles (John 20:19). The divine body was not recognized by the two disciples walking on the road to Emmaus; when they recognized Him at the breaking of the bread, His body suddenly became invisible (Luke 24:31). This same body later left the earth in the sight of all the apostles, began to rise and travel through the air as if on wings, disappeared from the apostles' view at an unattainable height, and entered heaven (Acts 1:9). The Protomartyr Stephen saw Himt in heaven, being led to this sight by the action of the Holy Spirit, and exclaimed: "Look! I see the heavens opened and the Son of Man standing at the right hand of God!" (Acts 7:56). With such preternatural qualities the God-Man showed and still shows His human body after the resurrection. These qualities are the incorruptible, spiritual crown with which the body of the God-Man was worthily crowned by Him, because He defeated and trampled upon death through death.[273]

It should not be thought that the body of Christ received such characteristics only after death.[274] No! As the body of the all-perfect God, it always possessed them, and after the resurrection it simply manifested them all the time. The following events demonstrate this. One day in the temple at Jerusalem, the Lord Jesus Christ made an allusion to His pre-eternal existence according to His divinity; the Jews picked up stones to throw at the God-Man who was speaking to them so openly about Himself. But the Lord suddenly made Himself invisible among them, and left the temple, passing through the crowd of His enemies (John 8:59).[275] On another occasion, the angry inhabitants of the town of Nazareth seized the Lord, who had been teaching in their synagogue, and led Him to the top of the hill on which the town was built, so as to throw Him over the cliff and kill Him; but the Lord made Himself invisible and, coming out from among them, He went on His way (Luke 4:29–30). The Lord acted in exactly the same way at His birth: He came out of the Virgin's womb without breaking the seal of virginity, without opening the doors of this wondrous temple of His, as the prophet Ezekiel prophesied, joyfully describing his visions: "This gate shall be shut; it shall not be opened, and no man shall enter by it, because the Lord God of Israel has entered by it; therefore it shall be shut" (Ezek 44:2). In its hymns the holy Church addresses the Lord in this way: "The Creator hath shown us a marvelous Creature, Who was incarnate of a Virgin without seed, rose from the tomb without breaking the seal, and entered bodily the apostles' room when the doors were shut."[276] "Thou didst arise, O Christ, and yet the tomb remained sealed, as at Thy birth the Virgin's womb remained unharmed; and Thou hast opened for us the gates of paradise."[277] And we hymn the Mother of God in this way: "Beyond all reason are your glorious mysteries, O Mother of God, sealed in purity and preserved in virginity, you were truly recognized as Mother, having given birth to the true God."[278] "Before the birth you are a Virgin, and at the birth you are a Virgin, and after the birth you remain a Virgin."[279] "To those who dare to say that the most pure Virgin Mary was not a virgin before giving birth, while giving birth, and after giving birth: anathema."[280]

The divine body of the God-Man was conceived in a divine manner and was born in a divine manner. The Virgin gave birth while filled with a most holy spiritual joy.[281] There was no pain involved in this childbirth, just as there was no pain involved in Eve being taken from Adam's rib. There could be no place there for pain, which is one of the punishments for the sin of the forefathers, as there was no place for this sin here, because the conception had taken place not only without male seed, not only without any sensation of carnal pleasure, but unlike ordinary conception, through the action of the Holy Spirit on the Virgin, through the placing of the most holy God the Word in her womb. The fact that the Virgin gave birth to the God-Man without pain is very clear from the simple and modest account we read in the Gospel: "She brought forth her firstborn Son," the Gospel says of the Mother of God, "and wrapped Him in swaddling cloths, and laid Him in a manger" (Luke 2:7). The Virgin gives birth, and immediately begins to serve. She wraps up the newborn Son and lays Him in a manger without needing any help, because she feels none of the pain or weakness intrinsic to women giving birth in sin to children conceived in wickedness (Ps 50:7), who give birth to them already dead from eternal death and unto eternal death. The Mother of God gave birth to Life and the Giver of life (John 14:6).

By conceiving and giving birth to the God-Man, the Mother of God was placed above all holy people and all the holy angels. According to the explanation of St Gregory of Sinai, the Mother of God was the only vessel into which God moved in His very essence. Even if other holy people become partakers of divine nature (2 Pet 1:4) and a habitation of God in three persons (John 14:23) through the action within them of the Holy Spirit, this happens in a completely different way than it does to the Mother of God[282] who alone received within her God the Word for at His incarnation. Receiving God in this way was, of course, a unique, unparalleled, and unprecedented event, unattainable either by holy people or by holy angels, and belonging only to the Mother of God. Just as the God-Man replaced Adam for the new generation of the chosen people who were to be saved, and became their Progenitor, so the Mother of God replaced Eve for these people, and became their mother. Just as the God-Man is the Heavenly King, the King of all people and angels, so the Mother of God is the Queen of heaven and of people and angels.

The Mother of God was born of holy and righteous parents, Joachim and Anna, the only fruit of their marriage, the answer to many prayers and tears; she was born after her parents had suffered many years of infertility, after an angel had foretold her birth to her parents, when they were already advanced in years. The circumstances of the birth of the Mother of God are very similar to those of the birth of St John the Forerunner, described in the first chapter of the Gospel of St Luke. The holy Orthodox Church sings of the birth of John with these words: "Let us now praise the Forerunner of the Lord, to whom Elizabeth gave birth for the priest from a womb that was barren but not without seed. For Christ alone passed into the dwelling that was impassable without seed. John was born of a barren woman who did not bear him without her husband, while Jesus was born of a pure Virgin by the overshadowing of the Father and the divine Spirit. But the prophet born of a barren woman revealed himself to be herald and forerunner for the One born without seed."[283] The holy Church views and confesses the Mother of God in a similar way. The barren, elderly Anna, bore a daughter to Joachim, and a Mother to God, but she did not bear her without seed: she took the seed in her womb from her husband, the righteous elder Joachim. Born of a holy couple, the Virgin became God's chosen one, a vessel sanctified by God, in which God the Word made His habitation, in which this Word and Creator of everything visible and invisible became incarnate, through the good will of the Father and with the cooperation of the Spirit, and served as the seed through His creative power. The God-Man born of Mary made the Virgin a Mother, and kept His Mother a Virgin. The God and Creator of the Virgin became Her Son, while remaining her God and Creator; by becoming her Son, He became her Redeemer and Saviour. The first Adam produced a woman without participation from her; the Ever-Virgin conceived and gave birth to the New Adam without the participation of a man. Despite all her greatness, the Mother of God was conceived and was born in accordance with the ordinary rule of humanity; consequently the general confession of the human race that it was conceived in wickedness and born in sins (Ps 50:7) also applies to the Mother of God. The humble and grace-filled Mary herself made this confession before the whole world, when she felt within her womb the presence of the longed-for Saviour, and spoke with spiritual, grace-filled joy the following marvelous and remarkable words: "My soul magnifies the Lord, and my spirit has rejoiced in God my Saviour. For He has regarded the lowly state of His maidservant; for behold, henceforth all generations will call me blessed" (Luke 1:46–48). The Mother of God confesses before all of humanity, from the Gospel read by all people, that the God to Whom she has given birth is at the same time also her Saviour. If God is her Saviour, then she was conceived and born in sin in accordance with the general law of fallen humanity. God is the Creator both of angels and of humans, but He is the Saviour only of humans. Regarding angels, who were not subject to the fall, He is their Lord, but not their Redeemer and Saviour. When God's reason-endowed creatures confess Him to be Saviour, they also at the same time confess their own perdition. The Virgin Mary was conceived and born in perdition, in fallenness, in the bonds of eternal death and sin; she was born in the state that is common to the whole human race. By giving birth to God, her own Saviour and the Saviour of all people, she became far greater than the sinless angels, who had not tasted the death of the soul and had no need of a Saviour.

The holy parents of the Mother of God, who were advanced in years and had subdued their flesh through many prolonged struggles, were consequently not subject in their conjugal intercourse to the strong passionate sensations that are inevitable for people in the prime of their lives, and whose disposition of soul is far removed from that of the devout Joachim and Anna. However, their intercourse was accomplished in the usual manner of human union, the manner that appeared after and as a consequence of the fall. In accordance with her conception and birth, the Mother of God took on the original sin and the sinful poison with which the whole human race was infected from the forefathers. Born of righteous parents, the Mother of God herself also led a most righteous life. Purity and humility were her main virtues. She was constantly engaged in contemplation of God, prayer, reading and study of holy Scripture. She was a stranger not only to mortal sins, but also to any deed or word that clearly opposed the law of God with which she was brought up and which she studied continually. However, despite the righteousness and purity of the life led by the Mother of God, in order to receive together with The Apostles the Holy Spirit that gave her Christian perfection, sin and eternal death showed their presence and dominion in her. We see evidence of this in the Gospel. Thus, until it was enlightened by the Holy Spirit, her mind, like the minds of the Apostles, remained in darkness, and she did not understand the words that the twelve-year-old Saviour spoke to her in the temple (Luke 2:49–50). St John Chrysostom, interpreting verses 46 to 50 of chapter 12 of the Gospel of St Matthew and verses 1 to 11 of chapter 2 of the Gospel of St John, shows quite clearly how the "old man" (Eph 4:22) was revealed and acted within the Mother of God.[284] The eternal death and sin sown in human nature could not but become apparent. This is the exact and true teaching of the Orthodox Church on the Mother of God in relation to original sin and eternal death, which have infected and seized the whole human race.

The Holy Spirit visited the Ever-Virgin twice. The first time was after the annunciation by the archangel Gabriel, when the Holy Spirit purified her, making her, already pure according to human understanding, pure through grace, and able to receive God the Word within her and to become His Mother. Her virginity was sealed by the Spirit. While she had until now kept herself foreign to any sensual intention or sensation, she now became inaccessible for these intentions and sensations. This befitted the Virgin destined to serve God incomparably more closely than the cherubim and the seraphim. She was not only to conceive and give birth to the God-Man, but to spend the rest of His life on earth in a very close relationship with Him. She breastfed Him; He spent His infancy and childhood in her arms, and He spent His youth with her until manhood, until He was thirty years old, when He revealed Himself as the promised Redeemer of the world. And for the three and a half years when the Lord was proclaiming salvation to mankind, the Mother of God was very often with Him, as is noticeable in the Gospel. The first time the Holy Spirit came down upon the Most-holy Virgin, He made her capable and worthy of such elevated service. The second time, the Holy Spirit came down upon the Virgin on the day of Pentecost, when He came down upon the holy Apostles (Acts 2:1–13), from whom she had been inseparable since the ascension of the Lord into heaven (Acts 1:14). On that occasion the Holy Spirit destroyed within her the dominion of eternal death and of original sin, raised her up to the level of Christian perfection, and made her a new person in the image of the Lord Jesus Christ. Having trampled on death through death, and having raised the human race in Himself and with Himself, the Lord first granted resurrection of the soul[285] to His all-pure Mother and to His Apostles on the day of Pentecost. St John the Theologian calls this resurrection of the soul the first resurrection (from the first death, that of sin, over which the second death, that is, eternal perdition, no longer has any power [Rev 20:6]). Perhaps it may seem incomprehensible to some people why eternal death was not destroyed within the Virgin the first time the Holy Spirit came upon her. We reply that this destruction of eternal death was the fruit of the redemption. It could not take place until redemption had been accomplished; thus, before being renewed by the Holy Spirit, the Apostles had received various grace-filled gifts such as healing diseases, driving out demons, and raising the dead; but the destruction of eternal death, the transition of the old man to the new from the state of the soul to that of the spirit was accomplished for them on the day of Pentecost and was a consequence of the redemption (John 7:39).

From all of the above, it is obvious how absurd the two opposing doctrines of the West regarding the Mother of God are. Of these, the doctrine of the Papists ascribes to the Mother of God conception free from original sin similar to the conception of the Saviour, and that of the Protestants does not recognize the Virgin as ever-virgin. The truth is foreign to all exaggerations and minimizations. It ascribes the appropriate measure and place to everything.

It should not be thought that the dogma that the Mother of God was free of original sin from conception (the "immaculate conception"/ "*immaculata conceptio*") is a contemporary innovation among the Latinists. It has simply been accepted officially and proclaimed by the Pope in our times.[286] Bergier, writing in the eighteenth century, says: "According to the common belief of the Catholics,[287] Mary was not implicated in any sin. At the entry for *conception immaculée* (immaculate conception), we explained that, although the Church has not formally determined that Mary was free from original sin, this is a belief based on Holy Scripture and on unbroken (ecclesiastical) Tradition."[288] At the entry for *conception immaculée*, Bergier pronounces the same doctrine even more firmly. He says: "According to the common opinion of Catholic theologians, the holy Virgin Mary, the Mother of God, was preserved from original sin *when she was conceived in the womb of her mother*. This belief is based on the opinions of holy Fathers who are most worthy of respect." But which fathers does the Latin writer cite? Only Latin ones belonging to the West after it had already fallen away from the East. He invokes the Council of Trent, which determined at its fifth session that all the descendants of Adam are born defiled by original sin, but that this does not extend to the holy Virgin; he invokes the Council of Basel in 1439 and the Council of Avignon in 1457, which recognized this teaching as unerring and belonging to the Church. The decree of the Council of Basel was accepted by the University of Paris, as a result of which its theological faculty ordained in 1497 that no-one could be awarded a doctoral degree if he did not first bind himself with an oath to confess the received dogma regarding the Mother of God. These facts, which have no merit for members of the Orthodox Church, show only that the heretical teaching about the Mother of God crept into the Western Church, following many other heretical teachings, more than four centuries before our time. In his articles supporting the new dogma, Bergier cites two writers who belong to the preeminent, universal Church: Origen and the blessed Augustine, who, however, made no mention of this dogma. Origen says in his Sixth Homily on the Evangelist Luke that the expression "full of grace" in Scripture is used only once, and that was solely in connection with Mary. This is recognized by the whole Church, but it does not relate in any way to the new papist dogma! As we have set forth and explained above, the grace of God received by the Ever-Virgin Mary exceeds incomparably both in quality and in abundance the grace conferred on any other holy person, as well as that possessed by the holy angels. In his book *De Natura et Gratia*, St Augustine says: "We know that she (the Mother of God) received abundant grace to vanquish sin in all its forms."[289] And these words do not in any way support the dogma of the papists. On the contrary, they contradict it: only a person who has sin living and acting within him needs and is able to receive abundant grace-filled power to vanquish sin. The holy Orthodox Church, as set forth above, has always confessed that the Holy Spirit came down upon the pure Virgin, on the unwedded bride—as the Church calls the Mother of God—and made the pure one all-pure, that is, made the one who was pure in nature pure beyond nature, full of pure grace, full of grace, receiving the grace of the Holy Spirit for sustenance and in joy. Partaking abundantly of the grace of God made the Virgin alien to carnal pleasure, and instilled in her a complete, resolute aversion to it. This was how it befitted the spiritual temple of God to be, the spiritual heaven, the throne of God, His holy of holies. One false idea is usually followed by a series of other false ideas. The papists, having recognized the Mother of God as free of original sin, deemed her to be free of all sin, completely sinless,[290] and consequently having no need either of redemption or of the Redeemer. She herself, however, the Ever-Virgin Mother of God, full of grace, closes the lips of the blind heretics and fanatics by confessing the God she has borne to be her Saviour. By ascribing sinlessness to the Mother of God, the papists show their lack of faith in the omnipotence of God. But the Orthodox Church glorifies the omnipotence and greatness of God Who made a woman conceived and born in sins incomparably greater than the cherubim and more glorious than the seraphim, who never knew sin and remained constantly in a state of holiness.

"My soul magnifies the Lord, and my spirit has rejoiced in God my Savior" (Luke 1:46–47), the grace-filled Virgin said in response to Elizabeth, when the latter, inspired by the Holy Spirit, exclaimed in a loud voice that the Ever-Virgin was the Mother of God (Luke 1:43). With these words, the most holy Mary not only closes the mouths of the papists who teach that God was not a Saviour for her, she also closes the mouths of the Protestants, who ascribe to her spirit joy not in God, but in carnal pleasure. In contrast to the dogma of the papists, the Protestants, sworn enemies of the virginity described in the New Testament, maintain that the Most-holy vessel and temple of God, the Mother of God, after giving birth to the God-Man, violated her virginity, became a vessel of human desire, and entered into matrimonial relations with Joseph and had other children. This is a terrible thought! A thought that is both bestial and demonic! A blasphemous thought! This thought could only have emerged from the depths of depravity. It could and can only be expressed by a desperate and ostracized adulterer. It can only be accepted and adopted by those who have fallen so far from the image and the likeness of God toward the likeness of beasts that they possess and can possess an understanding of human nature that is solely in its degraded, bestial state. To justify this monstrous thought, the ignorant and unhappy blasphemers refer to the Gospel.

Luther, who cast aside his monastic habit and took as his mistress[291] a nun who had also thrown off the habit—the union of Luther with Katherine of Bora cannot be understood otherwise than that the vows of chastity they made to God were obviously reversed—speaks out against Christian virginity. All Protestants together with Luther speak against it. They call virginity unnatural, against the will, blessing and command of God, Who after the creation of the first two humans immediately said to them: "Be fruitful and multiply; fill the earth" (Gen 1:28). It is possible to reply to the Protestants with the words said by the Saviour to the Sadducees: "You are mistaken, not knowing the Scriptures nor the power of God" (Matt 22:29). When the Protestants referred to the above words from Genesis, they did not notice that they were followed by a description of the virginity of the first two people, a state in which they remained until the fall, not even noticing their own nakedness, and that they noticed their nakedness and felt shame, a sign of the lust that appeared after the fall, and that the present relations of a woman toward a man, and her pain in childbirth, were pronounced as punishment for disobeying God's commandment (Genesis chapters 1–3). The Orthodox Church recognizes virginity as natural to humans, deeming the nature in which it was originally created to be essential human nature. The state of fallenness in which all humanity now finds itself is an unnatural, subnatural, and anti-natural state. But since all of humanity has been seized with the sickness of the fall, one might call this state of general sickness natural to fallen humanity. In this way, the characteristics of an ailment are natural to the state of a person suffering it, but they are unnatural to the state of health. In this case, we agree that virginity is now unnatural to humanity. For this reason, there are very, very few virgins among the righteous people of the Old Testament: the patriarchs and most of the prophets had to submit to the yoke of matrimony. But when our Lord Jesus Christ restored fallen human nature, he also restored virginity. He Himself was, in humanity, a most-holy virgin; His mother was a grace-filled, All-holy Virgin. Virginity, natural to human nature in its original state, unnatural to fallen nature, was returned, like a gift, to the human nature renewed by the Saviour. "The gift of God ... in Christ Jesus our Lord" is everything that constitutes our eternal salvation, our dignity, our perfection, all of which is signified by the general term "eternal life" (Rom 6:23). And the virginity of the New Testament is a gift of God, given by the Lord, as the Lord Himself said of it: "All cannot accept this saying, but only those to whom it has been given" (Matt 19:11). It is a gift of righteousness (that is, of a moral state that is more similar to that of our Lord Jesus Christ) given to those who wish for it with all their hearts and beg the Lord for it with the most heartfelt prayers.[292] Because virginity is unnatural to fallen humanity, it cannot be obtained by our own efforts alone: our own efforts tame the flesh, but true virginity is a gift of God, the result of constant, heartfelt prayer, often of long duration. True virginity does not consist solely in bodily purity, but more in alienating the mind from sensual thoughts and daydreams. The mind is incapable of renouncing sin unless it is overshadowed by divine power.[293] The battle of the mind against sin constitutes that greatest of labors during which a struggler sheds many bitter tears, and lets out many deep, heavy sighs, begging for help and assistance from on high. When the heart tastes spiritual sweetness, only then can it tear itself away from the delight of carnal pleasure; it cannot exist without pleasure. "Love is reflected by love, and the fire is quenched by the immaterial fire," says St John of the Ladder.[294] Numerous is the assembly of virgins in the Church of the New Testament, through the mercy and munificence of our Saviour; but they entered the state of virginity after proving their sincere desire for it through constant, arduous struggle with the desires of the flesh. This can be seen from the biographies of St Anthony the Great, St Pachomius the Great, St Symeon the Fool for Christ's sake, and many other great saints of God. But the Mother of God did not experience or know the struggle with carnal desires. Before lust could act within her, the Holy Spirit came upon her, sealed her purity, and granted her grace-filled purity and spiritual joy to which her heart clung never to let go again. The holy Church calls the Mother of God the "living book of Christ, sealed by the Spirit."[295]

The Protestants see the foundation of their teaching in the Gospel. The Evangelist Matthew, they say, in his account of the relationship between the Mother of God and her betrothed, Joseph, says of Joseph that he did not have intercourse with the Virgin until she had given birth to the God-Man, and that this serves as an indication of subsequent intercourse. The actual words of the Evangelist quoted by Protestants to support their opinion are as follows: "and (Joseph) did not know her till she (Mary) had brought forth her firstborn Son" (Matt 1:25). The blasphemers base their conclusion on the word "till," which in their opinion expresses a temporary abstinence from intercourse and the idea of intercourse following after the birth of the firstborn, and also on the word "firstborn," which they believe to indicate the birth of further children. However, it would be completely accurate to translate this verse of the Gospel as "Joseph did not know her, and she brought forth her firstborn Son." It is obvious that the words "Joseph did not know her" refer to the whole period of time when the Mother of God stayed in Joseph's house.

If we examine carefully the Evangelist Matthew's account of the birth of our Lord Jesus Christ (Matt 1:18–25), it becomes immediately apparent that the Evangelist was very assiduous in showing clearly and precisely that the God-Man was born of the Virgin without the seed of a man. This is why the Evangelist explains that the Virgin, betrothed to a man and without knowing a man, became pregnant from the Holy Spirit; this is why the Evangelist quotes the testimony of the angel appearing to Joseph in a dream and confirming that the fruit of the Virgin's womb was from the Holy Spirit; this is why the Evangelist quotes the prophet who foretold that a Virgin would conceive and would bear a Son, the Saviour of the world; this is why, already speaking of the birth of the God-Man, the Evangelist shows that Mary gave birth to Him while remaining a Virgin, just as she conceived, remaining a virgin. The Evangelist leaves without precise explanation the circumstances concerning the actual person of the Mother of God, which are not the main object of his description. The account of the Evangelist Luke of the birth of Christ has the same character. St Luke does not mention Joseph's perplexity and the appearance to him of the angel in a dream, but does relate the visit of the Archangel Gabriel to the Mother of God with the joyful news from God of her conception and birth of the Son of God, and that Elizabeth, inspired by the Holy Spirit, recognized Mary as the Mother of God. Like St Matthew, St Luke also calls Mary a virgin betrothed to a man (Luke 1:27), and he refers to the God-Man born of her as her Son and Firstborn (Luke 2:7). St Luke also omits circumstances concerning the Virgin herself; it is only indirectly that it becomes apparent from his account, as mentioned above, that the Virgin gave birth to the God-Man without pain. In vain, then, do the Protestants look for support for their blasphemy in the Gospel!

Unlike the Protestants, the holy Fathers of the Orthodox Church see the opposite idea in the words of the Evangelist Matthew quoted above: they see evidence that after conceiving the God-Man as a virgin, the Mother of God remained a virgin, gave birth as a virgin, remained a virgin after the birth and remained forever a virgin. "The Ever-Virgin," says St John Damascene, "remains a Virgin after the birth, having no relations with a man until her death." Although it is written, "and [Joseph] did not know her till she [Mary] had brought forth her firstborn Son", it should be known that the first child to be born is called the "firstborn" even if he is the only child. The word firstborn signifies the first child to be born, and does not necessarily indicate the birth of subsequent children. And the word "till" (ἕως), although it signifies a specific period of time, does not exclude the time that follows it. Thus the words of the Lord "and lo, I am with you always, even to (ἕως) the end of the age" (Matt 28:20) do not mean that the Lord will depart from us after the end of the age, because the divine Apostle says: "And thus we shall always be with the Lord" (1 Thess 4:17), that is, after the resurrection. Here the word "till," although in itself it signifies a specified period of time, has a completely different meaning as it is usually used in Holy Scripture. The Lord said: "you will by no means get out of there" (from the prison of hell) "till you have paid the last penny" (Matt 5:26). It is well-known that the torments of hell are eternal: the word "till" denoting a fixed period, as used here, means that a person imprisoned in hell will never get out of there, not having the possibility of repaying the debt of sin, which can only be repaid during one's earthly life through good works in Christ and by cleansing one's sins through repentance. It is said of the raven that Noah released from the ark that it "kept going to and fro until the waters dried up from the earth" (Gen 8:7); the raven did not return to the ark at all. Holy Scripture says: "The Lord said unto my Lord, Sit Thou at my right hand, until I make Thine enemies the footstool of Thy feet" (Ps 109:1); here the word "until," signifying a period of time, is again used to signify limitless, eternal time. It is obvious that the presence of the incarnate Son in humanity at the right hand of the Father, which signifies the highest state of glory, is not limited by the time taken to defeat the enemies of the God-Man, the fallen angels and impious people, but will continue eternally unto the ages of ages. The word "until" has the same meaning with reference to the Virgin as it has with reference to the written law given by God. "One jot," said the Lord, "or one tittle will by no means pass from the law till all is fulfilled" (Matt 5:18). The law is sealed by its fulfillment, and will remain eternally sealed, as fulfilled. The Virgin sealed her virginity through the birth of God the Word, and remained a Virgin forever, being sealed by through the birth of God. "And [Joseph] did not know her till she had brought forth her firstborn Son." "This means," says St Theophylact of Ochrid and Bulgaria, "that he never touched her, he did not know her either before the birth or after it."

Both evangelists emphasize, with an obvious particular goal, that the God-Man was a "firstborn." The Jews who had been promised the Messiah, for this reason particularly respected childbirth, and disdained infertility in women; for the same reason they particularly respected the firstborn among children, since one of the firstborn, in their opinion, was to be the long-awaited Messiah. And here was that longed-for, most glorious "Firstborn," say the evangelists, to satisfy the desire and the expectation! Since His birth, there has no longer been any reason for infertility in a woman to bring her shame, or for a firstborn child to have any special significance. Since then, glory has passed from matrimony to virginity, because the long-awaited Firstborn is a Virgin, and was born of a Virgin, while keeping her a Virgin during and after the birth.

The Holy Gospel makes no mention of the parents of the Mother of God, presenting the righteous Joseph as her protector and as the guardian of the infant Jesus. Her parents died soon after bearing their priceless fruit in their old age. "God arranged matters such," says St John Damascene, "that the young girl was betrothed to Joseph by the priests, just as the new book is given to 'a learned man' (Isa 29:11). This betrothal protected the Virgin."[296] The righteous Joseph was eighty years old[297] when he was betrothed to the fourteen-year-old Virgin. In accordance with Jewish law, the Mother of God was betrothed to him as a member of the tribe of Judah and the house of David, to which she also belonged. After staying in his house for four months, she heard the good news from the Archangel and conceived the God-Man. The humble Mary did not dare to inform her betrothed that the great Archangel had appeared to her and had told her that she was to become the mystical temple of God. When Joseph found out from the angel who appeared to him in a dream the great significance of the Virgin to whom he was betrothed, he understood the importance of his responsibility toward her, and became her servant, offering his holy service with reverence and fear, as St Theophylact of Ochrid and Bulgaria tells us. He acquired a feeling of deep respect toward her, similar to that felt and expressed by St Elizabeth, who was honored with a visit from the Mother of God. "But why is this granted to me," she exclaimed, why do I have this great honor, this great joy, "that the mother of my Lord should come to me?" (Luke 1:43). Not only were righteous people filled with reverence for the Mother of God: the Archangel Gabriel himself, who brought the good news, stood before her with reverence. He behaved completely differently toward St Zacharias when he proclaimed the birth of John, the greatest of the prophets. Yes, holy angels and holy people are reverent toward the Ever-Virgin. Impudent and blasphemous judgments about her are characteristic only of the rejected spirits that fill both heaven and paradise with blasphemy, and of corrupt people who unite themselves with the rejected spirits. St John Damascene is justified in observing that not only the deed, even the thought of violating the virginity of the Ever-Virgin could belong only to the most immoral, corrupted mind. How could the righteous Joseph, who had heard the great testimony about the Mother of God, and had seen the wondrous miracles that had occurred at the birth of the God-Man, attempt the gross transgression, the terrible offence ascribed to him by the Protestants! How could the righteous, eighty-year-old man be carried away by youthful lust, and, before the eyes of the God-Man, corrupt His Mother! No, no. Such terrible profligacy and evil was impossible for the holy elder. The righteous Joseph was honored with divine revelations that favor only those who are pure in heart and in body. When he was perplexed about the Mother of God, an angel appeared to him in a dream and said: "Joseph, son of David, do not be afraid to take to you Mary your wife" (Matt 1:20). The angel answered Joseph's thoughts directly. Joseph, suspecting Mary, had wanted to put her away quietly: the angel, witnessing to her chastity, commanded him to keep her with him, without any doubts, as she had not violated any marital duty. He then revealed that she had conceived from the Holy Spirit. And when the Son of God had to go away to Egypt to escape the murderous hands of Herod, the angel again appeared to Joseph, and no longer called Mary his wife, but the Mother of the young Child. The Gospel relates two further occasions when an angel appears to Joseph. In the appearance that is described in more detail, when he is commanded to return to the land of Israel, the angel again calls Mary solely the Mother of the young Child (Matt 2:13,19).

The Gospel mentions the "brothers" of the God-Man (John 7:3). The blasphemers of the Ever-Virgin point this out to support their opinion. But the authentic tradition of the Orthodox Church explains that it was the sons of the righteous Joseph, the betrothed of the Mother of God, by his first wife, who were referred to as the brothers of the Lord. They were called the brothers of the Lord in exactly the same way as Joseph was called His father. The Mother of God herself called Joseph His father. After finding the twelve-year-old Lord in the temple at Jerusalem, she said to Him: "Son, why have You done this to us? Look, Your father and I have sought You anxiously" (Matt 8:55; Luke 2:48; cf Luke 4:22; John 6:42). Contemporary Jews, unaware of the conception from the Holy Spirit and the virgin birth, assumed that the God-Man was the son of Joseph (Luke 3:23); but the Mother of God, the disciples, and those close to the Lord concealed the great mystery from the embittered Jews who did not cease to blaspheme against obvious miracles. What blasphemous cries would they have uttered if the conception by the Spirit and the virgin birth had been revealed to them? They remained unaware of this, and, in the opinion of the people, Joseph was considered to be, and known to be the father, and consequently his sons were considered and called brothers of the Lord. They were much older in years than the God-Man Who therefore could not have been the firstborn in relation to them.

The accusation that St Joseph attempted to violate the virginity of the Mother of God turns out to be meaningless: such an accusation is even more absurd in relation to the Mother of God herself. Thousands upon thousands of virgins have become spiritual brides of Christ, and have kept the seal of virginity intact. Surely the greatest of all virgins, the Bride and at the same time the Mother of God, preserved her virginity? Thousands upon thousands of virgins have preserved their virginity, with the help of the Holy Spirit, from the joy given through grace. Is it possible that the greatest of virgins, who held the almighty God within her womb, not through action of grace but through His essence, should not be able to preserve her virginity? Is it possible that she who was constantly in the closest contact with God could not do this? If the cherubim and the seraphim, through their closeness to God, have their minds and hearts constantly directed toward Him, and cannot tear them away from Him: is it possible that she who is incomparably higher than the cherubim and the seraphim, who conceived and carried God in her womb, who gave birth to God without pain, who nourished Him from her breasts and carried Him in her arms, who was with Him throughout His earthly life, did not have her mind and heart firmly joined to Him? Did she really descend to carnal sensuality? No! Such a thought can only arise and be accepted by those who have always groveled in carnal sensuality, never emerging from it. May this blasphemous thought be put away from us and go away to the darkness of hell and to the eternal flame prepared by the devil and his angels. We confess our Lady, the Mother of our God, to be virgin until she gave birth, virgin in childbirth, virgin after giving birth, ever-virgin.

Knowing and confessing the greatness of the Mother of God, we direct our hearts toward her with unwavering faith, with the greatest reverence, and in continuity from the holy apostles, we cry out to her in prayer: "Most holy Birthgiver of God, help us!"[298]

From several passages in the Gospel, it can be seen that the Lord replies to the Mother of God coldly and severely if judged by human criteria. This again serves as a stumbling-block to carnal minds. The stumbling-block is shown to be unjust when the actions and words of our Lord are examined from a spiritual viewpoint. Spiritual matters must be judged spiritually, said the holy apostle Paul (1 Cor 2:13–14). The deeds and words of the Lord "are spirit, and they are life" (John 6:63). While the old Adam was carried away by affection for the old Eve, and so transgressed the commandment of God, the New Adam—the Lord—shows Himself to be thinking only of the fulfillment of God's will, and for this reason is shown not to be distracted by the affection of the New Testament Eve and her care for Him. He does not even reveal any sympathy for this affection! By acting in this way, He redeems the passion of the forefather through His dispassion, and redeems the acceptance of affection that led to sin, by rejecting sinless and natural affection. He teaches us to guard against passions and being led astray by feelings, even for the most blessed reasons. Our lamp and our guide in our actions must be the law of God (Ps 118:105).

The parents of the Lord—this is what the Gospel calls the Mother of God and Joseph, speaking in this case in line with the custom of contemporary society—had the pious custom of traveling to Jerusalem every year for the feast of the Passover. When the Lord was twelve years old, they went to Jerusalem, taking Him with them. After spending the days of the feast in the holy city, Mary and Joseph left to return to their home-town, Nazareth, and the Lord remained in Jerusalem. At first the Mother of God and Joseph did not notice this, assuming that the Lord was walking with other worshipers. After they had already been on the road for a whole day, and had probably reached their lodging-place, they began to search for Him among their relatives and friends, but they did not find him, and returned to Jerusalem. There, after three days, they found the Lord in the temple among teachers of the law, who had been brought to amazement and fear by the word of God being spoken by the young God-Child. When the Ever-Virgin saw Him, she spoke the words filled with tenderness that we have already read: "Son, why have You done this to us? Look, Your father and I have sought You anxiously." To this the Lord replied, "Why did you seek Me? Did you not know that I must be about My Father's business?" (Luke 2:41–50).

In the reply of the Lord it is clear that His thoughts, and will, and love are dedicated completely to His duty toward God; His duties toward people are assigned their due place, as can be seen from the events that follow this reply (Luke 2:51). When a person does not accommodate his duties in the appropriate way, and does not give to each one the appropriate measure, then the fruit they bear cannot be virtue. The fruit will be sins and mistakes, all the more dangerous because their external attire is attractive.

At the time when the Lord was already preaching the Gospel, at Cana, a small town in Galilee, a marriage took place to which the Lord and His disciples and the Mother of God were invited (John 2). The Lord sanctified both the marriage and the wedding feast with His presence. During the feast there proved to be a shortage of wine. The Mother of God said to the Lord: "They have no wine." The Lord answered her: "Woman, what does your concern have to do with Me? My hour has not yet come" (John 2:3–4). This is a wondrous reply regarding the fruit of the vine, which has such a strong influence on people! This is the kind of reply that Adam ought to have given to Eve when she suggested eating the fruit that had been forbidden by God—a fatal act that infected the human race with the poison of eternal death. "Woman, why are you concerned with what I do?" These could have been the words of Adam—"you were created to be my helper: do not be my enemy. I am joined to you in the union of matrimony into one flesh; but if you did not listen to God, then I separate myself from you, as I am united with you to serve God, and not to act against Him." The second half of the Lord's reply contains within it a deep, mystical meaning. The Mother of God is merciful toward the celebrating people, who have run out of wine in the midst of the feast, and wishes to remedy this shortfall through the divine power of her Son. God the Word, Who, in His indescribable mercy, has come down in human form to fallen humanity which is perishing on earth from lack of spiritual food and drink, and has brought daily bread and a new drink—His body and blood, Himself, prepared for the sake of His love for mankind to grant this nourishment—alludes to the table prepared by God and already very close, and says: "My hour has not yet come." "My hour has not yet come!"—My hour has not yet come for salvific sufferings, My hour has not yet come to shed the life-bearing blood that is to save humanity from eternal death. That was the hour that the Lord wished for, the hour of salvation for mankind, the hour in which He would reveal all the abundance of His love, the hour for which He had come into the world (John 12:27). The request of the Mother of God did not in itself contain anything blameworthy, and it was granted. From this it can be seen that the original rejection of the loving request of the New Testament Eve only aspired to rectify Adam's agreement to the sinful suggestion of the Old Testament Eve. The meaning of the Lord's words can be interpreted as "you are concerned with the perishable food of people, but I love them with incomprehensible divine love. Guided by this love, I am ready and I wish to give them My very body and My very blood for food and drink; but this too will be accomplished in its hour, that is, in its own time, appointed and specified by incomprehensible divine counsel."

The holy evangelist Matthew relates that one day the Lord was teaching the people inside a house; the Mother of God and the sons of Joseph, who were known as the brothers of the God-Man, came and waited for him outside, wanting to speak to Him about something. The Lord was informed of this, but He replied: "Who is My mother and who are My brothers?" Then, pointing at His disciples, He added, "Here are My mother and My brothers! For whoever does the will of My Father in heaven is My brother and sister and mother" (Matt 12:46–50). Similarly, when a certain woman, hearing the wondrous teaching of the Lord, said to Him: "Blessed is the womb that bore You, and the breasts which nursed You!" He answered, "More than that, blessed are those who hear the word of God and keep it!" (Luke 11:27–28). In every situation, the Lord is constantly and equally true to His most holy ministry. "I have come down from heaven," He said, "not to do My own will, but the will of Him who sent Me" (John 6:38). This divine attitude of the Lord and His divine words toward the Mother of God do not in any way disparage her merit; they increase it. The Ever-Virgin is higher than all holy people, both because she became the Mother of the God-Man, and because she was the most constant, the most attentive hearer and fulfiller of the teaching He proclaimed. The first of these virtues is sealed with the second, and this is why the virtue of the Mother of God became greater than any other. The Holy Gospel says of the Mother of God: "But Mary kept all these things and pondered them in her heart" (Luke 2:19). This is said after the account of the shepherds to whom the angel appeared on the night of the birth of Christ and announced the news of the Saviour's birth. This verse has the following meaning: the Mother of God followed attentively all the events relating to the God-Man right from His birth, noticed them, and fixed them in her memory. Her heart served as a book for her in which these events were written down. The Gospel later repeats its testimony: "His mother kept all these things in her heart" (Luke 2:51). This is now said of the words of the Lord. She not only noticed every detail of the events relating to the Lord, but also His actual words, placing them in her heart, keeping them in her heart, like a priceless treasure in a treasure-chest that itself became priceless due to the treasure within it. It should be mentioned that the Gospel says this of those words of the Lord that were impossible for the Mother of God to comprehend given the state of her soul at the time, and became clear to her later, after her renewal by the Spirit. What hearing of the Word of God could have more power than the Word of God being placed into and kept in one's heart? The holy prophet David said: "That I should long to do Thy will, O my God; yea, Thy Law is within my heart" (Ps 39:9). What the greatest saints of God wished to accomplish, the Mother of God actually accomplished, through the divine grace she was granted. And how did she do this? First of all, her heart and her womb were overshadowed by the Holy Spirit; then her womb became a temple for the Lord Who had entered it. Spiritual joy from the presence of the Lord within her enveloped her whole being, as she herself bore witness. It is usual for holy joy to envelop people who have been honored to feel the Holy Spirit acting within them: the Mother of God was filled even more with divine joy. After the birth of the God-Man, she had a very close relationship with Him. He spent His infancy in her arms and in her embrace; He was inseparable from her not only in childhood, but in the years of His youth and manhood, right until He began His divine ministry, which lasted three and a half years. No-one else heard the Word of God more closely and for such a long period of time as the Mother of God; no-one followed the words and deeds of the God-Man with such close and constant attention, and no-one kept them so carefully and with such love. We considered the behavior of the Lord toward the Mother of God at the wedding in Cana of Galilee. Let us now turn our attention to the behavior of the Mother of God toward the Lord. When she received a stern reply to her request, she understood it in a completely different way to those who are scandalized by it. She did not see a rejection of her request in this reply, and so she went to those serving at the feast and said to them: "Whatever He" (the Lord) "says to you, do it" (John 2:5). After the Mother of God had issued this direction, the Lord turned the water into wine.

In the last three and a half years of the Lord's sojourn on earth, the Mother of God was not able to be with Him all the time. The Lord used this time to journey around the land of Judea, proclaiming the Gospel to the people; but even during this time the Mother of God often saw Him, often followed Him in the crowd of His disciples, listening to His most holy teaching, for which she had acquired an unquenchable thirst. She was particularly resolute in being with Him during His passion. The Mother of God shared in the sufferings of the God-Man; she participated in them most keenly and truly. As the old Eve in paradise made the old Adam a participant in her transgression, so the New Adam made the new Eve a participant in His sufferings, which redeemed the offense of the forefathers. During and because of the Lord's sufferings, the Mother of God was permitted the most terrible tribulation. Her heart was pierced with sorrow as if by a deadly weapon (Luke 2:35).

When the Lord had completed the redemption of the human race, and already intended, hanging on the cross, to conclude His redemptive effort with voluntary death, the Mother of God and his beloved disciple, John, stood in His presence at the foot of His cross. The Lord had already accomplished the redemption of humanity, He was already giving birth to humanity unto a new life through the sufferings He underwent before His death; He was already ready to complete this birthgiving through His death. Having become in this way the Progenitor of renewed mankind, by taking the place of the forefather who had been unable due to the fall to beget children unto salvation, and had begotten them only unto perdition, the Lord suddenly turned to the Mother of God, the participant in His sufferings for the redemption of mankind, who was standing before Him, and introduced her to her rights relating to humanity, the rights given to her by the God-Man and by her whole relationship with Him. He declared her to be the mother of the disciple whom He loved, and in him, as the Fathers understand and explain,[299] of the whole of renewed humanity. Just as the Lord replaced Adam with Himself, so He replaced Eve with the Mother of God. Eve, who was created a virgin, transgressed against God's commandment, and was unable to keep the holy state of virginity; her subjection to her husband was proclaimed to her as one of her punishments. The Mother of God, although she had been conceived and born in the sin of her forefathers, prepared herself through her chaste and God-pleasing way of life to be a divine vessel. Having become a divine vessel, she remained free of thoughts of and sympathy toward lust for a man, toward animal-like union, to which, as Scripture teaches us, women were subordinated following the fall. Constant communion with God, Who was at the same time also the Son of the Ever-Virgin, nourished her with heavenly, spiritual, holy thoughts and feelings. The apostle Paul said: "He who is joined to the Lord is one spirit with Him" (1 Cor 6:17). These words were fulfilled in their entirety in the Mother of God. They were fulfilled in a better way and more abundantly than in all the holy virgins from among the elect of humanity. The Virgin Mother of God was a virgin before she gave birth to the God-Man, she remained a virgin while giving birth, she remained a virgin after the birth. She knew no urges to be with a man, because she was wholly and entirely drawn toward and joined with God.

After the ascension of the Lord, the Mother of God, as we see from the book of the Acts of the Apostles, was inseparable from the apostles and lived in the same house, in constant prayer. The holy Evangelist Luke calls these prayers "prayer and supplication" (Acts 1:14), showing that all the activities of the Mother of God and of the apostles were focused on various modes of prayer, and that all their time was dedicated to prayer. It was in the context of this practice and way of life that the Holy Spirit came down upon the Lord's disciples on the day of Pentecost (Acts 2:1), for the Holy Spirit always requires a disciple of Christ to prepare himself with the most intensive, constant prayer, before coming down upon him and overshadowing him. On this day, then, the Mother of God received the most abundant gift of the Holy Spirit, enlightening not only her soul but also her body. Her soul and her body themselves became sources of light. The Holy Spirit testifies to this. The holy Church bears witness to it. Spiritual reason affirms it. For those who wish to hear historical testimony, we recommend here the account of the Mother of God written by her contemporary in earthly life, St Dionysius the Areopagite, a well-known and learned Athenian, who was converted to Christianity by the holy Apostle Paul (Acts 17:34). Three years after the Areopagite had first believed in the Redeemer, he visited the Mother of God, who since the Lord's ascension had been living permanently in Jerusalem in the house of the evangelist John. We quote the following from the letter of St Dionysius to the Apostle Paul:

> It seemed incredible to me, confessing before God, O our excellent leader and shepherd, that apart from God Himself on high there should be anyone filled with divine power and wondrous grace; no man can attain what I saw and comprehended not only with the eyes of my soul but with my bodily eyes. I saw with my own eyes the godlike Mother, holier than all the powers of heaven, of Christ Jesus, our Lord, whom I was granted to see through the grace of God, the condescension of the supreme apostle (John) and the unspeakable goodness and mercy of the most merciful Virgin. Again and again I confess before the might of God, before the grace of the Saviour and before the glorious honour of the Virgin, His Mother, that when I was brought before the face of the godlike, most holy Virgin by John, the head of the evangelists and

> prophets, who, living in the flesh, shines like the sun in the heavens, then there shone before me such a great and boundless radiance, not only outside but even more brightly from within, and I was filled with such a wondrous and varied fragrance that neither my weak body nor my soul could endure such and so many signs and elements of eternal blessedness and glory: my heart grew faint, my spirit grew faint within me from her divine glory and grace. I bear witness before God, Who dwelt in the most honourable womb of the Virgin, that if I had not remembered in my newly-illumined mind your divine teaching and commandments, then I would have confessed the Virgin to be God, and would have honoured her with the veneration befitting the one true God: because the mind cannot imagine greater honour and glory for a person glorified by God, than the blessedness that I, the unworthy, was granted to experience, being then entirely blessed and happy. I give thanks to my most good God on high, to the divine Virgin, to the excellent apostle John, and also to you, the highest and most solemn leader of the Church, who mercifully granted me such a blessing.[300]

The Mother of God possessed in even greater abundance the grace-filled gifts of the Holy Spirit in which the apostles abounded. She had not only the gift of prophecy but also that of spiritual discernment and of wonderworking, and countless other gifts known to herself and to the Giver of these gifts. Incurable diseases were cured when their sufferers touched her. Her virgin body, sanctified by God, became a vessel and source of miracles. Just as the image of the Apostle Peter made on the ground by his shadow performed miracles (Acts 5:15), so the icons of the Mother of God to this day perform miracles across the earth preaching, bearing witness, and sealing with signs the truth of Christ's teaching. The rays of the sun were the painters of the miraculous images of the Apostle. The apostles and the holy saints were the painters of the spiritual rays of the Sun of righteousness, of God and the Son of the Ever-Virgin, the wonderworking icons of the Mother of God.

On the third day after her blessed dormition, the Mother of God rose from the dead, and she now dwells in the heavens in soul and in body. She not only dwells in the heavens: she reigns there. As the Mother of the Heavenly King, she has been proclaimed the heavenly Queen, and Queen of the holy angels and of holy people. She has been granted special power and special boldness in intercession before God on behalf of humanity.

The holy Church, turning with requests to all the greatest saints of God, to all the angels and archangels, says to them: "Pray to God for us." Only to the Mother of God does the Church use the words "save us." The Mother of God is the greatest intercessor and helper of all those who labor to please God, and of all those who have dedicated their earthly life to serving God. When she appeared to a certain holy monk, she healed him from a grave illness and said that he belonged to her family.[301] She is a quick consolation to those who mourn and weep. She speaks for those who repent; she is a true refuge for sinners who wish to return to God; she is a fervent intercessor for them before God. Standing before the Mother of God, in deep reverence toward her greatness, in solemn bewilderment and astonishment, in the joy of faith and love, the children of the Orthodox Church bring to the Ever-Virgin the most joyful doxology. Accept, Lady, these infant voices, this infant prattling, attempting out of fervor of heart to define your greatness, and unable to do so from weakness of reason, from lack of words, from your boundless greatness.

Hail, tabernacle of God the Word!
Hail, Holy of Holies!
Hail, throne of the Almighty!
Hail, enclosure of the God whom nothing can enclose!
Hail, most holy chariot of Him who rides upon the cherubim!
Hail, best of all dwellings for Him who is above the seraphim!
Hail, height hard to climb for the thoughts of men!
Hail, depth hard to scan even for the eyes of angels!
Hail, tidings doubted by unbelievers!
Hail, undoubted glory of the faithful!
Hail, for thou provest devoid of reason those skilled in reason's art!
Hail, for the cunning disputants are shown to be fools!
Hail, for thou hast torn asunder the tangled webs of the Athenians!
Hail for thou hast filled (with spiritual knowledge) the nets (of faith) of the fishermen![302]
Most holy Birthgiver of God! Glory to you! Most holy Birthgiver of God, save us! Amen.

Appendix

A Short Biography of Bishop Ignatius (Brianchaninov)

The future Saint Ignatius was born on April 15/28, 1807, in the village of Pokrovskoye in the Vologda region of Russia. His given name at birth was Dimitry Alexandrovitch Brianchaninov. Of noble birth, his father was a wealthy provincial landowner. In due course the young Dimity was sent to study at the Pioneer Military Academy in St Petersburg to be educated as a military officer.

Even before entering the Academy Dimitry had aspired to the monastic life, but his family did not support these plans. Nevertheless, as a student he was able to find some time to devote to prayer and the inner life and to find other students with similar aspirations. Remaining obedient to his parents he remained diligent in his studies, winning the praise of his teacher and coming to the attention of the Grand Duke Nicholas Pavlovich, the future Tsar Nicholas I.

After graduating from the Academy he took up his first commission in the army but soon became seriously ill. This made it possible for him to request an honorable discharge and having made a full recovery to at last embrace the monastic life. He was duly tonsured as a monk in 1831 and given the name Ignatius. His spiritual father was the revered Elder Leonid of Optina. Shortly after his tonsure he was ordained as a priest.

Meanwhile, his absence from the army had come to the attention of Tsar Nicholas. As soon as he was able to locate Fr Ignatius in his small monastery near Vologda, he ordered him back to the capital. So, at the age of only twenty-six Fr Ignatius was made an Archimandrite and appointed as head of the St Sergius monastery in St Petersburg. He served faithfully in that capacity for the next twenty-four years.

In 1857 he was ordained to the episcopacy, serving as bishop of Stavropol and the Caucasus. This period of his life lasted for only four years, after which he withdrew into seclusion at the Nicolo-Babaevsky monastery in the Kostroma region of Russia. Here he was able to devote the remaining six years of his life to spiritual writing and correspondence with his numerous spiritual children. He composed five volumes of Ascetical Works, the fifth of which, The Arena, has been translated into English.

Bishop Ignatius reposed on April 30/May 13, 1867. The Russian Orthodox Church canonized him at their local council in 1988 and his relics now reside at the Tolga monastery in the Yaroslavl region of Russia.

Notes

All references to source material in the original text were to the classic Russian-language editions. The author followed a Russian cultural practice where one is not necessarily expected to provide all background detail and source material. Unless otherwise indicated, the quotations and their citations have been translated from the original text.

1. *Practical and Theological Texts. The Philokalia*, pt. 1, ch. 4. [English translation: *The Philokalia*, vol. 1, trans. G. E. H. Palmer, Philip Sherrard, Kallistos Ware (London: Faber and Faber, 1983).]

2. St Symeon the New Theologian, "Homily on faith." *The Philokalia*, pt. 1.

3. Saints Kallistos and Ignatius Xanthopoulos, *The Philokalia*, pt. 2, ch. 16 [Slavonic edition] [An English edition: *Writings from the Philokalia: On Prayer of the Heart*, trans. E. Kadloubovsky and G. E. H. Palmer (London: Faber and Faber, 1992).]

4. St Isaac the Syrian, Homily 48.

5. St Isaac the Syrian, Homily 71.

6. St Isaac the Syrian, Homily 41.

7. *The Lives of the Saints*, May 3.

8. *Sayings of the Desert Fathers*. [This work is known in Greek as the Apophthégmata tōn Patérōn and in Latin as Apophthegmata Patrum Aegyptiorum and refers to various collections of texts attributed the Desert Fathers of Egypt around the fifth century. An English language edition: *The Desert Fathers: Sayings of the Early Christian Monks*, editor Benedicta Ward (Penguin Classics, 2003).]

9. See St Peter Damascene, The Eight Stages of Contemplation, bk. 1, *The Philokalia*, Part 3. [English translation: *The Philokalia,* vol. 3, trans. G. E. H. Palmer, Philip Sherrard, Kallistos Ware (London: Faber and Faber, 1998).]

10. *On the Spiritual Law*, ch. 32. *The Philokalia*, vol. 1.

11. St Symeon the New Theologian, *Practical and Theological Texts*, ch. 4. *The Philokalia*, vol. 4. [English translation: *The Philokalia*, vol. 4, trans. G. E. H. Palmer, Philip Sherrard, Kallistos Ware (London: Faber and Faber, 1998).]

12. *Sayings of the Desert Fathers.*

13. St Isaac the Syrian, Homily 55.

14. St Tikhon of Zadonsk. Vol. 14, letter no. 4.

15. *The Ladder*, Step 28. [Available in English translation as: *The Ladder of Divine Ascent*, trans. Archimandrite Lazarus (London: Faber and Faber, 1959).]

16. St Peter Damascene, The Classification of Prayer according to the Eight Stages of Contemplation, bk. 1. *The Philokalia*, bk. 3.

17. From the interpretation by St Paisius Velichkovsky of the prayer "Lord have mercy."

18. St Nilus of Sora.

19 "Stand a while, until all the senses are calm. Then begin, not rapidly, nor yet too slowly, but earnestly and with a contrite heart, say Psalm 1, 'Blessed is the man...' quietly, with understanding, and attentively, so that the mind may grasp what is being said." Instructions on reading the Psalter.

20. See the commentary of St Theophylact of Ochrid and Bulgaria.

21. St Sisoes the Great. *The Lives of the Saints*, July 6.

22. *The Ladder*, Step 18: On insensibility or deadening of the soul.

23. St Isaac the Syrian, Homily 2.

24. Priest's service book. Directions for confession.

25. *Sayings of the Desert Fathers*.

26. St Isaac the Syrian, Homily 90.

27. *Sayings of the Desert Fathers*.

28. *Sayings of the Desert Fathers*.

29. St Agathon. *Sayings of the Desert Fathers*.

30. St Macarius the Great, Homily 1, ch. 11 and 12.

31. See the commentary of St Theophylact of Ochrid and Bulgaria.

32. *The Ladder*, Step 4, ch. 53.

33. *The Ladder*, Step 4, ch. 31.

34. St Isaac the Syrian, Homily 56.

35. Evening prayer of St John Chrysostom.

36. *The Ladder*, Step 7.

37. *The Ladder*, Step 1.

38. Service book. Service of confession. [In English: *Book of Needs of the Holy Orthodox Church*, trans. G. V. Shann (London: David Nutt. 1984) p.49.]

39. Ibid.

40. St John Cassian, *On the Eight Vices*; St John of The Ladder, Step 22, *On Vainglory*.

41. St Barsanuphius the Great, as cited by St Kallistos and St Ignatius Xanthopoulos, ch. 25, *The Philokalia,* pt. 2.

42. *The Ladder,* Step 4.

43. St Macarius the Great, Homily 4, ch. 3.

44. St Sisoes the Great. *The Sayings of the Desert Fathers*.

45. St Kallistos and St Ignatius Xanthopoulos, *On Silence and Prayer*, ch. 25, *The Philokalia*, pt. 2.

46. The Creed of St Athanasius the Great, Patriarch of Alexandria. *Book of Common Prayer*.

47. *The Ladder*, Step 1.

48. Life of St Ephraim the Syrian.

49. Claude Fleury, *Histoire ecclésiastique,* vol. II, bk. 27, ch. 28. [Claude Fleury (1640–1723). An English translation: *The Ecclesiastical History of M. L'abbé Fleury*, trans. John Henry Newman (London: Rivingtons, 1842)].

50. Fleury, vol. I, bk. 10, ch. 36 & bk. 11.

51. First Epistle to the Trallians.

52. St Ignatius the God-bearer. *Epistle to the Philippians*.

53. St Basil the Great calls the fallen spirit the father of passionate carnal weaknesses. Prayers against defilement, book of canons.

54. Abba Dorotheos, [*Church Slavonic*].

55. Claude Fleury, *Histoire ecclésiastique, vol. I, bk. 10, ch. 42.*

56. *The Ladder,* Step 15, ch. 48. Council of Laodicea, Canon no. 6.

57. Claude Fleury, *Histoire ecclésiastique, vol. II, bk. 20, ch. 24.*

58. Service for the Sunday of Orthodoxy.

59. St Symeon the New Theologian. From the prayers before Holy Communion. [See *Prayer Book* (Jordanville, NY: Holy Trinity Monastery, 2005) p.364.]

60. *The Ladder,* Step 26.

61. Resurrectional Troparion in Tone 5.

62. St John Cassian. Conferences 8, 9 and 10.

63. St John Chrysostom, Homily 8 on the Epistle to the Romans.

64. St Symeon the New Theologian. *The Philokalia,* pt. 4, in the words of Nicephorus the Monk.

65. Prayer-book. First prayer against defilement.

66. St Mark the Ascetic, Homily 7 on fasting and humility.

67. St Theophylact of Ochrid and Bulgaria, Commentary on Matthew 4:2.

68. St Theophylact of Ochrid and Bulgaria, Commentary on Luke 4:2.

69. St Theophylact of Ochrid and Bulgaria, Commentary on Luke 6:12–19.

70. St Isaac the Syrian, Homily 1.

71. St Isaac the Syrian, Homily 56.

72. This edifying advice comes from St Barsanuphius the Great. Response no. 261.

73. St Pimen the Great. *Sayings of the Desert Fathers*.

74. St Barsanuphius the Great. Response no. 401. St John Cassian. Conference 9, ch. 21.

75. St John Chrysostom. Moral teaching no. 46 in Homilies on the Evangelist John.

76. St Isaac the Syrian, Homily 68.

77. St John Damascene, *An Exact Exposition of the Orthodox Faith*, bk. 4, ch. 13.

78. Taken from St John Damascene, *An Exact Exposition of the Orthodox Faith*, bk. 4, ch. 13.

79. St John Damascene, *An Exact Exposition of the Orthodox Faith*, bk. 4, ch. 13.

80. St John Chrysostom, Moral teaching no. 45, *Homily on the Gospel of St John*.

81. *The Ladder,* Step 25, Here the words of St John of the Ladder are supplemented by ascetic explanations.

82. This is read at the beginning of the prayers before Holy Communion. [See Prayer Book (Jordanville, NY; Holy Trinity Monastery, 2005) p.331.]

83. Abba Pimen. *Sayings of the Desert Fathers*. In the prayer after the Nineteenth Kathisma, we read: "sweeten the bitterness of my soul by Thy precious Blood, wherewith vouchsafe me, who doth resist Thee, to drink."

84. This idea comes from St John Damascene.

85. As cited by St Kallistos and St Ignatius Xanthopoulos. *The Philokalia*, pt. 2, ch. 16.

86. Archbishop Veniamin Krasnopievkov, *Novaya Skrizhal* [This is a classic Russian reference book on the Orthodox Church.—Trans.]

87. St Basil the Great, Letter 93 to the patrician Caesaria.

88. St John Damascene, *An Exact Exposition of the Orthodox Faith*.

89. St John Damascene, *An Exact Exposition of the Orthodox Faith*.

90. St John Chrysostom. Moral teaching no. 46 in *Homilies on John*. St John Damascene, *An Exact Exposition of the Orthodox Faith*.

91. St Mark the Ascetic, *On the Spiritual Law*, ch. 118. *The Philokalia*, bk. 1.

92. Eucharist means thanksgiving. The sacrament is named thus because it is served with abundant thanksgiving and glorification of God.

93. Divine Liturgy of St Basil the Great. Priest's service book. [*The Divine Liturgy of Our Father among the Saints Basil the Great: Slavonic-English Parallel Text* (Jordanville, NY: Holy Trinity Monastery, 2020), pp. 181–3.]

94. Taken from St John Damascene, *An Exact Interpretation of the Orthodox Faith*.

95. St John Damascene, *An Exact Interpretation of the Orthodox Faith*.

96. St John Damascene, *An Exact Interpretation of the Orthodox Faith*, bk. 4, ch. 8, on the Liturgy of St Basil the Great.

97. [*The Divine Liturgy of Our Father Among the Saints Basil the Great*, p. 185].

98. "A sword will pierce through your own soul also," the holy God-receiver said to the all-holy Virgin. Luke 2:35.

99. St Ignatius was writing in the nineteenth century.—Trans.].

100. The suffering of the martyr Romulus. *The Lives of the Saints*, September 6.

101. The population of the Roman Empire in the time of Augustus totaled 100 million; by the time of Constantine the Great, three hundred years later, it had dropped to sixty million. The boundaries of the empire remained unchanged.

102. St John of the Ladder, *Ladder of Divine Ascent*, Step 18.

103. St John of the Ladder, *Ladder of Divine Ascent*, Step 1, ch. 6.

104. Abba Dorotheos. Instruction 1.

105. St Macarius the Great, Homily 1, ch. 2.

106. St Macarius the Great, Homily 7, ch. 4.

107. St Macarius the Great, Homily 7, ch. 4.

108. *The Lives of the Saints*, September 20.

109. St Isaac the Syrian, Homily 1.

110. St Isaac the Syrian, Homily 1.

111. *The Philokalia*, pt. 1, *On the Spiritual Law*, ch. 2.

112. As explained by St Pimen the Great, *The Sayings of the Desert Fathers*.

113. Humility received its name from the inner peace that it bears in our hearts. [The Russian word смирение (humility) is made up of the words с (with) and мир (peace).—Trans.].

114. The lips of the humble-minded speak the truth," said St Mark the Ascetic. *On the Spiritual Law*, ch. 9.

115. St Pimen the Great said: "Only in one place were the Israelites permitted to make sacrifices and to conduct public divine services. In the spiritual sense, this place is humility." *Sayings of the Desert Fathers*.

116. See our homily *On salvation*. [See Sermon 32. On the Twelfth Sunday: On Salvation. page 176.]

117. St Macarius the Great, Homily 20.

118. St Macarius the Great, Homily 37, ch. 2, 3.

119. St Nilus of Sora, Homily 3.

120. St Peter Damascene, *How to acquire true faith*, bk. 1, *The Philokalia*, pt. 3.

121. St Isaac the Syrian, Homily 84.

122. The weightier matters of the law [are] justice and mercy and faith"—Words of the Saviour (Matt 23:23).

123. St Dimitri, Metropolitan of Rostov, Chronicle. The saint takes this explanation of the words of Holy Scripture from St John Chrysostom, St Gregory the Dialogist, St Isidore of Pelusium, and St Pimen the Great.

124. See Cicero's speech against Mark Antony.

125 "The soul does not become humble if it is not deprived of bread," said St Pimen the Great. *Sayings of the Desert Fathers*.

126. To the patriarch and prophet Abraham.

127. St Dimitri of Rostov, *Chronicle*.

128. St Dimitri of Rostov, *Chronicle*.

129. Corporal punishment was widely used in ancient times. Even the most senior dignitaries of the Roman Empire and the Patriarchate were not exempt. For example, St Flavian, Patriarch of Constantinople, St Martin, Pope of Rome, and others, were subjected to severe corporal punishment.

130. Life of St John the Merciful. *Lives of the Saints*, November 12.

131. St Isaac the Syrian, Homily 89, *On the Harm Caused by Reckless Zeal.*

132. St John Cassian, *Collatio secunda, de discretione.*

133. St John Cassian, *Collatio secunda, de discretione.*

134. Papists.

135. Protestants.

136. St Isaac the Syrian, Homily 28.

137. Hebrew text [Ps 2:12].

138. St Symeon the New Theologian says: "What is the purpose of the Incarnation of the Divine Logos which is proclaimed throughout the Scriptures, about which we read and which yet we do not recognize? Surely it is that He has shared in what is ours so as to make us participants of what is His. For the Son of God became the Son of man in order to make us human beings sons of God, raising us up by grace to what He is by nature." *The Philokalia*, pt. 1, ch. 108.

139. The historical information in this sermon is taken from Claude Fleury, *Histoire ecclésiastique, vol. I, bk. 1.*

140. This is what the Lord said when He appeared to St Pachomius the Great.

141. The holy Apostle Peter mentions the fact that heresy implies denial of Christ in his second epistle: "There will be false teachers among you, who will secretly bring in destructive heresies, even denying the Lord who bought them" (2 Pet 2:1). Every heresy is a denial of the Redeemer. Even the heresy of iconoclasm, which apparently rejects only the icon of Christ, in essence rejects the incarnation of Christ, and consequently the Redeemer and the redemption. The rejection of Christian sacraments, without obvious rejection of Christ, is in essence a rejection of Christ; when the sacraments are rejected, essential interaction with Christ ceases and is destroyed.

142. "All rich men are appointees and stewards for God, and not owners. God alone is the owner and lord of every good thing and of all wealth; and He gives to whomever He wishes, for the benefit of all. If you punish your steward for the sake of the money you have lent him, for what he has spent it on: then the Lord will punish you for the sake of the riches He has given you, and you will give an answer to Him on the day of judgment for every rouble and what you spent it on and where." St Tikhon of Voronezh. Vol. 14, letter 29.

143. *Lives of the Saints*, December 23.

144. This homily is based on patristic texts, primarily Conference 9 of St John Cassian.

145. *The Ladder*, Step 28, ch. 64.

146. St John Cassian.

147. St Barsanuphius the Great. Response 71.

148 Homily 7, ch. 12, 11.

149. *The Ladder*, Step 28, ch. 61.

150. "The flesh has its own will," that is, its desire, said St Mark the Ascetic, referring to the apostle (Eph 2:3). Homily 4.

151. The word "daily" here is насущный, in the Slavonic, is literally "essential for life."—Trans.].

152. St John Cassian. Conference 9, ch. 21.

153. St John Cassian. Conference 9, ch. 21. This explanation of the daily bread by no means contradicts the monastic rule of saying the Lord's Prayer before meals: material bread serves as an image of the bread that "came down from heaven."

154. St Macarius the Great, Homily 7, ch. 4.

155. St John Cassian. Conference 9, ch. 23; St Isaac the Syrian, Homily 5.

156. Spiritual freedom bears no relation to freedom in the flesh. Slavery as a citizen has no influence on spiritual freedom, and, conversely, freedom as a citizen does not prevent a person from being enslaved in the spiritual sense. 1 Cor 7:21–23.

157. St John Cassian. Conference 9, ch. 24.

158. St Macarius the Great, Homily 7, ch. 19.

159. St Barsanuphius the Great. Responses 260, 261, 592.

160. St Isaac the Syrian, Homily 55, and other Fathers.

161. *The Ladder,* Step 28, ch. 1.

162. In the prayer before the Cherubic Hymn (see the priest's service book), the priest prays to be spared from an evil conscience, that is, one that is darkened by sin and false notions, through which evil is regarded as and becomes as if good. An evil conscience is particularly apparent in the activities of barbaric peoples; but to a Christian observer it is equally obvious in human activity in general, and especially in his own behavior.

163. St Macarius the Great, Homily 4, ch. 13.

164. Letter of George the Recluse of Zadonsk, bk. 1, p. 62, publ. 1850; Homily 106 of St Ephraim the Syrian *On the antichrist.*

165. *An Exact Exposition of the Orthodox Faith*, bk. 4, ch. 26.

166. From a troparion sung at the Hours of Holy Pascha.

167. St Isaac the Syrian, Homily 8.

168. St Peter Damascene, bk. 1, art. 2.

169. Interpretation of St Theophylact of Ochrid and Bulgaria.

170. This is included at Luke 14:24 in the Slavonic text but not in the King James text, where it is found only at Matt 22:14.—Trans.]

171. St Isaac the Syrian, Homily 85.

172. St Isaac the Syrian, Homily 2.

173. St Barsanuphius the Great. Responses 2, 6 and others.

174. This view of a Christian toward himself is completely different from "optimism," or the teaching that "everything in the world is getting better." Contrary to this teaching, Holy Scripture maintains that everything good is gradually declining.

175. St Macarius the Great, Homily 30, ch. 7.

176. See the life of the holy Apostle Peter, *The Lives of the Saints*, June 29. Pinetti, who lived in the late eighteenth and early nineteenth centuries, performed similar miracles, as have others.

177. St Ephraim the Syrian, Homily 106, *On the Antichrist.*

178. St Ephraim the Syrian, Homily 106, pt. 2.

179. St Macarius the Great, Homily 31, ch. 4.

180. St Ephraim the Syrian, Homily 106, pt. 2.

181. "An ascetic of prayer should look up at the heavens only occasionally for fear of the evil demons who are in the air, called spirits of the air for this reason. They produce various different delusions." St Symeon the New Theologian. *The Philokalia,* pt. 4. "On the Third Way of Attentiveness."

182. St Ephraim the Syrian. Homily 106.

183. Rev 13:2. "The beast which I saw was like a leopard, his feet were like the feet of a bear, and his mouth like the mouth of a lion."

184. St John Chrysostom, *Homily on 2 Corinthians 3.*

185. St Niphon of Constantia, Fourth reply to a brother.

186. St John Chrysostom, First homily on Pentecost.

187. St Isaac the Syrian, Homily 36.

188. St Isaac the Syrian, Homily 1.

189. Homily 7, ch. 4.

190. St Tikhon of Zadonsk. Vol. 15, letter 103, point 4.

191. Homily 56.

192. Homily 27, ch. 16.

193. Patrologiae L, LXXIII. De vitis partum, lib. IV, cap. XIII.

194. *Sayings of the Desert Fathers.*

195. Homily 34.

196. St Mark the Ascetic, *On Those Who Think That They Are Made Righteous by Works: Two Hundred and Twenty-six Texts*, ch. 6. *The Philokalia*, vol. 3.

197. *Sayings of the Desert Fathers.*

198. St Elijah the Recluse, Homily 27.

199. Abba Dorotheos, Sermon 7.

200. Response no. 130.

201. St Isaac the Syrian, Homily 37.

202. St Isaac the Syrian, Homilies 25, 26, 27 and 28.

203. *The Ladder,* Step 26, ch. 52.

204. St Isaac the Syrian, Homily 28.

205. Homily 89.

206. St Ephraim the Syrian, Homily 106.

207. St Isaac the Syrian, Homily 38.

208. This idea belongs to the holy martyr James the Persian. *The Lives of the Saints*, November 26.

209. The state of Christian perfection, the spiritual state, as opposed to that of babes in Christ (1 Cor 3:1), is mentioned in the New Testament (Eph 4: 13; Phil 3:15; Col 1:28; Heb 5:14) and in the writings of the Holy Fathers (*The Philokalia*, vol. 3. The Ladder of Divine Graces, by Theophanis the Monk; St Macarius the Great, Homily 3, ch. 12, 13, 14 ff). In the prayer after the seventeenth kathisma we read: "Perfect me with Thy perfection, and thus lead me up from my present life."

210. The exception to this is the Gospel of St Matthew, which was written in the Hebrew (Aramaic) language and translated into Greek. The Hebrew text was soon lost, and all the holy Fathers of the early centuries refer to the Greek text.

211. *The Philokalia*, vol. 4. St Symeon the New Theologian, *Practical and Theological Texts*, ch. 132.

212. St Mark the Ascetic, *On the Spiritual Law*, ch. 13, 14. *The Philokalia*, vol. 1; St Symeon the New Theologian, Homily on faith. *The Philokalia*, vol. 4.

213. 2 Peter 1:19 "And so we have the prophetic word confirmed, which you do well to heed as a light that shines in a dark place, until the day dawns and the morning star rises in your hearts."

214. Third petition in the Small Litany.

215. *The Ladder*, Step 28.

216. From Step 28 of *The Ladder*.

217. Saints Kallistos and Ignatius Xanthopoulos, *The Philokalia*, pt. 2, ch. 24.

218. St Nicephorus the Monk, *On Watchfulness and the Guarding of the Heart. The Philokalia*, vol. 2.

219. St Nilus of Sora, Homily 2.

220. Homily on Faith. *The Philokalia*, vol. 4.

221. *The Ladder*, Step 27.

222. Interpretation of St Theophylact of Ochrid and Bulgaria; St John of the Ladder, *Ladder of Divine Ascent*, Step 28, and others.

223. St Isaac the Syrian, Homily 90.

224. *Ladder of Divine Ascent*, Step 28, ch. 64.

225. See *A Discourse on Abba Philimon, The Philokalia*, vol. 2.

226. St John of the Ladder, *Ladder of Divine Ascent*, Step 28, ch. 61.

227. *Ladder of Divine Ascent*, Step 28, ch. 28.

228. St Macarius the Great, Homily 4, ch. 19.

229. Interpretation of St Theophylact of Ochrid and Bulgaria.

230. According to St Theophylact of Ochrid and Bulgaria.

231. St Theophylact of Ochrid and Bulgaria and many other Fathers.

232. St Isaac the Syrian, Homily 56.

233. St Barsanuphius the Great. Response no. 210.

234. St Isaac the Syrian, Homily 56.

235. St Isaac the Syrian, Homily 58, according to the reference of St Nilus of Sora.

236. St Gregory of Sinai, *One Hundred and Thirty-seven Texts*, ch. 19. *The Philokalia*, vol. 4.

237. Tsar Alexander II (1818–81).—Trans.].

238. St Isaac the Syrian, Homily 36.

239. St John of Karpathos. *Ascetic Discourse Sent at the Request of the Same Monks in India. The Philokalia*, vol. 1.

240. St Isaac the Syrian, Homily 35.

241. *The Lives of the Saints*. St Macarius the Great, January 19.

242. *The Ladder of Divine Ascent*, Step 4, on obedience.

243. St Mark the Ascetic, *On Those Who Think That They Are Made Righteous by Works*, ch. 35: "Prayer is called a virtue, but in reality it is the mother of the virtues: for it gives birth to them through union with Christ." *The Philokalia*, vol. 1.

244. See the *Trebnik* [monastic service book] Order of the Small Schema.

245. Abba Dorotheos, St Peter Damascene, and many other Fathers.

246. St Cyril of Alexandria Homily on the departure of the soul. *Psalter with Service Book*.

247. This homily was] written after arrival at the Babayev Monastery of St Nicholas in 1861.

248. The saints of God reach this state. See St Isaac the Syrian, Homilies 48 and 49.

249. [St Ignatius is referring to the siege of Jerusalem in 70 A.D. in which the Second Temple, the central place of worship for the Jewish people, was destroyed and Jerusalem, the Jewish capital, was besieged by Roman forces led by Titus who ordered its destruction. In 130 A.D. the Romans founded a colony dedicated to Jupiter on the site. —Ed.]

250. Bergier, *Dictionnaire de théologie*, Sadducéens.

251. St Tikhon of Zadonsk. Vol. 15, letter 32.

252. St Peter Damascene, *How to Acquire True Faith*, bk. 1. *The Philokalia*, vol. 3.

253. Homily 2.

254. This exposition was written at Stavropol in the Caucasus, in response to the request of several members of a society in which the new dogma of the Papists was the object of criticism. [This refers to the dogma of "immaculate conception," defined by Pope Pius IX in 1854. —Trans.]

255. St John Damascene, *An Exact Exposition of the Orthodox Faith*, bk. 4, ch. 13.

256. See St Isaac the Syrian, Homily 28, on how the reason of the flesh and of the soul is destroyed through faith and spiritual understanding is born.

257. "Those who from the beginning were eyewitnesses and ministers of the word delivered them to us" (Luke 1:2).

258. "The traitor takes the Bread in his hands, but stretches them out secretly to receive the price of Him who fashioned man with His own hands." From the Kontakion in the Second Tone on Great Thursday, translated by Mother Mary and Archimandrite Kallistos Ware, *The Lenten Triodion*, 2001.

259. "O Lord, the Jews condemned Thee to death, who art the Life of all," from the Troparion in the Sixth Tone in the Third Hour on Great Friday. "When the thief beheld the Author of life hanging upon the Cross, he said: 'If it were not God incarnate that is crucified with us, the sun would not have hid its rays nor would the earth have quaked and trembled. But, all-forbearing Lord, remember me in Thy Kingdom.'" Troparion of the Ninth Hour on Great Friday, *ibid.*

260. St John Damascene, *An Exact Exposition of the Orthodox Faith*, bk. 3, ch. 2.

261. According to the agreed opinion of all the holy Fathers of the Orthodox Church who wrote about this matter. St Gregory the Theologian, Homily 38.

262. St John Damascene, *An Exact Exposition of the Orthodox Faith*, bk. 3, ch. 2.

263. St John Damascene, *An Exact Exposition of the Orthodox Faith*, bk. 4, ch. 14.

264. St John Damascene, *An Exact Exposition of the Orthodox Faith*, bk. 4, ch. 14.

265. "In times of old Adam was once deceived: he sought to become God, but received not his desire. Now God becomes man, that He may make Adam God." Akathist to the Mother of God, 4th Stichera. [In English: *The Festal Menaion* trans. Mother Mary, Kallistos Ware (London: Faber and Faber, 1969), p. 460.]

266. St John Damascene, *An Exact Exposition of the Orthodox Faith*, bk. 3, ch. 28 and 16.

267. Passions are the human attributes in their diseased state, caused by the fall. Thus the capacity to feed oneself is transformed into an inclination to gluttony and sensual pleasure; the power of desire turns into whims and lust; the power of anger or energy of the soul into irascibility, rage, malice, and hatred; the capacity to sorrow and grieve into cowardice, despondency, and despair; the natural capacity to disdain a sin that demeans nature into disdain for one's neighbors and pride, etc. See St Isaiah the Solitary, Homily 2.

268. Here "spiritual" means "sanctified by the Holy Spirit," in accordance with the meaning given to the word by the holy Apostle Paul (1 Cor 2:15) and all holy writers of the Orthodox Church.

269. St Macarius the Great, Homily 4, ch. 3.

270. "You were transfigured on the mountain, Christ God, and Your disciples beheld Your glory as far as they were able: that when they saw You crucified, they might know that Your suffering was voluntary." Troparion and kontakion of the Feast of the Holy Transfiguration.

271. Troparion from the Hours of holy Pascha. [In English: *The Pascha Service*, eds. John Erikson, Paul Lazor (Scarsdale, NY: SVS Press, 1977), p. 54.]

272. An example is the novel derived from the Gospel entitled *The Dolorous Passion of Our Lord Jesus Christ* by Anne Catherine Emmerich.

273. St John Damascene. *Exact Interpretation of the Orthodox Faith*, bk. 3, ch. 28 and 17.

274. St John Damascene. *Exact Interpretation of the Orthodox Faith*, bk. 3, ch. 28 and 17. The Lord "accepted upon Himself the weaknesses of fallen human nature, such as hunger, thirst, exhaustion, death of the body itself, consisting of separation of the soul from the body," and the body of the Lord submitted to all of this before His resurrection, and stopped submitting to it after the resurrection. The flesh of the Lord was in itself deified from the moment of conception; it was already divine when conceived. "This flesh," says St John Damascene, "became one with God, and became God—not by joining or transforming, not by changing or mingling the two natures. 'One of the natures'—to quote St Gregory the Theologian, Homily 42—'deified, the other was deified, and, I say boldly, became one with God; and the one that anointed became man, while the anointed one became God.' And these things happened not by changing the nature, but by union through providence for salvation, that is, hypostatic union, by which the flesh was united inseparably with God the Word, and by the mutual penetration of the natures, similar to what we see in the heating of steel by fire." Just as divinity always has the same quality, being always the same as Itself and unchanged, so the quality of the soul and flesh of the Lord in relation to their divinity was always the same. This quality was the same throughout all the changes in human age of the God-Man: it was the same when God incarnate lay in a cradle as an infant, when He was wrapped in swaddling clothes, and when He revealed Himself in inexpressible glory on Mount Tabor, when He rose again from the grave, when He was taken up into heaven. This quality was the same in all situations to which the God-Man was pleased to submit Himself in His humanity: it was the same when the Lord stood bound before the Sanhedrin and Pilate, when He was showered with insults, beating and spitting, and when He was seated, after the incarnation, at the right hand of God the Father, when all the angels and archangels bowed down and fell at His feet.

275. According to the interpretation of St Theophylact of Ochrid and Bulgaria.

276. Akathist to our Sweetest Lord Jesus, Eikos 7. [In English: *Prayer Book* (Jordanville, NY: Holy Trinity Publications, 2005), p. 276.]

277. Canon of Holy Pascha, Ode 6, Tone 1. [In English: *The Pascha Service*, eds. John Erikson, Paul Lazor (Scarsdale, NY: SVS Press, 1977), p. 34.]

278. Resurrection Theotokion, Tone 2.

279. Resurrection Theotokion, Tone 7.

280. Service on the Sunday of Orthodoxy.

281. St Cyprian of Carthage, quoted by St Dimitri of Rostov. *The Lives of the Saints*, December 25. Homily on the Nativity of Christ.

282. Life of St Gregory of Sinai, written by his disciple St Kallistos, patriarch of Constantinople.

283. Ikos of the Canon of the Forerunner.

284. See the interpretation by St John Chrysostom of the Gospel of St Matthew; also St Theophylact of Ochrid and Bulgaria, in an explanation of the same passage in the Gospel of St Matthew (12:46–50), comments as follows on the circumstance described by the Evangelist: "The Mother of God did not show anything human, the power of a mother over a son: she did not yet understand all the greatness concealed within the God-Man. And that is why, when He is explaining His teaching to the people, she interrupts Him and calls Him to her, wanting from Him, as from a son, respect and obedience toward her. This is the reason why Christ, knowing the thought in her heart, says, 'Who is My mother? And who are My brothers? And I reach out My hand to My disciples, saying, here are My mother and My brothers: for whoever does the will of My Father in heaven is My brother, My sister and My mother.' He said this not to condemn the Mother of God, but to distract her from vainglory and from the viewpoint of the 'old man'."

285. See St Macarius the Great, Homily 7, ch. 11, 12.

286. Trans: The immaculate conception was defined as a dogma in 1854.

287. ie. Papists, Latinists.

288. Bergier, *Dictionnaire de Théologie*. Entry for *Marie/Mary*.

289. Bergier, *Dictionnaire de Théologie*. Entry for *Marie/Mary*.

290. Bergier, *Dictionnaire de Théologie*. Entry for *Marie/Mary*.

291. Trans. Martin Luther married in 1525.

292. According to the explanation of St Theophylact of Ochrid and Bulgaria.

293. St Gregory of Sinai, ch. 110 and 114. *The Philokalia*, vol. 4.

294. St John of the Ladder, Homily 15, ch. 3.

295. Canon of the Akathist to the Mother of God, Ode 1, troparion 1, trans. Mother Mary and Archim. Kallistos Ware.

296. St John Damascene, *An Exact Exposition of the Orthodox Faith*, bk. 4, ch. 14.

297. This and other historical information is taken from the *Lives of the Saints* which relates detailed church tradition about the Mother of God, i.e. the accounts and discussions of a great many holy Fathers.

298. This is what the apostles exclaimed when they saw the Mother of God who appeared to them after falling asleep. *Lives of the Saints*, August 15.

299. The blessed elder Seraphim of Sarov also explained this.

300. *Lives of the Saints*, the account of the dormition of the most holy Birthgiver of God, August 15.

301. This refers to the Blessed St Seraphim of Sarov.

302. From the Akathist to the Mother of God. [In English *The Lenten Triodion,* trans. Mother Mary, Kallistos Ware (London: Faber and Faber, 1984) p. 430.]

Subject Index

Scripture Index

Note: In citations the letter "n" and a number refers to the note number on that page; for example p. 255 n.8 refers to the text associated with note 8 on page 255.

Other volumes from

The Collected Works of St Ignatius (Brianchaninov)

VOLUME I

The Field

Cultivating Salvation

The field is a place of cultivation and of battle. The author instructs his readers in the cultivation of the field of their hearts, with the aim of producing a harvest of virtues both pleasing to God and of benefit to all humankind. *The Field* draws deeply on the teachings of the ascetic fathers of the Church, from the desert dwellers of Scetis in Egypt to St Ignatius's Russian contemporaries, the Optina Elders.

ISBN: 9780884653769

VOLUME II

The Refuge

Anchoring the Soul in God

Prayer is a refuge of God's great mercy to the human race. A refuge is a place of inner stillness and peace where the heart is fully opened to the embrace of God's love. This text is an exposition of the concrete actions one needs to take to live with and in God. It weaves together meditations on Scripture (from the Psalms in particular) and amplifies these with the wisdom of early Christian saints.

ISBN: 9780884654292

VOLUME III

The Threshold

Trials at the Crossroads of Eternity

In this third volume of St Ignatius's collected works, the saint examines the mystical boundaries that govern the life of a Christian: the one, between life and death; and the other, between the visible, physical realm and the invisible to most, but no less real, spiritual realm. He exhorts his readers to prepare themselves to cross the threshold into their final heavenly home: to cross from earthly into eternal life.

ISBN: 9780884654933

VOLUME V

The Arena

Guidelines for Spiritual and Monastic Life

This is one of the most important and accessible texts of Orthodox Christian teaching on the spiritual life, and not unlike the better known *Philokalia*. The author describes this work as his legacy "of soul saving instruction." In an age alienated from spiritual culture and rooted in materialism, his words pose an invitation to all who say to themselves "There must be more to life than this."

ISBN: 9780884652878